HOW DOES AN EAGER-TO-PLEASE, YOUNG CHINESE GIRL, OWNED BY THE UNYIELDING COMMUNIST GOVERNMENT, LEARN TO FIGHT FOR SURVIVAL BY BECOMING AN INDEPENDENT THINKER?

When Liu Yu, an impressionable Chinese girl, witnesses the venomous public trial of her mother's co-worker and friend during the Cultural Revolution, her life is changed forever. The incident silences her voice but not her desire to escape from poverty and the wearisome fate her mother endures.

At eleven, Liu Yu grabs her chance to avoid being sent to the countryside in the government's plan to re-educate its young people even though it means leaving her supportive family behind. She catapults to the top of Communist society by becoming an elite professional athlete, living the dream of every child in China. Prestige and material comfort, however, are quickly overshadowed by loneliness and a brutal training regimen.

After enduring nearly ten years of rigorous martial arts training, feuding coaches threaten Liu Yu's dreams of a national championship. She must then decide whether to follow her family's values and her heart or push for the championship she feels is within her grasp.

Guided by her grandmother's wisdom, the young woman realizes what she wants more than fame and fortune is the chance to control her own life. Liu Yu risks everything, finding the courage to turn against the cultural tide in China to seek her own destiny. In the process she rediscovers her voice, the one she lost as a child of the Cultural Revolution.

AWAKENING THE SLEEPING TIGER

AWAKENING THE SLEEPING TIGER

The True Story of a Professional Chinese Athlete

Liu Yu
and *Dawn Cerf*

San Luis Obispo, California

This story is true, although some of the names of people in the story have been changed to protect them. The authors and publisher have made every effort to ensure the accuracy and completeness of information contained in this book and, therefore, assume no reponsibility for errors, inaccuracies, omissions, or any inconsistency herein. Any slights of people, places, or organizations expressly named herein are unintentional.

Liu Yu
Wushu Taichi Center
P. O. Box 15955
San Luis Obispo, CA 93406
www.wushutaichicenter.com

Library of Congress Control Number: 2010909210

ISBN 978-0-9828262-0-1 (trade paperback)

Cover and Book Design by Dawn Cerf
Cover Photo: 1983 photograph taken in Nanjing courtesy of Liu Yu.
Interior Photos: courtesy of Liu Yu.
"Flying Tiger" calligraphy by Chen Xiaowang with his permission.

This book is dedicated to my grandmother,
NaiNai Xu Fengshi 徐房氏, and to my parents,
Liu Tian Ming 刘天明 and Xu Qiu 徐球.

This book is also a special gift for my daughter,
Han Ling Petredean 涵玲. Preparing to write this book by
asking my family questions enabled me to know my mother
deeply for the first time. My wish became that my daughter
would know me better by reading about my early life.

TABLE OF CONTENTS

Part One

Baoying, Jiangsu Province, China, 1962 (Birth) - 1974

Part Two

Nanjing, Jiangsu Province, China, 1974- 1985

Part Three

Beijing, China, 1985 – 1990

Part One

Baoying 宝应, Jiangsu Province 江苏, China 中国

1962 (Birth) - 1974

飛虎

虎年一旺

Baba

出生年月
部　　别
职　　务
专业技术

Baba's military ID card

THE HIDDEN YEARNINGS
OF A TIGER CUB

The confusion began as Mama eased herself gently down onto the bed, low moans escaping her throat. My beloved grandmother, NaiNai 奶奶, soothed my overanxious imagination, explaining everything was normal. Although nearly three years old, I sensed normal would never be the same again.

Banished from our dwelling, my "Baba 爸爸," the Chinese word for father, joined a noisy gathering of relatives and neighbors outside, chatting away as if attending a party. From time to time, many popped their heads inside volunteering their help, only to receive a sharp shake from NaiNai's head or a polite refusal from the unruffled midwife.

A loud knock at the door heralded the husband of one of my aunties—ladies Mama worked with who really weren't relatives at all. His arms brimmed over with a load of fresh straw tightly bound with string. I squatted next to NaiNai as she carefully arranged golden stalks in the wooden cradle we had borrowed, piling the excess alongside Mama's bed.

After a cursory glance in my direction, the midwife asked NaiNai for scissors, towels and paper. While NaiNai darted here and there, I scurried around in her shadow like a little tail behind her. Aiming to be helpful, I kept faithfully close until she shooed me from her side, busying herself by prodding the fiery coals in our small charcoal brazier. Instead of using it outside in the courtyard as she had always done before, she had set it up inside near the door over the carefully swept dirt floor of our cramped, windowless room. While puzzling it out, I stared hypnotically as dreamy tendrils of smoke mingled in dancing spirals with steam from the heavy pot of boiling water.

My thoughts strayed to the five children in my neighbor's family and how the boys always received special treatment. *If Mama has a boy,* I thought sadly, *Baba might not notice me as much as before.*

In my most treasured memory, Baba sat watching me draw at our little dining table. Each time his attention rested on me, my heart expanded, filling my world with sunny happiness. Reaching over, Baba picked up my hand, commenting that it was dirty. In the chill of winter we children didn't like washing our hands in the icy water collected from the river. Baba then led me to the washing stand, coming in close behind me. Putting his arms around me, he reached for my hands, carefully lathering and rinsing them above the washing bowl. What a rare feeling to have another person touch me. I savored that moment with Baba. This memory stood out because families rarely touched each other or showed affection. Words such as "I love you" remained unspoken. In our culture, we believed no one needed to speak about love and no one needed to hear it. Love was simply understood. Yet after that experience, deep within the stillness of my young heart emerged an inkling that something was missing, and I yearned to recapture that closeness.

Interrupting my reverie, NaiNai, holding a large rubber foot warmer, turned abruptly toward the boiling pot, nearly knocking me over. Exasperated, she said, "Xiao Yu 小玉," my name which meant Little Jade, "go somewhere else, out of this room." She swiftly motioned me out the door.

Both the narrow pathway to our door and the adjacent, tiny courtyard overflowed with people, everyone talking at once. Peering through a tangle of legs, I searched unsuccessfully for Baba, wishing he would lift me up and plop me down close to him on his shoulders. Too quickly, however, I found myself pushed up against the wall. As much as I wanted to spend a few precious moments with Baba, I sensed he was too distracted now to give me much notice. Scrambling alongside the building, I settled cautiously in a corner, amusing myself by drawing in the dirt with a craggy pebble and idly wondering where my older sister was playing. Accustomed to NaiNai's watching over me like a mother hen, I felt increasingly forgotten as time dragged on.

Finally, NaiNai's sharp voice barreled out above the commotion, "It's a boy!"

Everyone congratulated Baba for having accomplished something great, how he had secured the continuation of the family line. It made me think my birth as the third daughter had disappointed my parents, though they always treated me with kindness.

Eager to catch a glimpse of my new brother, I edged myself along the wall, only to find our door firmly closed. At that moment, feeling lost, not knowing quite where I should be, I wandered slowly down the walkway, away from the commotion. Perhaps I would find my sister in another courtyard.

My family lived in what was originally a long storage shed tacked onto the side of one of three gray brick buildings previously comprising one private residence. Before the Communist revolution, four generations of one family lived in the enclosed compound where three inner courtyards offered a modicum of privacy. When the Communists took over the country, people who owned large houses were forced to take in other families and share their living quarters. Now this house was home to ten unrelated families. When the government assigned my family to occupy this humble dwelling, my parents breathed a huge sigh of relief. After surviving the death of their infant daughter who was my first-born sister, my parents then witnessed a flood washing away their home. They had nowhere else to live.

When the other two courtyards failed to reveal my sister, I continued toward the creaky wooden door leading to the street. Raising myself on tiptoes, I peered through one of the eyeholes at the intriguing scene so close to me. What I did next was a clue to my innate personality, one that had already been beaten back by poor health and strict codes of social behavior. I opened the door without fear, stepping into a world I rarely saw and one I had never viewed lingeringly from the sidelines.

Remembering NaiNai had said I shouldn't walk by myself, I plunked myself down in front of a shop, mesmerized by the busyness before me. In this lively shopping district, bicyclists pedaled by chiming ding-ding-ding, their spinning wheels delightfully reflecting the warm October sun. Clusters of women in traditional peasant head scarves of white with blue tie-dyed designs chatted happily as they paraded by, baskets woven from shavings of bamboo skin hanging from their arms. Other baskets brimming with vegetables hung from the ends of poles balanced across farmers' shoulders. Two- or three-wheeled push carts wobbled by filled with either a mound of rice, squealing pigs, or caged chickens. One had a side basket carrying a young boy who glared at me with squinty eyes.

Eagerly, I looked around for the sugar artist, who would fill his straw from pots of five colors of sugary mixtures warming over a coal brazier. With the straw placed between his lips, he blew the sugar onto a stick while his hands shaped it into multi-colored animals, birds, or flowers. The most popular shape was the devious Monkey King, decorated with a golden shirt, dark pants and shiny boots. Most shapes cost one coin, but parents paid two coins for the Monkey King clutching the long, wooden staff he used as a weapon. Generally, children kept the sugar shapes for a day, stealing occasional licks, before finally eating the entire treat. Sadly, I didn't see the sugar artist on my street today.

Eventually, standing up, I watched a cobbler with a mouthful of needle-sized nails repair a leather shoe that was hooked onto a metal platform in his repair shop. To fix the worn heel, a wedge was inserted, affixed firmly with nails, and stained to match the shoe's color. Then he began stitching the sole of a cotton shoe. His left hand operated a tool that pierced through all the cotton layers of the sole while his right hand maneuvered a needle of thickly corded thread. Before long the old cobbler's gaze met mine. He smiled and then shuffled toward me with a curious expression. A lady followed behind him.

"Hello, little girl," the man said. "What's your name?"

"Little Tiger," I answered. Although my family called me Xiao Yu, they often reminded me of my birth in the year of the tiger. I always thought of myself as a little tiger.

"Where do you live?"

I pointed vaguely in the direction I had just come from, suddenly unsure if I knew which door would take me back home.

"Why are you out here all by yourself?" the lady asked.

"Everyone is busy. Mama has a new baby," I explained.

Just then, a familiar voice called out, "Xiao Yu, what are you doing?" NaiNai shuffled awkwardly on her bound feet toward me, concern written in her crinkly eyes. With a shaky hand, she reached for me, tightly gripping her thumb along my collarbone and firmly clamping my shoulder.

The cobbler explained how they had been trying to help me. NaiNai thanked them warmly before we turned to go home.

"Xiao Yu, why did you go outside? I told you *always* to tell me before you leave the courtyard," NaiNai scolded as the creaky wooden door swung closed behind us. And, then, with tension rising in her voice, she said, "What if you got lost or someone took you?" She gripped my hand tightly, saying with a dawning realization and deep emotion, "I could lose you."

Despite my feeling guilty for doing something wrong and making NaiNai so concerned, warmth flooded through me. *NaiNai really cares about me.*

Inside our home, my little brother, wrapped in a blanket, lay crying by Mama's side. I reached out carefully and touched the pink skin on his downy cheek, amazed at its softness and at how loudly such a small thing could cry.

"Mama," my Mama said to NaiNai, "maybe Xiao Yu would like to rock her brother in the cradle."

NaiNai gently gathered up the baby and set him down on the blanket-covered straw. "Not too fast," NaiNai instructed. She put my hand on the cradle and taught me how to rock it, slowly and rhythmically. After a few minutes, the baby stopped crying.

"You have the right touch," Mama said. "From now on, this will be your job." Ignoring the birth of my oldest sister who died, she added, "You are second sister now, Xiao Yu."

My brother became known as "Little Crooked Head" until sufficient time had passed that the jealous gods would no longer attempt to take away a perfect child. Only then could he safely be named. As an infant, Mama never wanted to awaken him when his head needing straightening. Despite the aunties' predictions his head would become permanently crooked, Mama always spoiled him by letting him sleep with his head scrunched in a funny position. After all, silence was precious because my brother cried too much.

Although three years had transpired since the end of China's Great Famine, food remained scarce. While my brother cried because he was always hungry, I suffered from a lack of appetite and was plagued by periodic bouts of dizziness and fatigue. I learned never to complain, even when Baba, who worked as a doctor, made me drink his bitter herbal remedies to rid me of my anemia. Without a word, NaiNai communicated with her stern looks that complaining was inappropriate. NaiNai, who lived with her crippled, bound feet, provided signals on how to behave. I tried to follow her example of combining grace with silent tolerance

Mama always said I possessed a good memory for my early life, although it helped that relatives enjoyed reminding me. I remembered my brother's crying was tolerated with little attempt made to teach him manners. Naturally, he garnered tremendous attention as the young emperor of the family, and I came to know my place as a female in Chinese society ranked below his.

When my brother was a few years old, Baba delighted him with a wooden gun he had carved, filling me with wistfulness. Although, due to my family's poverty, I never had any toys, not even a doll of any kind, it wasn't my brother's toy that I envied. I craved Baba's attention like I did the feel of the sun to dispel shivers of cold. I worked hard at school and in my free time tried to read Baba's books, struggling through vocabulary too advanced for my years, in the hopes he would notice and offer some small murmur of praise. *Some day,* I vowed, *Baba will be proud of me for something I accomplish.*

My future may have appeared to be written. I had only to follow my mother's footsteps toward a factory job with long hours, little pay and no free time to spend with one's family. Things were changing in China, however. Already in my mother's generation, women could choose their own husbands and China outlawed the barbaric practice of footbinding— breaking the bones of a woman's foot and bending the foot under until the toes were positioned at the bottom of the heel, creating the tiny golden lily feet that pleased husbands. I hoped for more changes. After all, the founder of the People's Republic of China, Chairman Mao Zedong-毛泽东, had proclaimed that women held up half the sky.

Something inside me allowed me to see possibilities, though I had yet to learn to develop them. Perhaps my birth in the year of the tiger gave me the extra insight and someday I would trust it. According to the time-honored Chinese astrological calendar system, tiger people are considered noble and brave, earnestly cultivating deep inner strength in their lifetimes. Circumstances in my life, however, inhibited the growth of the small tiger cub I concealed inside. I knew it was there, but to everyone else I appeared to be sickly and shy, certainly not qualities characteristic of a valiant tiger.

Amid overwhelming political chaos, at the delicate age of four, I buried my true nature deeper after witnessing an alarming scene that left me anxious and frightened. From that moment on, I tread carefully as if stepping across an expanse of smooth, slippery ice, my tentative footholds never fully confident and secure. To become the brave tiger I knew I could be and earn my father's praise, I needed to discover a way to overcome my anemia and fearfulness. *Surely a tiger can accomplish it.* But troublesome memories complicated my resolve, making the task all the more daunting.

Baoying, Jiangsu Province, China, 1967

Piercing voices from the nearby town square blared over the thunderous loudspeakers, summoning the townspeople to another political rally.

"SPIES! TRAITORS! HEAR THEM CONFESS!"

My head jerked up as the familiar harsh sounds torpedoed over the rooftops, invading my solitude in the small, barren courtyard. For many months now, the town square rarely remained quiet during this time of Chairman Mao's Cultural Revolution. Heated accusations against political prisoners and entreaties for sentences of jail or death often reverberated over the tops of our walls. The insistent noise reminded me of a loud, obtrusive dragon wielding its importance with heavy footfalls and fiery invectives while demanding everyone's undivided attention. Instead of the mischievous dragon that chased us children for fun on New Year's Day, this raging dragon with imaginary bulging, demonic eyes and scissor-sharp talons was bullying its way into my world, leaving behind a swath of fear.

Shuddering at the angry screeching, I drew on the calming protectiveness of the familiar courtyard walls elegantly topped with curly-edged tiles, breathing a sigh of relief that Baba was only a whisper away inside our home. While squatting next to a steaming pot of soup that rested on my family's outdoor brazier and idly guarding the precious food from bird droppings, I wondered anew how life outside these walls could be so crazy. Many times my tender four-year-old mind struggled to comprehend the nature of the meanness and hostility that gripped the townsfolk. Yet, in spite of feeling fearful and confused, I remained curious as was my nature. Maybe, I hoped, Baba would take me to the nearby square, not to witness the handiwork of the dragon, but for the comfort of companionship I would share with my father.

NaiNai hobbled toward me to fetch the soup. She paused briefly, tilting her head upwards to catch the fiery commands. As her eyes met mine, I saw her jaw set in that disapproving yet determined way of hers that meant she would thrive no matter what obstacle awaited her. I watched her skeletal-like body bending down while her knotted fingers carefully wrapped rags around the handles of the soup pot. Between us, we silently carried the load into our modest home for the family's noontime meal.

Six of us—NaiNai, my parents, my older sister, my younger brother, and I—lived in the makeshift, dirt-floored home containing two tiny rooms connected by a short hallway. Old wooden doors served as walls with only one tiny window-like opening set too high to look out. To prevent the freezing winter wind from penetrating our heatless home, we mixed flour and water together to paste newspaper along the cracks between the doors. In the summer, we removed these wooden doors by lifting them off their dowels to welcome any breeze, though we gave up all privacy to keep cool.

Shivering slightly in the fresh spring air, I sat on a stool next to the open door. It was left ajar to allow light to spill into a room we used both for dining and as my parents' bedroom. It also admitted noise from clamorous chanters accompanying a parade of political prisoners on the street. My family and I listened while we sipped salty broth and chewed on the cooked vegetable roots and greens we fished from our bowls.

Within minutes of eating, my baby brother began his ritual of mealtime crying. No one tried to comfort him because it never did any good. Even though annoyed, I had already learned it was proper never to show my emotions, but my brother was too young. My family sat there stoically knowing only a full stomach could satisfy him. Baba quietly sighed in resignation.

Usually, I dawdled over my food. Today, however, I forced myself to finish my soup quickly because I wanted Baba to take me to the square.

Baba turned his head toward my sister. "Da Jing 大静," Baba said, calling her by a variation of her name, "would you like to come to the square with me?"

I guessed her response. My sister, though older than me by three years, generally avoided things that made her uncomfortable. Shuffling her feet she said, "Baba, I would rather stay and play with my friend in the courtyard."

Raising myself up to sit taller on the stool, I eagerly awaited Baba's invitation. It would be improper to ask him myself. As soon as his eyes met mine, he permitted himself a small smile. "Okay, Xiao Yu," he said using my birth name, "you can come."

Warmth filled me inside, and I basked in the enjoyment of Baba's invitation, knowing that soon my brother would be old enough to be asked first.

NaiNai turned around, peering into my empty bowl and nodding her head in approval. She grabbed a piece of clothing off the rack and handed it to Baba. "Here's an extra shirt if she gets chilled."

Along with devoting her time to keeping house and preparing food, NaiNai raised my siblings and me in place of Mama. Sadly, Mama's long hours at her job as a seamstress rarely allowed her to spend much time with us. As a result, I often felt motherless and grew to depend on NaiNai. She was a strict disciplinarian but I had no doubts she cared about me.

Baba and I walked along the brick path between the buildings of our compound while the din over the walls grew louder. We exited the narrow front door sandwiched between a shop selling firecrackers and a shoe repair business and found ourselves on the edge of a moving horde of people.

Briefly, I regretted my decision until Baba bent down, picked me up, and placed me on his shoulders. My family, like all families I knew, never showed affection on the outside by hugging or kissing, so this rare physical contact helped me feel braver and safer. I lived for these moments of closeness with Baba. As we fell in step with the movement of the crowd swarming toward the square, I settled myself comfortably on Baba's strong shoulders and craned my neck to see what lie ahead.

The square was actually a wide intersection of the town's two main streets and its principal shopping district. Within its center, prisoners stood with bowed heads and hands tied behind them. They were displayed on a makeshift platform of several dining tables the Red Guards had confiscated from nearby dwellings. Perched atop the tables pushed together was another table with a chair stacked on top of it. One prisoner stood precariously on the towering chair with the other prisoners encircled below on the bottom set of tabletops. Baba had explained to me how dangerous it was to stand on a chair or a table, and I worried the prisoner might fall.

When we found a good viewpoint and stopped moving, I peered more closely at the prisoners. Vacant eyes were surrounded by chalky skin. Their jackets were sweat-soaked despite the cool air. One prisoner wore baggy trousers that showed a wet patch in the front and down the inside of his trembling legs. Just then a sad image popped into my mind of a defenseless dragonfly whose wings were being thoughtlessly pinched by a neighbor boy's quick fingers. I imagined that was how it would feel to be standing up there, only worse because everyone you knew was judging you. The loudspeakers, thundering in praise of the Cultural Revolution, the revolutionary people, and Chairman Mao, were enough to make my own legs tremble.

I breathed a sigh of relief when I spotted the giant poster of Chairman Mao being carried by two teenaged boys in Red Guard uniforms. This meant I didn't miss my favorite part of the rally and the chance to view my idols. My eyes eagerly sought out the group of girls in their stylish Red Guard uniforms who positioned themselves in front of the poster in two neat rows. Showing deep emotion, the eight girls who were about fifteen years of age began singing, "Our Great Leader, you're the sun in our hearts." While singing, they turned and waved their arms with animation toward the picture, opening them wide to pantomime the round sun and pressing their hands dearly to their hearts. They danced as they sang, "We want to share with you what's in our hearts and let you know how much we're devoted to you. We have so many songs we want to sing to you."

I admired the girls' zeal and the pretty picture they made among the shabbiness of the onlookers. Their white shirtsleeves, rolled up over their beige army jackets, made white cuffs above their elbows. Three red dots stood out: two bars on their collars and one five-pointed star on their caps. The uniforms hugged their budding figures and army belts showed off their tiny waists. I envied their ability to inspire the crowd to sing along with them. A wisp of aspiration nestled in my heart that someday I would accomplish something worthy of respect.

After the girls finished, the chanting began, which impassioned the spectators. A Red Guard, a boy about seventeen years of age, stood with one hand on his hip and his spread legs planted firmly on the ground. He held a bullhorn in his clenched fist and shouted slogans while the crowd repeated them with a roar.

"LONG LIVE OUR GREAT LEADER! LONG LIVE CHAIRMAN MAO! LONG LIVE THE RED TERROR! LONG LIVE THE GREAT CULTURAL REVOLUTION!"

Powerful emotions stirred up the air around me, and I flinched at the intensity of the voices. With the refrain of each slogan, fists punched the sky. Baba couldn't raise his arm because I was sitting on his shoulders, but otherwise he would be required to follow everyone or draw unwanted attention his way. The only safety lay in not being different. If a person stood out in the crowd in any way, he would be picked off by the terrible dragon and gobbled up. The dragon had cast a net of suspicion over the town and through its trickery coerced the people to do its bidding.

Through the bullhorn, the young Red Guard then began his condemnation of the prisoners. He pranced around the tables while his fierce voice spewed accusations. "Look what we've dug out of the ground. Snakes that were hiding in their holes. But we've trapped them."

Scowling at the prisoners, he abruptly whipped off his belt, snapping it at one of the prisoners who had leaned his head over to the shoulder of his jacket to wipe his dribbling nose. The belt knocked his glasses to the ground.

Anyone who wore glasses was marked as part of the educated class the Red Guards denounced. Even though the Red Guards were educated, they believed Chairman Mao when he said their "Red" education under the Communist flag made them pure in heart and mind. "Black" influences had not yet tarnished them.

The bullhorn emitted an ugly screech, and the Red Guard holding it pointed at the prisoner and exploded, "Who told you to move? You think you can do whatever you want? You don't think you're wrong?"

Two outraged Red Guards jumped up on the table. One of them grabbed a fistful of the prisoner's hair, jerking his head and neck back. Red flags waved and the crowd yelled its approval.

The malicious incriminations continued. "This man before you once owned a large store. He used poor people to make his money. He has criticized our Great Leader and his words."

The young Red Guard pointed accusingly at the prisoner. "If you're against Chairman Mao, you're against the people, against the Communist country."

The accuser's words inflamed the onlookers as more flags waved and cries of *zuo feiji*, "make the prisoner fly," erupted all around me. In a *zuo feiji* position, a prisoner bent forward shamefully with his arms raised behind him as if he were flying.

In response to the crowd's plea, the angry-looking Red Guards knocked the prisoner forward, forcefully slamming his head down in a submissive posture while cranking his arms unnaturally high behind him.

Someone yelled savagely, "Tear off his arms." When it turned into a hungry chant, I looked around me in fear and amazement at the purplish faces of the spectators bursting with hostility. The dragon's evil intent had infected them through their exposure to the ruthless young men in uniform.

The Red Guards then yanked the prisoner's hair and wrenched him back to a standing position with his head and neck arched back. I looked from the expressionless face of the prisoner to the intensity in the Red Guards' eyes and cringed at the ugliness. I barely comprehended why they had to be so mean. The Red Guards were clearly enjoying their power over the prisoner. While watching them, I felt my own bravery slipping away like boats floating downstream. Baba's hands had been casually resting atop my foot, but now they reached up and tenderly held my ankles. I felt the warmth of Baba's protection and found the courage to watch what would happen next.

Throughout his ordeal, the prisoner didn't flinch and maintained a serious face. Showing any emotion or revealing he felt any pain would only further incite his tormentors. The best action was to be stone-faced so the Red Guards would be convinced of the prisoner's complete submission and give up in boredom.

During the commotion, the tabletops shook and I saw the prisoner on the top wobble unsteadily. Although all the prisoners wore similar gray trousers and jackets, there was something different about the prisoner on top. Then, it hit me. The prisoner on top was actually a woman. I looked closely and gasped when I recognized her in spite of her *yin-yang* head. The hair on one side of her head—the white side—had been shaved off while the other side was left short and choppy—the dark side. Heavy chalkboards hung from the necks of all the prisoners on which their crimes and names were scrawled, although I couldn't read them. Large red x's slashed through the name parts. Also strung around the lady's neck was a pair of worn-out shoes with holes in the bottom, a symbol I didn't understand but knew to be disgraceful. *Oh, no*, I thought, *she must feel so ashamed.* It scared me to look at her, but then I couldn't pull my eyes away.

Immediately, my mind flashed back to over a year ago on the day before Chinese New Year. Mama had walked my sister and me a few doors down to the tailor's shop where she worked.

"I have a surprise for you both," Mama said as she held open the door.

My sister and I eagerly scampered inside, quickly greeting the clerk at the counter and slipping past to the back room where the sewing ladies worked. At Mama's sewing station, a beautiful New Year's outfit was draped over her machine. On the front of it, Mama had sewn a rooster and flowers by embroidering the outlines and filling in the colors with free-form machine stitching. My eyes and mouth grew round as I admired its loveliness. Even though tomorrow wasn't the beginning of the year of the rooster, Mama chose a rooster because she was proud of her birth sign.

Then I watched with growing alarm as Mama picked up the outfit and held it to the front of my sister. "It looks like the right size. And, here Xiao Yu," Mama said as she handed me the outfit that had been underneath, "this one's for you."

I took one look at the plain-looking outfit and burst out, "I want the pretty one! I want flowers and a rooster!" Then I started crying, not in a calm and quiet way, but loud and indignant.

Wang Zhao Xia 王朝霞, whose name meant Morning Glow, worked alongside Mama. She rushed over and put her hands on my shoulders. "You look so unhappy, Xiao Yu," she said.

"I want the same as Da Jie!" I wailed, calling my sister not by her name of Jing but by Older Sister, as was custom.

Mama took the pretty outfit and slipped my arms through the holes as she said, "Let's see how it looks on you, Xiao Yu."

Morning Glow stood behind me, reaching around and carefully rolling up the waistband of the apron-like smock. As she tied it in the back, Mama commented to her, "This is the first time I've seen the tiger in her. She's always been so quiet and sickly."

I was proud of my tiger birth sign, but I bristled at hearing myself referred to as sickly.

"I've always called her my peaceful cat," Mama continued. "Tigers that are born in the morning are supposed to have full stomachs and sleep peacefully in the sun all day. They're never supposed to starve."

Mama reached over and smoothed out my wrinkled waistband. She smiled and said, "I guess I've stirred up a sleeping tiger!"

"Can I take her around and show the outfit to the other ladies?" Morning Glow asked.

"Yes, thank you, and in the meantime I'll have a discussion with Da Jing."

Morning Glow held my hand and said, "Xiao Yu, do you feel better now?"

I nodded my head.

"Let's show the ladies how beautiful you look in the pretty rooster dress."

After I had received many compliments from the ladies, Morning Glow squatted down in front of me. "Xiao Yu, your mother worked hard on this dress. She wished she had more time to make Da Jing's older one pretty, too. This new dress isn't just for Da Jing; it's for you, too. You and Da Jing are growing. Soon, it will be too small for Da Jing and you will have it for yourself. Then it won't hang too long and you won't have to worry about tripping on it if the sash comes loose. But you're lucky to be the first one to wear it. Will you let Da Jing wear it now?"

I remembered thinking hard about that decision before finally agreeing. I wanted Morning Glow to think well of me because I appreciated her kindness as she tried to calm me down.

Mama had learned that day I wouldn't tolerate injustice. Now, as I watched a suffering Morning Glow up on the chair amid the noisy spectators, my entire body reacted to the unfairness of it all. It didn't make sense to me. I could barely understand how men could become spies against Chairman Mao, much less this tiny, gentle woman. What could a little lady like that have done that was worse than what the men were accused of doing? How could such a small person affect the powerful government?

I watched the red-faced young man with the bullhorn motion the other guards to leave the table. He then began prancing again, informing everyone, "Today, we present you with a spy we have captured. Her brother is a Nationalist soldier hiding in Taiwan. In a letter he sent his sister, he asked her to pass on information to his Nationalist spies. THEY WANT TO TAKE OUR COUNTRY BACK! WE WON'T LET THEM!"

Red flags waved and echoes of "WE WON'T LET THEM" ricocheted left and right.

The Red Guard signaled everyone to stop and raged, "IN ADDITION, THIS LADY REFUSES TO ADMIT HER GUILT!" With his red armband standing out prominently, he pointed to the tight-lipped woman and shrieked excitedly, "It's your duty to admit you're an enemy of our Great Leader. The only way to escape severe punishment or death is to repent. Admit your wrongdoing. Admit you're a spy!" He turned to his excited audience and shouted repeatedly, "CONFESSION OR DEATH! CONFESSION OR DEATH!" Everyone chimed in.

After several minutes, the crowd obeyed his signal to stop chanting, and the Red Guard yelled, "ADMIT YOU ARE GUILTY!"

Morning Glow continued to stare straight ahead with angry eyes. Her thin, bluish lips were pinched together with determination. At that moment, I ached inside because I knew she was devastated and I couldn't do anything to help her like she had helped me. I also sensed big trouble.

When Morning Glow refused to answer, her interrogator fumed, "We have ways of making you admit your guilt. BRING OUT THE SNAKE." All around me, the crowd exploded in loud cheers.

At the mention of the snake, I jerked in Baba's arms. What were they going to do with the snake? How was the snake going to make her talk? Baba didn't wait to find out. He turned around and headed for home.

It was several hours after dinner before Mama came home. The adults sat down at the tiny dining table, and NaiNai poured lukewarm tea from the tall thermos into cups for the adults. As a result of the usual evening power outage to save energy, the room lay in semi-darkness. Normally, I enjoyed the light from our oil lamp while it danced around but tonight its flickering cast eerie shadows on the walls like troublemaking ghosts ready to inflict a pestilence of bad luck.

Baba looked at my sister and me and instructed us to get busy. "Da Jing, practice some of your writing. Xiao Yu, do some drawing. We're having an adult conversation." Da Jie went to work nearby on her bed in the tiny hallway. My brother was asleep on my parents' bed. I grabbed a quilt, wrapping it around myself and gently easing down next to him. To look busy, I began pushing my snub-nosed pencil around on a piece of scrap paper.

My parents and grandmother huddled together and began whispering over their tea. I liked to listen to them when they talked, and tonight I was especially interested to hear what happened to Morning Glow. I couldn't ask for information because I knew it was impolite. I waited anxiously, pretending to be absorbed in my drawing.

"Poor Morning Glow," Mama murmured. "They've accused her of something that happened when she was barely a teenager."

"What did she do?" NaiNai asked.

"Her older brother skipped with the Nationalists to Taiwan in '49 and wrote her a letter from there. Even though the letter was confiscated at the post office and she never received it, the Red Guards said she was supposed to deliver it to enemy spies, that she belonged to an enemy group. She finally admitted it. I don't understand how she can be a spy."

"It doesn't matter whether she is or not," Baba said quietly. "If they think she is, they will do anything to make her say she is. When they put that snake into her pants, they knew she would say yes. She would sign anything they put in front of her after that."

Although my parents probably knew I was listening, it was a good thing they didn't look at me or they would be alarmed by my panic-stricken face. I thought about how it would feel to have a snake put down my pants and my skin recoiled in terror.

"Poor lady," NaiNai lamented. "She's had some bad luck."

"They even marked her with *po xie,* like an unfaithful wife," Baba added.

Po xie meant ruined shoes.

"They arrested her husband today," Mama said. "Even though this happened long before they were married, he's guilty by association."

NaiNai's spunky voice rose a little higher. "It's lucky they didn't have any children yet."

The room fell quiet for a moment before NaiNai added sternly, "I know you girls are listening." I looked up to see her sharp eye directed toward me and then at Da Jie. "Never talk about anything you hear in this room to anyone outside. NEVER!"

I quickly shook my head. I didn't want to get my family in trouble. We were all connected. If one of us encountered trouble, all of us would be punished just like the lady's husband. I trembled, thinking I didn't want anyone putting a snake down my pants to make me say bad things about my family. Although I tried as hard as possible not to worry, I could never shake my fear. My frazzled brain imagined the Red Guards taking away my family while I was left with vindictive snakes lurking everywhere to bite me.

The next autumn, just before my fifth birthday in November of 1967, my family got a scare. A group of us were boisterously playing in the courtyard, our moods more carefree than usual. Not only were our parents home most of the time, but school had been cancelled. Although I was too young to attend school, it meant the older children were around to play. Of course, we were aware of the increased fighting going on in the street and were restricted to staying within the protective walls of our compound. We lived close to the town square, and more fighting occurred here than in any other area of the city. Yet, to us, these days resembled holidays.

All of a sudden, we heard an unusual noise. It sounded like someone breaking clay tiles or pots. We looked up to see two men running on the rooftop.

"Baba, Baba, what's going on?" Da Jie yelled.

Children were scattering when Baba came running out. He had heard the footsteps on the roof from inside the house. He looked up to see men carrying guns. "Quickly, everyone rush home and get inside your houses," he ordered the children. He picked me up and grabbed Da Jie's hand, pulling her inside.

While tending to my chore of cleaning the oil lamp and trimming its wick, I realized the chaos from the street was closer to physically violating the safety of our home. That realization filled me with dread.

I knew from eavesdropping on conversations between my parents and NaiNai that the Red Guards were out of control. Some of the townspeople were angry and had formed rival groups to fight the Red Guards, which split the town into factions. Each side claimed to be the true followers of Chairman Mao's dictates, both trying to rally the support of the army. When the army gave some of them guns, I overheard Baba say he couldn't figure out why the army would do such a thing. Meanwhile, the growing violence in the town alarmed everyone.

With so much fighting going on, many businesses closed because it was too dangerous to go to work. Of course, the hospital was never closed. Whenever we heard gunshots or yelling in the street, Baba elected not to go to the hospital. It was too dangerous for him to be on the streets. If a messenger pounded on our door, however, Baba grabbed his brown satchel with the Red Cross emblem and rushed away. While he was gone, every sound from the street made time stand still and the waiting unbearable.

A few weeks later, Da Jie was sent across the street to purchase soy sauce at the market. Everything was calm when she left, but while she was in the store, groups gathered outside to fight each other. Baba worried Da Jie would get scared and try to run home. My family watched through the peepholes in the front door of our building, mentally willing Da Jie to stay in the store. I kept my hand over my mouth as I winced in alarm.

While we stared out onto the street, shouting reached a fever pitch and a gun fired. We gasped to see someone go down. When the groups broke up and moved away from each other, Baba ran across the street to the store and grabbed Da Jie's hand, rushing her back home. With terror in her eyes and a trembling chin, Da Jie slumped against Mama who wrapped her comforting arms around her frightened daughter.

A small crowd had gathered around the fallen man. Baba went to examine him and found him shot in the head. The dead man was the soy sauce salesman on his way into the store where Da Jie was shopping. He wasn't involved in the fighting, simply in the wrong place at the wrong time.

I wondered to myself how people could die so easily. How could a bullet be so powerful that it could kill someone? That night at home, NaiNai warned us children, "Be smart and always look around. Life is precious and parents can't always protect their children. It's up to each of you to be aware of danger."

That night, I dreamt my recurring dream of being surrounded by blackness. People were running around me, but my feet were mired in mud. I sensed snakes behind me and knew the gunfire and dreadful voices booming over a loudspeaker were directed at me. I always woke up out of breath in a sweaty tangle.

That winter, rumors circulated that Red Guards were more avid about entering people's houses to remove anything of value. Treasured objects and antiques were taken away and used to redistribute the wealth. If the Red Guards decided you came from a wealthy family, big trouble resulted. An investigation would determine if you were part of the elite class the Communists had revolted against. Everyone wanted to avoid this because then they would become one of the prisoners on display.

One evening, NaiNai told us she'd made a decision and wouldn't be swayed from it. "I don't want to make trouble for this family," she announced. "We must burn some of the furniture."

Mama was shocked. "But why? This furniture was your dowry."

Just before NaiNai married, her father gave her some beautifully carved cherrywood furniture—a bed with three carved sides and a wooden canopy, two nightstands with drawers, a large wardrobe, a trunk for storing blankets, a lady's grooming table, and a set of table and chairs. We admired the beautiful furniture with its delicate bronze handles and finely detailed carvings.

"I don't want this family to be accused of being wealthy or coming from a wealthy family." NaiNai informed us the Red Guards had taken a relative in for questioning earlier that day. Three past generations were examined in any investigation, and the Red Guards might discover the families of NaiNai and her husband had owned farmland. Even if the family had no money now, it didn't matter; you could be branded.

"Do we have to burn all of it?" Da Jie asked.

"No, but I think the bed's too fancy. We can remove the carved panels. The table and chairs must be burned. Maybe we can keep the other pieces."

The next day, behind closed doors, Baba took an axe to the incriminating furniture. He had negotiated with NaiNai to make an unadorned table with stools from the scraps and save as much wood as possible for future woodworking projects. She agreed but sighed, saying, "It's such nice wood just to build ugly furniture, but better that than to see it all burned."

Baba removed what offensive decorations he could with the axe or a handheld planer. Our hearts heavy, Dai Jie and I sanded the bare wood and carefully bagged all the shavings. NaiNai would use the shavings as kindling and the chopped filigreed wood as fuel when she cooked on the big stove we were assigned to use. The government had instructed us to use the large kitchen stove of the wealthy family next door who used to own the house. Although they were no longer rich, we still thought of them in that way. Generally, NaiNai avoided using their stove whenever she could use our portable mini-grill instead. She knew the other family was uncomfortable sharing with us and NaiNai tried to be respectful of their privacy.

Gossip spread that in other compounds people alerted the Red

Guards about their neighbors' suspicious activities. My family always tried to mind its own business and show respect for our neighbors, so we hoped they would ignore the unusual noises coming from our apartment.

During the furniture chopping, NaiNai withdrew into herself. Her normal resilient manner disappeared, and we knew to leave her alone.

In the middle of the afternoon, NaiNai and Mama left the house. After they returned, NaiNai announced, "I've decided we can't keep our fancy dishes."

She explained that anything with words, fortunes, good wishes, or pictures with special meanings would be considered part of the old way of thinking. We watched in horror as she took out her beautiful china bowls and began smashing them with a hammer. Then she removed some poor quality rice bowls from her shopping bags. They were ugly and plain with one little decorative stripe. NaiNai looked sadly at their uneven roundness.

Hastily, NaiNai stood up and said, "Let's see if there's anything else in this house that has any value or is sentimental." She began going through every drawer.

I brought out a little curved abalone shell, holding it up in the palm of my hand. Many times I had calmed myself by gently stroking its marbled smoothness and rocking it in the sunshine to capture the shimmering rainbow swirls. Quietly, I asked, "Can I keep this, NaiNai?"

"No, don't make trouble," she answered, snatching it out of my hand. I bit my lip to keep from crying when the beautifully colored shell lay smashed on the floor.

When NaiNai saw my sorrowful expression, she tried to console me. "Just remember, the life of every family member is more valuable than anything owned. Don't get too attached to things because you may have to give them up. Later, if things change, you can try to make up for what was lost."

That night as I lay on the newly barren bed I shared with NaiNai, I felt her shifting around. When she couldn't sleep at night, I knew she was busy thinking. At one point when I awoke in the middle of the night, I thought she might be crying but I couldn't be sure. I lay there, wishing there was something I could do to comfort her, but I only knew to give her privacy.

In the darkness, I thought about the crazy world. I thought about Morning Glow who was forced to admit to being a spy and about her husband who I learned had been beaten to death in jail. I thought about the soy sauce salesman dying unfairly. My heart went out to NaiNai who gave up her pretty things to protect our family. It seemed everyone had little control over their own lives.

When I looked at my own life, the only thing within my control was my behavior. I always tried to be an obedient child, and I was grateful for that. I wanted to help NaiNai as much as I could, to ease her burdens, and to pay her back for her kindness to me. I couldn't wish for an end to the craziness because it was all I knew and it never occurred to me that one day it might end.

NaiNai had taught me it was better to choose the path of least hope as it had a better chance of coming true. Silently, I vowed not to make trouble for my family. But then, like little dancing fireflies, tiny faraway thoughts about accomplishing something special momentarily twinkled. With a sigh, I watched them fade and die out. To stand out in any way invited trouble. That's what the dragon taught me. Contributing to the harmony of the family was what really mattered after all. As I slowly drifted back to sleep, however, my dreams belied my vow. I dreamt that a bit of the glory my naïve mind associated with the spirited Red Guard singers and dancers belonged to me.

Liu Yu, Mama, Liu Jian Guo, Baba, Liu Jing

2   *A SLEEPING TIGER OPENS ONE EYE*

Squeezing my way through the dense throng of chattering people, I reached the center of the square and smiled as I spied my friend standing in front of the performance area. Cao De Mei 曹德梅, nicknamed Pretty Green Snake after a feisty opera character, motioned me over with barely restrained enthusiasm. After I joined her, she leaned close to me and said, "Let's watch all the entertainers and decide who we want to be." I readily agreed.

The date was August 1, 1971, China's annual Army Day celebration. I stood in the square where four years earlier Morning Glow, the little seamstress lady, had been publicly tried and shamed. The setting triggered that dark memory as it always did, but I pushed it away and anxiously awaited the start of the festivities.

Colorful paper umbrellas, straw hats, and fluttering fans dotted the crowd as everyone stood in the intense 100-degree heat with its sweltering, high humidity. Small, red flags hung limply in spectators' hands without a whisper of wind to enliven them. To shield out the blinding mid-day sun, I adjusted my cap squarely over my eyes. My dingy long-sleeved cotton shirt and pants protected my skin from burning but left me smoldering in the oppressive summer heat that softened the road tar, causing a noxious oil smell to foul the air. As I shifted my feet, my plastic sandals stuck slightly to the surface of the road.

Spending long periods of time in the sun always sapped my energy, and I worried I might faint in today's heat. My poor health had never shown signs of improving, no matter how many herbal remedies and acupuncture treatments Baba had tried on me. We were determined, however, not to give up. I desperately wanted to be healthy and rid myself of my curse.

A young man with a bullhorn moved through the crowd, his commanding voice barking out, "Everyone move out of the way." The crowd shifted to allow the marching army to enter, quickly swallowing up the gap behind them.

The local army was composed of factory workers, both men and women, mainly in their twenties. They wore navy blue caps, dull white tee shirts, and overalls hanging heavily in the suffocating heat. They shouted out orders as they moved in unison. "Gun to shoulder. March, one, two, three. Look to the right, turn right. Gun ready, thrust." They stabbed their bayonet-tipped guns forward with precision. I enjoyed the performance, but ever since I saw an innocent man gunned down in the street, marching with a gun wasn't appealing.

Teenaged Red Guards performed next by singing their special songs. Although I had admired them when I was little, their violent acts had appalled me, and I knew I didn't want to be like them anymore.

During the singing, my eyes wandered aimlessly around the square until I saw a sight that made my throat tighten. Baba was standing in the crowd off to the side, and next to him was Jian Guo 建国, my younger brother, now six years old.

Baba spent a lot of his free time with Jian Guo, and I understood why. Jian Guo was his only son, but the main reason, I believed, was that Jian Guo needed supervision and coaching. He was the kind of child who was easily distracted. Baba was trying to help him control his impulsiveness. Still, the sight made me wish I were the one standing next to Baba.

Familiar scratchy music began playing over the loudspeakers, and I turned my head, noticing the next group of performers had entered the square and taken up their positions.

"Oh, look," Pretty Green Snake said excitedly, "it's Raise the Red

Lantern."

This was our favorite of the eight simple military operas revering Communist heroes that Chairman Mao's wife had approved. We knew all the songs and stories by heart because we heard them so often. The Communists had banned the older traditional Chinese operas because of their elitist vocabularies and themes, replacing them with our limited repertoire of entertainment. Some people grew bored of watching and acting out the same propaganda-filled dramas over and over, but Pretty Green Snake and I still found them entertaining. We didn't know anything else.

The performer playing the father character in the play held up his red lantern as he began singing. He wore the uniform and cap of a railroad worker. The famous Beijing actor who played the role in the movie version had two unusual facial muscles bulging under his cheeks. Pretty Green Snake and I believed those muscles had developed because he sang so much. We watched the actor in the square try to imitate having those special muscles by scrunching up his face while he sang. His efforts made us burst out in giggles.

The family in the Red Lantern play wasn't a real family. They had each lost all members of their real families and had formed a "Communist family." In a sorrowful song in the last act, the grandmother began telling the young girl named Iron Plum the truth about how her "Communist father" had sacrificed his life in the revolutionary struggle. Suddenly, Iron Plum gripped her long braid with two fists in front of her chest and jutted her elbows. She sang in a screeching, opera-like voice filled with emotion, vowing to take over her father's mission in the revolution. Symbolically, the grandmother passed the red lantern to Iron Plum who tossed her head with determination, snapping her long braid behind her.

"That's my favorite part," Pretty Green Snake said. "I want to be Iron Plum. What about you?"

Reluctantly, I admitted, "I'm not a good singer. I don't want to be that performer."

Dancers with long swirling red ribbons performed next. Their whirling streamers led me to imagine butterflies aimlessly gliding in a sun-drenched, flower-filled garden, although I rarely saw flowers. Chairman Mao, born a farmer, had decreed land should be utilized for living or growing food. He showed disgust at the sight of flowers, grass, or fruitless trees. Fears of being branded as enemies of the new China spurred people to remove signs of prosperity—destroying furniture and gardens, wearing false patches on their clothes, and making their homes appear ugly. The undulating strips of bright red color before me seemed like bright flowers in my washed-out, gray world.

Next, the ribbon dancers tied drums around their waists and took up wooden batons to thump out a snappy beat as they twirled, danced, and sang. I knew dancing was something I was capable of doing, but I didn't want to be like them because of the bright smiling faces they wore. I told Pretty Green Snake I thought their expressions looked phony.

"You don't like all the best parts," she complained.

When the final performers entered the clearing in the square, the crowd, shedding its thermal-induced stupor, buzzed with renewed excitement and enthusiastically pounded the air with red flags. A sense of pride welled up among the spectators as they watched their home-grown athletes prepare to entertain them with demonstrations of *wushu* 武术.

Chinese martial arts, known as *wushu*, made its debut in Baoying in the last couple of years, and how the people hungered for anything new. Although *wushu's* existence extended far back into China's history, it only recently became a sport the common people were permitted to learn. Before the Communist takeover, *wushu* was the closely guarded secret of elite martial arts families. Now, as a national sport unique to the country of China, *wushu* fulfilled a need for entertainment that reflected the spirit of the culture rather than the policies of the ironhanded government. *Wushu's* immense popularity at holiday celebrations enlivened and recharged the poverty-stricken, war-weary, and revolution-jaded populace.

Among the usual group of young men readying themselves to perform today, I noticed a couple of teenaged girls around the age of sixteen and, surprisingly, one boy about my age. Some of the men wore old Chinese Army uniforms with belted waists. Others represented revolutionary fighters, with men in denim overalls and girls with scarves tied around their heads. All had applied the modern face painting entertainers usually wore, darkening their eyebrows and making the cheeks of both the men and women rosy. I anticipated seeing a marked improvement in the abilities of the *wushu* athletes since their last demonstration. And, I was especially curious to see how well the boy executed his movements compared to the other martial artists.

Wushu had undergone a transformation under the Communists. In a bold move to eliminate street violence, the Communists outlawed *wushu* as a defiant fighting art with face-offs between rivals and converted it into a government-controlled exhibition sport with choreographed fighting rounds between partners. For solo performers or groups of athletes performing in unison, difficult *wushu* movements were blended into standardized athletic routines similar to gymnastics floor exercises.

Now, one at a time, sets of two or three *wushu* athletes performed fighting routines wielding various weapons against each other. The soldiers used gun-shaped or straight sword wooden weapons and poles crowned with spear tips amid a fringe of red yarn. The others employed scythes, benches, and hammers, any kind of weapon that fit the flavor of the Cultural Revolution and its revolutionary army of farmers and workers. In spite of following mapped routines, however, the athletes brought a competitive edge and daring to their movements. The risks taken by the athletes were real crowd pleasers. One false move and the opponent's weapon would no longer be narrowly missed. More than once their daring stole my breath away.

Next, the entire *wushu* troupe performed its bare-handed routine, moving dynamically in unison. My eyes were immediately drawn to the boy who was my age performing in front alongside the older athletes. I envied the strength and confidence he exhibited with his warrior-like stances, solid punches, and precision kicks. Like a panther, he advanced, leaping with deliberateness, unleashing his potent energy upon his imaginary opponent. While watching him, something happened that I had never felt before. A powerful strength welled up inside me.

I pointed my red flag in the boy's direction and shyly confided to Pretty Green Snake, "His movements look good."

"That's Young Soldier. Out of everyone in the youth class, he's been doing *wushu* the longest. He started when he was four because his father's the coach. But he's not very nice. He thinks he's so important."

Pretty Green Snake had started *wushu* lessons last year, when, with haughtiness in her voice, she had announced she was joining the *wushu* group. For weeks thereafter I felt dejected because we could no longer play together after school. I had envied her situation, but it wasn't until now that something significant shifted within me.

It started with a thought. *If I were doing wushu, nobody would think I looked sickly anymore.*

In that instant, and despite my frailty, I knew I had to learn *wushu*. I yearned to make the movements my own. I had been searching for something that would bring me the healthy vitality I desired and I sensed learning *wushu* was the answer.

I realized something else as well. For years I had subconsciously buried my desires, believing it wasn't right to want things I couldn't have or my family couldn't afford. I still remembered the feeling I had at three years old when I cried to wear a pretty New Year's outfit. I had almost forgotten what it felt like to want something new that badly, to release the tight grip I held on myself, allowing my mind to dream.

Sadly, I knew having a dream didn't mean it would come true. Getting invited to join the *wushu* class would be difficult, especially for someone as unhealthy as me. After all, the coach might think it was a waste of his time to teach someone who appeared to be a poor athletic specimen. I decided, however, I would try to find a way.

When the performance ended, the crowd burst into cheers and enthusiastic applause. I marveled at how the abilities of the *wushu* athletes evoked such a feeling of pride in the spectators. *To have caused that reaction must be such a great feeling.*

Without warning, a wave of dizziness hit me.

Unaware, Pretty Green Snake looked at me and asked, "Have you decided?"

Momentarily flustered, I responded, "Decided on what?"

"Which performer you want to be?"

"Oh, well, I think I want to be my own person."

Pretty Green Snake's eyebrows rose quizzically.

I looked down at my tar-stained sandals, feeling shy about admitting the truth. "I want to be a girl out there doing *wushu*."

"Wouldn't it be great if you could join me?" She smiled briefly before her face fell. "But I don't see how. Coach Dai teaches for fun. The fathers of all the kids in the youth class are Coach Dai's friends. Your father doesn't know him."

"I know."

Asking the coach if I could join his class would be ill-mannered. It seemed all I could do at this point was wish.

Baba was waiting for me on the corner with Jian Guo. After Pretty Green Snake left with her family, the three of us walked the short distance back to our apartment.

In the courtyard, I held a stick, scraping the tar and pebbles out of the cracks in my sandals. Baba did the same for my brother. Casually, I asked, "Baba, how did you like the *wushu*?"

"It was great. The movements were impressive."

Oh, good, he likes it.

Baba and Mama never had the opportunity to play sports. They lived through the Japanese War, the Communist revolution, the famine, and the tumultuous beginning of the Cultural Revolution. All their energies had been directed toward surviving. Mama didn't even have time to obtain a good education.

As I prodded the sticky tar that wouldn't budge, I wondered how my parents would feel about my desire to learn *wushu*. It might seem strange to them that a child who lacked robust health would feel a strong affinity for *wushu*.

At school I was a good student and my favorite pastime was trying to read Baba's books. But I often felt there was nothing special about me. Although I was born in the year of the tiger, my family had remarked I was more like a sleeping tiger. I worried I looked so sickly that the tiger in me appeared unrecognizable.

I tried not to let it bother me that I didn't have anything I could call my own. I shared my bed with NaiNai. My clothes were hand-me-downs from my sister, and hers were reworked from Mama's old ones. The shoes I wore could be from my sister or my brother, but the toes had to be cut out if I received them from my brother. Toys were rare, and I didn't own any. My sister and I didn't have any dolls. My brother was lucky to have received the wooden gun Baba had carved for him. My siblings and I collected a few postage-stamp-sized pictures of Chairman Mao and exchanged them with friends. The fancy ones were molded from iron or made of plastic. Owning them, however, didn't fill the void I felt inside. By allowing myself to dwell on my lack of ownership, I justified why I should be given the one thing I decided I now needed.

As soon as the new school year started a couple of weeks later, I lingered at the end of the day, talking with Pretty Green Snake before her coach showed up for *wushu* class. Standing by the school's wooden gate, we were making arrangements to walk to school together the next morning when a piece of chalk sailed by my head. I turned and quickly ducked the next chalky missile.

The coach's son and another younger boy who looked like his brother held fistfuls of chalk they had taken from the drying area. As a fundraiser, the elementary school made and sold chalk to other schools.

After the school's machine pressed out pieces of chalk, they were set out in a corner of the playground to dry. The students in each classroom had to meet a quota of packaging so many boxes of chalk per week.

"Go away," Young Soldier yelled. "You don't belong here."

Pretty Green Snake came to my defense. "I'm talking with my friend."

"Anyone not taking *wushu* has to leave," he shouted and threw another piece of chalk. The younger boy copied him and they both laughed.

Humiliated and angry, I hastily said to Pretty Green Snake, "I'll see you tomorrow." Instead of bolting out of the playground like a scared baby, however, I stood tall and walked regally through the gate. I ignored a piece of chalk flying past me as I continued walking while my heart raced. Halfway down the street, I passed the coach. Too bad he hadn't come a few minutes earlier.

Pretty Green Snake had been right when she said Young Soldier wasn't nice. *If I join the wushu class,* I vowed, *I'll never act rude like him.*

I knew how it felt to be tormented. Other children at school teased me whenever I fainted, calling me a little sick girl. They also made fun of my "left" voice, something I inherited from Mama. This hurt more because I didn't know how to change it. "Left" voices sang off-key and lacked the high-pitched, girlish intonations of "right" voices. After suffering through my classmates' teasing —"you could never become a teacher with that rough voice"—I shied away from talking in front of the class, unwilling to reveal how unladylike I spoke. The teasing hurt because I secretly wanted to become a teacher. Today's ridicule by the coach's son deepened my pain.

At home, I kept the teasing to myself. My siblings and I learned early to avoid complaining about other children. Sometimes neighboring parents went to other houses when there was a problem. "Your daughter is doing such-and-such," they said.

But at our house, we received no support from NaiNai or our parents. NaiNai would inform us, "Those kids aren't good. If you're getting into trouble with those kids, then you found the trouble yourself. You must think about what *you're* doing wrong and not what somebody else is doing wrong." We learned it was better to avoid trouble because nobody would protect us.

Confiding in my family about the teasing would only bring warnings to stay away from people or situations that could lead to problems, something I generally did anyway. But there was something else I had decided to talk to Baba about.

After dinner, Baba asked me about my new third grade teacher.

"She's different than Teacher Li," I said. Li Yun Xin 李云欣 had taught my first and second grade classes and was understanding and kind, but I wasn't sure how comfortable I felt with my new teacher. "She expects a lot."

"Good," Baba said.

My new teacher expected the students to participate in class by answering questions, something that was difficult for me. That afternoon, when the teacher had called on me, I rose from my chair feeling everyone's eyes on me. I knew the answer to the teacher's question, but too quickly my cheeks burned and my mind went blank. Although I desperately wanted to overcome this embarrassing fault, so far nothing seemed to help. But that wasn't what I wanted to share with Baba.

I mustered up my bravery and said, "Baba, my friend, Pretty Green Snake, takes *wushu* lessons. Do you think if I took *wushu*, it could improve my health?" This was the strategy I had worked out in my mind. If Baba thought my taking *wushu* had some merit, then maybe we could find a way for me to join the class. I breathed uneasily while I waited for his response.

"Maybe it could," he answered as he eyed me thoughtfully. "Do you want to take *wushu* for that reason . . . or because your friend takes it?"

"I want to take *wushu* because I think I'll like it," I said truthfully.

"Well, in that case, I'll think about it."

"Thank you, Baba."

He could easily have said no like many fathers, but he hadn't. Still, I wondered how long it would take to get a response, if any.

飛馬

庚申年

一旺

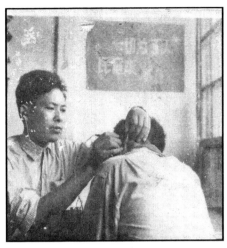
Dr. Baba

THE SIGN OF THE HORSE

The red-hot sun shimmered in wavy shafts of heat, rebounding after hitting the schoolyard bricks. A double dose of heat from both above and below made my head feel as if it were stuffed with dry rags. Sweat beaded my brow and dribbled down the valley of my back beneath my hand-me-down cotton shirt and pants now a dull gray from repeated washings in the murky river. My plastic sandals thankfully shielded my feet from the bricks baking in September's oven of feverish temperatures.

In the schoolyard, my classmates and I were arranged in a circle. A large red ball zigzagged wildly from one child to another. No one wanted to be caught with the ball when the teacher clapped her hands because then they would have to perform—sing, dance, or tell a joke or a story. I learned to be quick with the ball to avoid revealing my unmusical "left" voice.

When the ball accelerated toward me, my reactions were sluggish, and it pounded against my chest. Embarrassed, I threw it back. Although I knew I was drawing attention to myself and would incur ridicule, I left the circle to approach my teacher.

"I feel dizzy," I whispered. But before the teacher could respond, my body slumped limply at her feet.

A foot messenger rushed to the hospital to contact Baba. When he arrived, I felt shaky but better as I rested on a small cot in the school office.

Baba bent over me and pressed his hand to my forehead. He took hold of my wrist, examining the balances in my pulse.

"Xiao Yu, are you feeling worse today?"

"I got so dizzy," I admitted, feeling embarrassed to have dragged Baba away from his job to tend to a sickly daughter one more time.

"Your teacher says you fainted in the sun again. Do you think you'll faint if you get up?"

"No, Baba."

Baba extended his hand. "Here, let me help you. I'm going to take you home."

As I placed my right foot on the floor, it wiggled around loosely. "Look, Baba, the strap on my shoe is broken."

"Don't worry, I'll repair it," he said.

I shuffled across the schoolyard next to Baba with my book bag in my arms. After closing the sturdy wooden gate behind us, he picked me up and positioned me on the triangular bars protruding from the front of his bicycle. I kept my toes pointed up while my sandal dangled loosely. Instead of riding, Baba walked alongside pushing the bicycle forward and providing a backrest for me with his arm.

We headed down the narrow brick lane that resembled an alleyway with its low-roofed buildings and shops opening right onto the passageway with no protruding entryways, sidewalks, or places for plants to grow. The absence of greenery, combined with the lack of shade, sharpened the effect of the cloying heat radiating from the dogged afternoon sun.

Baba's words resounded near my ear. "The other day you mentioned a children's *wushu* class. You said you'd like to join them."

At the mention of the *wushu* class, I snapped to attention. After fainting yet again, I was afraid Baba would never consider it. My heart quickened as I answered him with a mixture of fear and hope. "Yes, Baba, *wushu* is something I really want to do."

As we rounded the corner onto the busy main street, Baba's voice rose, sounding resolute. "I've been talking to the other doctors about it, and we feel you'll become stronger and develop a better appetite if you begin *wushu* lessons. I'll find out how you can join."

I gasped, hardly able to believe my ears, then quickly moved forward with the second part of my plan.

"Baba, the older boy who lives in the building next door takes *wushu* classes in the mornings before he works. Maybe we can ask him to introduce me to the teacher."

"That's a good idea, Xiao Yu," Baba said approvingly.

A warm feeling flowed through me. "Thank you, Baba," I responded, feeling grateful to have his support. Rarely had anyone made me feel special until now.

Moving in silence alongside a wide avenue, Baba nodded to people he knew. He wasn't one to talk much, unless it was to tell his children the importance of things like working hard. The culture dictated that fathers should be stern and appear as proper role models at all times.

My father's silence didn't bother me; it was something I had learned to accept. I grew satisfied with his quiet acknowledgment of me, shown by an approving glance or a sense of nearness. Inside it felt good having Baba's attention resting on me now. As a busy doctor, he rarely spent time with his children individually. Having an older sister and younger brother had its disadvantages.

Continuing through the streets of Baoying, Baba and I passed busy shoppers in the town square where the first two-story buildings housed a department store and a candy shop. We lived around the corner on Red Flag Boulevard in building number 93.

When Baba and I entered our apartment, we discovered NaiNai wasn't home. Suffocating heat blasted us because the stove still burned the remains of coal from lunch. NaiNai never let the stove grow cold, as it would take too much time and fuel to restart.

Two years ago, the government authorized improvements in our living conditions. At no cost to us, workers had bricked over the dirt floor and built new walls, one with the novelty of a large window, though it had no glass and remained uncovered in the summer. They extended our living area so that it protruded into the third courtyard, making room for our own brick stove, an immeasurable improvement that banished the cold from our home during the long, icy winters. As part of the expansion to make room for the stove, my parents received permission to move their bed and my brother's bed into an old servants' room accessed by a door in the building across from our front door.

After giving me a cup of water to drink, Baba poked a metal rod into the fire and reached for my sandal with his large hands. When the metal was hot, he pressed it against two ends of my broken shoe strap. The plastic melted enough so that when he pinched the ends of the straps with his fingers, they fused together. To wear them, I simply adjusted the buckle to a new hole. If the strap became too short to reach the buckle, a strap from an old pair of sandals was added on.

Baba handed me the shoe and said, "Xiao Yu, maybe you should try to sleep for awhile. You have a little time before your sister and brother come home from school."

"I'll try," I answered, appreciating his concern. Naps were considered a luxury and rarely indulged in except as a treatment for illness. To be given permission for a nap was considered a gift.

In the dim bedroom—our renovations had only allowed for a small slit of a window in this room—I pulled aside the draped mosquito netting and lay down on the bed. Many years ago, I had shared my bed with Da Jie until my parents discovered how wildly she slept, kicking me, pushing me out of bed, and stealing all the blankets. I liked sleeping with NaiNai better.

I settled myself and smiled, thinking about having spent special time with Baba. Just before I drifted off to sleep, however, a worrisome thought encroached on my happiness. *What if the coach didn't accept me as a student?*

A little later, I awoke with a start, feeling nearly smothered from the heat. Outside, movement and voices resounded in the courtyards. I decided I better get up.

In the kitchen, NaiNai worked over the stove. She shoved some soup at me with her small bony hands. "Here, drink this."

"Yes, NaiNai," I answered dutifully. I thought it was too hot to drink soup, but I learned a long time ago never to argue with NaiNai. I pretended to drink the soup until it had cooled enough to suit me.

I sat down across the table from my father, who was reading. It surprised me to find him still at home. I pulled out my notebook and fountain pen and carefully practiced my Chinese characters. Occasionally, I noticed Baba's eyes resting on me, and a happy feeling billowed up inside me.

Baba, known as Liu Tian Ming-刘天明, trained first in Western medicine and later in traditional Chinese medicine. He wanted everyone to be as healthy and strong as a horse, which was his own Chinese astrological sign. Having a horse for a father meant obedience and respectfulness at all times. His serious and formidable demeanor with his children disallowed any horseplay when it was time to settle down to the business of chores or homework. Once Baba made up his mind on something, he seldom changed it. He was usually successful at influencing others and persuading them to adopt his own strong beliefs. Rarely revealing his feelings, he often seemed remote. What I didn't know then was horses hide their faults and worry about what others think of them. Baba was a typical father, molded by the culture to be the leader of the family.

"Baba," I said breathlessly as I waited for his eyes to turn toward me. "I'm feeling shy about asking our neighbor to introduce me to his *wushu* teacher. Do you think after dinner you could ask him for me?"

"Yes, Xiao Yu, I'll do that." Relief flooded through me.

I finished my writing assignment just as I heard my siblings outside in the walkway. My snake of a brother, Jian Guo, entered the room first. Although he was born under the sign of the snake, he claimed to be a little dragon instead.

"After all, they both have scales," he said, "and I don't want to have a snake as my birth sign."

People believed astrological signs predicted personalities and directions lives could take. As the symbols of emperors, powerful dragons were more popular than egotistical snakes who believed their irresistible appearances and personalities brought them many admirers. The rest of the family called my younger brother little emperor because he always tried to get his own way by whatever means necessary. This often meant he resorted to tantrums, exaggerations, devious schemes, or attempts at charming his way in or out of situations.

When Da Jie entered the room, she eyed me suspiciously. Maybe she envied my sitting with Baba, but I knew her perfectionist nature made her uncomfortable when the usual order of things was disrupted. She was astrologically a pig, preferring the comforts of her usual surroundings where the unexpected never happened.

"Baba," Da Jie inquired, "what happened to Xiao Yu today?"

"She fainted again, but she's feeling better now." Baba folded his newspaper and laid it on the table. "Jian Guo, come here."

Jian Guo slithered up to the table as if he feared some punishment.

"Xiao Yu wants to join the children's *wushu* class. I think it would be a good idea for you, too."

Disappointment flooded me because I wanted *wushu* to be something I could call my own. Then a worry flashed through my mind. *Does Baba think* wushu *is really for boys?*

Upon hearing Baba's suggestion, Jian Guo broke into a cunning grin. He tried a few choppy martial arts movements aimed at Da Jie and me, backing us against the wall.

In a stern voice, NaiNai said, "Jian Guo, there will be no practicing in this house!"

"Yes, NaiNai," he answered as he slunk away.

Whenever more than three people congregated in the kitchen at the same time, it was chaos. Now with five, we had no room to move and feelings of confinement deepened in the oppressive heat. The paper normally covering the kitchen window in cold weather had been removed so the air could circulate in and out, but it didn't help.

NaiNai then turned to me. "Xiao Yu, do you feel well enough to go to the river with Da Jie for some water?"

"Yes, NaiNai, I can do that." I quickly drank down my cooled salty broth before joining my sister outside.

From the side of the house, Da Jie and I retrieved our pole and the medium-sized wooden bucket Baba had made. Adults could carry two buckets each, but my sister and I weren't tall enough yet for two. Before we left, Da Jie asked NaiNai if there were any vegetables she wanted us to wash in the river.

"No, just get the water. And be sure you don't get into any trouble there," she warned, shaking a cooking utensil at us.

Da Jie reassured her. "No, NaiNai, we won't."

It was a relief to leave the stuffy room, and I looked forward to being at the river. Outside on the street, Da Jie and I headed west along the busy tree-lined roadway. A nearby alleyway offered access to a narrow water inlet winding behind the department store, but the hot weather and the promise of a diversion prompted us to walk farther to the river.

For the next few blocks, we strolled at a leisurely pace as we passed the public bathhouse and various shops. The street vendors hawked their colorful displays of food staples, dark clothing, shoes, and household items. Tempting aromas wafted in our direction from stalls selling fried sweets and warm buns. At this point Da Jie normally complained about how hungry she was, but today she kept silent.

At the river we removed our shoes and rolled up our pants, anxious to feel the cool water on our feet. This was our secret pleasure. NaiNai always cautioned us against this, saying we could be swept into the current. We didn't know how to swim. No one did. If we got caught in the current, no one would try to save us.

While at the river, Da Jie and I acted more like friends than sisters. We sat on the riverbank and watched as two-person fishing sampans, makeshift barges, and flat-bottomed houseboats floated by. The graceful movements of the men maneuvering their long poles behind the boats had a mesmerizing effect when combined with the gentle lapping of the water at our feet. The river was known as China's Grand Canal, transporting goods and people along the route from Beijing in the north to Hangzhou in the south.

My sister and I usually dreamed aloud about traveling to other places, though we reluctantly agreed with one of NaiNai's pronouncements. "Life on a riverboat is no life for children. They have no school to attend and no friends," she asserted irrefutably.

Today, Da Jie was surprisingly quiet. I tried to engage her in a conversation, but she only gave me short uninterested responses.

I always addressed my sister respectfully by her title as older sister. It would be disrespectful to call her by her real name, which was Liu Jing. "Da Jie," I inquired to break her silence, "do you want to count the sampans and decide which one we would like to be on?"

"No, I'm not interested in that anymore," she answered haughtily, kicking her feet in the water and tossing her head high.

Shrugging my shoulders, I wandered along the edge of the river looking for anything worthwhile that had floated in from the boats. I casually watched a graying, older woman squatting nearby, rhythmically swirling her rice-filled sieve in the turbid current. Her vegetables glistened in the sun as they dried on the rocks.

Too soon, we filled our bucket with the brown water. Usually, we were careful not to overfill, but today in the heat we didn't mind if the water sloshed out as we walked. We threaded the pole through the handle of the bucket, putting the pole on our right shoulders with the bucket between us. Behind me, Da Jie steadied the bucket with her left hand as we walked home. We then emptied the water into a tall earthenware jar kept outside our apartment door. By repeatedly turning its handle, a filter purified the water and the dirt settled to the bottom. We were almost finished, and Da Jie had yet to tell me what had caused the silence. Despite my burning desire to press her for an answer, I knew better than to ask her directly.

NaiNai's vigilant eyes never missed anything, and I saw her peering at Da Jie and me as we worked quietly side-by-side. When we finished, Da Jie abruptly left to find her friend in the courtyard. I turned around to find my grandmother standing behind me.

In her matter-of-fact way, NaiNai answered the question I'd been dying to ask. "I think Da Jing's jealous that your father wants you to take *wushu*. She'll get used to it, but I know you won't make it worse for her by acting special."

"No, NaiNai," I agreed.

She then handed me a carefully wrapped bowl of warm food. While we were gone, she had prepared Mama's dinner. Delivering it was my special job, and one I loved. It gave me a chance to see my mother whom I barely knew. I looked forward to sharing my news with her, but NaiNai's remarks and Baba's wish to have my brother join the *wushu* lessons had put a damper on my happiness. Now I could only hope Mama would make me feel better.

Mama

MAMA AND THE
CLOTHING FACTORY

The guard at the nearby factory waved me through, repeating one of his usual greetings, "I know you. You look just like your mother, Xu Qiu 徐球."

Inside the massive, busy beehive workshop, the whirring noise of the sewing machines and the loud voices of the women talking reminded me of noisy holiday firecrackers. While winding my way between long tables lit by fluorescent lamps, women on all sides yelled their greetings, never once missing a stitch. I used to worry they would injure their fingers under the furiously moving needles because they looked up at me and not at their work. It seemed like such a happy place, although working there was hard on the women's bodies. Eyestrain, backaches, and deafness were common complaints. And the women became so accustomed to talking loudly they didn't realize their voices were just as loud at home.

Mama glowed with pride when I came to visit, and it pleased me to brighten her day. The aunties at Mama's table always welcomed me with friendly greetings.

"How's school?"

"What have you been doing?"

"Look, you're getting taller."

Handing Mama her dinner, I blurted out my news, purposely omitting the fact that Jian Guo shared it. "Mama, Baba says I can join the children's *wushu* class."

On all sides, I heard, "You're a lucky girl."

Mama exclaimed, "That's wonderful, Xiao Yu."

I basked in momentary glory until I remembered my episode at school. Suspecting someone else's child might come in and mention it, I decided to admit it. "Mama, it was so hot today at school. I got dizzy while we had class outside and fainted. Baba had to come and take me home."

She wrinkled her brow. "Xiao Yu, you make me worry."

Then a stream of advice flowed from the ladies.

"You should eat more."

"Drink more soy milk."

"Yes, soy milk is good for you."

Mama motioned me closer. "Come and stand by my fan to cool off." The weak flow of warm air coming from the ladies' fans had little cooling effect in the overcrowded factory. More than a gentle breeze was needed to clear the musty, stagnant air.

"Thank you, Mama. But please don't worry. I'm feeling fine now."

These were precious moments I spent with Mama. Although we lived in the same home, Mama's work schedule left her with limited time to be with her family, especially after the government combined all the local seamstresses into one large company to handle foreign contracts that made clothing items for shipment overseas.

NaiNai insisted Mama spend her leisure resting and have no household responsibilities because she worked twelve to fourteen hours each day. Although entitled to one day off each week—with no yearly vacations—workers were often asked to give up their Sundays off to meet contract deadlines. The company officials didn't want to lose face by being late with an order, and the workers earned double pay they felt they couldn't turn down. Although Mama worked hard at the factory and put in extra hours whenever possible just to earn additional money, her pay amounted to a paltry sum per hour.

Sometimes Mama seemed like a distant relative. Sadly, we simply had very little time to get to know each other. Once I rudely voiced my objection to her long work hours. Mama put her hand up and stroked my hair, telling me her job wasn't something she would spend time thinking about liking or disliking because she had no other choice. It was just something that had to be done.

Mama was born a rooster, a very hard-working person who is adaptable in a life filled with many setbacks. Roosters create ways to make a living out of nothing but never seem to strike it rich. They grow impatient towards those with no ambition but are always willing to help others succeed. Roosters make extremely loyal friends. But never criticize roosters because they're fragile and can easily develop inferiority complexes.

Unlike the generations before her, Mama's life was very hard. The Japanese and civil wars drained money from many families, especially Mama's, because her father died when she was nine years old. The wars interrupted her education and, although she learned to read, her reading lacked broad Chinese character recognition. She felt badly about this and encouraged her children by telling us, "If my reading was good, I would have a better job. You must study hard and learn as much as you can." Knowing how she struggled, I vowed to study hard at school to make both my mother and father proud.

In the dimly lit factory, Mama finished sewing a seam and put her work aside. As she uncovered her dinner bowl and began eating, I looked up and casually surveyed the entire factory of women diligently working elbow-to-elbow as they slumped over their whizzing machines. Although I knew these women were grateful to have jobs, they had sacrificed too much of their lives and health to be here. Even though I never heard Mama complain, it seemed to me she enjoyed very few of the important things in her life, especially her family. I silently hoped I wasn't seeing my future and that my diligence at school would pay off in a better job. I didn't want to be stuck in a job that was all-consuming.

Mama interrupted my thoughts by saying, "Xiao Yu, the company is selling bags of fabric scraps tomorrow. Maybe you want to take a look."

"Yes, Mama, I'll do that."

I wandered over to inspect the shapes, sizes, and colors of the scraps. My favorite ones were printed with delicate pink, red, and blue flowers on an ivory background. The government-owned clothing stores in China never sold anything colorful. Even the old-fashioned Chinese silk was no longer available. As part of Chairman Mao's destruction of China's four olds—old ideas, old cultures, old manners, and old customs—only three main colors were acceptable to wear—a dark navy blue, an army khaki color, and white, which was worn in the summer. The only other color visible on store-bought clothing was a little bit of red on the uniforms of the army soldiers. Chairman Mao wanted everyone to look like country people or soldiers.

The company sold the scrap bags for a little less than one hour's worth of wages per bag. We used these scraps to make patchwork blankets, book bags, and the soles of the black cotton shoes we wore in the winter. Our family also traded the scraps with relatives in the countryside for precious nuts, grains, and seeds, which we saved in jars for our New Year celebration. Adding bits of color to my gray existence helped chase away weariness, especially in the bleak winter months.

While inspecting the colorful fabrics, a bent over woman carrying a washing bucket shuffled by. I knew right away who she was and my heart filled with sadness. It was Morning Glow, not the same kind woman who had once helped me, but a shell of a woman who shunned eye contact with everyone. After spending a couple of years in jail—which meant sleeping at the jailhouse and working each day in unwanted jobs such as repairing cracks in roads or cleaning government offices—she was released and given a job, not as a seamstress like she had been before but as a washerwoman, the lowest job possible at the factory.

I had seen Morning Glow on the street with her head bent low in shame, always sneaking by on the farthest edge of the street, as far away from other people as possible. One time as I walked with NaiNai, I saw boys throwing rocks at Morning Glow as she scurried on her way.

"NaiNai, look at what those boys are doing to Morning Glow."

"They shouldn't do that. When people have a hard time, Xiao Yu, you shouldn't make it worse for them. It only draws attention to yourself and could bring trouble. Leave the unfortunate people alone. You can't help them without someone saying you're sympathizing with an enemy of Chairman Mao. Morning Glow understands that. She wouldn't want you to get in trouble, too. Just open your eyes and learn from what you see. Don't be the one who gets caught, who trips and falls with no one to help you."

As I watched Morning Glow hobble away to attend to her cleaning chores, I recalled NaiNai's words and knew I couldn't say anything to this poor lady. Seeing her reinforced my desire to avoid trouble at all cost. I didn't want to be as lonely as I imagined she was with no husband, no children, and no friends.

Even though it was my dinnertime, I lingered while saying goodbye to Mama and the aunties. At home, NaiNai asked me to summon my sister and brother. After finding them in the second courtyard, I slowly walked back to our apartment so I wouldn't have to feel angry at Jian Guo for shoving past me to wash his hands and gloating over getting served first. Even if he didn't rush, he would still get served first because he was the only boy in the family, the little emperor. Once I asked him, "Why don't you just relax? We'll let you have dinner first." But he just looked at me like I was crazy to take all the fun out of it for him.

NaiNai cooked steamed greens with sliced water lily roots, the local specialty. These roots were sliced, shredded, or ground up and became part of one of the recipes at each meal. Yummy packages of sweet red beans surrounded by sticky rice were also served. NaiNai prepared them by wrapping the ingredients in leaves, shaping them like lilies, and carefully tying them before boiling. Meat rarely graced our plates.

The steamy heat from the cooking hung in the sweltering room, reducing my appetite. Poking my food around with chopsticks, I watched Jian Guo stuff his mouth and begin crying because there was no more food. Ever since I could remember, he cried during meals, especially in the wintertime when we only had rice and pickles to eat. Although Jian Guo didn't have anemia, he suffered from a lack of proper nutrition. Da Jie was the only one of us children who was lucky enough to be born at a time when everyone ate plentiful meals at communal kitchens.

I turned my attention away from my whimpering brother to thoughts about starting *wushu*. I noticed a restless, anxious sensation bubbling in my chest like it did at the start of a holiday. It felt strange to have something new to consider in my life. I never spent much time thinking about what I didn't have, but now my thoughts turned to what I could have.

Unwrapping the leaves of my sweet rice packet, I watched the steam escape into the humid air. As I did, a secret yearning glowed brighter inside me. Was it possible I would be allowed to learn *wushu*? I would practice hard in exchange for the honor and diligently try to conceal my low level of endurance. I idly savored the memory of my rare private conversation with Baba earlier that day. If I were accepted to start *wushu*,

I knew I could make Baba proud of me. *Maybe, he won't see me as just a health problem he has to remedy or one more mouth to feed.*

"Xiao Yu, stop slumping and sit up straight," NaiNai instructed as she sat in the empty chair across from me, placing her bowl of food on the table. Baba was served his dinner first, and then we children ate when there was room at the table. I was a slow, picky eater and usually the last one done. Baba hoped *wushu* would help me gain an appetite.

In the evenings, after completing my homework and bathing in the big oval-shaped wooden tub placed in the kitchen, my sister, brother, and I hurried along to play. Except in extremely hot weather, all the children in our building gathered together in one of the courtyards for play-acting or storytelling, leaving our apartments free for the adults to take turns bathing and tidying up.

Storytelling ranked as our favorite after-dinner activity. When I was about five or six, the lively tales told by the oldest son of one of the families in our building attracted all the children. Each family carried a portable bed, a stiff bamboo slab placed across two benches, out to the courtyard. Expectant children sat or curled up on their bamboo beds, listening to scary stories. Our neighbor—who seemed so grown up because he was in high school—tried to frighten us so we would run home or have bad dreams, but it didn't work. Even though we felt chills down our spines and bumps on our skin, we were thrilled and enjoyed it immensely. When our storyteller moved away, it saddened us and forced us to play games instead. Games disappointed me, however, as they often led to competition and cheating by the boys involved.

On especially hot nights like this, all the families moved into the street to be cooler. The roadway was wide, much wider than any of the courtyards. A long, narrow strip of rocks made a divider in the middle of the road, and patterns of rocks and bricks embedded in tar filled out its sides. During the day, bicyclists covered the road along with an occasional government car. In the evening, it was like a big party out in the street. This was the only time my sister, brother, and I were allowed to play outside our building. There would be music and singing and other neighborhood children. Best of all, a skillful storyteller from a nearby building kept us enthralled. Part of me couldn't wait to join in the fun, while the other part of me fretted over whether my neighbor would agree to my request.

What if he didn't help me? What then? Baba and I would have

to find some other remedy for my poor health. My future demanded it. Whether I became a teacher as I hoped or ended up working day and night in a factory like my mother, I needed to develop enough stamina to do my job or risk losing it and never having enough to eat.

飛馬

虔心筆

一旺

Liu Jing

Liu Yu

Liu Jian Guo

 STREET PARTY

Leaving our building, I immediately scanned the area for my neighbor who I hoped would introduce me to the *wushu* coach. Disappointed at not finding him, I joined a cluster of children standing alongside the road watching families prepare their own special areas of the street.

I watched Baba lug a bucket of water he carried from the house, emptying it onto our part of the road to cool it down. Next, he fetched the bamboo bed so NaiNai had a comfortable place to sit. Little by little, the street filled up with older children. After chores were finished, more adults would come with their younger children in tow.

Skipping over to greet me with long braids swinging behind her, a schoolmate asked me, "Liu Yu, what happened to you on the playground?"

I looked shyly down as I explained, "I fainted from the heat, but I'm feeling better now."

Then, our favorite storyteller from one of the nearby buildings strolled over, and all the children quickly encircled him. "Let me tell you a tale that's true," he started. He sat down with his back to the building while we clambered for positions around him.

His tales revealed bravery in battles, intrigue among the rulers of the dynasties, and love stories with unfavorable outcomes. Sometimes we heard old Chinese legends about mischievous dragons or how the stars were formed. During the height of the Cultural Revolution, many stories weren't allowed because they represented the old way of thinking, especially any stories with a religious connotation.

When our storyteller finished, no one moved, but we all cried for more. "Maybe later," he said.

No longer distracted by the storyteller, I searched again for my neighbor. More adults were coming out, exchanging friendly greetings, glad to break the routine of work and enjoy each other's company. When I spotted our *wushu* neighbor, I looked around for Baba. He was engaged in a conversation in front of the large post office window where the most recent newspaper was displayed for poor families to read for free.

I ran over to Baba and patiently waited for him to notice me. When he looked my way, I reminded him he agreed to speak to our neighbor for me. Baba nodded and we made our way over to the other side of the road.

Baba exchanged greetings with Liu Zheng Qiang 刘正强, our neighbor, whom I called Da Liu, or Big Liu. Baba cleared his throat. "I heard you're taking *wushu* lessons at the park."

"Yes, Dr. Liu, that's correct." Even though our neighbor was out of high school and working, he was part of a group of older students who received lessons at the park each morning with the children.

"I believe my daughter and her younger brother would greatly benefit from *wushu* lessons. I would like to get them an introduction to the teacher."

"Oh, yes, *wushu*'s a very good thing." Then he turned to me. "Let me see how flexible you are. Reach down and touch your toes."

I didn't know he would ask me to do anything for him, but I didn't hesitate to comply and was proud of my flexibility.

"Good, good. Now, can you do the splits?"

That, too, was easy for me.

"How high can you raise your leg while standing?" He nodded his head approvingly at my leg lift.

"Do you want to test my brother?" I asked.

"No, that won't be necessary." He turned to my father and said,

"Yes, Dr. Liu, I'll give them an introduction." Directly asking a teacher to join his class was considered impolite. Instead, an introduction was necessary. The person doing the introductions vouched for both parties, thereby bearing some responsibility if problems arose in the future. This method also allowed a teacher or *sifu* to make a decision without embarrassment.

"Before they start, I think it would be a good idea for me to teach them a few stretches and movements so they won't feel out of place."

We made arrangements to meet the next afternoon, after our half day of school on Saturday. Baba was pleased and thanked Da Liu. I thanked him, too.

"We're lucky tonight, Xiao Yu," Baba reassured me.

I agreed with him. "Thank you, Baba."

Anxious to share my good news, I joined NaiNai on the bamboo bed. "NaiNai, Da Liu has agreed to introduce me to the *wushu* coach."

"I'm happy for you, Xiao Yu. You know, however, it'll be hard work. You're going to have to eat more if you want to have the stamina you need to keep up."

"Yes, NaiNai." I knew she was right. I often found it difficult to finish my meals, something my brother couldn't understand. Glancing around and noticing how thin my neighbors looked, I wondered how I could possibly get enough food to build up my endurance and improve my health with my family's meager rations, and with so much of it going to my brother.

At that moment a musician began playing a lovely, high-pitched melody on the *erhu*, a two-stringed violin. The familiar music—an older, traditional Chinese style—meandered through the neighborhood wrapping and uniting everyone in a deep sense of camaraderie.

Amid the soothing music, I noticed a mysterious longing deep within tugging at my heart. Although I wasn't used to idle fantasizing, my mind kept returning to images of myself performing *wushu* with determination and grace. I imagined my body filling with strength until all my weakness was gone. My fainting spells would disappear and then my classmates wouldn't stare at me and snicker behind my back. In my reverie, I imagined Baba smiling with pride and saying, "We did it, Xiao Yu. You won't be sick again."

My daydreaming was interrupted when Mama's workplace let out, a whole stream of ladies filling the street with their loud voices. It was extremely rare that Mama didn't work overtime. Usually, she came home after I was already asleep.

Mama carried her empty dinner bowl as she made her way through the street full of beds and sat down beside me. I passed my good news on to Mama, inwardly smiling with contentment at her happiness for me. To keep Mama sitting by my side instead of going home to bathe, I took this opportunity to ask her a question that had been tumbling around in my mind.

"Mama, how did I get my name? Is it because I'm so precious?" I asked as I beamed up at her in hopeful innocence.

One of the meanings of *yu* is jade, a highly valued green or white stone carved into jewelry or statues that is believed to have protective properties. I always considered jade to be the meaning of my name. Yet, several meanings can exist in the Chinese language for each written word, depending on its spoken tone or inflection or its combination of Chinese characters. Was it possible there were other meanings to my name?

Mama didn't respond right away but eyed me thoughtfully. Finally, she said, "Do you want to know the truth?"

"Yes," I said, wondering what she might say.

She sighed and looked away briefly before beginning. "When I was pregnant with you, everyone was starving. We didn't have enough food to feed ourselves. It was much worse than now. During the harvest before you were born, we traveled to my family's village to pick produce whenever I received a day off from my job. Occasionally, your father helped a farmer in exchange for a little rice or maybe some meat if the farmer had to kill a starving cow. Sometimes, your father was forced to take little bits of food from the hospital, which made him uncomfortable."

I listened respectfully but wondered what this had to do with naming me.

"Often in my sleep, I dreamt about food. In my dream the night before you were born, I was walking in a cornfield. The Chinese character for corn is *yumi*. Separately, *mi* means rice and *yu* means having the shape of a jade stone. I didn't think about jade when I named you. I thought about food because I was starving."

What a disappointment to find I was named after corn by a starving parent. I wrinkled my brow. "That's not a very dramatic name," I said.

Mama patted my hand lightly. "When you were born I didn't call you corn because it wasn't a good name. I decided to give you only the

Yu part because Yu is a well-known girl's name, and I thought it was pretty."

NaiNai had been listening to our conversation and jumped in, "Your full name is Liu Xiao Yu." Liu was my father's family name and Xiao meant little. "You were supposed to have three parts to your name and shouldn't have changed it."

"Well, I'm not always going to be little," I said with a touch of defiance. "When I'm older, I'd still be called little."

I remembered clearly how angry NaiNai was when she discovered I used a blob of black ink to mark out the Xiao part of my name in our family's identification book. We never had birth certificates, and the only record of my full name existed in that book. I was quite young and didn't want anyone to see my middle name. It embarrassed me. Several years later our family had to apply for a new identification book. How pleased I was when the new book came back indicating my two-name status.

NaiNai whispered so our neighbors wouldn't overhear, "I'm glad the government didn't find out. It would have made trouble for our family. No one was allowed to change a name at that time."

On the sidewalk in front of the candy store, a group of boys, Jian Guo included, talked loudly, waving their arms around trying to appear bigger than they were. "Mama, tell me what my brother's and sister's names mean."

I saw my mother glance in Jian Guo's direction and nod her head.

"The meaning behind your brother's name is 'to build up a country.' Your sister actually changed her name, too. When she was born just before the famine, everyone wanted to select names for their children showing their support for the revolution. Her first name, Jin, meant 'move forward or you will fall behind,' a slogan popular at that time. She didn't like it and changed it to Jing, which means quiet."

"But, she didn't take away one of her names," NaiNai said, warming to an argument.

Choosing a name in China was serious business. Names were believed to guide and influence what kind of person the child will grow up to be. Before my sister changed her name, she was briefly a Red Guard trainee. She proudly wore a red armband and scarf to school. These were awarded to any student who excelled. One time, she borrowed a Red Guard hat and coat to have her photo taken. After she changed her name, it seemed to change her personality. She gave up her interest in being a Red Guard and chose to go back to being quiet and calm.

"NaiNai, how'd you choose Mama's name?" I asked.

"It was different before the revolution. We had to think about the family tree. Everyone in your mother's generation had to have a first name that began with the same Chinese character. Her first name means ball, something round."

"Ball doesn't make much sense for a girl's name."

"By the time your mother was born, a lot of the good names were taken. I chose from names that were left."

It took two Chinese characters to write out Mama's first name of Qiu. The first character was the one signifying her generation within the Xu family. It was combined with a second character to make up the meaning. When a name was read, people wanted to be able to place it in the proper generation. After the revolution, customary naming practices were abandoned, as were many things traditional.

NaiNai took the opportunity to suggest that Mama go home and rest. I didn't want to be selfish because I knew extra rest was precious to her, but I felt sad to see her go.

Suddenly, a lone voice began singing a fiery and spirited marching song. People nearby eagerly picked up the tune. Soon everyone up and down the street joined in with passion in their voices. They didn't sing the song because they were nostalgic for the past; they just liked how it made them feel proud. I'm sure all the vocalists would agree, however, they were relieved when the fighting ended. During the beginning of the Cultural Revolution, just a few years back, this street where we now enjoyed the outdoors wasn't a safe place.

After the dust settled on the commotion stirred up during that time, we discovered Jiangsu Province had fared better than most of China. The people in our province were generally better educated and had studied Confucianism with its principles of maintaining justice and peace. The uneducated people in other provinces reacted more violently and didn't always understand the meaning of the Cultural Revolution. Instead of forcing affluent families to share their homes and wealth, they used the Cultural Revolution as a justification to kill them.

In Jiangsu Province, many wise merchants—including the wealthy family that lived next door—predicted the revolution and turned over their holdings to the townspeople so they could claim they were now like everyone else. In this way, negative consequences were avoided. The townspeople rationally understood the merchants were willing to cooperate and abide by the new dictates of the country. This tempered animosities and smoothed the transition to a new form of government.

I was glad the fighting in the streets had died down, making our town a safer place. Our family had been lucky. The secret NaiNai carried about her ancestors' having once owned land remained undiscovered. Mama wasn't singled out by the Red Guards and criticized like her former co-worker, Morning Glow. And Baba could easily have been trapped on the streets during a skirmish as he rushed to and from patients' houses on emergency medical calls. I hoped no fighting flared up again.

Baba strolled over and suggested it was time for the family to go inside. He picked up the bed and we walked toward Jian Guo. Da Jie came out of nowhere and joined us. As we walked back, I couldn't decide if the queasy feeling in my stomach was an anxious happiness or nervousness at the possibility of the *wushu* coach rejecting me and sending me home in disgrace. Although he could say no, he could also say yes. I hoped for yes.

Mama, cousin, Liu Jing, Baba, NaiNai

6   *A DRAGON IN THE HOUSE*

Before the clouds blushed in response to the morning sun, the dragon in our house roused everyone from their slumbering beds. NaiNai ruled our household as if she were indeed a dragon, the sign of her birth. Dragons act as commanders, expecting everyone to bow to them and respect their authority. These successful individuals are fearless in the face of a challenge, exhibiting confidence and enthusiasm. People are warned to choose their battles carefully with dragons because dragons are intolerant and make ferocious opponents.

    True to her birth sign, NaiNai cooked, cleaned, washed clothes, and maintained order in the house with her own fiery zeal. She was the first one up in the morning and the last one to bed. With one look from her penetrating eyes and a firm hand on her hip, she demanded our attention. We children learned to obey before we were caught in a wrath of words from which it was hard to escape.

    I needed no prompting today to drag myself out of bed even after sleeping fitfully during the night. While brushing my teeth outside in the courtyard and then washing my hands and face indoors over the washing bowl, I shuddered with apprehension about whether my plan to take *wushu* lessons would work. In an attempt to keep my mind off my anxiety, I turned my attention to my chores.

Morning chores included the dreaded cleaning of the smelly commode. In our entire housing compound no one had a bathroom. Instead of a flushable toilet, we used a wooden chamber pot. At 5:30 the village farmer collected the contents of our commode, using it as fertilizer on her crops. In exchange, she occasionally brought us some white cabbage or other vegetables. The service she provided was invaluable, saving the city people from the problem of waste disposal. Once our commode was emptied, NaiNai made sure it was thoroughly cleaned.

My favorite job each morning was helping an elderly neighbor whose son incurred trouble during the Cultural Revolution. People said the son talked too straight, saying things he shouldn't have said. This prompted the government to send him to live permanently in another village. The father of this boy now lived alone in a one-room apartment in our building with no family to care for him.

After I brought my neighbor a bottle of water that NaiNai had freshly boiled, the neighbor gave me enough money to buy one long loaf of bread and two little Chinese bread buns at the market across the street. As compensation, he gave me one of the little buns, which I took home to eat with my breakfast.

Jian Guo, overtly eyeing my bun, asked, "NaiNai, could I have the bun for a change?"

"No, it belongs to Xiao Yu. She deserves it for being nice and helping our neighbor."

I learned a lot from witnessing the kindness NaiNai showed others. Sometimes Baba's patients paid with fresh fish, shrimp, or vegetables. Then NaiNai cooked extra and shared it with many of the neighbors, who returned the favor on other occasions. This was one way we were able to enjoy a variety of foods. As a young girl watching NaiNai's generosity to other families, I learned how to get along with other people.

After breakfast my siblings and I departed for Saturday's half day of school. With my attention elsewhere, I squirmed in the classroom and frequently lost my concentration until I looked up and saw my teacher's disapproving expression directed at me. My face reddened, and I tried harder to focus on my work after that.

Finally, the afternoon arrived and Jian Guo and I met Da Liu in our courtyard for our *wushu* lesson. He taught us a stretching routine and some stances we needed to know before the practice at the park the next morning. Jian Guo was being very attentive and didn't try to hog all the attention for once. He seemed a little intimidated because our neighbor was older.

"Don't worry about memorizing the routine today," Da Liu said. "It'll be easy to follow everyone else. At least you know what the stretch or stance is supposed to look like."

Still worried about tomorrow, I tried to discern whether Da Liu had any qualms about introducing us to the coach. I didn't notice anything until Da Liu hesitated before speaking again.

"I've noticed that a few children find the *wushu* lessons too hard. Others think the intense stretching is too painful. Sometimes, they quit. Coach Dai is a strict teacher. He doesn't tolerate talking or not paying attention," he warned. "But I'm sure you both will do fine."

He sounded confident the coach would accept us. I wished I shared his belief.

We arranged to walk to the park with him early the next morning and thanked him for his help.

Da Jie then came out into the courtyard to inform me that NaiNai needed my help. "I'm leaving because I have important things to do," she announced.

"What are you doing?" I asked her.

"I'll be stringing firecrackers with my friend," she boasted and turned to leave. This was her way of saying I couldn't come with her because I wasn't old enough, but I knew she was just jealous because she had been excluded from the *wushu* lessons.

Da Jie helped her friend's family by braiding firecrackers together to make long strands. She earned money for the family in this way, and it made her feel important, like she had a real job. She didn't like housework, preferring instead to work away from home.

Inside, I found NaiNai preparing to soak her feet, which she did faithfully each week because it was important for her health. When NaiNai was very young, her family began the process of binding her feet. Families with daughters had to make them desirable for marriage, and parents would never consider a marriage for their son if the prospective bride didn't have small, delicate feet. Therefore, from approximately six years of age, parents of high breeding painstakingly bound their daughters' toes and midfoot so that they curled beneath the soles of their feet. The children were then forced to walk on their bound feet until the tiny foot bones broke, allowing the foot to be manipulated into a new shape.

Before a husband's family agreed to any marriage, they first checked the size of the girl's feet. The men found the three-inch golden lily feet beautiful and erotic. Even the women developed a certain amount of pride in their tiny feet and looked on the foot nature shaped as mannish and ugly. Since the Cultural Revolution, binding a woman's feet was no longer an acceptable practice, frowned upon as part of the Four Olds. But many older women, like NaiNai, were still alive who had them.

Now, I watched as she took off her little shoes and two pairs of socks and put the bent-up feet in the tub of water to relax and clean them. Her feet were so little, her bones so small. The shape of each foot was in a crooked pattern with the top of the foot bent underneath, and the bones all smashed together. She supported her weight on her big toes and heels as she walked. As I glanced at her crippled feet, it repulsed me to imagine the pain she went through as a girl.

NaiNai's tiny feet were considered perfectly sized, which was a sign of proper upbringing, much as education was valued by the culture today. I compared them to the feet of our neighbor who formerly owned the building. NaiNai's feet were faultlessly smaller, an indication she was highly born and raised.

Each week I helped NaiNai by trimming her calluses, something her failing eyes prevented her from doing. After she finished soaking her feet, I snipped away the dead skin carefully with scissors, trying not to cut too deep and draw blood. Da Jie avoided this task because the smell emanating from NaiNai's feet nauseated her. It didn't bother me as much.

Baba once told me I had the talent to become a doctor like him— though I fancied the idea of becoming a teacher instead. Sometimes, I noticed Baba's look of disappointment when he saw how repulsed Jian Guo was by the sight of blood. I suspected Baba wished Jian Guo would follow in his footsteps.

With my small hands, I gently massaged NaiNai's swollen legs to get her blood moving. Sinking into the chair, NaiNai tucked a loose stand of hair carefully back into place, and I thought about how NaiNai always tried to look her best.

NaiNai's clothes were old but always clean. She pressed them with her hands until the wrinkles disappeared. She once told me, "Being poor isn't something to be ashamed of because sometimes there isn't any other choice. But, Xiao Yu, you have to make people respect you by being neat and clean."

I noticed people did respect her. This taught me about having my own sense of dignity and self-respect, though I had to counterbalance it with my desire not to bring trouble to the family. Showing too much dignity wasn't a good thing.

I felt sorry for NaiNai because traditionally women with *shan chun jing lian* feet were supposed to have servants to do heavy housework. Becoming newly impoverished due to wars, the Cultural Revolution, or early widowhood left many crippled women to cope with formidable chores. Even with swollen legs at day's end, however, I never heard NaiNai complain.

By watching NaiNai and Mama, I learned that a woman's life wasn't easy. I didn't have NaiNai's bound feet and wasn't prevented from studying hard at school like Mama, yet I knew some new oppression could come along. There were no guarantees my life would be any easier. A new war, another severe famine, or a second Cultural Revolution could happen at any time. As a result, fear permeated our lives despite some improved conditions over the past twenty years since the Communists had taken over China.

As I gingerly rubbed NaiNai's misshapen feet, I asked, as I always did when rubbing NaiNai's feet, about her life and Mama's.

"My parents raised me to act like a lady," she replied in a dignified tone. "I had private schooling and learned to read." Then her voice grew softer as she added sadly, "When my husband died young, your mother was only nine years old. I had to raise my children without his support."

NaiNai paused and idly smoothed out the socks in her lap. Then she looked up at me with an unusually tender and sentimental look, one that deep down in my soul made me feel loved.

"I had a very comfortable life, but then everything changed. Life can go up and down, Xiao Yu. Everything you have could disappear very fast. Today you own this, but maybe tomorrow you won't have it. The most important thing is what kind of person you are on the inside. And, you must study hard. That's the way you can prove yourself."

Having so little in my life that was actually within my control, I had eagerly taken up the challenge of being a top student. Becoming well educated was going to make a difference and help me beat the odds someday. However, I knew my unhealthiness put me at a disadvantage. If I could conquer this weakness, my chances of a better life would increase dramatically. My determination to begin *wushu* grew stronger the more I sensed it would help me eliminate the weakness that made me unequal with everyone else. Again, I hoped the last part of my plan—having the coach accept me—came true.

Wushu class students in Baoying
(Liu Yu is in the back row, third from the left,
and Young Soldier is in front of her)

THE ONE-ARMED TEACHER

Dreams slipped away as the customary wake-up song aired over the loudspeakers.

The sun rises, the east becomes red.
A Savior is born for China.
Mao Zedong is like a sun, so bright.
He amasses fortune for the people.
Hu-ya Hey-ya.
He is the people's liberating star.
Chairman Mao loves the people.
He is our guide to create a new China.
Hu-ya Hey-ya.
He leads us forward.
The Communist Party is like the sun.
Wherever it shines, there is light.
Wherever there is a Communist Party,
Hu-ya Hey-ya.
There the people are saved.

The familiar lyrics danced in my head, as they had every morning at 5:00 for as far back as I could remember. In the Sunday morning blackness, I woke up feeling uncertain about what the day would bring. My stomach churned as I slid out of bed, quickly dressing before NaiNai came to rouse me.

I found NaiNai shuffling around the cooking stove, stoking the fire. My job was to wake up my brother who was asleep in our parents' room. I tiptoed into the room so I wouldn't disturb my parents and shook Jian Guo gently until he tumbled out of bed with a sleepy look of reluctance. We quietly slipped out of the room into the darkness of the pre-dawn morning. At one of the courtyards, we joined our neighbor to walk to the park for our first *wushu* lesson.

Sounds of a city coming to life broke the spell of peacefulness that had enveloped me. In the darkness street sweepers were already out with their long brooms made from tree branches, sweeping away the prior day's debris. I wished I could sweep away my insecurities that easily.

When Coach Dai began teaching *wushu*, it was to high school-aged students first. Two years ago, he started a children's group, though his older son began receiving instruction before that. All the students were children of his friends. I feared the teacher would wonder why he should spend time teaching me *wushu* when he didn't know my family and I would be way behind the other children.

When we arrived at the park, I looked around at the children eyeing me suspiciously. Young Soldier huffed, his face glowering with displeasure. Being rejected meant I would face humiliation and endless teasing.

When Da Liu walked toward the teacher, Jian Guo and I respectfully held ourselves back. My breathing became shallow and my heart hammered in my chest. I overheard our neighbor say, "Coach Dai, I brought my neighbors, Liu Yu and her brother, Liu Jian Guo." He pointed in our direction. "Their father is Dr. Liu. They really want to join the *wushu* class and hope you'll admit them."

I watched the coach pause. His bushy black brows furrowed as he considered the request.

Da Liu quickly added, "If you're concerned they'll be behind the other students, I can help them learn the basic stretches and stances."

When, at last, he pointed to the back of the group and said, "Okay, just go there," a whoosh of air escaped my lungs.

During the practice I tried very hard to keep up. Out of the corner of my eye I saw Coach Dai look over at Jian Guo and me a couple of times, evaluating our abilities. I knew the lessons were considered mostly for fun and no one needed to be outstanding in order to participate, but some spark inside pushed me to do my best.

One of Coach Dai's older students led the group in various stretches and drills. Da Liu had explained on our way to the park that Coach Dai didn't give any special teaching or individual attention to most of the students. This was the Chinese way. First, beginners had to prove themselves worthy of special training. They had to follow the group as best as they could and learn the routine by themselves. Most Chinese teachers waited to see if the students really wanted to learn. Teachers didn't want to put much energy into teaching if the students didn't stick with it. This was the way the teachers tested students' commitment.

When the class stretched, I stretched. I knew I wasn't doing it correctly, but little by little I began to figure it out. Fortunately, I was flexible because otherwise catching up would have been even harder.

At the end of that first instruction and despite the incredible disadvantage I felt for being such a beginner, I realized I had never been so happy in all my life.

Pretty Green Snake rushed over and questioned me, "How did you manage to get in?"

"Da Liu is my neighbor and agreed to introduce me," I said carefully, trying not to leak too much of my bubbling emotion for fear of what she might do should she know how desperately I wanted this

To my surprise she said, "That's great," and joined us on our walk home.

Even though I became part of the morning *wushu* group, I wasn't considered a member of the children's *wushu* class and couldn't go to practices after school. Seven mornings a week, Jian Guo and I practiced at the park alongside the other children and our neighbor's group who were about fifteen to twenty-five years old.

Learning the rigorous *wushu* maneuvers wasn't easy for a sickly child like me. Yet, as I tried to imitate the leader's movements, in my imagination I was moving with the grace and power displayed by the *wushu* athletes I had seen performing in the town square. A new feeling of vitality stirred within as my inner tiger cub yearned to develop her muscles.

Over the next three months, I began noticing my stamina slowly improving, although anytime I didn't eat enough, I became too weak to do well, suffering dizzy spells in class or on the way home. It became a challenge not to let the coach notice anything was wrong with me.

As wintertime descended on Baoying, our class began a half hour later and lasted only sixty minutes instead of ninety minutes. For protection while walking to the park on bitterly cold mornings, my brother and I piled on extra clothing. We wore gloves, scarves, hats, and special handmade jackets Baba made from two shirts sewn together and stuffed with cotton. I giggled at our fat dumpling shapes. Before class, we shed the extra clothes. After a sweaty practice, the dampness made us cold again and we quickly donned our protective layers.

We didn't have any boots to wear. When we stepped on the ice, we could feel the cold coming up through our gigantic shoes stuffed with cotton. Whenever the temperatures warmed up a bit and melted the ice in the road, we made a game out of avoiding the puddles to see who could keep their shoes the driest. On muddy roads, we challenged each other by jumping atop the bricks somebody had tossed across the expanse of mud. To our amazement, my brother and I learned for the first time to have fun together.

On really cold mornings after slipping out of bed in the dark, I pulled my rough cotton clothing out from their warm spot between my blankets, grabbed my warm jacket and shoes hanging by the stove, and padded across the icy courtyard to rouse my brother from his slumber. I yanked on his arm, saying through clattering teeth, "Jian Guo, wake up. Come with me to *wushu* practice." I wanted his company while walking the long distance in the dark, but it was getting harder and harder to nudge him awake.

One day in the middle of winter, after I pulled back Jian Guo's covers, exposing his warm body to the cold air, he grabbed the quilt and tucked it back in around him. "Go away, I want to sleep. It's too cold today." Reluctantly, I turned away, deciding to make my own way to the park.

That evening, Baba questioned Jian Guo about going to *wushu*.

Jian Guo fidgeted but finally blurted out, "It's too cold. I don't want to go to *wushu* anymore."

Baba looked so disappointed to find out Jian Guo didn't have the determination to stick with *wushu*. All I could think about was: *What about me, Baba? I'm not quitting.*

That winter Coach Dai must have noticed I was getting better because he told me I could join the class after school. Beginning around 4:00 in the afternoon, we often practiced in the dark, unlit schoolyard. If it rained or snowed, Principal Gao 高校长 kindly allowed us to practice in one of the classrooms. We moved benches and tables over to the walls and practiced on the brick floor. None of the classrooms was heated, and in the cold dampness we shivered our way through rigorous stretching and increasingly difficult warm-up exercises. Though thoroughly chilled, my happiness and determination kept me going.

The hardest thing was running long distances around the outskirts of town for forty minutes a few times a week. Feeling competitive that first day, I charged through the beginning of the route. I was good at sprinting and wanted to capture the coach's attention. No one had told me to pace myself. By the time we reached the shores of the Grand Canal, I nearly collapsed from fatigue while the freezing wind off the water shot icy barbs through my clothing and into my lungs. Soon all my classmates passed me up. *Just keep up, keep up,* I kept telling myself. Even after I learned to pace myself, running long distances was always torture for my weak body.

Sometimes on frosty mornings as I lay snuggled in the reassuring warmth of my quilts, I hesitated climbing out of bed for the stone cold walk to practice. Then I would remember NaiNai's words to me after Jian Guo had quit *wushu.* "If you quit one thing, you're likely to quit something else. It's better to learn how to stick with something." I appreciated the interest NaiNai showed in my continuing *wushu.* Determined not to be a quitter, I pushed myself out of bed.

Coach Dai must have noticed my efforts because he began giving me some individual instruction. He came up next to me and showed me how a move was supposed to look. He demonstrated the correct way and the incorrect way so I could see what I was doing wrong. The more personal instruction I received, the more I knew Coach Dai was pleased with my progress. This made me enormously happy. I continued working hard to get the teacher's attention in class, even though I noticed a few resentful looks from Young Soldier and a few other students.

Some students didn't take the class seriously. They thought they were smarter than the teacher. When Coach Dai wasn't looking, the students didn't work as hard and made the exercises easier by standing higher or doing fewer repetitions. But the teacher knew what was happening. Later, when he chose students to learn some special movements or a form using a weapon, these students weren't chosen. Sometimes they complained to their parents. If parents tried to make a polite inquiry—often accompanied by a clandestine gift of cigarettes—Coach Dai told them, "Ask your son why."

Coach Dai Jia Yu 戴家余教练 taught martial art forms and weapons with only one forearm and hand. Though we were all curious, no one ever asked him what had happened. Many years later my sister told me his story.

Coach Dai grew up in Baoying and went away to a teaching college in Beijing. While in Beijing, he studied with a famous *wushu* master, later entering *wushu* competitions. After graduation, he came back to Baoying and received a full-time job teaching physical education at the high school. He was young then, in his middle twenties. Outside school, he started teaching *wushu* to athletes in their late teens and early twenties, at the peak of their athletic ability.

When Coach Dai came back to Baoying, the Cultural Revolution was in full force with two or three separate groups fighting each other for control. As a young, new teacher at the high school, Coach Dai became involved with a group of high school students who were making homemade bombs. One time, he realized something had gone wrong. Quickly, he evacuated all the students from the room. He was the last one to jump out the window. When the bomb exploded, his left arm still gripped the windowsill. He was lucky to lose only his forearm and hand; he could have died.

After Coach Dai recuperated, the people in control of the government had to determine whether he was good or an enemy. Those who were found to be enemies could be killed but were generally sent away from Baoying to the countryside and not allowed to return. What saved Coach Dai from this fate was his ability to teach *wushu*, which was seen as a valuable asset for the community. The *wushu* team was a source of pride for the town and a major form of entertainment. Coach Dai lost his job as a teacher at the high school but was allowed to resume teaching *wushu* to older students. In this way, Coach Dai began to earn back some of the good favor he'd lost as a result of his activism. Eventually, he was allowed to return to the high school part-time and later full-time. Knowing *wushu* brought Coach Dai luck.

Wushu was bringing me good luck, too, because Baba began taking more interest in me. Completely out of character, he surprised me with a treasured gift, the first one I ever received from my family.

Baoying *wushu* girls
(front center is Liu Yu, front left is Little Sweetie,
and rear center is Pretty Green Snake)

8   *A TREASURED GIFT*

When Baba entered our apartment with a rolled up poster tucked under his arm, Jian Guo quickly pounced on him. "Is that a new poster for the New Year?"

Posters depicting the ideals of the Cultural Revolution decorated our walls. Each New Year we bought different ones to freshen the apartment, and the New Year was nearly upon us.

"No," Baba answered, "this is a special poster I bought for Xiao Yu."

A flood of excitement washed over me as Baba handed me the poster. I carefully unrolled it, finding a grid of photos depicting *wushu* athletes wearing silk uniforms of every color of the rainbow. They posed in the foreground of China's famous parks and shrines like the Temple of Heaven in Beijing. But what captured my attention the most was seeing that many of the athletes were just a little older than I.

Looking up at Baba, I smiled with amazement. "Oh, Baba, thank you."

I realized happily Baba was proud of my *wushu*. At that moment, I felt like the pampered daughter of a generous emperor. Baba made me feel special and a strong connection was growing between us. *I'll make Baba even prouder yet.*

Baba took the poster from my hands and applied a water and flour paste to its edges. He went over to a patch of wall and flattened the poster against it, instantly brightening the drab room with colors as vibrant as brilliant flowers.

The purpose of the poster was to elevate the status of *wushu*. Even though the Cultural Revolution seemed less intense than before, China continued with campaigns to promote Communists ideas. *Wushu* was considered a cultural treasure and its professional athletes had become stars.

Briefly glancing at Jian Guo, I noticed he looked a little lost. He could have been good at *wushu* if he had been willing to work hard. I wondered if he regretted his decision to quit.

Over the next half hour, I couldn't take my eyes away from the poster. I examined every detail, admiring the way one girl held her neck, her posture so erect when she lifted her leg high, and the firm bow of strong legs in various stances. As I tried copying the poses, I began to believe if I practiced hard, I could improve my skill to nearly the level of these athletes.

One of the girls in particular inspired me with her flexibility and fame. Whenever I stared at her photo, I was filled with awe that anyone could be so good. Her exceptional abilities had won her the title of women's *wushu* champion for five years. In the cramped, simple room, this poster served as a tiny opening that breathed vitality into my lackluster life.

My biggest idol wasn't a *wushu* athlete, however. As a member of China's national gymnastic team, she had won a world championship in gymnastics at about the age of ten. Her poster caught a breathless moment as she floated mid-air in a beautiful jump directly over the balance beam with her legs spread in perfect splits. I often wished I could learn to hold my body suspended in the air like my gymnastics idol, but Baoying was like many small towns in China—it didn't have a gymnastics teacher. Luckily, I had someone like Coach Dai who could teach me *wushu*.

Whenever I passed that poster at the sports center in Baoying, my thoughts turned to amazement at the gymnast's accomplishment. To achieve something that made your family proud was a conceivable goal, but to cause the whole country to burst with pride seemed an impossible dream. Her becoming famous at such a young age and doing something so great for our country inspired me to work hard both at school and at *wushu* practice. I vowed not to waste any chance that came my way to become successful, even if that success only meant I avoided the oppression that weighed down NaiNai and Mama.

Ever since I started *wushu* lessons, a new hope filled my days and nights. When Baba presented me with the poster, it seemed as if he were giving me permission to dream. I idly envisioned becoming so good at *wushu* that I would make not only my family proud but everyone I knew. In my reverie, I never allowed myself to imagine I could become as successful as the athletes in the poster, but I was convinced it was only a matter of time before *wushu* solved my health issues. Reaching optimal strength and vitality was my ultimate goal. Along the way, gaining pride in my developing abilities gave me more confidence, though I had to be careful not to appear arrogant or conceited to avoid being harassed.

As my favorite holiday, the New Year, approached, I was in the mood to celebrate even though I wasn't chosen to perform *wushu* with some of my classmates for the festivities. I understood why because I was still so new.

All year I had looked forward to special foods, a wondrous parade, gifts of coins, firecrackers popping everywhere like little automatic machine guns, and over a month's vacation from school. Everyone became one year older on the New Year rather than on their birthdays. It was a time for celebration.

To prepare for the holiday, everything had to be cleaned, including ourselves. In the hot months, we bathed daily using a wooden tub placed in the kitchen. Some families bathed in the river where the current wasn't too strong. In the cold winter months, the water had to be heated on the stove, so we didn't bathe as often. NaiNai told us cold baths in the winter chilled the body and led to sickness.

Bathing at a public bathhouse just before Chinese New Year was traditional and felt like a luxury. Da Jie and I walked to one side with Mama and NaiNai, and Baba accompanied Jian Guo to the men's side. I loved the hot, steamy atmosphere and stayed as long as possible, happy to wash the dirt from my body and hair.

As gifts, we received New Year's coins from friends and relatives, treasures wrapped in red paper envelopes. These coins were used to purchase supplies needed for school. I was embarrassed my family couldn't afford to buy me new notebooks and workbooks. At the hospital,

Baba collected used paper, blank on the back, and carefully bound the sheets together. I used these notebooks to practice my Chinese characters and my mathematics problems.

All year we looked forward to the fancy food served for the New Year celebration. Trading bags of fabric scraps with our country cousins enabled them to make cotton shoes while we gained precious beans and nuts not available with our monthly food rationing coupons. Jars and tins of soy beans, red beans, dried fruit, peanuts, watermelon seeds, sunflower seeds, sesame seeds, and pork fat were squirreled away during the year to make delicious homemade treats for the New Year.

My favorite New Year's treats were sticky round sweets balls with two kinds of fillings, sweet red beans and black sesame seeds. To make them, NaiNai soaked a pound or two of rice in fresh water to soften it. Da Jie and I then carried the wet rice to a special place for grinding. We didn't mind standing in the long line because we felt joyful with anticipation. NaiNai borrowed a large bamboo tray from my uncle who worked at a Chinese medicine store and used it to spread out the wet rice flour for drying. My siblings and I then took turns watching over the tray in the courtyard to protect it from cats, birds, chickens, and airborne particles like feathers. To pass the time, we used chopsticks to draw pictures and write Chinese characters in the flour like it was sand.

When sweet red bean filling wasn't bubbling in a pot, black sesame seeds roasted in a dry pan. I hung around the stove with my sister and brother allowing the wonderful smells to enchant me, causing my mouth to water and my belly to rumble gently. After grinding the roasted sesame seeds, we added sugar with a little bit of pork fat and rolled bits of it into balls called *Yuanxiao*. The adults whirled these sesame seed balls around in a sticky rice flour mixture, and then they did the same with dollops of sweet red bean paste.

We made these treats on the eve of the New Year but couldn't eat them until morning. Nothing tasted better to me than NaiNai's homemade goodies. Da Jie, on the other hand, didn't like the taste of pork fat or sticky rice, but NaiNai insisted she eat some of the sticky rice balls.

"You must eat *Yuanxiao* balls the first thing on New Year's morning so you'll have good fortune all year. It'll keep our family together. Eating big or small balls doesn't matter, but you must eat double numbers. You can't eat just one. Two is always a lucky number, but you can eat four or six." Da Jie crinkled her face as she quickly popped the tiny balls NaiNai rolled especially for her into her mouth. We laughed, happy there were more for the rest of us.

That New Year was my most joyous holiday ever. Although I still worried about catching up with my classmates in *wushu* and having enough energy to do well in class, I felt lucky finally having the means to improve my health. It was happening slowly and steadily, bit by bit.

Sometimes during the year, NaiNai made special food for Mama and occasionally for Baba. "You kids can't have this. It's for your mother because she works so hard."

Now that I was practicing *wushu* over three hours a day, NaiNai began buying one egg, which she fried for me.

Jian Guo became jealous. "I want an egg, too." It was hard for my brother because, as the boy of the family, he was usually indulged before the rest of us.

NaiNai insisted, "The egg's for your sister because she's doing such hard training and has to keep up her strength."

At first I protested, thinking I didn't want special food made for me. "No, no, don't do that. I don't want it."

"No," NaiNai ordered, "you have to eat it. It's good for your health. For the amount of energy you put out, you have to eat to get the energy back." She always watched out for me.

Eggs were precious and eaten only on special occasions, so I felt honored to be given one occasionally. Instead of gifts, children usually received one egg on their birthdays to ensure good health and good luck for the upcoming year. The birthday child was presented with a hard-boiled egg carried in a pouch worn around the neck so the egg would hang down on the chest. Everyone at school knew it was your birthday when they saw the dangling egg pouch. The hard part was waiting to eat it.

The extra food NaiNai purchased for me helped increase my stamina at *wushu* practice. Already accustomed to never feeling good physically because of my illness, I found I could tolerate the pain of the increasingly rigorous workouts. I knew my *wushu* was improving when traces of jealousy popped up in class. If I weren't careful, however, I could end up without any friends.

Liu Yu posing with sword

9   *SHANGHAI BOUND*

Pretty Green Snake, another girl named Chen Hua 陈华, and I were *wushu* competitors as well as friends. Signs of jealousy appeared as I began to catch up with the other girls in the class after less than one year. Then I surprised and upset them by learning a difficult maneuver before they did.

Coach Dai was teaching us the waist turning movement, which would help us learn other difficult movements such as the aerial and the butterfly. It was hard for us at our young ages to trust ourselves as we attempted to open up our bodies to the new movement. We crossed our legs, held out our arms, leaned back, swung right, and then turned left to spin like a fan while keeping our eyes glued the entire time to one fixed point behind us.

I practiced daily at home in the courtyard, fighting waves of dizziness. Coach Dai had advised us our lightheadedness would subside the more we practiced. Determined not to let this obstacle hinder my progress in class and knowing that I had to work harder than the healthy kids, I trained as much as I could. I hoped to get beyond the dizziness so Coach Dai wouldn't see any weakness in me.

After several days something clicked, and I developed a feel for the movement. Then Coach Dai surprised me in class by saying, "Everyone, watch Liu Yu do the waist turning."

As the first one to accomplish it, I glowed inwardly with pride. Now I really felt I had caught up with my classmates.

After class, my friends wouldn't talk to me. Chen Hua huffed and said, "Okay, I have two friends, but not you." She waved me away.

This hurt, but instead of feeling sorry for myself, I spent my time practicing more *wushu*. The unfriendliness didn't last long, as I knew it wouldn't. Soon we were playing together again outside *wushu* class.

Chen Hua earned the nickname Little Sweetie when she brought Pretty Green Snake and me some sweet cookie crumbs from the bottom of the cookie jar at her father's bakery. One of our favorite diversions became visiting the bakery where Little Sweetie's father worked. We put together any money we had and bought cookies. Then Little Sweetie's father always gave us a little bit extra. We thought his job was the best anyone could have.

In the summer before the one-year anniversary of my participation in the *wushu* class, Coach Dai made an announcement. He was making arrangements for the class to take a trip to study with a special children's *wushu* team in Shanghai-上海. Any student could go, but the family had to pay for the train to Shanghai, food, and bus rides in the city. Oh, how I longed to go, but my parents wouldn't have enough money to send me.

When Pretty Green Snake announced she was going on the Shanghai trip, I dearly wanted to join her. "NaiNai, Pretty Green Snake's going to Shanghai. Please, can I go?" I asked her so many times.

NaiNai was in charge of the money in the household. All the extra money, even the money Da Jie earned stringing firecrackers, went to NaiNai. She alone decided how it would be spent.

I don't know how it happened or what sacrifices the family had to make, but somehow they got the money together for me to make the trip. This put a lot of pressure on me because I felt I had to do well in order to justify the money spent. And, although I had finally caught up with my peers, my health began slipping as the weather turned hotter, sapping my energy.

Fifteen children were in the *wushu* class, but only four girls and Coach Dai's two older sons went to Shanghai. To save money, we stayed in the home of Coach Dai's college friend. We called him our uncle, sleeping on the floor in his hot, low-roofed attic. During the day, we rode a bus to the Shanghai Youth Recreation Center where the youth *wushu* team practiced.

One night we slept fitfully while heavy rain drummed the rooftop, the awful humidity inducing suffocating dreams. Our uncle roused us as an eerie gray light seeped into the room. Pressing our faces against the tiny attic window, we saw the streets flooded with nearly two feet of water.

Downstairs in the kitchen, we nibbled our breakfast buns and discussed our options. "The buses won't be running while the streets are flooded. If you don't want to miss your training, you could walk. It'll be warm in the rain," our uncle suggested. We unanimously agreed.

Holding hands, we snaked our way down the middle of the streets and across the huge People's Square. Of course we were wet when we arrived, but it was summer, and we didn't mind. Coach Dai carried a plastic bag of clothes and shoes, which we sorted through upon arrival, claiming our dry belongings.

Coach Fong, a retired professional athlete, was the *wushu* teacher at the Shanghai school. He kindly let us join his youth *wushu* team in their warm-up exercises. We marveled at the luck of the Shanghai students who practiced indoors in a room with a large carpet laid over hardwood floors. They had racks of weapons on one wall and colorful uniforms hanging on hooks.

Coach Fong's students spent some time teaching each of us different forms and different weapons. I longed to learn the popular flying rainbow sword form I saw the Shanghai students practicing, but I didn't get to choose which weapons I could use. Only a certain number of students were chosen for each type of form or weapon. When some of the students were assigned the straight sword, I was given the broadsword. I was taught the staff when other students were given the opportunity to select the spear. In my heart of hearts, I wondered if maybe I had to learn the weapons no one else wanted because my parents weren't actively involved in *wushu* training or because they weren't close friends with Coach Dai. More likely, the reality was that Coach Dai had to think about our group learning as much variety as possible. However, it all worked to my advantage later, when I began competing, because I stood out with my unusual weapons.

In addition to individual forms, we learned fighting sets for two or three people. The fighting sets were with bare hands or weapons. Pretty Green Snake and I were partners in a straight sword fighting set. Another set involved one girl with a broadsword fighting against two boys with spears. Of course, the girl was allowed to win. We didn't have a snapshot or video camera, so Coach Dai kept busy writing down everything we learned in case we forgot.

We crammed as much learning as possible into the month we spent in Shanghai. While there, one of the female Shanghai teachers complained we disrupted her students' efforts, so we were told to practice only during the regular students' breaks. While we waited for our turn on the carpet, our eyes remained glued to the students practicing at a more advanced level. "Look at how good they are! We can be like that," we asserted.

Coach Dai had taught us some basics and two traditional *wushu* forms, but now we felt flashy with our more modern *wushu* forms and weapons. Before we left Shanghai, Coach Dai bought one broadsword and a set of double straight swords for us to use in our performances. He also obtained an old-fashioned reel-to-reel tape of some classical Chinese music to play while we performed. We felt so important and proclaimed ourselves the Baoying Wushu Team.

After returning home, we passed on what we had learned to the other students who weren't able to go. We improved so much in Shanghai that many students had trouble catching up with us. We developed such a professional demonstration that the children's group was now given the honor of being the last group to perform, the older *wushu* group preceding us. Coach Dai then decided to focus his teaching on our age group instead of the older students who were busy with their jobs, having limited time to practice. He understood if he wanted to raise a good *wushu* team, he had to start with the younger ages.

In Shanghai, I acquired my first pair of *wushu* shoes. The tops were white cotton with rubber soles. These shoes couldn't be purchased in Baoying. Mama then sewed a cotton uniform for me made from Baba's old khaki military uniform. We bought a black stretchable belt for it and a bow for my hair. This was the first time I got something new to wear instead of a hand-me-down from Da Jie.

Baba had my first weapon made for me—two metal rings eight inches in diameter and one-inch thick, one for each hand. He found some brightly colored tape at the hospital, which he wound around and around the rings to make eye-catching stripes.

Our group was in big demand in Baoying because we had uniforms, music, weapons, and fancy routines. We performed for the local schools, at special events when dignitaries came to town, at holiday celebrations, and for schoolchildren from other towns visiting Baoying on field trips. The only other entertainment at a performance was the Communist-related singing and dancing. When our music started, one-by-one Coach Dai called out our names as we ascended the stairs to the school's stage. A great feeling of pride swelled up within me each time I heard my name announced to the audience.

Surprisingly, my relationship with my sister, Da Jie, improved after my trip to Shanghai. She became proud to have a sister whose ability at *wushu* stood out in our community. In addition, all her best school friends now liked me.

Each year, my sister had her picture taken at a photographic studio and received a small postage stamp-sized photo. This year, when her photo didn't turn out, she offered me the re-take coupon.

"You take this coupon and make a picture with a *wushu* pose," she proffered.

"Oh, no, this is for your photo. You earned it by bringing money in for the family," I said. But Da Jie insisted and accompanied me to the photographer's studio where I posed with my sword and my only store-bought piece of clothing, a red sweatshirt my family recently asked friends to buy for me in Shanghai. Da Jie's generosity made me realize how grown-up she was becoming, and I caught NaiNai smiling at her as I showed my family the photo.

I admired the kindness my sister showed me while she faced a hard decision that would affect her entire life. In the fall of 1968, Chairman Mao decreed that one child from each family could remain with the child's parents and all other children must serve the government. To fulfill this edict that first year, many Red Guards were sent to remote areas for re-education, to learn the ways of the common peasant. Reports circulated of horrifying conditions and extreme hardship, especially for the girls. Parents' efforts to legally pull back their children—whose futures appeared to be permanently locked onto the governments of the rural areas—resulted in frustration.

One day, I overheard a neighbor whispering to NaiNai about her cousin's daughter who had been sent to the countryside. After over a year away, she was finally allowed to come home for a short visit. Her parents became concerned when they noticed how withdrawn she acted. When it was time for the girl to return to the countryside, she cried and begged to be allowed to remain home. The parents finally found out she had been ruined against her will by a local official there and was pregnant.

The neighbor explained, "My cousin and his wife deliberated about what to do. If they let her stay and defy the authorities, the whole family would be investigated and probably be sent to jail, or worse. The family felt helpless, finally deciding they had to push her to go back. It was so sad. The poor girl went back, but then the family was notified that upon arriving back in the country the girl hung herself."

"Oh, poor girl," I heard NaiNai say.

I shuddered as I listened and told Da Jie about it later. We both agreed we wanted to avoid going to the countryside if at all possible.

High school students who were Red Guards were the first ones sent to the countryside. Da Jie had worn a Red Guard armband and scarf in elementary school like everyone else but then decided she didn't want to continue and become a Red Guard if it meant being sent away. Within two years, that decree changed. All high school students, whether they were Red Guards or not, were also being sent for re-education in the countryside.

Families electing to keep one child at home faced intense pressure from officials and the community if the child was in high school. Many times parents were coerced to reconsider when interrogated about why they wouldn't want their child to serve the country in the same way as the child's classmates. Even if the parents remained strong, their child could still be sent to the countryside if a permanent job wasn't found after graduation. Permanent jobs were difficult to find without community support.

Da Jie was only in middle school, but she was already deliberating her future. She told my parents she was thinking about not going to high school even though she was a top student and would surely face a lifetime of working at inferior jobs as a result of her decision. She said she couldn't bear the thought of moving away from the family and living in poor conditions. Baba and Mama told her they would support her decision.

My reaction to my sister's being allowed to stay home was that my family would have no choice but to send me to the countryside. It became a deep worry brewing in my gut. Part of me wondered if this whole thing meant my parents loved my sister more. I tried to rationalize it away, but it wouldn't completely disappear. Fear prevented me from talking about it with my parents. I didn't want to hear what I suspected was the truth. Instead, I buried my fear.

Resigned to being sent away eventually, I began practicing my *wushu* harder. At least I could make myself tougher, healthier, and stronger to endure the suffering in the countryside and to fend off unwanted advances. I didn't realize how my hard work would pay off in another way.

Fighting set
(Liu Yu on the left holding broadsword)

Little Sweetie

Baoying teammate

Baoying teammate

Baoying *wushu* team in Xuzhou preparing for
tournament (Liu Yu fourth from right, Coach Dai behind,
Little Soldier is fourth from left, Little Sweetie is second
from left and Pretty Green Snake is third from right)

10

BE SOFT LIKE THE GRASS

B irthdays weren't recognized in a big way, except ten-year and
twenty-year birthdays. When my tenth birthday rolled around,
my uncle presented me with a gift. It was a pair of blue socks I
loved and proudly wore often. This gift also caused me sadness. Several
months later at the river on washday, I saw one blue sock floating on the
surface of the water. I tried to grab it, but it drifted just out of my reach.
Unable to swim, I let it go.

I remembered what NaiNai had told me. "What you have today
could be gone tomorrow." I fervently hoped nothing would happen to
take *wushu* away from me. My remaining sock became a keepsake holder,
storing little treasured things, like my tiny pictures of Chairman Mao.

The next day in class when Coach Dai said he had an announcement,
I was ready for good news. "I'm pleased to let you know Baoying has
been chosen to host the Yangzhou 扬州 County *wushu* competition in
June. The purpose of the competition is choosing one team of six boys
and six girls to represent our county at the Jiangsu Province competition
coming up this fall in the city of Xuzhou 徐州. In addition, one boy and
one girl will be chosen as alternates. The alternates will be competing, but

their scores won't count in the final tally to see which team wins."

Everyone's eyes widened with excitement. It was the dream of every *wushu* student to be chosen to compete at a provincial competition. Held every two years, this was the highest competition for nonprofessionals and the only time they would be competing against professional team members. It was the premier athletic event in the province with thousands of people attending. While most athletes imagined being discovered as a potential star athlete by the coaches and then asked to join the professional team, I didn't think I was ready. Sometimes in class I surprised myself with my newfound skill, but psychologically I still felt behind the others. I wondered when that feeling would go away.

Coach Dai continued, "More good news. The Jiangsu Province Professional Wushu Team will be coming to Baoying for the selection tournament. Let's all work hard to prepare ourselves."

Perfecting our skills in preparation for the tournament consumed us. In class I quickly developed the habit of competing intensively in an attempt to raise my skill level. Young Soldier always led the group in kicking, jumping, and acrobatic drills and I pushed myself to top his ability. He was my model. When it was my turn, I tried to jump higher or kick higher than he did. It was as if my inner tiger sprang to life during practices and then afterwards went back into hiding so no one would be offended.

Tournament day finally rolled around. Without an indoor gymnasium, Baoying held the competition outdoors on a concrete basketball court. I was nervous about executing my acrobatic maneuvers on the concrete but decided to ignore it and try my best. My expectations weren't high, but that didn't keep me from wishing I would be chosen.

At the tournament, the professional team members exhibited incredible power and great athletic ability. Their performances captivated me and fueled my imagination. These gifted athletes were the idols of Chinese children everywhere. I also caught a glimpse of competitors from nearby cities and small towns within our county who provided stiff competition.

When it was my turn to compete in each of my four events, I focused on the inner competitiveness I had developed in class. With no experience competing, and having performed at only a few local events, I was surprised my nervousness didn't seem to affect my performance adversely. I kept my inner tiger bottled up so much of the time that when I began my routines, I felt that tiger spring to life during those brief moments of freedom.

First, second, and third placements were awarded in each event. As expected, I didn't win first place in any event. Winning second place in the longfist *(changquan* 长拳) and third place in the staff form, however, allowed me to walk away happy about how much I was able to show my skills.

The names of the fourteen selected to compete in Xuzhou wouldn't be announced until the next day. After the tournament, the coaches of the various city teams would negotiate among each other and with the professional team coaches to fill as many of the twelve slots as possible with their own students.

Just before the tournament concluded, the coach of the professional team stood up and called out the names of a few athletes. Young Soldier, Pretty Green Snake, Little Sweetie, and I were among those asked to come forward. Some of these children were prodded forward by mothers anxious to have their child's skill recognized.

"Please come stand over here," the professional coach said as he motioned to the area in front of him. "I want you to squat down and then jump as high as you can." Jumping high was something I excelled at, maybe because I was so thin and lightweight.

"Now, do the splits." Being flexible was something that came naturally to me as well.

"Make a bridge," the coach instructed. A bridge is bending over backwards from a standing position until the extended hands touched the ground.

The coach watched us carefully and then said thank you. I went back to the sidelines, feeling honored to have my name called. I caught a few jealous looks from my classmates and worried that being singled out might cause problems for me later.

The next day Coach Dai posted the results of those selected to compete in Xuzhou. I eagerly scanned the list naming three boys from Baoying, including Coach Dai's two older sons, as well as Pretty Green Snake, Little Sweetie, and another girl from Baoying. Near the bottom, my name appeared as number thirteen. I made the team, but as an alternate. Although filled with disappointment, I wasn't embarrassed because I was still so new on the team with only two years of lessons, compared to six years for Young Soldier.

I didn't let this loss affect my desire to continue. If I was this close with only two years of lessons, anything was possible. I used this motivation to work harder.

The competitive team held a week of special practices in the city of Yangzhou to prepare for the Xuzhou tournament. Even though I was only an alternate, I attended every practice. My plan was to practice as if my scores counted because I was number one on deck and could be switched if one of the six girls canceled.

Two days before the tournament, Coach Dai approached me during group warm-ups. "Liu Yu, I've just heard one of the Yangzhou girls is sick. You'll be one of the six team girls."

After a sharp intake of breath, I smiled secretly to myself.

Buoyed by my good fortune, I performed flawlessly that day at practice, my inner tiger imbuing me with deep-rooted power and steadfast movements. At one point, I caught a look of surprise on Young Soldier's face. Until that moment, I don't think he seriously considered me a competitor.

It was the fall of 1973 when I arrived in Xuzhou for the Jiangsu Province Wushu Competition. The day before it was set to begin, I sat in the stands and watched athletes of each county team practice during their assigned hour on the thick red wool carpet serving as the performer's ring. I stared with disbelief that I was part of such a talented group.

The Xuzhou city team had its own training facility and dormitory. With surplus funds from regional coal production, Xuzhou financed its *wushu* team, which was the only sport promoted in the area. These older athletes trained one-half day and attended school one-half day. When they claimed the floor for practice, many coaches and team staff cheered loudly, boosting the team's confidence. As the athletes took turns on the floor, they demonstrated their best moves. I bit my lip, fearing I didn't have the experience to match their skill.

When it was time for the Yangzhou team to practice, I tried out various flips so I could judge the area of the carpet. I didn't want to over rotate and receive a deduction for landing out of bounds. The only sense of spacing we had prior to this was from chalk lines Coach Dai had drawn on concrete.

One move I was told to practice was slamming my staff down on the carpet. A staff is made from a branch of a wax tree that reaches from the floor to the top of a raised arm. When I practiced in Baoying, I had to hold back for fear of breaking it on the cement. On the carpet, I was encouraged to let go and slam it down fiercely. I was rewarded with a loud smack.

The next day, butterflies circled my stomach as I took my place in a line of *wushu* athletes. We were about to parade through an auditorium filled to capacity with 6,000 spectators. I looked down and smoothed out a wrinkle in my uniform. The slightly worn and simple khaki cotton uniform my mother had sewn for me over a year ago made me feel self-conscious, but my parents couldn't afford something new. Even though my uniform wasn't fancy compared to what my teammates wore, I forced myself to shrug it off. I could do nothing about it.

As we entered the auditorium, my eyes were drawn to the thousands of people aligned in rows reaching up to the distant ceiling. I felt like an ant engulfed by a mountain. The spectators were standing and clapping for the famous *wushu* athletes who were part of the group of both professionals and other amateurs like me parading around the competition floor to loud Chinese marching music. A combination of hard work and luck awarded me this opportunity to compete against my idols. The crowd energized me, and an inner determination emerged to show them my best. I would attempt to ignore my jitters and the sweat that was already dampening my uniform in the hot, sticky arena.

While I considered it an honor to join six boys and five other girls in representing my area, a part of me felt I didn't belong here. After all, I didn't consider myself a formal team member, only an alternate. If I could perform without any major errors, then I would have the satisfaction of justifying my place on the team.

After the judges followed protocol by walking the perimeter of the auditorium, the competition got underway. I collected my weapons and chose a place on the sidelines to warm up.

My biggest worry was failing to hear the announcements signaling the start of my events. Some of my team members were accompanied by one of their parents. My parents couldn't afford it, which meant I must listen to the announcements myself. My teacher was here, but he was busy with his own sons, and I couldn't count on his help. I refused to dwell on the fact that I was alone. Besides, my family taught me to be independent and take care of myself when necessary. When I was older, I came to realize that growing up in such hard times had made us more mature as kids. We acted like little adults, forced to be obedient and self-disciplined in response to the scariness of the Cultural Revolution.

On the sidelines, practicing my *wushu* movements relaxed me. My expectations weren't high. After all, I was competing against professional athletes, and they always won the top spots. Just being at the competition was the fulfillment of my dream. Although I secretly hoped a professional coach would see me and offer me a chance at professional *wushu*, I didn't expect it. Even though I had tried to overcome my feelings of inferiority, inside I still considered myself behind my *wushu* classmates.

Each time the crowd cheered, I stopped my warm-ups and glanced up. Generally, the audience was responding to a professional athlete or a Xuzhou team member moving on the carpet. Sometimes when I watched, I saw nerves affecting athletes' performances when they had seemed so confident yesterday. Whenever the spectators gasped or laughed, I knew the athlete had made a major mistake like slipping or faltering while landing an acrobatic movement. Each time that happened, I took a deep breath and hoped I didn't make any mistakes my teammates could tease me for later. More than anything, I wanted to prove myself worthy of being a team member.

An announcement finally called my first event, and I hurried to the performers' waiting area, watching the action until my turn. One competitor surprised everyone when her staff made an unusual cracking sound as she slammed it on the carpet. Holding her broken staff, she attempted to slow down her movements so nothing dangerous would happen. When she whipped the wooden pole around her body, however, the tip of it broke off and whizzed past a judge's ear, receiving a big deduction Momentarily fearful of the same thing happening to me, I decided I wouldn't let it affect me. I wouldn't hold back.

When I heard my name called, I wiped my sweaty hands on my uniform and grasped my weapon. My staff was the first weapon I had learned and the one with which I had the most experience. In my routine, I twirled the staff until it made a whirling windmill noise and then slammed it down with a satisfying smack on the carpet. Executing one of my special staff movements, I turned a cartwheel with only my staff end touching the ground while my hands gripped the staff pole.

With each movement, I shed more inhibitions. The shy and fearful part of me faded. I became all the things I wasn't in real life. Brave and confident, I floated through the air, landing with dynamic power. It felt like someone else was performing the moves and I found myself wishing my life could be like this. I didn't want that seductive feeling of freedom to end. At the close of my performance, I bowed to the judges and quickly trotted off the carpet, slipping back into my inconspicuous persona. The head I had held so high now dipped forward, my mask firmly in place, inoffensive and dull. Only inside did I allow relief to flood my body, rejoicing I had made no mistakes.

In between routines, while I practiced on the sidelines, my nervousness returned. Yet, in my next routine an undercurrent of surprise rippled throughout me as once again I broke through my defenses, setting them aside while wielding a single broadsword, my steady hand hitting the right marks. I then competed without any noticeable mistakes in the double rings, the weapon my father had made for me. Somehow, I was able to block out the terror of having thousands of people watching me while giving myself permission to feel free on the mat, to explore that carefree side of myself.

Afterwards I stood to the side and caught my breath, amazed that my legs hadn't given out. My buoyant feeling on the carpet surprised me. I knew my inner strength was responsible aided by the fact that I had no expectations of winning against such experienced athletes. Although not the youngest athlete competing, I was probably the one with the least experience with only two years of lessons before and after school.

It still astounded me that my shyness at school didn't carry over into competitions and *wushu* performances. While performing, I didn't have to worry about offending anyone or feeling embarrassed that someone would tease me unless I stumbled. Although I lacked confidence in speaking, in athletics I performed with a sense of ease. That was part of why I was attracted to *wushu*, because somehow it fit me perfectly. Not only was it bringing me better health, but through *wushu* I was discovering my inner spirit, one I controlled everywhere except on the mat. That was the only time I allowed my true self to shine and the feeling fascinated me. To let myself show my emotions in everyday life would bring hurtful accusations from my peers and scolding from my family. Not controlling one's feelings was like a show of defiance in the face of my culture, like Morning Glow standing on the tabletops so long ago with a look of determination that brought down a ballast of wrath upon her. As much as I desired freedom in my real life, I knew the danger. For now, I was happy to have the opportunity to practice *wushu*, and I was determined to give full reign to my dreams in my last event.

The longfist, a bare handed routine, was the only event in which I competed against my hometown classmates. As we lined up for our chance to compete, Young Soldier pointed to himself and moved ahead of me in line. He wanted to be first in everything or closer to the action. He often said he would be chosen for the professional team soon because his father was a *wushu* instructor and he had started much earlier than anybody else. He was definitely good, but on several occasions I had outrun him, jumped higher than he did, and showed more flexibility. Maybe his father did have connections, but Young Soldier's boasting put tremendous pressure on him to perform. It seemed to me that Young Soldier, who was also born a tiger, was letting his tiger loose in areas of his life where he shouldn't. My friends and I actually liked Coach Dai's middle son better. He wasn't as bossy, although he often got into trouble for following the ideas his older brother dreamed up.

To be competitive and attract a higher score from the judges, a competitor needed to perform a specialty movement no one else could do. My specialty was the butterfly twist, a maneuver I had worked hard to perfect over the past year. In the butterfly twist, the body is thrust into a high move parallel to the ground with a half twist in the air before scissor kicking the legs and landing in the splits. If several performers executed the same movement, then the judges decided whose jump looked more graceful in the air or was the highest. My butterfly twist always reached a higher level than the jumps made by my teammates, probably because I was so skinny and light. I decided to try excelling in my jumps today and suppress any doubts creeping in my mind that I might falter.

The longfist was my favorite event. I loved the strength in each movement, and I gave my performance every ounce of energy and dynamism possible. For several brief moments, I floated weightless in the air. Tasting freedom from gravity, I forgot the risk should I fall. Then suddenly I was back on the mat, the crowd cheering. My heart did a flip. I had done it. I had conquered the fear that I carried with me through the rest of my life like a cloak.

Brimming with newfound confidence, I felt the satisfaction of having done my best, earning my place on the team. I would be able to hold my head high should anyone tease me about being only an alternate. Slightly out of breath, I waited for the five judges to hold up their scores. Surprisingly, my scores were very good, over nine points out of ten. Feelings of happiness and accomplishment washed over me as I watched the rest of the competitors.

It was a pleasure to watch the professional team athletes who seemed to float through the air. Their performances had a high degree of difficulty, which meant they occasionally fell or wobbled on a balance, bringing down their scores considerably. If they made it through without a mistake, however, they earned extra points for the difficult maneuvers.

The longfist event ended too soon for me. Before competing, I blocked out as much as I could to mentally prepare myself for my next routine. Now I was finished and had a great view from the edge of the carpet but could enjoy watching only the few remaining competitors. At least I would see the professional team members claim their medals for the longfist.

After each event, the competitors lined up and faced the judges as they waited for the three place winners to be called. The head judge stood in the center of the carpet with the three medals. When I heard my name called as the third place winner, I thought my imagination had taken over. *Who me? No way!* But when the judge looked at me and motioned for me to step forward, my pounding heart told me this was real. After receiving my medal, I stood in awe as the professional team members came forward to claim their silver and gold medals alongside me. Being an amateur who won a spot against the professionals seemed unreal. From then on, I would always try to recapture the magical carefree feelings of this tournament, but it wasn't to be. Never again would I attend a competition without a burning desire to win, and never again would the win be so meaningful.

As I collected my weapons on the sidelines, a deep feeling of happiness I couldn't share ballooned inside me. It wasn't my nature to be boastful or proud. If NaiNai ever caught me looking too happy with myself, she would rap me on the top of the head with her chopsticks.

"Xiao Yu," she would say, "calm down and don't show so much on the outside. If you're too obvious or unbalanced, you're going to break first. If you're soft like the grass, then when the wind blows or when stones roll by you'll survive. By acting like a big tree and sticking out, you'll be the first thing broken."

I didn't expect any offers of congratulations or comments of a job well done because they were rarely given. No one said anything to me—not my teammates or my teacher. On the bus back to Baoying, I pretended to be sad that my teammates didn't win instead of me. It was better to avoid out-of-control jealousies by acting humble, by keeping my tiger carefully hidden.

Inside, however, I looked forward to telling my family about my win, especially Baba. When I did, I saw a glimmer of pride in his eyes though he didn't express it verbally. A gentle nod of his head and the beginnings of a smile communicated his feelings.

Thoughts about my win swirled through my head for days. I decided I had beat out my teammates because I didn't feel the same stress they felt. I knew Young Soldier in particular wanted more than anything to join the professional team. His parents put a lot of pressure on him. I, on the other hand, had no expectation of joining the professional team because I thought many of my classmates were still ahead of me in ability. Consequently, I was more relaxed at the competition and able to perform better. Yet even after winning, I still didn't believe I was really better. It turned out we all had a mistaken notion of what the professional team was looking for.

Yangzhou County *wushu* team trial athletes in Xuzhou
(Liu Yu is fifth from right in front, Little Sweetie is
third from right, Pretty Green Snake is fourth from left)

Summer camp participants
(Liu Yu is rear left)

Coach Wang's
monkey staff form

DREAM OFFER

Three months after the Xuzhou tournament, Coach Dai surprised us at the end of class when he announced, "Two of you have been chosen to attend the professional team's training camp during the winter school break, Young Soldier and Liu Yu."

Me? How can that be? My heart beat faster at the thought. Coach Dai held out a piece of paper. "Liu Yu, this is the information for your parents."

Feeling shocked, I took the paper, careful not to look at Pretty Green Snake and Little Sweetie, saving them any embarrassment. I examined the paper until they departed.

I walked home in the dark by myself, thinking my family had already paid for my expenses to go to Shanghai and Xuzhou. The paper explained that families were responsible for the costs of food and transportation as well as supplying their child's bedding and incidentals. How could my family afford it? How could they spend all their extra money on me and not on my sister or brother? Maybe I wouldn't be able to go, which would be a shame because I was warming to the idea. By the time I entered my apartment, I had convinced myself I didn't want to miss such a special opportunity.

Baba sat next to the lamp reading the information on the paper as I waited impatiently across the table for his decision. Baba's breath flowed rhythmically while I could hardly breathe.

"Xiao Yu, do you want to go to the training camp? It'll be a lot of hard work."

"I know, Baba, but I want to go."

He gazed at me long and hard, his face masked and unreadable. He turned to NaiNai, asking about the family funds. She busied herself tallying our expenses while I fidgeted nervously with the strap of my school bag.

"We don't have enough money to make it to the next month if Xiao Yu goes," NaiNai said as my heart sunk. "But," she continued, "we could borrow some money from Neighbor Chen to tide us over."

Baba sat thoughtfully and looked up at me before saying, "I want you to have this chance. If we can borrow the money, you can go."

I fought hard not to break out in a smile and elicit a rap on the head from NaiNai for showing my feelings. "Thank you, Baba."

Neighbor Chen had given us short-term loans before and agreed to NaiNai's request on my behalf. I worried about what sacrifices my family would have to make paying it back. After delivering his water bottle and bread buns the following morning, he said, "I hear you're getting a great chance for special *wushu* training. Work hard."

I replied, "Yes, I will. And thank you for helping me."

With my family spending so much of their limited money on me, I knew I had to push myself as hard as possible at the camp. Being invited to go there meant I had a chance at joining the professional team, though at this moment I could hardly believe it. For the first time, I dreamed of being chosen.

A fear that had been lurking in my subconscious now surfaced, followed by a comforting thought. If my dream came true, I wouldn't be sent to the countryside. Becoming a professional athlete would fulfill Chairman Mao's mandate to serve the government. Instead of going to some backward area with horrid conditions, I could make my family proud and spend many years doing what I loved.

The one-month winter training camp was held in the town of Qidong-启东, north of Shanghai. Approximately fifty team hopefuls had been invited from all over the province to join the training sessions. I was so excited I didn't even care about missing the New Year celebration.

A local elementary school, empty because of winter break, became our training facility. With no heat whatsoever and inadequate indoor space, the training conditions were the poorest possible. We learned this had been planned to weed out some of the hopefuls who couldn't take the frigid weather conditions.

The purpose behind the training camp was twofold. One aim was seeing if we team aspirants could take the hardship of the training regimen and keep up the pace set by the professional athletes. The other purpose was to show the professional athletes they needed to work hard because all these other children were ready to step into their shoes if they didn't fulfill the coaches' expectations. Professional athletes had no job security and could be dismissed at any time by the whim of the coaching staff.

Attired in coveted workout uniforms, the professional athletes appeared to move confidently as they led our kicking and jumping drills. They inspired me to the point of intense longing. I hungered to be like them. Knowing I needed to make myself stand out in some way, I began strategizing how I could win the attention of the coaches. I decided I needed to put out more effort than everyone around me, something I knew wouldn't be easy. But I knew I had to try.

Following behind the professional athletes, I swung my leg with assurance, slapping my foot each time with a loud crack. In my jumps, I sprung with the lightness of a kitten to reach heights I hoped were higher than anyone else. When everyone began running, I sprinted with all the power and sure-footed speed of a tiger, though I nearly blacked out by the end of each race. *I'm going to show them I want to be chosen.* Training with my idols inspired me to tough it out.

While watching the professional athletes, it occurred to me they weren't too far ahead of me in ability. When I saw their butterfly twists, my eyes opened wide in amazement, and it wasn't because they were so good. It was because I knew I could do it as well as they could. At that moment, I gained confidence and tried to show it in everything I did.

At the end of the day, wearily crawling onto my bunk bed set up amid many others in the freezing classroom, I listened as the wind howled outside, shaking the window panes. Bundled in multiple layers of clothing, I huddled in the lumpy sleeping bag Baba had made from two blankets sewn together and stuffed with cotton. Before drifting off to a deep sleep, I thought two things: *I can be as good as them and, thank you,*

Coach Dai.

When the wake-up bell clanged in the dark stillness, I silently groaned with each movement of my aching, unresponsive body. After sliding out of bed, my sore muscles became rigid and then shook involuntarily with spasms in the below-freezing temperature. My constant dizziness prepared me to handle never feeling good, but that day I had to dig deep within for the drive to push myself. I had five minutes to ready myself for a warm-up run. Thankfully, I slept fully dressed to keep warm at night.

Strength training was held twice a day on the icy playground, which chilled my bones but helped me learn I could go past my imagined limits. With my breath vaporizing before my eyes, I attempted to stand still in a low *wushu* stance as instructed. I soon discovered, however, stillness was impossible. After fifteen minutes of no movement to help warm up my body, my tense muscles began shaking uncontrollably. If the coaches looked at my face, however, they would see my carefully sculpted expression of indifference despite my quivering jaw. I tried to act as if this torture was nothing. Thinking about the sacrifices my family was making motivated me to continue.

Sometimes, my determination collapsed at mealtimes when I overheard the idle talk of the city coaches and teachers recruited to help the professional staff. On several occasions, they spoke about the girl from the opera family named Little Sparrow and her friend.

"Maybe those two will be selected," they mused.

I never heard them talk about me.

Pretty and vivacious, Little Sparrow had big eyes and a showy personality that captivated everyone. One evening, Little Sparrow was asked to sing an operatic tune in the middle of the cafeteria. With total confidence, she belted out a lovely high-pitched wail, bringing tears to everyone's eyes. I knew I couldn't compete with that. My quietness was my downfall. To counteract it, I continued to unleash my power during practices.

On one of our Sundays off, a group of team candidates planned an expedition. "I've never seen the sea," one girl said, "and we're so close to it, only a couple of hours away if we walk. Would you like to go?"

It didn't take me long to decide. "No, I think I'll stay here and relax." I was curious about the sea, but my body needed to rest so I could keep up my efforts.

Each pair of pants I wore at the winter camp developed a hole on the inside of the knee corresponding to the bruises and scabs I acquired from doing the splits on concrete. Mama packed a needle and thread in my bag, and every Sunday I sewed up the hole to give my knee some cushion. By the end of the camp, my puckered pants bunched up at the right knee and hung crookedly.

Before everyone was due to leave, the professional team coach announced that some of us might be asked to train again at the summer camp. When I heard that, I sighed with disappointment. I knew I wouldn't be receiving an invitation to join the team anytime soon. More work lay ahead. To me, training in hot weather was worse for my stamina than the freezing conditions here. However, I would do my best to prepare because I couldn't give up on my dream. I remembered the nice training facility in Shanghai, and I imagined a gymnasium with thick carpeting at the professional sports camp. *That's where I want to be.* I held tightly to my dream.

After I returned home, I began training for the summer competition to be held in Baoying. I wanted to impress the professional team coach by showing some improvement since the winter camp. My classmates and I were more focused now, and this seemed to influence the parents, who became more competitive with each other over whose child was better.

Baba typically rode his bicycle to the school to pick me up after practice and talk with the other parents. A few parents used to come for fun to watch our practices. Now, many arrived early, suddenly more serious. They wanted their child to outperform the others and be number one. It made me feel proud that because of my skill Baba received more respect from the other parents.

As a young girl, I was closer to NaiNai, but now my relationship with Baba became deeper for the first time. It pleased Baba that *wushu* was returning my health to normal. And although he never told me, I knew he was proud of my abilities because sometimes he brought little cookies for me. Wrapped snugly in our silent companionship, I rode home on his handlebars feeling the breeze on my face and the sweet taste in my mouth. Before *wushu*, Baba had never spent any special time with his children. Having this attention from my father felt good and motivated me to work harder.

Shortly before the tournament, I sat with my classmates as Principal Gao addressed the students for an end-of-school-year assembly.

"Recently, a group of teachers came to Baoying so we could exchange teaching information. The little *wushu* team performed for our guests. I was proud to tell my guests that besides being good at *wushu*, these athletes are the best students at my school. They're models for the school."

Her comments created a warm feeling inside me.

Principal Gao continued by saying, "I would now like to announce the outstanding student of the year who excels in studies and sports, is talented in an extracurricular activity, has a perfect attendance record, and shows high political integrity." High political integrity is considered a combination of honesty, respectfulness, and good moral values. Principal Gao looked out over the group of students as she said, "The award goes to our fifth grade student, Liu Yu."

My face immediately reddened when I heard my name called. All I could think about was how honored I felt to receive the award. *Wushu* was indeed bringing me luck, and I hoped my luck would continue.

The competition in Baoying wasn't an area-wide competition like the previous summer, but it did include the professional team. Young Soldier and I became more intensely competitive because the winter training camp put us on a level slightly higher than everyone else. Young Soldier had been bragging about his abilities ever since he'd attended the summer training camp prior to my starting *wushu*. He fueled the competition between us with comments to his teammates like, "If anyone gets to go to the team from this place, it'll be me." I didn't react to his bragging. Instead, I restrained myself and stood back. When I got the chance to show my *wushu* in the Baoying competition, I gave it everything I had. That day, I beat out my teammates in all my events. Afterwards, Young Soldier stood to the side, sheepishly avoiding my eyes.

At the end of the competition, everyone begged the team coach for a demonstration. Coach Wang Jin Bao 王金宝教练 was a big star with more national *wushu* championship titles than anyone else. He'd recently visited the United States as a member of a Chinese friendship delegation and performed for President Nixon at the White House. He readily agreed to demonstrate his monkey staff form 猴棍 for us.

With his staff lying on the ground, Coach Wang dragged it backwards with the toe of his shoe and flipped it up behind him. Our jaws dropped as we watched him twirl his body around and catch the staff without ever looking at it. Acting like a monkey climbing a tree, he defied gravity by stepping on the upright staff and spinning around it as he raised his body. At the top, he momentarily jutted his elbow across his chest, shading his darting monkey eyes with the back of his hand—in a kind of cockeyed salute—as if he were scanning a forest.

We ducked our heads, marveling at Coach Wang's control, as he whipped his staff over our heads. He then did something with one hand that we had only seen done with two. In front of his chest, his right hand gripped the middle of the staff. With the rotation of his wrist, he began to spin the staff in two vertical circles, oscillating from one side of the body to the other. Gaining momentum, the staff looked like two fan blades protecting his body, moving so rapidly it appeared to be two spinning poles instead of one. The vibration caused a whistling noise we felt as well as heard. At this point Coach Wang began his monkey walk by standing up on the tips of his toes almost like a ballet dancer, stepping bow-legged toward us with his thrumming weapon. We hustled ourselves out of his path, and the crowd separated into two sections.

We roared with approval while Coach Wang caught his breath. He then shared a bit of his wisdom. "I wanted to be the best at the monkey staff form, so twice a week I took a bus across town and sat in front of the monkey pavilion. I studied the way the monkeys moved their bodies and eyes. I believe you have to develop a passion for *wushu* and show it when you perform."

We sat in awe that anyone could be so great. Later I learned that Coach Wang was known as the monkey king in *wushu* circles. The monkey king was a famous traditional opera character but also an appropriate name for someone displaying such an amazing talent.

After the competition, Coach Wang approached Coach Dai, telling him he was in the process of selecting a second team he would personally train. Coach Dai's face flushed with excitement as he praised the abilities of his son and the overlooked potential of Pretty Green Snake, whose father was a close friend of his. Coach Wang had heard this speech on other occasions but could never disclose the team's plans or preferences. At this time, however, Coach Wang informed Coach Dai the team was interested in having Little Sweetie and me try out by attending the summer camp and staying with the team at its completion.

Coach Wang told me this story more than one year later. "Did you know how hard it was to talk to Coach Dai about having you try out for the team?" It made me uncomfortable to hear it, but Coach Wang insisted I listen.

Coach Dai was my first teacher and loved teaching the children. He generously imparted his knowledge of martial arts. He helped us with our math when we went out of town for competitions so that we wouldn't get behind in school. I appreciated the Shanghai trip he arranged because it was a turning point for me, greatly improving my *wushu* skills.

When Coach Wang told me that Coach Dai had said I wasn't as good as some of the other students in his class, I winced. Coach Wang informed me of his reply. "I told him your current ability didn't matter, that I would train you. I explained that I also considered your future potential before I made my decision."

Still, Coach Dai had insisted that other students were better and had more potential. It went on like that, back and forth. Coach Wang finally told him he had known for a while he wanted me to try for the team.

I was hurt when I found out Coach Dai had tried to sabotage my chances in order to give his son a better chance of success. While Coach Dai gained face in Baoying for having a student try out for the professional team, he lost more face because his own son didn't go. Some people asked him straight out, "Why didn't your son go?" Although embarrassed by this rude question, Coach Dai carefully covered up his distress.

After Coach Wang spoke to my teacher, he spoke to Baba. "We would like to have your daughter try out for the professional team. Would you be willing to let her go?" Trying out for the team meant training on a trial basis and at some point either being sent back or being asked to join the team permanently. Baba wanted to discuss it with me before answering.

Many reasons for joining the team came to mind. I wanted to discover for myself how far I could go, how good I could be. And, the idea of being on my own and not needing my family's support meant they would have one less mouth to feed. My parents had put so much money into helping me that I didn't want to disappoint them. If I didn't go, my family and I wouldn't be able to hold our heads up in public. The overwhelming reason to accept, however, was because I viewed becoming a team member as a way of getting out of my obligation to be re-educated in the countryside. My sister had left high school after attending for only two months because she feared being sent away from the family. My team service, if I became a permanent member, would satisfy the government's requirement for me, but a risk was attached.

Baba explained if I wasn't selected to stay permanently—a process that could take up to two years—then I would be behind my classmates in my class work when I returned. It would be extremely difficult to catch up, and any possibility of going to college—a dream Baba had for his children—would fade.

"What do you want to do, Xiao Yu?" Baba asked me gently.

"I want to try for the team." He nodded his head as if he expected this answer.

After the decision was made, Baba completed the necessary paperwork. Someone from the team measured my ankle joints and wrists to determine their widths. Mama's and Baba's body types were evaluated to predict how my body would develop. No doubt this was the reason why Young Soldier and Pretty Green Snake weren't considered. Their parents didn't have the genetic leanness their children needed to be high jumpers and fast movers.

Before my application could be approved, a family background check was made. Unlike the Red Guards who had once hunted with a magnifying glass to find incriminating evidence against families, the local district officials used the close-one-eye approach. Baba's stint in the Air Force meant we were deemed a Red family. The father's side of the family was considered more important, and Baba's family had also been poor. Even though NaiNai's family was once wealthy, she never benefited from it and was poor before the Communists took over the country. The local officials ignored her heritage because she was well respected. They were also proud to have someone from Baoying serve the country by possibly becoming a professional athlete. In fact, the whole town buzzed with the news.

While my approval came through easily, Little Sweetie wasn't so lucky. Sadly, her family's political file revealed a problem with her father speaking out when he was younger. Although he didn't suffer during the Cultural Revolution, he was considered an outsider as far as the townspeople were concerned. For me, everything happened quickly, and I was told to report to the sports camp in a couple of weeks.

Behind my back, a group of parents enlisted the help of Baoying sports commission officials, trying to change Coach Wang's mind about limiting his selection to me. Instead of asking directly for a favor, it was customary to give gifts or bestow benefits and then ask for something in return. Coach Wang was invited to a banquet, but he turned them down flat. Next, they invited him to have drinks with them, thinking this would work because Coach Wang liked to drink.

"Liquor is too expensive," Coach Wang told them. "If I drink it, then I'll have to do you a favor. I know what you're planning, and I won't go with you for drinks."

When those tactics didn't work, the group decided they might as well get something out of the situation. They convinced Baba it was his duty to give a banquet for everyone because his daughter was being honored with an invitation to join the team. This was a huge financial burden for Baba, but he felt cornered.

When Coach Wang found out about it, he politely declined the invitation and said, "If my boss finds out I went to the banquet, he'll think the father of my new recruit bought me and that he promised to give me a banquet if I chose his daughter. I can't go."

Everyone finally agreed if Coach Wang wouldn't go, then the banquet was cancelled. Of course, Baba protected me at the time and didn't tell me what had happened.

Before I left Baoying, our family kept a low profile. We didn't want anyone saying we acted proud because I was getting favored treatment. I knew how much the families of Young Soldier and Pretty Green Snake wanted their children to be on the team. I worried I would never see them again because now they might be sent away to the countryside. Nothing would ever be the same.

While Baba and I sat at the dining table together, he gave me a lingering look, saying, "You must work hard for Coach Wang and listen to what he says. And don't neglect your mind. I hope you also keep up your studies. Don't become another poorly educated athlete."

Then Baba told me what he had said to Coach Wang. "You have my permission to take my daughter for the team. I pass her to you. Now she's your daughter, your responsibility." I could feel Baba's sadness when he said this to me. I knew it was hard for him.

Although I was excited, I felt tremendous pressure to realize my dream. I had been given many opportunities and people expected me to become successful. And though I tried to ignore everyone's attention toward me, when I went out on the street, I overheard people whisper, "That's the girl who's going to Nanjing to try to make the *wushu* team." It made me nervous because when two soccer team hopefuls were sent back from Nanjing, people commented, "Those guys couldn't take all the hard work." They always blamed the athlete when maybe the reason was another athlete came along who was better. I didn't want to disgrace myself or my family.

The morning of my departure for Nanjing, Mama surprised me by staying home from work and holding my hand as we walked to the bus station. My parents worried I might have a hard time on the team. We said goodbye, but no one hugged or kissed me. Waiting for the bus to leave, I watched my family through the clouded, half-closed window. They yelled their last-minute parting instructions.

"Work hard and do your best," Baba shouted.

"Listen to your coach," NaiNai reminded me.

And Mama yelled, "Don't forget to write."

Da Jie and Jian Guo just stood there. My family looked so forlorn standing by the side of the bus waiting for me to go. I was torn between feelings of excitement about the possibilities ahead and the fear that being separated from my family would be overwhelming.

No one outside the family gave me going-away wishes or farewell greetings. Pretty Green Snake didn't come to say goodbye. Most likely, everyone assumed that because I was going on a trial basis, I might be sent back like the soccer players who didn't make the cut. But I knew inside I would never return. I could work hard. I had to believe my anemia wouldn't hold me back. This was a dream come true for me, one that meant I wouldn't be wasting my life toiling twelve to fourteen hours each day in a factory like my mother. I wouldn't be sent away to the countryside with only a vague hope of ever returning home. Naively, however, I never stopped to wonder if I was really escaping oppression at all.

Part Two

Nanjing 南京, Jiangsu Province 江苏, China 中国

1974 – 1984

392 steps at Zhongshan Ling

EATING BITTER

Day after day during my first year on trial, I endured bone-tired fatigue, inferior health I struggled to keep secret, and loneliness— missing my family and wondering how they were doing. Too much competition among my teammates prevented any of us from becoming friends. Besides, we never knew who would be dismissed next. It was better not to get too attached if it meant adding to the heartache we already suffered. By day, Coach Wang's tortuous program toughened our bodies and attempted to strengthen our minds. Each evening, he patched our flagging spirits by reciting stories filled with inspiration and determination.

The general anxiety I lived with prevented me from getting the sleep I needed to revive myself and face the next day. Each night, I fell into a fitful sleep where dreams morphed into nightmares filled with fear about meeting the coach's expectations and never seeing my family again. With no end in sight to the harsh demands, I became a robot. My only shred of dignity lay in the fact that I wouldn't give up.

My days started before dawn when shrill metallic bells pierced the darkness. Like other slumbering athletes, I lurched into consciousness, attempting to quell my surging sense of fear and dread. We slept in our workout clothes to save time and avoid an undesirable late penalty. Within five minutes, we rushed to put on our shoes, use the bathroom, splash a little water on our faces, and silently line up in the dormitory's courtyard in neat team rows, all before the 5:35 a.m. whistle blew.

After a team count, the team leaders shouted in army fashion.

"Soccer team all here."

"Basketball team all here."

"Gymnastics team all here."

"Ping-pong team all here."

"*Wushu* team all here."

Everyone stood at attention in the semi-darkness, listening to the echoes of team leaders of every type of Olympic sport in other dormitory courtyards all over the camp. Though it was the start of a new day, there was rarely anything new about it. The training program went on day after day, year after year, and like the other athletes, I habituated myself to the demands. Now, one leader's voice filled the warm air. "The soccer team was here first. Okay, every group on your own." The camp became a flurry of activity as athletes from each dormitory group rushed to their designated team areas.

After lining up at the *wushu* training area, a gaunt, middle-aged man who was the Communist Party liaison and *wushu* team leader puffed up and scolded, "I noticed one of you was almost late. When you're late, you drag down the whole team. It's everyone's responsibility to be here on time. No excuses are tolerated."

Along with my *wushu* teammates, I waited to hear our punishment for the morning, but not for almost being late. The rigorous morning training sessions were so dreaded they might as well be punishment. What new torment would we go through this morning? We had learned our bodies had no limits when it came to endurance. We were forced to go far beyond what we believed was physically possible, but the brick wall never came, except for a tragic few.

Coach Wang Jin Bao, the coach for the second string *wushu* team, ignored any subtle signs of distress when he announced, "Everyone, run to Zhongshan Ling 中山陵." He waved his arm with a flourish and clicked his stopwatch. We took off running and were soon swallowed up in the silent darkness, our only consolation being the gentle breeze blowing on our faces.

The city of Nanjing fanned out along the southern banks of the Yangtze River as it flowed toward Shanghai, emptying into the East China Sea. Only a few bicycle carts and one or two foul-smelling trucks creaked down the road in the hush of early morning. It was the end of summer and the smothering humidity suppressed all desire for activity. By midday, the greedy heat would turn the climate into a steamy, sweating stew. Residents endured the normal 105-degree mid-day summer temperatures with a measure of reluctance, which would have increased had they known about air conditioning.

Coach Wang rode a bicycle alongside the panting team. First, he pedaled to the front, goading the runners to increase their pace. Then, he circled around to the back of the line where I pumped my legs as fast as I could. "Liu Yu, why are you always at the end? Speed up," Coach Wang urged.

I groaned inside. I could sprint short distances, but running fast for a long distance was very difficult for me, especially in the sweltering humidity. My strength was still a little behind the others, the remaining sign of my childhood anemia. My determination, however, was strong and I knew this run wasn't our longest, so I sped up, at least temporarily.

Zhongshan Ling was the mausoleum of Sun Yat Sen 孙逸仙, who fought against the powerful warlords and founded the republic in the year 1925. The twenty-acre complex with its tree-lined avenue rested amid the lovely Zijin Mountains 紫金山. The memorial hall, a squat cement structure topped by an elegantly curved blue-tiled roof, was reached by a climb of 392 granite steps. Everyone on the team hated this place.

We seldom noticed the beauty that surrounded us. All we saw was a formidable mountain of steps, a grueling ordeal as we ran up and down each of the 392 steps as fast as possible. Twenty times up and twenty times down!

I struggled with controlling my fear and keeping my forward momentum from propelling me downward to crash against the unforgiving granite. In a recent fall, one of my teammates was lucky—no broken bones.

One-foot-wide strips of flat cement sloped downward and edged the steps, which were interrupted by a series of platforms. Coach Wang stood at the bottom and couldn't see us at all times, but he appeared formidable with stopwatch in hand. Out of the corner of my eye, I caught some boys cheating by running down the steep, flat strip. We girls knew better than to tattle, because the boys could make our lives more difficult. We didn't want punches and bruises dispensed behind the coach's back.

Coach Wang trained our team extremely hard. He constantly pushed our endurance levels to new heights so at competitions we would give one hundred percent of our energy to the entire routine of blended martial art movements, even at the end. As much as we hated the morning body conditioning, we didn't hate Coach Wang. We felt he was training us to be champions.

Everything we did turned into a competition. Coach Wang announced the fastest runner at every lap, which was always a boy who cheated. Yet, we tried for first place every time. Competition infected our blood. We competed against each other on a daily basis for almost everything and tried to outperform each other at regional competitions. Even at local demonstrations, Coach Wang always encouraged us to show our best, by being fast, sure-footed, and energetic.

I competed against the girls who were training at the camp on a trial basis in the hopes of filling empty slots on the second team. After this long year, only one other girl remained who had started the same month I did. The athletes who didn't make it were sent home because they didn't work hard enough or couldn't take the pain of stretching and working out. Occasionally, an injury caused dismissal. This usually occurred in the winter when athletes' muscles weren't warmed up enough before rigorously working out in the cold *wushu* gymnasium. If we couldn't take the arduous training or the painful stretching, we were disposable. A never-ending line of athletes waited to get in and try out for the team.

After finishing the laborious training on the cliff-like steps and running the two and one-half miles back to the sports camp, we arrived feverish and winded. Coach Wang directed us to the running track, to sprint one hundred meters ten times at our top speed. Coach Wang, a powerhouse of athleticism just under age thirty, stayed in shape by running with us. Because he got a head start, we had to run hard to catch up with him. Sometimes, he had us sprinting for a grueling thirty minutes.

Stretching was next on the concrete basketball court and flexibility was mandatory. Like hand washing your clothes by rubbing them back and forth, the body's muscles and tendons had to be stretched and toughened until their smoothness and elasticity allowed the body to move easily in all directions.

Coach Wang assisted our daily stretching by pushing on our bodies at the most prime spot. As I did the front splits—with one foot in front of me, my heel resting on top of a brick, and the other foot behind—Coach Wang pressed his foot to my lower back while pulling my raised arms up and backwards, increasing the arch in my back. He pushed my lower back forward with his foot for side splits—both feet out to the sides of my body while I leaned forward with stomach and head to the ground. For those athletes who weren't as flexible as I was, this was torture.

Stretching was followed by what we called our one hundred one hundreds (100 100's) because they seemed to go on forever—one hundred front kicks, one hundred side kicks, one hundred snap kicks, and one hundred back kicks, outside crescent kicks, inside crescent kicks, and cross kicks that kicked toward the opposite ear. Jumps were next, and each day we did thirty repetitions of each type of jump—front jump kick, tornado kick also known as an inside jump kick, outside crescent jump kick, aerial, butterfly, and butterfly twist. The endless repetitions of various types of kicks and jumps caused the air to vibrate with the sounds of rhythmic slapping of shoes and pounding of feet. I suppressed a giggle when I saw Coach Wang kick the bottom of a teammate to lift him higher in the air while screaming, "Go higher, higher. Again, again."

When we trained, Coach Wang never distinguished between what boys could do and what girls could do. He often said, "There's no difference between girls and boys when training." During training, we all competed against each other, not just boys against boys and girls against girls. We knew girls could jump just as high as boys and boys could be as flexible as girls.

The butterfly twist was the most difficult jump to master. First, stepping in a spiral pattern and then abruptly changing directions created momentum as the legs separated and thrust the body up in the air. In that moment while parallel to the ground with arms and legs stretched to all four corners, the body resembled a butterfly in flight. Then after briefly facing the ground, both legs scissor kicked together to roll the body 360 degrees like a mermaid spinning in water. After completing a full spin, the legs separated again, and the athlete landed on the ground in the splits with a straight back and arms held out proudly like a flying bird.

"You need to relax into it to get the height out of it," Coach Wang prompted from the sidelines.

A similar jump was a butterfly without the twist. Butterflies were done in a series with high scissoring leg kicks fueling the momentum.

Some of the boys easily completed thirty to fifty nonstop rotations of the butterfly, and those who couldn't were often seen practicing on their own whenever they got a chance. No excuse was accepted for not doing something correctly. If an arm was not strong enough for a one-arm weapon move, then we learned to keep at it until it was. Fear and competition drove us to master each move. Otherwise, we would be turned away and sent home in disgrace.

Coach Wang set our daily training program in advance. He expected perfect form for every kick and jump, and we didn't want to draw attention to ourselves with anything mediocre. We were happy if Coach Wang had nothing to say to us. That meant we were doing fine.

After dismissal from practice, we ran instead of walked to change clothes before breakfast even though our energy reserves were depleted. We grabbed our spoons and the two white tin bowls we took to each meal, one for a serving of rice and one for a vegetable and meat dish. After our meals, we rinsed out our bowls and drank tea out of them.

Instead of chopsticks, we used spoons because they helped us eat faster and quickly grab more food. My sister teased me when she found out, saying, "Only babies and young children use spoons."

Our appetites swelled as we joined the noisy throng of hundreds of other athletes at 7:30 in the morning. Breakfast consisted of an assortment of eggs, porridges, buns stuffed with meat or red beans, all kinds of bakery goodies I had never seen before, and powdered milk, though occasionally fresh boiled milk was offered, but only in the mornings. Fruit was available at lunch for team members only. Now and then, Coach Wang shared a little of his fruit with one of us trainees as a reward.

Sometimes, I felt guilty because of the quantity and variety of high quality food the cafeteria provided, knowing my family couldn't afford many of the things the cafeteria served. Even though I was gone and there was one less mouth to feed, I knew my family suffered because of me. They had been subsidizing my training by paying the team for my incidentals such as bar soap, toothpaste, soap for washing clothes, and toilet paper. We had to provide our own toothbrush, comb, towel, shower basket, slippers, street shoes, and eating utensils. At home, I knew my family still struggled to feed themselves, and I didn't want to be a burden to them. By becoming a permanent team member, my family wouldn't have to pay anything for me again.

After breakfast, we younger athletes attended school in rooms built under the bleachers of the running track. Camp officials didn't want us forgetting what we had learned before coming to the camp and falling too far behind former classmates if they had to let us go. Some children tried out for the team as young as age five, though usually they were eight or nine. I came at age eleven and had completed fifth grade. I was always a good student, and at home I had read a lot of Baba's books. This put me at an advantage, though the camp school was one place where competition was conspicuously absent.

I enjoyed learning from the teachers at the team school and thought they were nice. Even though the training camp hired teachers who were the best in their field, they weren't always prepared for teaching arrogant athletes. Some of the boys were trouble, acting vain and disrespectful, like little emperors. One teacher walked out, saying she couldn't teach us. "You kids don't want to learn, so why should I waste my time," she told the class before she quit. It was true. Some of the kids just didn't want to learn anything. They felt too important as athletes to study Chinese and mathematics. They didn't realize they might need these skills later in life. I tried to imagine what the teacher was feeling because I had secretly desired to be a schoolteacher before joining the team.

Our new teacher was smart because she understood the kids weren't afraid of her. When the boys stopped paying attention and talked with each other, she patiently told them, "Okay, I'm going to speak to your coach." That calmed them down immediately. Some of the kids, however, never tried to learn. Baba encouraged me to be an athlete with a brain. Fortunately, I enjoyed learning things, and this was the reason why I remained a good student.

Lunch followed our school session, and then I mentally prepared myself for an afternoon of tough training in suffocating heat. Walking to the training gym, I carried a bucket in one hand and a thermos of water in the other. We only drank warm or hot water, never cold, because the Chinese believed it was healthier. Our bucket was stocked with bar soap, comb, towel, and our change of clothes. Following afternoon training, we would head directly to the showers.

The first and second teams shared the *wushu* gymnasium. The choice of training times went to the first team. They preferred to take a nap after lunch and train later, so the second team—combined with trainees like myself—had to practice directly after lunch.

As my eleven teammates and I entered the dim, cavernous

gymnasium, Coach Wang's booming voice issued his command. "Time for body conditioning. Everyone, handstands against the wall."

I cringed inside but was careful not to show any reluctance. Tucking a misshapen tee shirt into the elastic band of my sweatpants, I took a deep breath, preparing myself for the ordeal. I went through the motions of facing the wall and bending forward at the waist. Positioning my hands on the worn parquet floor, I locked my elbows and kicked up my feet until they rested against the crumbling cement wall that never earned a coat of paint. Blood rushed to my head as I attempted to numb my mind to the impending anguish. Before closing my eyes, I glanced at Coach Wang who began his vigil by stretching the powerful muscles of his squat, athletic body.

Everything about Coach Wang reflected his drive to succeed. As a man, he flaunted his confidence and his competitive spirit. As our coach, he demanded an obsessive dedication to training with the resolve that we mirror the qualities of the weapons he taught us to wield—the toughness of a wooden pole smacking the floor with a jarring thud, the flexibility of a thrusted broadsword vibrating with power, the exactness of a straight sword piercing its target, and the quickness of a three-section staff whipping around from behind to strike an imaginary opponent. Coach Wang's training rigor required we athletes mentally prepare ourselves as best we could to endure the worst. Not everyone was successful.

At first, the handstand felt good and allowed my shoulders and back to stretch out. Finding my body's centerline permitted me to hold myself in the most relaxed position possible, delaying the inevitable. I recognized the familiar odor emanating from the red wool workout carpet five feet shy of the wall. Its mustiness grew from years of sweat dripping daily from bodies kicking, spinning, flipping, and jumping in drills from one edge to the other and from routines bursting with every ounce of athletes' energies and abilities. Feeling sealed off from the world in an entombed gymnasium, my teammates and I struggled through the monotony and pain of endless days, weeks, and years of arduous training while waiting for the moment when we could claim our deserved rewards.

Time elapsed with aching slowness during Coach Wang's demanding body conditioning exercises. Within ten minutes, the strain of trembling arms and shoulders weakened my defenses, and fleeting pictures of my family flashed through my mind.

During my most difficult periods at the sports camp, my longing to be with my family crippled my drive to excel at the challenges Coach Wang imposed. When I recalled happy memories to distract my mind during tough training, they quickly transformed into heartache, matching the pain my body was experiencing. I learned the hard way that avoiding memories of my former life was my only safeguard while under duress. Making a conscious effort to block further thoughts of my family from my mind, I concentrated on my breathing, which helped to counteract the aching numbness in my hands and wrists.

After twenty minutes of heels-over-head agony had crawled by, deep fatigue set in. Athletes who are required to hold a weight-bearing position that long without moving their burning and screaming muscles feel those minutes lengthen into eternity. Depression spread through me with the realization I had around fifteen minutes more to endure.

In this moment while upside down, I cried in frustration without wholly understanding its cause. Control over my feelings had been learned at a young age, and my survival in the Chinese culture depended on it. Showing weakness led to intense teasing bordering on harassment. In a crowded society that revered the hard shell of an unreadable face, we built protective armor to survive. Add to that the enormous pressure placed on athletes to perform at their highest level at all times, and the result was a balloon waiting to deflate. Crying meant failure, and my inability to stop humiliated me. Soon the running flow from my nose trailed down and mixed with my tears.

Despite shaky breathing, I summoned what little determination remained within me and attempted to prevent my aching arms from bending at the elbows. Fear kept my teammates and me quiet until, eventually, we reached a point where we stopped caring. Next to me, sobbing openly, a younger teammate pleaded in her shaky voice, "Coach Wang, I can't hold it any more."

"What do I hear? If you aren't ready to become champions, why should I waste my time on you? Reach inside yourself and find the flame of desire for greatness. I did it, and I know you can do it, too. It's all in your own mind. If you think you can do it, then you can keep going. Don't quit." Coach Wang decreed.

As soon as Coach Wang recognized our dwindling morale, he told us a story to distract us from the gripping pain in our arms and shoulders and the pounding in our heads. After the story, Coach Wang paced along the edge of the red practice carpet, urging each of us to keep going. Over and over again, we were pushed to the limit of our endurance, and then we had to go a little bit further than before. We lived the true meaning of the Chinese words *chi ku*, which meant "to be capable of enduring hard work." We must eat bitter before we can taste something sweet. To become champions, we must continually push the limit of our abilities to new and higher levels.

Coach Wang insisted emphatically, "You have to take the pain now so you will never think about giving less than your full ability at a competition. You have to know deep down inside that there is no limit to what your body can handle. Pain no longer matters. All that matters is giving one hundred percent."

At some point in our upside down torment, time stood still. Excruciating pain became our existence. Thoughts of quitting dissipated and were replaced by a numbness of mind, a yielding of will. Taking the next conscious breath was our only goal.

After an indeterminable amount of time, Coach Wang finally released us from our misery. As my body crumpled into a pile on the floor, relief flooded my limbs. My blood began flowing again, but it took several minutes before my wrists unlocked from their ninety-degree angle and my arms cooperated to move the few inches necessary to wipe my nose and eyes on my sleeve.

After Coach Wang decided we had recovered from our intensive body conditioning, he switched us to forms training. We followed his training formula of doing many repetitions. One person after the other, we practiced the first section of our longfist routine until we had completed it twenty times. Then we completed twenty drills for each subsequent section, followed by two sections together twenty times, and, finally, three sections together twenty times. As always, my lips turned white from the exertion, something I desperately hoped Coach Wang wouldn't notice.

Each time I completed a part, I marked the blackboard next to my name with one stroke of a five-stroke Chinese character randomly chosen that meant "straight." This made it easy to count up all the fives. I noticed a couple of the boys bravely mark two or three strokes with the chalk instead of one. They thought Coach Wang wouldn't catch on, and sometimes he didn't. Today, however, Coach Wang must have been counting because he abruptly yelled for everyone to stop.

"You guys are a team. If one person makes trouble, everyone must start over again." With agitation, Coach Wang swiftly erased the marks on the blackboard. Sometimes, we girls hated those boys!

Before we could start over, Coach Wang selected one stance from the form. "Everyone hold this pose." He walked around the carpet and adjusted our stances. He made all the boys bend their knees until their stances were as low as possible. After twenty minutes, sweat dripped down our faces and into our eyes. Our legs shook, but still we couldn't move. Burning sensations tormented our inner legs like hot pokers skewered through them, but we learned to endure it. Finally, Coach Wang released us, ordering us to resume our training.

It helped to move again, but each repetition of the form took a huge toll on our bodies. Muscles ached with every movement, and our clothes were dripping wet. We learned to block out any mental distractions because all our concentration was needed to keep moving.

If we incurred minor injuries during training, Coach Wang always had a tough approach. "It's just a cut," or "It's only a twisted foot. Don't make such a big deal out of it." When a bumblebee hit the middle of my forehead during running, his words were, "What'd you do to that bee? Bad luck! Keep going."

One afternoon, I was injured during the practice of a two-person spear and staff fighting set. To build our skills and teamwork, my partner and I completed back-to-back triple forms. Soon, fatigue set in and my partner made a mistake. The chipped and roughened end of her staff poked the soft tissue between my eye and eyebrow. Even though I felt blood running into my eye, I knew I couldn't stop my form. After we completed it the third time through, I stood still, pretending nothing was wrong. Coach Wang didn't like us to show any weakness. We had to look brave, ignoring the problem until he noticed it.

Coach Wang casually called out, "Liu Yu, come here. Something's dripping." I walked over, devoid of any expression. After he examined my eye, he shrugged. "Go to the hospital wing and get that cleaned up."

Coach Wang always insisted, "Finish the form. That's the number one requirement." Until the coach gave permission to stop or see the doctor, you had to continue. He told us if one person on the team showed weakness, it ruined the whole team. We weren't allowed to think only about ourselves. If we felt any pain, we must endure it. We heard many times from Coach Wang, "If you don't have a strong spirit in practice, you can't compete well."

If we got a nod from Coach Wang, this was as good as a compliment.

If he corrected us, we heard about it at subsequent practices. No one wanted to be reminded they had made a mistake. Mistakes were painful for us athletes because the punishment—extra repetitions—simply prolonged the pain until muscles refused to work anymore. Additionally, the risk was always there that the whole group would have to start over again. Once a mistake was made, Coach Wang's attention zoomed in at that point every time to see if the mistake was permanently remedied. If not, his temper flared, and he shouted in outrage, sometimes hitting the boy or kicking the girl who had erred. We tried not to attract his disfavor.

We didn't want our life becoming worse by incurring penalties and we didn't want to be disgraced and lose face. But more importantly, we didn't want Coach Wang to think badly of us. We desperately wanted to make the team even though we knew we could be replaced at any time if someone came along who was better. This put tremendous pressure on everyone and created fear in our hearts. We used this fear to drive ourselves to become better. We trained well beyond the brink of exhaustion.

Following practice, we limped to the open shower area containing about thirty showerheads for all female athletes at the camp. We didn't give our lack of privacy much thought because showers were considered a luxury in China. Most cities only had two or three places where the townspeople could either shower or bathe in a tub. On hot days, however, we shunned the warm water and opted for cool water to douse the heat inflaming our weary muscles.

Whenever we could, we washed some of our clothing, especially our underclothes, while we showered. This was the only hot water on campus. The designated laundry areas were the cold-water sinks next to our toilets. Doing laundry in the showers was forbidden, and a stocky team leader policed the area. We positioned the tall female basketball players in the front to block the team leader's view. If we were caught, we had to pay a fine and admit our guilt in our weekly forum meeting.

Our training schedule varied day by day. Jogging was the usual warm-up. My least favorite run was up the steep mountain. Even though the run around the old Nanjing city wall took the longest, the mountain run had the added element of fear. We didn't follow a path; instead we made our own way up and down, dodging obstacles like loose rocks and scrubby weeds that could trip us. While going down, it was hard to stop. We ignored our fear of losing control of our steps because competition drove us to be fast. To slow down, I reached out and grabbed trees several times, holding them briefly to catch my breath. Reaching the bottom unscathed was almost impossible. We often skinned our legs while sliding and hitting rocky surfaces.

Sometimes we practiced jumping by utilizing ping-pong tables when the ping-pong coach wasn't around. Coach Wang devised various jumping combinations we followed until fatigue caused our shins to scrape against the edge of the table. Despite any pain or discomfort, Coach Wang wouldn't give us permission to stop. After dozens of repetitions, the stepping pattern was altered, and we started over again. Those sturdy ping-pong tables took our pounding without cracking. Many times the ping-pong players exchanged gymnasiums with us so they could enjoy playing with our weapons.

Occasionally we trained with other camp teams, like the weight lifting team. Weight training for girls was different than for the boys. Our objective was building strength by using many repetitions while keeping our postures erect. Often, Coach Wang wanted us to strengthen particular muscles. When we learned short weapon forms, each individual forearm muscle had to be identified and strengthened. Muscles in the back had to be built up for the staff and broadsword.

All coaches at the camp shared their knowledge with each other's teams. The weight lifting coach guided our muscle-building exercises. The gymnastics coach offered suggestions on improving flexibility. The short distance running coach shared his experience with us. And researchers at the hospital studied kinetics to improve the efficiency of our muscles. We attempted to copy the fluid motions of the rhythm gymnasts without success. A frustrated Coach Wang told us, "You're doing the forms too straight. You need to be more graceful." He arranged for special ballet instruction, making us think about our postures and learn how to hold our heads correctly.

Our most famous athlete at the camp was a world champion female fencer. We all knew the story about one of her international competitions in France. During the competition, a French girl's fencing sword accidentally pierced her upper arm and poked out the other side. She didn't let that stop her, though, and she went on to win. When she returned home, Chinese coaches everywhere wanted their athletes to learn from her competitive spirit.

On Wednesday afternoons, Coach Wang challenged other second teams—like soccer or basketball—to compete with us at *their* sport.

Then he demanded, "I don't want you guys to lose. Even though they're professional, it doesn't matter. Get them!" The competitive gleam in his eyes when he instructed us to win at all costs showed us how desperately he wanted to win. He pushed us hard to win and raised our spirits so we believed we could do it. We also knew if we lost, we would have to do some long-distance running and hundreds of sit-ups. Coach Wang didn't call it punishment for losing, but we knew he used it as motivation so we would win.

When playing the other professional teams at basketball or soccer, we used every advantage possible. Sometimes this meant grabbing the other team's clothing or even scratching them so we could beat them. The tall basketball players saw how agile we were and how quickly we changed directions. We were also fast runners and high jumpers. When we played against the soccer team, we blocked a line so the other team couldn't get through. The other teams complained when they had to play us. They knew we didn't play by the rules. The coaches, who were good friends with each other, probably planned these competitions to help each other's teams work harder.

One day, as the coaches sat laughing and watching the game on the sidelines, the soccer team coach abruptly whistled to get our attention and yelled, "Stop! Do that again!" We followed his finger pointing to Huang Jun, my shortest male teammate who was also the most limber of the boys.

Huang Jun's-黄俊 chest puffed up with pride as the other team threw the ball in his direction. He turned away from it, jumped high, and snapped his foot to kick the ball over his head backwards before landing softly on his upper back in the grass, then "kipping up" to his feet in one swift motion. In a kip up, a martial artist propels his lower body to flip up and out without pushing off with his arms or hands; the momentum pulls his upper body with him, and he lands firmly on his feet.

After conferring with Coach Wang, the soccer coach announced to his team that Coach Wang would be teaching them how to do this jump kick. This turned out to be easier said than done.

Coach Wang enlisted our help in demonstrating. We started with jumping and kicking our legs high in the air. When the soccer players copied us, we laughed hard because they couldn't kick their legs any higher than their waists. Coach Wang tried to get them to relax while kicking without much success. Next, he had us show them how to fall correctly on their upper backs. It was obvious that teaching them to do a kip up would take a lot of training.

After the practice, one of the soccer players complained to us, "Your coach is trying to kill us." We laughed.

In turn, the soccer coach taught us *wushu* athletes how to use our feet to control the ball as we ran forward. We loved moving the ball more freely, although we could never do it as well as the soccer players. They got their chance to laugh at us.

The jump kick lessons didn't last too long. The soccer coach soon gave up. He saw how much difficulty his team was having in learning the movement.

Day after day, rigorous training went on, except on Sundays, when the whole camp took a day off. Everyone except the second *wushu* team. The sport at the camp that most closely resembled *wushu* was gymnastics. They trained as hard and also selected their athletes at young ages, but they didn't have Sunday practices.

Coach Wang laid out his reasoning. "Your body doesn't have Sundays off. If you take one day off, you waste three days to get your body back to the same level of conditioning. Then you're going backwards. And, besides, you aren't church people."

So, instead of Sundays off, we trained for half a day. The other camp coaches often threatened their teams with Sunday practice, saying, "We should be just like the little *wushu* team." Trying to mold our attitudes, Coach Wang used his persuasive abilities to inform us *wushu* training was different. He explained it was more critical for us to keep building ourselves than for athletes in other sports. During a *wushu* form, there was no rest; *wushu* movements must show maximum vitality every second of the performance.

Before practice on Sunday, we cleaned our room, washed our laundry, and went to the small camp store to purchase supplies Coach Wang had approved in advance. We weren't allowed to leave the camp like the older athletes. I often took this opportunity to get a book from the library. All I wanted to do with my free time was just lie in bed and relax while reading.

The Jiangsu Province Sports Training Camp 江苏省体育工作大队 was a huge gated facility akin to a university campus. Each team had its own gymnasium or outside training area and shared the use of a huge running track, swimming and diving pools, and plenty of tennis and basketball courts. Dormitory rooms were often grouped by sport. When I arrived at the camp, the girls' *wushu* rooms were full, so four of us *wushu* girls combined with nine gymnasts across the hall in Room 308. We always wished we could move to the *wushu* room because their room was on the sunny south side. Our dormitory rooms didn't have any heat in the frigid winter, making the sun's warmth highly valued.

The camp was self-sufficient with its own hospital, store, post office, library, and school. Masseurs were available, but we decided only weaklings used them. For superficial muscle pulls, Coach Wang massaged our aching limbs as a way to check our injuries. The camp officials tried to think of everything we needed so no one had to go off campus.

The other professional teams thought Coach Wang was the most competitive and toughest coach at the camp. When a vote was taken to select this year's team with the best training, we were chosen because the other teams saw how hard we worked. We had mixed feelings about winning the honor.

After the vote, one of the kitchen workers who had known Coach Wang as a boy came over to our table in the cafeteria, heckling him. "You little monkey, I saw you grow up. Now you're the big coach. Why are you training them so hard? They're just little kids." Then the man turned to us and said, "You guys aren't human." He said it with a serious face, but then he laughed, his big belly shaking. We had never heard anyone talk to Coach Wang in that way, and we were glad he didn't take offense. Although our coach laughed about it, we were too afraid and kept any semblance of a smile off our faces.

Coach Wang chose different locations for our training. In the summer, we might go to the countryside for two months. Our training included running circles around cotton fields. The suffocating summer weather sapped our energy and made us desperately thirsty. We couldn't drink water when we wanted it because water in the stomach during training was believed to harm one's body. When we could, we stopped and only rinsed our mouths with water.

One teammate felt so parched it made him a little brave. He snuck into the kitchen where they stored the water and guzzled it down, but his absence was noticed. When he reappeared, Coach Wang questioned him in a loud voice. "I think you went to the kitchen and drank some water. Did you drink it?"

The boy answered in a quivering voice, "No, I didn't."

"DID YOU DRINK IT?" Coach Wang thundered.

Again, the boy denied it.

"You're lying to me," shouted Coach Wang, who began angrily kicking the boy.

Sometimes, the coach hit, kicked, or spanked the athletes who disobeyed his rules. We understood all coaches had this right, but it made us very fearful of him, especially at such a young age.

Although Coach Wang possessed a booming voice commanding instant obedience and shooting fear into our hearts, he also knew how to relieve some of our tension by kidding around with us. He enjoyed making us laugh by exaggerating a wrong move as a clown might do. This lighter side of his teaching helped to offset the tyrannical image of him in our minds.

To prepare for the national competition held each year in late fall, training went into overdrive with longer workouts and an extra session each evening. Even though the second team wasn't competing yet, we still had to follow the pre-competition training. Because competitors never knew what time of day their events would be held until the competition started, it was important to be accustomed to performing at any time of the day, whether it was first thing in the morning or late at night.

The training focus for the second team was the longfist. An even and spirited pace had to be maintained as we practiced the whole form for twenty times followed by twenty double forms and twenty triple forms. A single *wushu* form was like sprinting 400 meters. A triple form was doing the form three times back-to-back without stopping. We had to finish it in about ten minutes, and the third repetition had to be as fast and energetic as the first. Triple forms were killers, turning my lips white because it took all my oxygen to get through the form while showing the strongest vitality possible at every moment.

Coach Wang made us train under many different conditions. We trained so often on cement—even in winter—that our pants got holes in them and our legs became bloody while doing the splits. We also practiced flips on the concrete, which terrified us while we were learning. Falling the wrong way jolted and bruised our bodies as we banged the unforgiving surface. Coach Wang explained, "You need to be tough. If you can perform well on concrete, you'll do even better when you're more relaxed on a carpet. It's good for you. You'll appreciate it later."

If the weather was really bad, we might run laps through the dormitory up and down the stairs on each side. During rainy weather, however, Coach Wang usually had us training outside. He said, "You have to train under all kinds of conditions so you'll be prepared." We thought this was crazy. Competitions were always held in big arenas or gymnasiums with roofs. However, we learned quickly to have sure footing on slippery cement, which helped us develop stronger stances and better balance.

One year, at a national competition, the host city was building a new gymnasium, but it wasn't finished. The roof hadn't been completed. Even though the competition wasn't held during the rainy season, it surprised everyone when it rained for the few days of the competition. The carpeting, soaked with water, was slippery. We couldn't complain because the conditions were the same for everyone. At that time, our team really appreciated the training Coach Wang had given us.

As time went on, the grueling workouts became harder to endure as my body had greater difficulty recovering from the punishment it suffered. It was the sense of it never ending, of going on forever, which made me question my sanity. Whenever my teammates and I thought our bodies couldn't take anymore and we were barely holding on, Coach Wang stepped in and steered us away from entering a darkness from which we might never escape. But darkness seemed to follow us.

China's 1974 Friendship Tour to the U.S.
(Clever Treasure is second girl to the right from President Nixon--her head just above his wrist--and Coach Wang is the full figure standing to the left of Nixon)

1974 *wushu* performance in White House Rose Garden

 13

COACH WANG'S STORIES

Camp life was hard with few compensating rewards. Fear constantly plagued me that my body wouldn't be able to handle the demands dealt out by Coach Wang. When my body threatened to revolt, I thought about my family and the shame I would bring them if I quit, and NaiNai had ingrained in me never to be a quitter. Yet, sometimes I missed my family so much that I caught myself wallowing in self-pity.

At those times, Coach Wang knew how to boost our languishing spirits. Just after the time of spring competition—though we were still too young to compete—and before the team geared up for the national tournament held in late fall, our training schedule was more relaxed. On summer evenings, Coach Wang gathered my teammates and me around him and spun a web of magic that fed our dreams, seducing us into thinking we were all moving along brilliantly in the master plan he had devised for us. He inspired us with revelations about his life and what he had accomplished.

Shifting slightly in his chair, Coach Wang sipped tea from his cup while my teammates and I sat on the grass at his feet. Even though Coach Wang was good at creating competition among us, after practice he encouraged us to act like brothers and sisters. During practice he said there was no difference between boys and girls, but after practice we girls must be in our rooms or in a group with him. The boys had more freedom but generally wanted the encouragement Coach Wang offered. We girls were given crayons if we wanted to draw, while the boys lazed beside us.

Coach Wang told us stories we never tired of hearing, sometimes with a twist or a new piece of information added, but always filled with inspiration. We loved hearing about his days spent training, competing, and winning. The late 1960's and early 1970's were golden years for Coach Wang when he won multiple gold medals and was honored several times with the title of China's All-around Wushu Champion. Although the competitions held during the beginning of the Cultural Revolution were friendship competitions rather than official national competitions, they were attended by the same teams and considered the same thing. Then at the 1974 national competition, a few months after my move to Nanjing, Coach Wang was awarded five gold medals in the categories of compulsory form, compulsory straight sword, individual longfist, individual staff, and all-around champion. We thought he was the best *wushu* athlete there ever was, making us feel proud to have him as our coach.

Coach Wang's voice took on an edge of excitement as he recited a favorite story before his gathered audience. "When I went to Beijing to train for the 1974 friendship tour to the U.S., eighty athletes were invited from all over China to try for the delegation team. Only thirty-two were selected for China's first trip to the U.S. The competition was intense. The officials looked for the best athletes at longfist, broadsword, and all the different weapons. Some children were also selected to go."

As the oldest on the second team, I assumed the role of big sister. While Coach Wang talked, I kept an eye on his teacup. Whenever it became half full, I poured more hot water from the thermos into his cup. I knew he appreciated it, though he never acknowledged it.

"Those kids worked hard. One of the youngest chosen, Li Lian Jie 李连杰 (later known as Jet Li, the movie star), was very good. He really wanted to be selected and was always practicing, even when he could be taking a break." Coach Wang employed silence for emphasis by taking a moment to let his words sink in while he sipped from his cup again.

As I listened to his stories, I was also idly drawing on paper with colored crayons. Yet, I never missed a word Coach Wang said. Hearing about the children who trained to go to the U.S. made me wish I had been chosen to be on that special team.

Coach Wang gently put his teacup down and cleared his throat. "I had two friends from other provinces, Zhang Ling Mei 张玲妹 and Chen Dao Yun 陈道云. We worked hard during the daily workouts and evening practices, but we felt that wasn't enough. We had to practice more. After bedtime, we snuck out in the dark for secret practice at a nearby construction site where we could train. We just had to be the best."

"Coach Wang, what was America like?" someone asked.

"It wasn't exactly as we expected. The people were friendly, polite, and so educated. They clapped their hands very hard when we performed. I couldn't believe the little lady who worked for the Asian cultural association in New York could organize everything and make it just right. It inspired me the way everyone listened to her and how she got things done. American people were the opposite of what I believed they would be like."

We sat very still, our attention riveted on his words. "There were beautiful, fragrant flowers growing everywhere in Hawaii. They string them together and put them around your neck when they greet you. We stayed in first-class hotels with bouquets of flowers in each room. And, oh, there were so many cars and tall buildings. We visited Honolulu, San Francisco, New York, and then met President Nixon in the White House Rose Garden in their capital city of Washington, D.C. We were proud we could show *wushu* to the West."

Coach Wang paused momentarily before continuing, and I knew he was about to say something important. "Of course, we had to be very careful with what we said because we were told the Americans would be spying on us. We weren't allowed to watch television there because they show the women wearing almost nothing when they swim, and we Chinese know that'll brainwash you. We couldn't always eat with chopsticks. We had to learn a new way to eat before the trip, using forks and knives. We were told, 'When the people look at you, they'll see China. You belong to your country. Everything you do there is for your country.' It was an honor. This applies to you, too. You represent the Jiangsu Province Wushu Team. You aren't just representing yourself. You must think about the group. You must be careful how you present yourself."

Coach Wang always had a point to make when he talked. We knew he used psychology to get us to work harder, but because he was such a great champion, we believed him.

Many years later, a funny story surfaced about Coach Wang's trip to America. His roommate in Hawaii who became the coach of the Singapore team told me, "Jin Bao was so curious about the television. He looked it over and finally couldn't resist pushing buttons. When the television suddenly sprang to life, he panicked, trying several buttons to turn it off. I laughed to see him so alarmed, but he was smart and followed the electrical cord, giving it a quick yank. He then lay on the bed, wiping sweat from his forehead, asking me not to report him. Of course, I had to do it. They chastised him during a meeting, but he didn't get into big trouble over it."

Sometimes, Coach Wang recited stories about athletes of other sports. In the 1960's, a top female ping-pong player on the national team injured her hand the night before her world championship match. People were irate when they heard an unknown assailant had attacked her and whacked her wrist with a ping-pong paddle. With poor relations between China and Taiwan, rumors circulated that maybe Taiwan was responsible.

All Chinese eyes and ears followed the national ping-pong team in its bid for world glory. To the horror of the country, the athlete broke down and finally confessed during the investigation she had injured herself. The enormous pressure she was under contributed to her overwhelming fear of what would happen if she lost the match. She was afraid of bringing dishonor to her country by losing. That same pressure spilled over onto me, and on some days I found that I couldn't go anywhere, perform any function without the fear of failure looming large, tying my stomach into knots.

Coach Wang explained to us that athletes all over the world have pressure, but in China there's more pressure. Only the gold medal brought honor to China. Top government officials believed they could compel athletes to win by putting fear in their minds. Athletes were commanded to win, especially when they faced an enemy of China such as Taiwan or our Cold War enemy, America.

Athletic competitions became battles between countries. Winning was a matter of our country's honor. As a result, the spirit of competition was lost for these athletes and for me. We were told we belonged to the government and owed a responsibility to the farmers who fed us. We were ordered to *beat* our opponents. We *had* to win.

Coach Wang explained, "If China points its finger at you, you have to go where you're sent and do what you're ordered. You're part of the government and you have to serve its leaders. You must train hard so your only desire is doing your best at all times. This is how you will feel confident."

Working harder was always Coach Wang's remedy for what ailed us. Sometimes I felt trapped when my exhausted body and resentful mind threatened to stop cooperating. I knew, however, I couldn't express that resentment. I tucked it away inside me until the middle of the night when it tormented me. In order to keep my sanity, I knew I had to follow Coach Wang's plan. Always, the fear of being sent home in disgrace and being laughed at was worse than anything Coach Wang had put me through so far.

On other evenings, Coach Wang talked about how his childhood training was different from our training. "In the 1950's life was hard. People sold their children to the *wushu* master because they couldn't afford to keep them. The training was much harder than what you go through. Even if the *wushu* master beat a child almost to death, the parents couldn't get the child back. I teach the traditional way with lots of repetitions and maximum stretching, but I already adjusted my teaching. You think I'm hard, but you don't know what hard is. You'll be very grateful someday for all this training."

He sipped from the teacup he cradled in his hand before continuing. "My mother didn't want me to study *wushu*. She wanted me to get a good education. When I was young, I watched the Beijing opera whenever I could. When I read my favorite book about the three kingdoms, I imagined myself acting out the story in costumes with weapons. At eleven years old, I secretly started formal *wushu* training. I snuck out to train with Master Yu Bao Hui-于保惠 in my hometown of Jiang Yiang-姜堰. Master Yu's specialty is the big broadsword. He's also famous for his ability to absorb punches, which he learned by practicing what's known as hard qigong-气功 as opposed to soft qigong, the practice of breathing and internal energy development. Whenever I went to practice with Master Yu, I jumped in the river afterwards to take a bath and then let my clothes dry on me before I went home. In less than two months I entered a provincial competition and won first place in the Southern boxing style of Nanquan-南拳."

Some traditional forms or older styles had slower movements than the longfist but required more strength to execute power releases. Instead of a typical *wushu* horse stance—standing with the legs bowed like riding a horse—solid bridge stances that took many years of work to learn were common. The Southern style of Nanquan focused on more use of the fist with many sweeping arm movements. The Northern style of *wushu* used the longfist, employing more flashy kicking techniques, high jumps, and fierce punches.

Coach Wang swatted a mosquito on his arm. "I became a professional team member when I was twelve in 1958, the year our training camp opened. The professional *wushu* team coach, Wang Feng Gang 王风岗, helped me prepare to compete the next spring at the very first big game competition held every four years thereafter. I won a sixth place medal for my monkey staff form. Right after that, I was selected for the China National Youth Team and studied with the national professional team coach, Professor Cai Longyun 蔡龙云, who's from Shanghai and has written many books on Chinese martial arts. I felt honored to represent China when I traveled to Czechoslovakia and Cambodia. I saw Chairman Mao speak at Tiananmen Square 天安门广场 for the national ten-year anniversary celebration and traveled with Zhou Enlai 周恩来 to Cambodia. At the second big game competition held in 1963 in Shanghai, I won all-around champion. Everything happened so fast, one, two, three," he said as he snapped his fingers.

Knowing Coach Wang had undergone training similar to mine and surfaced as such a famous athlete encouraged me. Hearing how badly Coach Wang wanted to be the best was contagious and strengthened my trust in him. Although his words inspired me, they didn't neutralize the fear I carried around and kept hidden from Coach Wang. He didn't know how much I struggled with my weak body.

"Although I was a natural at *wushu*, I also had to be really good to survive. It's not enough to love *wushu* and be eager to learn as much as you can. You also have to train hard. The key is to focus on a particular goal, like developing the highest butterfly twist. If you can accomplish this one thing, then you can do anything later on. You can be number one at the national competition," he declared with clear conviction.

"How can you distinguish yourself from every other *wushu* athlete?" he asked us as he leaned forward in his chair. "You all have basically the same training and that means you have an equal chance at winning."

We raised our heads, listening intently.

"The answer is: who's mentally stronger? That means every moment that you're out there competing on the carpet, you're showing your *best*. If you can show the best you can do, then you'll be a winner, even if it's only winning second place. It all depends on how strong your mind is. So don't waste these valuable years of basic training. Even though I train you hard, I have a master plan to make you champions. You just have to follow my training schedule with one hundred percent of your effort."

How could I argue with that? I felt compelled to put my faith in him by training, living, and breathing as if one day I, too, would become a champion. There was an end to the training somewhere out there in the future. I just couldn't think about how far away it was and what had to happen in between.

"During my early training, I worked hard to develop my flexibility. I wanted to get my leg closer to my head in the one-legged splits stance. Before I went to sleep at night, I raised my left leg straight up to the side of my head and tied my leg to my head. I slept that way. No one told me to do it, I wanted to."

My ears were still attuned to what Coach Wang was saying, but my eyelids had nearly closed and the crayon tilted limply in my hand. I was too tired to draw and the mosquitoes were annoying. Finally, Coach Wang dismissed us. Like lead weights, my weary feet thumped up the dormitory stairs.

Without any cooling fans, the heavy air inside the building stood as motionless as a steam bath. The boys were lucky. Coach Wang allowed them to sleep on the rooftop where it was cooler. Girls, however, weren't allowed outside their locked rooms at night. We didn't have the same freedom as the boys. We convinced ourselves Coach Wang was protecting us like our fathers would. And because I missed my father so much, I appreciated Coach Wang's concern. It helped ease my homesickness to claim that someone at the camp cared about me, and I needed to feel connected. I found myself trying to please Coach Wang to earn his attention like I had once done with Baba.

After brushing my teeth, I filled up my empty thermos with cool water and poured it on the shaved bamboo skin bed mat I used in the summer. It would make it feel a little cooler for a while. Too soon, however, the oppressive heat would filter back in and make it difficult to sleep.

Before lights went out and doors were locked, I heard a familiar shout in the hallway, "boys coming up." The boys' rooms were on the second floor of our dormitory and we girls occupied the third floor. Whenever the boys wanted to reach the roof—though they usually slept on the rooftop of the hospital next door—or if they wanted to find someone, they stood at the bottom of the stairs and yelled. We girls screamed because in the hot weather we didn't wear much clothing—bra and underwear for older girls and just underwear for us younger girls. Annoyed, I rushed over to slam the door to our room shut.

When I finally lay in bed trying to sleep, I thought about Coach Wang's motivating stories. Just to see what it felt like, I extended my leg up and pressed it against the wall to keep it in place. I knew Coach Wang had been encouraging us to try it. It wasn't hard to put my leg up, but I found it difficult to fall asleep in that position.

Training during the day wasn't easy to endure and my sleep was never peaceful because I worried about meeting the demands of the next day. As much as I longed to show Coach Wang how good I could be, I decided the extra stretching at night was overkill and could affect my rest. Whatever deep sleep I could get became my most precious reward. Without it, I feared empty motivation and looming insanity. I forced myself to remain tough.

As I drifted off to sleep, my mental resolve melted and doubts crept in to persecute me. *What if Coach Wang discovers my secret?* I feared he would say, "Why should I waste my time on such a sick girl." Every day, I pushed myself in practice so he wouldn't find out because otherwise he would surely dismiss me. I felt a sword aimed at my chest, ready to thrust and pierce my heart at any moment. I couldn't be sent home. I just couldn't.

Clever Treasure and Liu Yu

14 *PROMOTION WITHOUT FANFARE*

Every Wednesday evening after six to eight hours of practice, I carried my folding stool under my arm, reluctantly dragging myself to the group political forum with Team Leader Chen. As the representative of the government, he was required to make sure we followed all the rules of the camp and the government. In the weekly forums, which began all over China during the Cultural Revolution, each of us was commanded to share with others everything we did wrong during the week. Most of the time the revelations were mundane and tonight's tiresome disclosures were no exception. In the room's oven-like temperature, it was hard to concentrate, and I drooped on my stool, my back collapsed from fatigue.

One teammate squelched a yawn, confessing wearily, "Oh, this week I didn't work hard enough during Saturday's training."

Another revealed, "I'm sorry I forgot to wash my workout clothes and they're dirty."

After each athlete shared, Leader Chen's voice droned on explaining in great detail why it was important to eliminate wrong action and wrong thinking. He pried into our lives by asking very personal questions. We thought we couldn't hide anything from him because we suspected he snooped through our rooms. Also, we were accustomed to revealing every detail about our lives to Coach Wang, who made each of us write in a daily journal.

We were required to disclose in our journals the condition of our bodies each day, including any aches or problems. Coach Wang wanted to know how well we ate and what we were thinking. He then wrote some short responses in our journals like, "I don't think so!" or "Good job!"

If we were involved in any arguments or witnessed any fighting or problems with other teammates, we had to include it. One time, a teammate forced one of the girls to lend him her radio. When he wouldn't give it back, she complained to Coach Wang in her journal. It turned out he had taken it apart and couldn't put it back together again. Coach Wang gave him a hard time.

Although we risked a teammate's revenge, we preferred a few covert punches to anything Coach Wang doled out. Yet we didn't always know where to walk the line. If Coach Wang discovered we omitted something, we faced extra workout penalties, something we wanted to avoid at all costs.

There was one thing we all tacitly agreed to keep hidden from Coach Wang. We were supposed to include in our journals how we slept, but we were afraid to admit that we regularly lost sleep because we worried about being able to withstand the next day's training. We couldn't let the coach know we lived in a state of constant fear of failure. We knew if he found out, we would be gone.

The forums and journals robbed us of any sense of privacy. We adjusted to it just like we got used to never having closed doors except at night. In our minds, we believed Coach Wang knew everything, and we couldn't hide anything from him. If he became suspicious of someone, his penetrating stare caused the suspect to shake all over. We learned it wasn't worth the effort to be sneaky. Sometimes a boy thought he was smart and could get away with something, but he was rarely successful.

I tried following everything Coach Wang said, so I had very little to disclose at the forum. Usually the last one to confess, I was still shy about speaking in front of people. When I knew my turn was coming up, my heart drummed harder. Instinctively, my arms wrapped protectively around my torso. When the team leader nodded in my direction, my voice came out in a soft whisper. With downcast eyes, I said, "I could have worked harder at our distance runs this week."

The forum meeting went on and on as usual despite our fatigue. Periodically, I wiped my brow on my sleeve and pressed my tee shirt against my back to absorb the dripping sweat. Just when we thought the meeting was over, Coach Wang began talking. I listened as I swatted a mosquito on my leg. "As of today, Liu Yu is now an official member of the second team. Okay, dismissed."

My heart beating wildly, I stole a glance at Coach Wang, but he had already turned away and was heading for the door. Immediately, I buried my joy for fear of what the others might think, and sure enough I heard the hushed whispers, the jealousy in the murmur that erupted through the room.

From behind, a resentful voice grunted, "Huh, she's Coach Wang's favorite." I recognized it as coming from a girl who had been here longer than me and who still hadn't made the team. Her cousin had recently been assigned the job of assistant coach, though he still competed on the first team. I never expected to make the team before the athletes who had been here longer and certainly not before someone who had team connections. It only proved Coach Wang didn't do favors for people.

No mention was made of what steps Coach Wang had to take to get me approved for the second team. The first team coach, the team leaders, and the camp leader had to agree. Then paperwork was filled out and sent to the appropriate Jiangsu Province government officials. I suspected my approval was unusual for the short length of time I had been training at the camp. Slowly, I filed out the door, trying not to show any emotion to minimize the jealousy. After all, my teammates would view my promotion as one less position available for them to fill.

While walking back to the dormitory in the safety of the darkness, I allowed happiness to bubble inside me. My parents could discontinue paying a subsidy for my training, and with my salary I could now send them money. I looked forward to Sunday when I could write my parents about the good news. I took a deep breath, relieved I had accomplished my first goal. Now I was on my own. If something happened and I were forced to leave the team, at least some kind of menial job would be given to me so I would never be a burden to my family again. Being sent away to the countryside was no longer a threat and for that I was truly grateful.

As I tried to go to sleep that night, I smiled to myself, feeling overjoyed Coach Wang thought I could take the hard work. With my promotion, a new set of fears began lurking in the back of my mind. There was no security in being a team member. I could still be asked to leave at any time if I couldn't do the work or if someone better came along. With each doubt, my resolve to become a champion grew stronger. I could do it; I knew I could. I was a tiger, and I believed I could accomplish anything if I set my mind to it. Someday, I would even learn to speak easily in front of people.

My promotion changed my life in a couple of ways. I now received a salary, but I had no spending money. Coach Wang held my earnings in a separate bank account and kept track of my incidentals in a notebook. If I wanted to purchase stamps and envelopes at the camp store, I was required to ask his permission first. He then subtracted my expenses from my earnings in the notebook he kept for me.

Coach Wang now began more serious training with me. After breakfast when it was time to go to school, he pulled me aside. "You don't need to go to school today. You already know enough. I want you to train with the gymnastics team." So, I went to practice with the second girls' gymnastics team two or three times a week. I didn't mind, and it was nice to get to know the other camp athletes better.

Training with the gymnastics team required great care. They had a high rate of injury, often breaking bones while tumbling. One day, I witnessed a gymnast fly off the uneven bars and smash into the wall. She was badly hurt and had to be sent home.

The gymnastics coach needed a replacement athlete. She liked me because I was very flexible and had the right body type for gymnastics— slender with strong, long legs. Later, she asked Coach Wang, "Would you let Liu Yu change to the gymnastics team?"

Coach Wang quickly responded, "No way!" Although athletes sometimes changed sports at the camp, Coach Wang wasn't the type of coach to lose a potential investment willingly, despite the coaches' friendship.

I loved *wushu* too much to ever consider changing sports. I came from a small town with more traditional Chinese values and felt *wushu* fit my personality better. Sometimes, my gymnastics roommates got into verbal competitions with *wushu* athletes. They always acted so proud of themselves for being in an Olympic sport. To me, they seemed to think of themselves as little ballerinas. We defended ourselves by saying, "We like our uniforms because they're Chinese-style, not Western leotards."

We said "Western" like it was a dirty word. We also countered with, "*And we can eat as much as we want.*" They couldn't argue with that.

The gymnastics team had to conscientiously monitor their weight. The girls weren't allowed to eat much or drink hardly any water, especially before a competition. The coaches didn't want any water weight. This was especially true of the rhythm gymnasts, who were chosen because they looked pencil-thin. Occasionally, the gymnasts who shared my dormitory room asked us if we had any water in our room they could drink. In contrast, Coach Wang always encouraged us *wushu* athletes to eat enough so we could sustain the difficult workouts.

Coach Wang now focused on me more in class. One day during my barehanded fighting practice with both male and female partners, Coach Wang expressed frustration. "Liu Yu, you're too afraid to hit your opponent back hard. It has to look real and match your partner's intensity. I want to see sparks flying off in all directions. Spectators should feel you're throwing flames at your partner's head." He then paired me up with the most aggressive boy whose fists painfully rammed into my face when I failed to block him. Instead of using the flat section of the fist between the first and second finger joints to inflict less pain, he smacked me with his knuckles. I quickly learned to release my inhibitions, fighting back with all my might. I brought that lesson of creating forceful movements to all my forms, which raised my *wushu* skill to a new level.

After becoming a permanent team member, Coach Wang started giving me private lessons during his morning break. He drilled me on one side of the huge gymnasium while the first team practiced. These lessons were a big honor, but they scared me and were tough to endure. My teammates confided they were envious I was receiving special attention from the coach, but they were also glad it wasn't them. They wanted to escape more torturous training.

Although my health was improving, I had great difficulty keeping my energy level high. For three hours when my teammates were in school, Coach Wang locked his attention on me, prohibiting me from enjoying a moment's rest. I pushed myself to show Coach Wang I could work hard, while desperately trying to mask my inadequate health. I found myself wishing my teammates were there so I could hide behind them to catch my breath and relax. I didn't want Coach Wang to think I couldn't keep up the pace he expected because I had a bad attitude or was lazy. The harder I struggled to keep going, the more doubts flooded my psyche.

Maybe I can't physically handle the excessive work.

When my teammates worked this hard, their faces became beet red and their lips purple from the exertion. In contrast, all color drained out my face, my lips turning white from the strain. There was nowhere to hide. When Coach Wang paused from issuing constant directives, the eerie silence put me on guard. Then, in a frustrated, booming voice, he yelled, "You little sick girl! Stop right now!"

I immediately froze, my breath coming in short, uncontrollable gasps as I tried to recover from my exertion and stem my panic at the same time. *Coach Wang now knew my secret.* For several moments he stared hard while my imagination ran wild. *Please don't give up on me. I don't want to go home.*

"I'm going to contact your father," he said at last. "We need to discuss what can be done so you can train harder. I want him to come to Nanjing." My spirits plummeted with his words. *How could I train harder when I could barely manage the current level?*

Recently, the camp doctors had tested everyone's blood. They found the level of iron in my blood was low and prevented enough oxygen from being carried by my blood cells. I now clung to the hope my father and Coach Wang would find a solution to allow me to remain on the team.

The day Baba arrived at the training camp, he, Coach Wang, and I embarked on a secret trip to the best hospital in Nanjing. After a thorough check, the doctors recommended a bone marrow test.

I could tell Baba was anxious, thinking they might find cancer. They stuck a tube into my hipbone and inserted a needle through it to pull out a bone marrow sample. The procedure was painful, but I clenched my jaw with determination. Once and for all I needed to know what was wrong with me.

During the test, Coach Wang told the doctors I ate well. Actually, I didn't have a big appetite, but I learned I needed to eat a lot to keep up with the training. I desperately wanted to remain on the team. The greatest *wushu* champion was my coach, and his sole ambition was to mold me into a champion. I *had* to know if he could take me there, and I resolved to die trying to achieve our joint dream.

Thankfully, the bone marrow test didn't reveal any problems. The doctors strategized and decided on a plan. Every day, I would get a shot of Vitamin B-12 and iron at the camp hospital. Baba and his brother would make a liquid concoction of herbs, and I would drink one tablespoon of it at bedtime. Coach Wang would arrange for the kitchen to prepare a special soup made from pork liver for me to drink every day at lunch. The soup tasted good, but I quickly grew tired of drinking it every day.

My teammates noticed the specially prepared soup. Although I tried not to appear different in any way to avoid making my teammates jealous, they teased me that Coach Wang liked me best. I couldn't tell them it was because I wasn't healthy. Coach Wang tried to cover up my weakness when he casually asked for the shots and soup. My intuition told me if the first team coach found out about my health problem, Coach Wang couldn't prevent him from turning me away.

Although I struggled through the extra private practice, I continued to try my best. Sometimes, I caught Coach Wang's look of disappointment as he watched me. I knew he felt helpless, thinking I wasn't strong enough to reach a higher level. I began anticipating he would reach a limit and let me go. Each day, I breathed a sigh of relief after I made it through the private lesson and was thankful Coach Wang allowed me to continue.

When I first arrived at the camp, Coach Wang changed one of my weapon specialties. It made me very happy to discontinue the broadsword and train with the straight sword instead, which Coach Wang said fit my slender body better.

One day during my lessons, he expressed some frustration. "You've picked up some bad habits from Coach Dai when you're holding a weapon. You forgot about your left hand. Its movements should coordinate with your whole body. I know your old coach was missing his left hand, but you never thought about needing to use it."

One focus of my extra training was to perfect my tornado kick jump, a spinning jump that slapped the foot and was followed by landing in a seating stance with my feet tucked around my body. Coach Wang got fired up as he commanded, "Kick higher. Again. Again." More than twenty times, I kicked without stopping.

Although my workouts were brutal, they didn't feel like punishment. I believed Coach Wang had some insight about how to guide me. Even though I had difficulty in keeping up, I tried my best. Knowing the purpose behind his training made a difference. I fortified myself by repeating mentally that Coach Wang was trying to help me achieve something great.

Each day following my private lessons, I had to lead a group of teammates in their workout without any rest in between. Coach Wang tried everything he could think of to help me overcome my anemia, except allow me to get the extra rest I probably needed.

Each morning as the earsplitting alarm sounded, my overworked body resisted my commands. My knees refused to bend. My legs were so heavy I had trouble moving them off the bed. When I dragged my weary body to the toilet, I glanced in the mirror at my puffy face and swollen eyes, splashing a little water on them to wake myself up. I knew I needed more sleep to recover from the harsh extracurricular training, but I never got it.

I looked to one of the first team girls for inspiration during this time. Clever Treasure, whose Chinese name was Zong Qiao Zhen 宗巧珍, was my role model and inspired me not only because she had once been Coach Wang's top female student, but also because she worked extremely hard at *wushu* practice without ever babying herself. She often gave me a pat of encouragement, and I appreciated her friendship and wise counsel.

When Coach Wang began his coaching career, he personally recruited athletes for the first team from the poorest families in the countryside because he felt they would work hard for the opportunity to succeed. I remembered the worn *wushu* uniform I wore for the Xuzhou tournament and chuckled now to think that simple uniform had probably worked to my advantage.

One top male athlete on the first team came from a needy family living in the countryside in faraway Xuzhou County. His early martial arts background was limited. Before he joined the team, he performed on the street in exchange for coins using a few martial arts movements he learned as a child. Clever Treasure's father peddled a three-wheel bicycle taxi or pedicab. On that low-income job, he fed a wife and four children.

Coach Wang selected athletes with above-average feminine beauty and masculine good looks, and Clever Treasure's beauty never faded. Her personality, however, was different from her looks. Standing still, this pretty, feminine-looking girl appeared demure. As soon as she moved or opened her mouth, that image vanished. Her boyish mannerisms and husky voice actually made her all the more alluring.

Clever Treasure had the kind of flexibility that only came from working exceptionally hard. Many of us could do the standing splits, with one unbent leg extended straight up next to the ear. The loose translation of the Chinese name for the pose was "smoke from burning incense rises to heaven." Clever Treasure was the only one of us, however, who didn't have to use her hand to hold her leg to her head.

In the under-fifteen age group, Clever Treasure and Jet Li became China's Youth All-around Champions in 1974 after earning coveted spots on the 1974 friendship delegation to the United States. Clever Treasure's specialties were the double straight sword and single straight sword, and in 1974 she won the gold medal in individual straight sword.

During my private practice, Coach Wang told me, "I trained Clever Treasure to become successful. I can train you like that." Coach Wang always claimed if one athlete could accomplish something, another athlete could learn to do it just as well.

Coach Wang never trained me to copy Clever Treasure's movements because he saw I was flexible in a different way. Competition forms displayed individual athletic abilities but were becoming increasingly compulsory and rigid. My forms highlighted my specialty of kicking my leg back until it hit the back of my head. I believed and trusted Coach Wang when he said he could train me to be as successful as Clever Treasure. I tried to show I could work as hard as she could.

One day, I was walking side-by-side with Clever Treasure across the camp to our dormitory from the building where we showered. We each carried a water bottle in one hand and a plastic shower bucket in the other. Our buckets, which we used as a sink in the evenings to wash our faces and on Sundays to wash our clothes, were now heaped with dirty clothes, soap, shampoo, and comb.

I didn't know the first team girls well and wasn't sure how they felt about their former coach after the first team coach had taken them over, but I bravely asked Clever Treasure, "Tell me a little bit about the time you were training with Coach Wang. How did you learn to do the smoke-from-burning-incense-rises-to-heaven pose so well?"

Her eyes lit up brightly and she gave me a devilish answer, "The truth is every time Coach Wang made me hold that pose, I yelled at him."

My eyes grew big and I said, "No way! No one can yell at Coach Wang."

"Well," she admitted proudly, "I could do it. He made me hold it so long my face got all sweaty and I had tears in my eyes. I got so mad that I screamed, 'Why'd you pick me? You're a monster. Why do I have to hold this pose longer than anyone else?'"

"No," I argued, "you didn't!"

"Your team's too shy, too *chicken*," she teased me in her boyish voice. "I'm the brave one."

I looked at her pretty moon face and knew I could never be that brave. Then, I asked, "Didn't Coach Wang get mad? Didn't he punish you?"

Clever Treasure chuckled. "Coach Wang just laughed. When I yelled at him, he always said he liked it. Of course, I'd never do that outside of training. He told me, 'Good, you're in very high spirits today,'" she said in a throaty voice while imitating Coach Wang's manner by waving her arms around. "'You're lit up like a fire now. You're my kind of girl. Just keep going.'" Clever Treasure was a great copycat and could parody Coach Wang's demeanor with ease.

The next moment, however, Clever Treasure became serious. "Well, he was right. After crying, sweating, and feeling my neck ache numerous times, his words finally came true. He was the one who helped me become the youth champion. He took me to my highest level. I got what I wanted. My hard work paid off. Just do what Coach Wang says and you'll become a success like me. Sure, he's the prince of the devil, but he has some kind of magic power to make dreams come true."

I admired Clever Treasure's honesty and appreciated her encouragement. Her words stoked my inner fire, pushing me toward new levels of achievement.

To counteract all the pressure I put on myself, I savored the few inspiring and relaxed moments that came my way. Now, as an official team member, a new benefit brought a smile to my face and sweet moments to each day. I often closed my eyes and relished the crunch of a juicy apple or the sweetness of a slice of watermelon at lunchtime. To have fruit whenever I wanted was something so decadent in China that it made me feel like an emperor's daughter. It was a joyful reminder of my new status and the accomplishment of one part of my dream.

As I gained confidence, however, I yearned for more. A budding desire to become an inspirational champion like Clever Treasure grabbed hold of me, but I didn't know if my body could take me there. The alternative was giving up on my dream and bringing dishonor to my family, so I forced myself to endure.

Liu Yu with siblings

Liu Yu in opera make-up

HOME VISITS

The long-awaited home visit followed the national competition at the end of autumn. For a brief two weeks each year, the endless routine of rigorous training was gratefully suspended. Athletes hurried home with two missions, resting their weary bodies and visiting with families left behind. With great anticipation, I sought relief from pushing myself physically, which I hoped led to several nights of deep, untroubled sleep. I wanted to feel like a normal person again but with one added difference. A personal reward for my hard work would be seeing a glimmer of pride in my family's eyes over my accomplishments.

A dreamlike familiarity enveloped me as I walked home from the bus station, my arms weighted down with bags of gifts. With a quickening pulse I dodged bicycles across well-known streets, passing forgotten storefronts, each with its own shopping allure. Hearing the local dialect spoken by chattering passersby played kindly in my ears. My dreams of being home had finally materialized. I was floating on air, especially when my presence at home created a festive mood, and everyone, even my brother and sister, beamed with pleasure.

I plopped my bags onto the brick floor and eagerly dug into them, proudly producing special gifts I stashed away during the year. I brought NaiNai tiny, yummy cakes, some like shortbread rich with oil and others we called egg cakes with many precious eggs in them. She fussed, saying, "You shouldn't have brought me anything, Xiao Yu." But her hands lovingly accepted the gifts I knew she would enjoy and share with everyone.

At the national tournament, athletes received a chocolate bar to snack on for energy. Instead of eating mine, I saved it for Baba. Later, after he sampled it, he said, "This chocolate tastes bitter, like medicine. I don't think I like it very much, but I'm glad I was able to try it." I didn't know at the time it was more like unsweetened baking chocolate and not as creamy as chocolate from other countries.

I pulled out instant milk powder and cocoa mix for Mama. She giggled like a little girl and waved her hand in front of her face, saying I shouldn't have.

Da Jie and Jian Guo flashed big grins when I presented them with athletic shoes and socks. At the camp, we were offered all kinds of training clothes and shoes. We each possessed half a dozen pairs of athletic shoes. Shoe sizes were irrelevant, and we often crammed our feet into shoes we had outgrown, with the result that our toes grew crookedly. Before my home visit, camp athletes and I exchanged new and used shoes with each other to get different sizes to take home to our families. My sister and brother rushed to try them on, and I smiled knowing their friends wouldn't have any shoes as nice as these.

"NaiNai, I have some money for you," I said as I pulled it out of my pocket.

"Oh, no, I don't want your money," she said, shaking her head.

"This money is a team benefit," I explained. "All the athletes get it so we will eat well at home and are ready to train hard when we return." The coaches demanded we continue with the highest quality food available.

"They give us enough money so everyone in the family can eat well, too," I said. NaiNai's expressive eyes revealed her amazement.

"I also brought you some coupons I didn't use during the year." The Chinese government issued tickets so we could buy rationed goods, including sugar, meat, cooking oil, rice, soap, and even bicycles. Each ticket could be used toward the purchase of a specific item. I tried not to use my tickets and saved them to take home to my parents. The most fulfilling part was contributing toward making my family's lives easier.

"Look at all of this you brought us," NaiNai exclaimed. "Extra money for food, even purchase coupons for the store. Thank you, Xiao Yu." Yes, it was definitely like a holiday and I enjoyed playing the rich auntie.

After that first year, I asked Coach Wang for some extra money to bring home to my family. It made me feel proud to give it to my parents. One year, Mama put her hand to her mouth and said, "I can't take this from you. I want you to save it for yourself." But I insisted she keep it. Finally she said, "Okay, I'll keep it for you."

Once, when I was able to do some shopping on a visit to Shanghai for a team demonstration, I searched all over for some special socks. NaiNai could never find socks in Baoying to fit her tiny bound feet. She bought regular socks, cut off the toes, and stitched them closed. When I finally found special socks for bound feet, I bought dozens of pairs to bring her. NaiNai usually didn't want me to waste my money buying things for her, but she glowed with appreciation when I presented her with those socks.

The next year, Mama pulled me aside, "You did a wonderful thing for NaiNai by buying her those special socks last year. She was so proud of that gift. She gave several pairs of socks to each of her friends." That made me happy.

During my first visit after I made the team, Baba asked, "What salary did they give you?" When I told him, he was amazed. "That's higher than my salary and I've been a medical doctor for thirty years." That's the way China's system worked. Professional athletes were at the top pay level along with military leaders and air force pilots. It made me uncomfortable to see Baba looking a bit dejected.

While at home, Baba encouraged me to visit Coach Dai as soon as possible and bring him a gift. After thanking me, my first coach asked me to give a demonstration for his students. I felt proud of my accomplishment but tried not to show it, knowing it would make everyone think poorly of me. Young Soldier was unusually quiet. I could tell he didn't want to see me because he always thought he would be chosen as a team member over everyone else. He avoided going to the countryside when his family selected him as the one child they would keep at home, forcing his next brother to face his fate. The younger brother joined the Army rather than be re-educated in the countryside.

I learned that Coach Dai had received a monetary bonus from the government because of me. The prestige he gained from training an athlete who joined the professional team also earned him a higher benefits score, something that was calculated from a person's education, number of years working for the government, and special successes. Higher scores aided a person in qualifying for certain government benefits, which included receiving a larger apartment in a newly built complex. Coach Dai also received a promotion from high school physical education teacher to superintendent with a higher salary.

At home, I offered to ease my family's workload because I knew they had extra chores without my help. NaiNai let me help some, but she said, "You need to spend time resting because you never get to do that." Da Jie threw a jealous look my way, but I hoped the special things I brought home eased her objections.

Almost every year, as soon as I relaxed at home, I got sick. I was never sick at the camp because I never let my guard down. The pressure I put on my body was so intense that I often felt like a machine spitting out martial art forms. Although I suffered through a cold or fever at home, my body revived with the extra rest.

While walking the streets of Baoying, I attracted a lot of attention but not because anyone recognized me. Team members received a warm, double-breasted winter coat with a fur collar, and wearing it was a status symbol. Only high military officials had such nice coats. Wherever I went, people stared at me, but I knew they were looking at my coat. Although I felt guilty having people envy me, I wore the coat to get over my sickness as quickly as possible. Returning to camp in any condition other than full health would incur Coach Wang's wrath.

Seeing positive changes in my family's living conditions made me happy. One year, my family used some of the money I sent them and applied to the government for the installation of a water pipe in the kitchen. This meant they didn't have to carry buckets to the river for water. Only two families out of the ten who had apartments in the housing complex had water pipes. NaiNai beamed as she proudly told me how she had them install a separate pipe extending beyond the kitchen window into the courtyard. Now other families could come to her window and ask for a bucket of water. They would leave a few coins on the windowsill to show their appreciation. It was a big improvement for my family to have something so progressive in their home. Seeing their happiness reminded me of when I was a little girl, vowing to do what I could to make NaiNai's life easier. The feeling it gave me went a long way toward offsetting the pain and suffering I enduring while training.

Visiting former Baoying teammates and school friends made my visits fun. In November 1978, before anyone had married, we had a reunion and marked the occasion by taking a photo together. We scribbled on the photo silly words about old friends meeting again just like Army buddies. Soldiers made a big deal about their reunions.

To avoid going to the countryside, Pretty Green Snake had used her martial arts skills to land a job at the local opera company. After Chairman Mao died, traditional operas enjoyed a revival. Pretty Green Snake played the well-known role of Green Snake, her namesake, in the White Snake Opera. In the story, White Snake needed the help of her companion and personal servant, Green Snake, to secretly communicate with her fiancé. Green Snake used her wisdom and courage to fight the evil Monk Fa Hai 法海和尚 who tried to break up the couple. The role of the feisty character fit Pretty Green Snake's personality perfectly.

One year, Pretty Green Snake encouraged the make-up artist for the Baoying opera to paint my face. He applied the white base coat to my face and then embellished it with color around my eyes and on my lips. I donned a blue silk costume with elaborate red embroidery and an elegant headdress. When I looked in the mirror, the person who looked back appeared strange and unrecognizable. While looking at my masked face, I recalled my audition with the opera company, which took place before I joined the professional team. Pretty Green Snake had won out because she had a good singing voice.

Although the opera company's pay was small, Pretty Green Snake avoided re-education, learned new skills, and kept her residency with her hometown. In contrast, many young people who were sent for re-education became locked into their new location with no hope of moving back home. The opera actors had hard lives, however. They traveled endlessly to small towns, living like gypsies. They couldn't afford to stay in hotels, which was no life for a husband or children. In my eagerness to avoid being sent to the countryside, I had tried to become an opera singer. Now I realized that kind of life could easily have been mine, had my singing voice not forced me into a new direction. I breathed a sigh of relief, knowing I had chosen wisely.

Little Sweetie was lucky. Her older sister was sent to the countryside, guaranteeing Little Sweetie could remain at home. Eventually, her parents arranged a marriage for her with a man in Nanjing.

My brother never dropped out of high school to avoid re-education. The year before he had to choose between the countryside and the Army, the policy changed. The family was overjoyed. Gradually, some of Baoying's lost children found their way back home to be welcomed by their families. Many others had married in distant provinces and couldn't obtain permission to move their families to Baoying, although they were able to visit if they could afford it.

Da Jie's choice not to attend high school to avoid re-education in the countryside resulted in years of low-paying, menial jobs mostly obtained by my parents begging favors. Each year when I went home to visit, Mama told me about the temporary job they had scraped together for Da Jie.

Da Jie's first job was using a loudspeaker to make announcements to a crew dredging the bottom of the Grand Canal while Baba managed their first aid station. She held other temporary jobs, such as breaking bricks, peeling bark from weeping willow tree branches for baskets, making mops from fabric scraps to sell to boat people, and pulling feathers from dead ducks to be used in down-filled quilts. A job of dyeing paper red preceded cleaning duties at Baba's hospital. This job caused jealousy at the hospital and complaints she was too young. Da Jie then went to work for Mama's company as a messenger and trainee to the seamstresses. The job paid only 9-13 *Yuan* a month, approximately $1-3. This was Da Jie's first permanent job. Mama tried to discourage Da Jie from making a seamstress job her life's work. Da Jie admitted it looked like laborious work but didn't know what else she could do.

One year when Da Jie was about seventeen, she came to visit me in Nanjing. As she marveled over the food and the prestige of my being on the team, I saw that with each comment she descended deeper into a dark and unfriendly depression. She complained of her heavy responsibilities at home because she had to take over my chores in addition to her own. Da Jie jumped to her feet, scorn written in the newly formed lines on her face. "You don't have to cook. You don't have to clean commodes. You have hot water showers every day."

How could I explain the hardships of camp life to my sister? I couldn't tell Da Jie about how hard my life really was because I didn't want my family to worry. I didn't want them to know how hard I pushed myself to be tough, even though inside I knew it wasn't natural. I shrugged off injuries because nobody would feel sorry for me if I got hurt. Keeping up with my teammates became a fixation. Falling behind would mean my dismissal from the team, an outcome too shameful for an honored athlete to imagine. I knew I was disposable and could be replaced at any time with another athlete who wanted a chance at greatness.

Having missed several years of regular schooling, I knew I couldn't rejoin society if I were forced to leave the team. If I didn't succeed, only a menial government job like taking tickets at an arena awaited me. My fear of failure and my desire to avoid bringing dishonor to myself and my family flung me into the middle of a spider's web. Never smiling, I stuffed my true feelings and personal desires down a deep, dark hole. I ceased to think of myself as a real person.

I knew I was missing a lot—a regular childhood and friendships with other teenagers. I learned to act like a little adult and mimic the expressions I saw on my coaches' faces. Thinking about my needs was replaced by thinking only about what adults thought of me. Competition impeded my finding solace in my teammates.

Instead of dwelling on what I lacked, I learned to put all my energy into practicing. All desires except one—becoming a champion—were purged from me. It became a matter of survival. I succumbed to the pressure to be perfect and strove to meet my coaches' expectations.

The hardest time for me was at night as I lay defenseless against the fear of being unable to withstand the next day's arduous physical tasks and meet my coach's increasing demands. Fear mocked me until my confidence evaporated. It robbed me of sleep. To keep myself from mentally collapsing, I naively clung to the idea my hard work would pay off, that I was in control of my fate. I knew I couldn't communicate all this to Da Jie without upsetting my family, so I tried to bury my frustration like I buried everything else unpleasant in my life.

Standing before Da Jie, I threw up my hands and paced the short length of my dormitory room. "You only see your hardship. What about mine? My training is exhausting. I even have to help clean the dormitory room and do my own washing."

But Da Jie only grunted and turned as if she were through with me and my complaints. As far as she could see, I had a perfect life and a job that people respected. She couldn't see the hardship in my life, and I, in turn, didn't fully comprehend the frustrations in hers. As I watched her leave, my heart twisted painfully. *No one who cares about me understands what my life is like.* Feeling abandoned and isolated, I couldn't hold back my tears and they flowed unrestrained.

My saddest visit home was when NaiNai was seriously ill. She had slipped on the icy ground in the courtyard and broken her hip. When I arrived home, a bedridden NaiNai couldn't talk anymore. It made me sad to see how frail and helpless this spirited woman had become. I sat beside her for most of my visit, holding her hand and talking to her. I kept her feet warm with a heated water bag, propped her up with pillows in her bed next to the kitchen stove, and combed her hair. Afterwards, I ground up cookies and cakes I brought from Nanjing and mixed them in a little water. NaiNai ate them after a little porridge or soft egg. Her soulful eyes expressed her gratitude. The attention I showered on my grandmother helped Mama and Da Jie enormously. Mama worked during the day and cared for NaiNai at night by feeding and bathing her.

As I stroked NaiNai's hand, I told her about some of my early memories. "I remember when I was four years old and you used to visit your friends for afternoon tea. I always made sure I was home so you would invite me to the tea. I was so excited each time you reached into the jar where you kept those large dried persimmons my uncle gave you and pulled out a piece of the dried fruit to share at the tea. I thought I was so smart to be included and receive a little sliver of the fruit."

I paused to chuckle and saw NaiNai's aged eyes crinkle in fine lines as she attempted a small smile. "Do you remember how the ladies teased me? They always asked, 'What's your name?' I tried to puff up with importance when answering, 'Little Tiger.' You used to smile each time I said that."

All I could think about was how inspirational NaiNai had been for me. She grew up as the only girl in a prosperous family and was used to getting her way as a child. The hard times she went through as a young widowed mother shaped her into the lady I knew who never got depressed, even when the family didn't have enough food to eat. I witnessed some of our neighbors looking enviously at what other people had, but NaiNai never did that. She charged through her day with the energy of a dragon, yet she knew how to balance her life by allowing herself a little time with friends each day.

Although NaiNai couldn't talk, she communicated to me through her eyes, soul-stirring eyes that showed how much she loved me and how proud she was of my accomplishments. I knew it made her happy that I was maturing and had found something that would offer me a measure of security for life. I sat beside her, soaking up all the tenderness and affection she shared. I would use it to give me strength during the hard times.

One evening, after Mama had returned from work, she and I sat talking quietly while NaiNai slept. "A few months ago," Mama began, "when NaiNai was still able to talk, she told me she didn't want to die in town because then her body would be burned." Burial wasn't allowed because land was scarce and used for growing crops. "NaiNai says she wants to be buried next to my father in the Xu village cemetery," Mama whispered. Although it was against the law, bodies were still buried quietly in the countryside.

Mama took my hand in hers. "NaiNai asked to be moved to the Xu family village before she dies but not until after your visit." She had been lying in bed for nearly a year before I arrived. I bit my lip and fought the emotions that welled up within me. How like her to be so stubborn that she waited for my visit before dying. She wanted to see me one last time, and I was so grateful to spend these days with her. Saying goodbye to NaiNai at the end of my visit was harder than anything I had been through so far. Walking away from my family home to the bus station, I suppressed my tears while feeling my heart break in little pieces, my motivation to work hard slipping away.

After I left, my family moved NaiNai to the Xu village where my aunt took care of her until her death. Mama went to see them every weekend, usually by walking many hours through cold winter weather. When Baba wasn't working, he chauffeured Mama on the back of his bicycle while she balanced a basket of food on her lap. I sent Mama as much money as I could, asking her to buy things for NaiNai, whatever she liked.

Several months later when I received word that NaiNai had died, I rushed to see Coach Wang. Barely able to control my overwhelming grief, I stood face-to-face with him outside his faculty dorm room in a hallway cluttered with shoes, washstands, and garbage bins. "Coach Wang, my father telephoned to say my grandmother has died. Please, may I have permission to attend her funeral?"

He replied as I expected, without emotion or sympathy. "Liu Yu, you know there's a competition coming up. Your country needs your services right now. It'd be difficult to change the schedule. Your routines with your partners are too important. In a few months you'll be home for your yearly visit."

I didn't argue with him because in some small way I understood. Being a member of the team was special. The government had provided years of training, the highest quality and variety of food possible, a top-level salary, and every kind of clothing I needed. I knew my duty to the government must come first; however, a part of me wanted to explain how close my grandmother and I had been. We shared the same bed as I grew up, warming each other on cold nights. She encouraged me to keep up with my *wushu* and not be a quitter. She taught me, not in words but through her example, to make the most of a bad situation. This lesson served me well through my years of repetitive, grueling training. I longed to tell Coach Wang I didn't want to shoulder this grief alone, but people never speak about their feelings in China. Everything must be locked away inside.

Usually, after a week of visiting in Baoying, a telegram arrived at our home. Coach Wang, always nervous about letting us go, issued his summons for my return. Instead of a two-week training reprieve, I was lucky to stretch the time to ten days. Upon our return, Coach Wang explained, "You athletes don't need to stay home too long. It'll take you two months to get back to the same training level!"

Although treasured, the fleeting visits with my family never made me wish I could remain in Baoying. I slowly understood I didn't belong there any more, especially after NaiNai had left the family. Never able to confirm her death by seeing her lifeless body, I fooled myself into thinking she was only temporarily gone.

These visits home were the only marker for the passage of time. As the years piled up, my memories were jumbled into a giant mound because nothing ever seemed to change at the sports camp. We athletes never knew how old we were because birthdays were irrelevant in China and forgotten while on the team. Hearing our families say how much we'd grown during the year was our only measure of aging.

Before I left, Baba always offered some bits of encouragement like he did my first year home. "I never thought you'd be on a professional team, that my daughter would be an athlete, a martial artist. But, it was your decision. Even though it sounds like hard work, don't quit halfway. If you quit one thing, you're going to quit something else. You always need to remember to try hard and stick with your decision."

I saw concern in Baba's eyes. Somehow, without my saying anything, he intuited how difficult my life was. After all, he was the one who knew how hard I had to work to compensate for my anemia. I also perceived how proud he was of me. It was a tender moment and I felt close to Baba, a closeness that had gradually developed between us because of *wushu*. I knew I would never give it up. Still, I silently worried whether I could improve enough to please Coach Wang.

Liu Yu, brother Liu Jian Guo, and sister Liu Jing

Young Coach Wang   Coach Wang

16   *COACH WANG'S SECRET*

O ur bus rattled along the bumpy road in the poorest and most northern part of Jiangsu Province. Across the aisle from me, Clever Treasure pulled out her small hand mirror, inspecting the curls she had formed around her pretty face. Beneath her long pants, this brave girl wore high-heeled shoes, something I'd never dare to wear. It wouldn't fit my personality, but I envied how stylish and comfortable Clever Treasure looked.

Over three hours earlier, we left the large city of Xuzhou where we had performed in a jam-packed arena the previous evening. The gymnastics athletes, rhythm gymnasts, and acrobats who performed with us headed back to camp while our *wushu* group ventured north to visit the hometown of one of our male first team members.

We drove up to the edge of a small village where the bus halted, vibrating to a stop. I followed the group into the village, passing tiny shacks made from dried mud. Alongside us, the few children and adults we saw stopped their chores and stared. We were escorted to the best house in the village and the only one made from real bricks—subsidized no doubt from a portion of their son's salary.

My teammates and I took turns entering the house and returning the family's greetings. Both parents were farmers, and my fellow *wushu* athlete's younger sister and brother also worked the land. The pitched-roof home contained a single room with a large brick stove on which sat steaming pots of food. No beds were visible in the room, but blankets and bedding hung from the roof's crossbeam.

We were soon served Chinese-style pancakes of white flour and chopped long beans in homemade bowls. This was all the family could afford to offer us, but it was delicious.

After our meal, Coach Wang led us on a walk through the village. News had spread that we'd arrived, and the village now teemed with residents. Older people hovered in their doorways, staring at us. As Coach Wang approached each family, he kindly offered the best brand of cigarettes to each man. This broke the ice and the people relaxed, laughing and talking with Coach Wang and each other. Soon, the women were asking Coach Wang for cigarettes, too.

We heard the people's comments as we passed them. "Look at that curly hair."

"See how white their faces are." Farmers with sun-toughened faces viewed our pale faces as a sign of a higher class.

"Look how funny," the women blurted out with pointing fingers. "That girl put a little block on the heel of her shoes."

My teammates and I cordially nodded and greeted the people, while inside we were startled by the poverty. These people were poorer than my own family, especially the children following closely behind us. Young girls up to the age of eleven or twelve wore no tops. The younger boys were naked, some acting shy about it in front of us.

Visiting the poor village elicited the effect we were sure Coach Wang desired. It gave us a greater appreciation for being team members, prompting us to work harder. Coach Wang thought working hard was all in our minds. I wondered if I were the exception as the only one whose weaker body didn't follow the dictates of the mind.

Training day after day, month after month, made it difficult to stay enthusiastic and keep our minds focused on attaining new skill levels. My teammates and I welcomed any change in our routine, viewing the change as a holiday.

Our boredom was greatly alleviated by traveling to different cities within Jiangsu Province to demonstrate our abilities. In a large city, the invitation to perform might also include gymnasts, rhythm gymnasts, and acrobats as it did in Xuzhou. Our accommodations were always the best the city could offer, and the specialties of the local cuisine were lavished upon us.

Our training didn't stop when we traveled. When we worked out, the local people peeked in through gymnasium windows or surrounded us in the park, their eyes growing big as they watched every move. Each of us remembered when we were younger and coveted a glimpse of the professional team. Our egos inflated as we thought, *We're the team!* A little glory went a long way toward feeding our enthusiasm to train hard.

We gave our best performances to crowds that probably encompassed entire cities or towns and their dignitaries, sometimes as large as ten thousand people. The crowd especially enjoyed watching how good we *wushu* team children were and our exciting fighting set routines. We steeled our minds as if these performances were competitions, vying for the prize of winning the coach's approval.

In two-person fighting sets, a barehanded athlete could be matched with an opponent wielding a dagger or spear as well as with another bare hand. Various weapon matches were between two straight swords, the three-section staff against a regular staff or a broadsword with shield, and the spear against the double broadsword, the staff, the long handle broadsword, or the broadsword with shield. Different styles of martial arts can oppose each other, like the drunken form against the eagle claw or a combination of two opponents of internal styles, such as *baguazhang* 八卦掌 (circular footwork with various palm and kicking techniques), *xingyiquan* 形意拳 (explosive boxing attacks), or *taijiquan* 太极拳 (defensive techniques usually practiced in slow motion). Three-person fighting sets were often barehanded fighters or two spears against a broadsword, a double broadsword or a bare hand. Two fighters could also wield broadswords with shields against a third fighter with a three-section staff.

My two-person fighting set specialties were two straight swords, the staff against the spear, and the three-section staff versus the broadsword and shield. When three opponents fought, I defended myself against two male fighters using bare hands and was part of a group of two spears against the broadsword. Each athlete's timing had to be superb because we stopped just short of weapons piercing or jabbing the other person. It had to look real to thrill the audience.

After our performances, we toured the surrounding areas. Whether we were in large cities like Wuxi 无锡 or Xuzhou or in a smaller town in the countryside, we were favored with departing gifts of some local specialty, like pottery or candy, which made us feel special.

Chinese New Year performances were the most requested. Coach Wang explained why we couldn't go home during the biggest holiday of the year. "The people work hard and pay their taxes. The farmers feed you. You all benefit from that. Now, it's time for you to serve the people."

One Chinese New Year, we performed in a small town. The February weather was below freezing, and there was no heat in the performance area. By this time, we were experienced enough to know we had better keep our body warmed up and prepared before the performance.

As I jogged around the outside of the old gymnasium in my thick sweat suit, the cold wind stung my face and hands. My feet landed on patches of thin ice, making loud crunching sounds. After three times around the building, my feet and back started warming up.

Inside the building, I stood briefly, watching the crowd filling the stands. Family and friends laughed and talked among themselves, having a great time. Sunflower seed shells littered the ground, reminding me of all the good food being enjoyed for the New Year. I thought about my own family at home celebrating with all the special foods I loved. At that moment, sadness spread through me. I deeply missed sharing this special time with my family. I knew I couldn't dwell on my sadness, however; I had to mentally prepare myself to perform.

Like Chairman Mao had said, we must serve the people. My duty was entertaining the townspeople who rarely had the opportunity of seeing athletes perform. I donned my thin silk uniform, adding my sweat jacket on top, and went into the hallway to practice some longfist movements.

I gave the second performance of the evening to an enthusiastic crowd. Checking the schedule, I learned my double hooks demonstration was 25th on the program, probably a half an hour away. Inside the performers' waiting room, a little coal stove provided scant heat to the athletes crowded around it. While shivering, I tried to worm my way toward the stove to warm my hands. It wasn't easy, and I felt frustrated. Too soon, someone called out, "Liu Yu, you're next." I threw off my jacket and grabbed my freezing metal hooks just in time to take the center of the carpet in the icy gymnasium.

The result of not properly warming up for my double hooks performance was that sometime during my routine I hooked one of my molars. It broke the tooth in half. I didn't notice it until later, and then I told Coach Wang about it.

"Why'd you do that? I didn't teach you to do that movement," Coach Wang shouted unsympathetically. A few moments later he inquired, "Well, does it hurt?"

My tongue slipped over the jagged edges, and then I admitted, "No, not hurt. It just feels weird."

"Okay, if it doesn't hurt, then it's nothing." And Coach Wang forgot about it. No one suggested I go to a dentist. Much later, after I came to the United States, I saw a dentist for the first time. He couldn't believe it was my first dental visit. Eating very little sugar and few snacks coupled with brushing my teeth daily kept them in good condition. The root of the damaged tooth was still healthy over ten years later and was fitted with a cap.

A feeling of isolation permeated the training camp. We athletes were generally ignorant about life outside except when it came to politics. Everyone, no matter what their age, followed prescribed political indoctrination. We learned training was secondary to showing our Red hearts to government representatives.

The day I heard over the loudspeakers that Chairman Mao had died, everyone seemed to overreact. Some fainted, while many held their hands in front of their faces, crying like their fathers had just died. Athletes wearing black arm bands lamented their sun was gone. "What will we do?" they asked. Although I knew many pretended, I was surprised at the outpouring of emotion coming from a society that prided itself on its unreadable faces. Of course, I acted sad as the occasion warranted, but I found it hard to shed fake tears.

After the ensuing arrest of the Gang of Four 四人帮, which included Madame Mao Jiang Qing 毛泽东夫人-江青, camp officials decided our education should include watching the political trials on television. We stuffed our pockets with food from the cafeteria, oily patches spreading on the fronts of our jackets. Happy for a training reprieve and a change in our routine, we munched and socialized our way through the trials. We watched Madame Mao talk persuasively to no avail. One of her cohorts didn't try to say anything, knowing it wouldn't make any difference. Deng Xiaoping allowed the Gang of Four a chance to defend themselves, but everyone knew it was a token gesture.

After the Gang of Four was sent to jail, people across the country celebrated. They cheered regardless of whether they agreed or disagreed that those people should be punished. The philosophy was to uphold whoever was the winner. Whether a person was good or bad didn't matter and no one felt sorry for a loser. The only thing that counted was being on top. As an avid history reader, Chairman Mao had learned political tricks employed in previous dynasties and used them to incite his enemies to fight each other. His success came from always knowing how to stay on top.

Although Deng Xiaoping 邓小平 formally declared the Cultural Revolution was over in 1976, it wasn't until 1978 that millions of former Red Guards who had been banished to the countryside were freed. Political prisoners languishing in jail since the Cultural Revolution were also released with some given their old jobs back.

When the rest of the country began attacking Chairman Mao's supporters who had perpetrated crimes during the Cultural Revolution, the camp followed suit by holding its own trials. We athletes didn't mind that our training was suspended once again while we listened to how people suffered at the hands of the Red Guards. It was like a revolution inside the camp grounds with the camp population split into two different sides.

The most colorful trial included a husband and wife, newly released from jail, who gave testimony against the treatment they suffered at the hands of a Red Guard, now a sports camp official. The husband had followed Chairman Mao on his Long March. When he had retired from the Army, he was appointed as a provincial high official. During the Cultural Revolution, Chairman Mao tried to eliminate officials who he deemed a threat to him, regardless of whether they had once been supporters. That's when the husband and his wife were arrested.

The wife's testimony was an emotional tirade against her tormenters. She wailed about beatings and torture that caused her to go crazy in jail. Her demented behavior while in jail included ripping her clothes off, pulling out her hair, and smearing blood everywhere. As she spoke, my teammates and I were mesmerized by her tales. She made all of us hate the Red Guard who had attacked her. At the end of the trial, the former Red Guard was sent to jail.

The wife, who was later appointed as a team leader for rhythm gymnasts, scared me because I couldn't get rid of the image I had of her laughing like a crazy woman at the trial. Her children ran around on the street without proper care, which made me suspicious. I avoided her whenever possible.

Her husband was invited to speak to us about the Long March. Dressed in the Mao jacket and straw shoes he always wore, he told us, "You should appreciate your food, your clothes. During the Long March, we had to eat grass and roots as we climbed snowy mountains." He wasn't much of a talker. A shy man from a poor family, he eschewed everything modern and proudly rolled his own cigarettes from a bit of tobacco and newspaper. These rigid Maoists were some of the people who controlled the political meetings at the camp.

I grew to hate the political scheming and righteous dogma. Ignoring it would have been political suicide, however, because team leaders at the camp set traps for us and were ready to pounce whenever we said the wrong thing. I kept my mouth shut and my eyes and ears wide open for any sign of danger.

Several months later, our team made a trip to Suzhou 苏州, located near Shanghai. The day after our demonstration, Coach Wang made a casual announcement that three of us, myself included, would take a walk around town later, something a bit unusual for him to do. I was eager to go because we weren't allowed to walk around on the street unless accompanied by a coach or team leader.

A few moments later, an older first team girl pulled me aside. "Do you know why you're going out to look around Suzhou?" she asked me.

"I have no idea."

"Well, I know why you're going," she admitted. "Coach Wang's old girlfriend lives here."

I looked at her with surprise. She continued when I didn't say anything. "Ten years ago she was one of the top gymnasts at our camp. Of course, it was against the team rules for them to be together as boyfriend and girlfriend. The government had to break them apart. Because Coach Wang was such a big star at that time, they couldn't get rid of him. So they sent his girlfriend away. She had to go back and live with her parents. She was one of the prettiest girls and very good at gymnastics."

Usually I didn't waste my time listening to gossip, but this captured my attention. "That's so sad. Did Coach Wang like her a lot?" I inquired.

"Not liked, I would say loved. They really loved each other," she told me with a sigh. "You know the girls' gymnastics coach now?"

"Yes."

"Well, they're sisters."

Visiting a former girlfriend when both parties were married to other people was against Chinese propriety, especially if they were alone. That's why Coach Wang brought some students with him.

Before the Cultural Revolution, many large homes in the wealthy city of Suzhou rested comfortably on generous lots situated alongside the city's peaceful canals. Marco Polo had once called Suzhou the Venice of China, and it was still lovely when we visited, although the homes were now owned by the government and occupied by multiple families.

After we arrived, we marveled at the fancy home where Coach Wang's former girlfriend lived. It had a second story that was topped by a slanting roof layered in gray tiles edged in ruffled curlicues. The woman's elderly father was waiting for us in the large tree-filled courtyard. He greeted Coach Wang warmly. "Oh, Jin Bao, come in, come in."

At that moment, I knew how sad this was for Coach Wang. Despite the fact that the woman's father was high in the government and genuinely liked Coach Wang as a person—and therefore probably once approved of him as a prospective son-in-law—he had no power to stop the government from separating the two lovers. Romances among camp athletes were strictly forbidden.

I speculated Coach Wang's girlfriend must have been truly beautiful. Of course, all the gymnastics girls were tall, slender, and attractive, but I thought this one had to be something special. When she walked into the room, it hurt my heart to look at her, not because she was as beautiful as I imagined, but because she looked too old for her age. When I turned my head to watch Coach Wang, I saw tenderness in his eyes. Though everyone spoke formally and acted properly, I could feel the underlying current of affection. In that moment, I felt a glimmer of pride in Coach Wang for remaining friends with his first love.

I learned after the government sent the girl home from the sports camp, she was hospitalized for a nervous breakdown. This must be the reason why she had aged so much. Her younger sister, the gymnastics coach, was a good friend of Coach Wang's, but the difference in appearance between the two sisters made them appear to be farther apart in ages than they were. The older sister had married, but it must not have been a happy one.

The rule against romances between camp athletes still existed, although penalties were becoming less strict. Some of the older girls defied the ban, but I vowed never to be stuck in the same kind of situation Coach Wang had faced.

Coach Wang never confided in us about the purpose of our visit in Suzhou or about that part of his history. Coaches never told the younger generation about anything unfavorable. The only thing Coach Wang ever said to us was, "Don't give anyone a chance to disrupt your goals. You don't want trouble. Girls should always act like princesses. Of course, when you're getting older, there'll be people who could distract you. Don't even think about it. Now is the time for you to focus on training and studying. Keep yourself standing on solid ground."

After hearing about the sad story of Coach Wang and his former girlfriend, I took those words to heart. I had never fancied any boys at the camp anyway. Sure, they were handsome, but their bravado was offensive and masked their immaturity and lack of intelligence. I vowed no one would separate me from my dreams of winning a championship. However, some things were outside my control, especially eluding the jealousy of others as I climbed the steps toward success.

Entrance to the Arena at the Jiangsu Province
Sports Training Camp. The structure survived the
Communist Revolution and was formerly the Chi-
nese Nationalist Government Arena.

Jiangsu Team preparing for demonstration

THE THREE FAR AWAYS

At the age of fifteen, after almost four years of living at the sports camp and while on the brink of becoming a national competitor, I learned I possessed a higher destiny.

It happened during a short visit to the lovely city of Yangzhou where Coach Wang's wife lived. My eleven teammates and I had spent the previous day giving a team demonstration, a welcome break in the monotony of our daily training. Before returning to the sports camp, my coach gathered us together after breakfast and instructed everyone to remain in the hotel. He then turned to face me and ordered, "Liu Yu, come with me." I ignored the raised eyebrows of my teammates and scurried out of the room.

As my coach strode briskly away from the nondescript hotel, his wife and I automatically advanced our pace to keep up. We passed several shopkeepers methodically arranging their wares, before turning down a narrow side street into a weary residential neighborhood of aged brick walls supporting slanted roofs layered with gray ruffled tiles. Following my coach through the faded red gate of an older, genteel-looking home, I trembled, wondering anew where we were going and for what purpose.

Coach Wang guided us down a narrow brick entryway, passing an arched door to an inner courtyard where a young dwarf maple tree bursting with fresh red leaves stood alone in the center.   Underneath one of the branches hung a circular bamboo bird cage, its green cover bunched at the top to reveal a tangerine-colored parrot with milky feathers surrounding its eyes in a sideways teardrop shape like face paint applied for an old-fashioned Chinese opera.   The bird stared at us as it stood on its thin bamboo perch next to two dainty porcelain bowls decorated with painted blue flowers.   On sunny days in the park, bird cages hung in trees all over China while nearby the owners conversed on benches.

"Good morning, pretty bird, how are you today?" my coach's wife inquired.   The bird alternately picked up first one foot, and then the other. We giggled.   "Look, he's dancing for us."

My momentary pleasure in watching the dancing bird beneath its lacy red canopy was interrupted when Coach Wang called out and impatiently motioned us over.   We quickly obeyed, stepping over the flood barrier of the open doorway into the warmth of a cherry wood-paneled room reminiscent of an earlier era of Chinese history.   Amid the simple furniture my curious eyes spied objects of beauty tucked here and there within the room's shadows.   I wondered how they had outlasted the purging of the Cultural Revolution.

Coach Wang replaced his normal blustery manner with a show of respectfulness as he addressed a stooped, elderly gentleman.   During our introduction, Master Li's 李先生 steady eyes examined me intently, warming my ear tips as I shifted the weight of my long, slender frame.

Master Li took a seat at his writing table and then turned to me, asking in a lilting voice, "What is the date and place of your birth?"

I snuck a suspicious sideways glance at Coach Wang before answering.   "I know I was born in 1962, in the year of the tiger, in the city of Baoying."   When I gave him my actual birth date, I watched as he converted it in his head to the old Chinese calendar date.

"You're a tiger with a predominating water element," he said with interest.   "What time of day or night were you born?"

"I don't know exactly.   My mother told me I was born just as the sun was rising, about six or seven o'clock."

"It matters whether you were born before or after seven," Master Li said.   Chinese time was divided into two-hour segments of astrological significance.   For instance, I knew six o'clock was known as the Chinese time of the earth, while midnight was considered the time of heaven.

"I don't think my mother knows my exact time of birth," I said shyly. "I was born at home with my grandmother and a midwife present, but there wasn't a clock in my mother's room." As an afterthought, I added, "She always called me a peaceful cat. She was glad I was born in the morning. It made me a full-stomach tiger. She said I would never starve."

My mother had actually told me more. A precious memory of this gentle woman fluttered brightly into my mind. On a day made unusual because my mother was home, she sat on a stool at our tiny kitchen table doling out food for my little brother to eat. As we watched him grab bits of rice and pickles with his fists and stuff them in his mouth, she said to me, "If you had been born at night, you'd be a hunting tiger. Then your personality would be very aggressive. But you'll never attack anyone. You'll always get along with your brother and sister and be the peaceful one in the house." She turned to look at me, smiling as she said in her scratchy voice, "Your personality is like a little cat. Once your stomach is full in the morning, you'll sleep peacefully in the sun all day."

Master Li studied me thoughtfully. "Are your mother and father alive?"

"Yes."

"Well, then," he said with confidence, "you weren't born after seven o'clock."

I wondered how he knew that, but then I recalled hearing that some people superstitiously believed children born at certain times caused their parents to die young.

With wrinkled hands, Master Li stroked his chin thoughtfully. "I believe you're not an only child. You must have a sister and maybe a brother."

"Yes, I have an older sister and a younger brother."

This delicately boned man with snowy white hair nodded in satisfaction.

By now, I figured out the purpose of this visit, which was to obtain a scholarly reading of my Chinese horoscope by an esteemed Taoist astrologer. Although banned by the Communists along with religion, horoscopes were secretly sought by people who still respected the old ways of countless generations. Coach Wang read forbidden Taoist and Buddhist books he obtained from an underground source. Though illegal, many people secretly read about religion and horoscopes either for fun or because they were serious believers. I kept alert for clues about how much credence Coach Wang would place upon this prophecy.

Master Li gently dipped the bristles of his tapered calligraphy brush into the saucer of black ink and wrote down my birth information in various grids of a parchment. Then, with wrinkled fingers, he opened and flipped through pages in a thick black book covered in faded brocade silk. This elderly man surely found a secure hiding place for that book during the country's upheaval. As Master Li copied information from the book, I glanced around.

My eyes were drawn to a petite glass vial on the bureau, and I bent over for a closer look at its hand painted insects and flowers. Finely detailed renderings of a dragonfly and a cricket amid bright red blossoms graced the inside of the glass, finished off with a mustard yellow wash of color. Objects of beauty were slowly reemerging in China since Chairman Mao's death two years earlier in 1976, and they created happiness in my heart whenever I encountered them. Although my fingers itched to examine the other side of the bottle, it wasn't in my nature to be bold and presumptuous.

"It was painted by my grandfather," Master Li volunteered with eyes that smiled before returning to their perusal of the astrology book. That explained why he took care to keep it safe. My coach's wife came over to take a look while Coach Wang stood beside Master Li, trying to read over his hunched shoulders.

I wondered whether Coach Wang wanted my horoscope read to bolster his confidence in me or to allay his fears, but I thought I knew the answer. Coach Wang's normal overconfident manner quieted my suspicions.

Coach Wang's contagious love of *wushu* had brought him here. He placed his devotion to *wushu* above everything else, even his own family and, at one point in his life, his own happiness. The eyes of this powerfully energized man indicated an inner will of steel no one could miss. The fullness of his elongated earlobes, curling out slightly from his head, added a Buddha-like look of intelligence. He emanated strength and power, although to some he appeared egotistical. Yet, he was generous when it came to sharing his knowledge and was the only coach who'd earned the respect of the athletes he trained.

My thoughts were interrupted when Master Li put down his brush and stood up to face me. He explained that latitude, longitude, recorded weather disasters, and configurations of the stars and planets connected to the time and place of my birth affected my life.

"The moment of your birth predicts how your life's supposed to unfold. Whether your life actually follows that prediction or not depends on the person. If you work harder, you can do better. If you get a chance at something and grab it, this can change your prophecy."

My chance had come four years ago when I followed my heart. Although it seemed contradictory that astrological fortunes could change, I learned it was based on Taoism, a folk religion that teaches harmony and balance. According to Chinese astrology, people receive a series of opportunities in life, which are triggered by cosmic forces and furthered through the choices made. Possibilities exist for people who are truly motivated. Their destinies can reach well beyond those of others who don't do anything with their lives. Change can be good or bad, depending on which path the individual decides to take. Yet, even if a seemingly wrong path has been taken, other paths may open up later to bring the person back to their original fortune. The forces that are acting upon an individual's life still operate regardless of which path is followed.

"Tigers," Master Li said in his sing-song voice, "are noble yet warm-hearted, independent yet hard-working, and can be very dynamic. Pressure makes tigers perform at their best, but they must take care to avoid being defiant and quick-tempered. This is where you're lucky. The water element serves to soothe any fire threatening your character. You're more stable, more open to advice than other tigers, and you love to entertain others. But water tigers also seek change and adventure. This last aspect is in conflict with you now."

Yes, I longed to end the monotony of my training routine. Everything about my life was controlled, from the time I was told to wake up in the morning to the time I was allowed to sleep. Water tigers or not, everyone at the camp yearned for change, but we wanted it in the form of success.

Master Li gazed steadily at me. "You'll experience a different life than your sister and brother. In your future, you won't live close to your parents. You'll live far away from your hometown, far away from your parents, and far away from your siblings. These are called the 'three far aways' and make the prediction stronger."

It was true that the sports camp was located in Nanjing, a day's journey by bus from my hometown. I wondered skeptically what Coach Wang had told Master Li about me, but intuition told me it wasn't much.

When the old astrologer paused to look at the parchment to double check something, I glanced over at Coach Wang and immediately recognized the intensity behind his eyes. I knew that look. It meant he waited impatiently for the rest of the prediction.

Master Li cleared his throat to claim our full attention. He looked pleased. "Your future is as a teacher and a writer. You'll receive a high education."

Warmth quickly rushed to my face. *Oh no, that will never be me.*

I could tell Master Li had a lot of confidence in his prediction, but I thought it was silly. I would make a very bad teacher because my hometown classmates' teasing had made me too shy to talk in front of people. Although I had secretly desired to be a teacher when I was younger, I never believed it could ever happen. And, in such a highly populated country where people rarely left their family, hometown, or job, and relocation required government permission, I doubted a remarkable life change could happen to me not once, but twice. This fortune wasn't what I had planned for my future.

As I prepared to leave, Master Li offered final words of warning. "Great change is coming. Be observant in the next year of the tiger and especially in 1989 in the year of the snake when a red star will influence the earth. Those are important years for you."

An exchange was then made between the two men, money for parchment. Everyone bowed. We thanked Master Li and said goodbye.

As we exited the courtyard, I caught Coach Wang's eyes. He looked puzzled, but not displeased.

Out on the street, Coach Wang's wife said, "It sounds like great things will happen for you, Liu Yu."

Before I could comment, Coach Wang responded over his shoulder as he increased his brisk stride, "She doesn't need to think beyond her training. After all, the prediction didn't say she would become a champion athlete. Nor did it say she wouldn't. Nothing has changed."

Even though Coach Wang told us athletes many times our hard work would pay off, I suppressed a smile upon hearing him refer to my becoming a champion. As Coach Wang's oldest student, I knew he saw me as the first of his students likely to succeed. When I allowed myself to think about the future—which I rarely did because it made it harder to deal patiently with the overall sameness of the present—I hoped I was close to something big and that my chance to become a champion loomed in the near future.

The special training Coach Wang had been giving me was a sign of good luck that translated into harder work for me. As I approached the right age to begin competing nationally, noticeable changes occurred in his teaching. When he corrected my movements, his frustration was less apparent. When he told me to freeze my motion, he altered the tilt of my hand ever so slightly or gave me an instruction to add more fullness to the bow of my arm—something barely noticeable. In essence, he was polishing my technique. Sometimes he motivated me by relating a classical story about a famous Chinese heroine. He guided me into believing I was that warrior girl showing great courage. A thrill of excitement caught me unawares when I sensed my life about to change.

Yet now, as I followed Coach Wang down the old residential street, a little niggling worry crept into my mind. What if I had chosen the wrong path? What if my father had been right, that I should have continued with my education instead of becoming an athlete? His dream had been that I go to college, and he correctly predicted the education the camp offered would be substandard. Out of habit, I took a deep, calming breath, forcing myself to slip back into survival mode, a state of heartfelt confidence in my athletic abilities and unquestioning loyalty to Coach Wang, a man I now considered my surrogate father.

I knew I shouldn't allow myself to take Master Li's prediction at face value; Coach Wang wouldn't. Too much was at stake. Too many years went into my training. Like Master Li, who secretly continued his work even though the Communists had banned Taoist astrology, I couldn't question whether I was on the right path. This required holding on to my vision and summoning my raw willpower to continue.

As we turned onto the market street, now busy with mid-morning shoppers, I realized with relief that Master Li predicted I would never be sent back to Baoying. My future lay elsewhere. For four years, fear of failure had never left me. Maybe, I could release some of that fear today.

My desire to fulfill Coach Wang's aspirations for me by becoming a winner suppressed all other dreams. I hadn't allowed myself to look beyond that goal. I knew it was futile to think about living another kind of life where the physical and mental torture of training didn't exist. The government owned me and even my family couldn't help me now if I chose a different path. My pride and perseverance kept me going.

Yet, as the hotel came into view, my mind toyed with thoughts about Master Li's prediction. Unexpectedly, a vague idea tickled my imagination. Just maybe, I would have the opportunity one day to choose something different, follow my own desires, make my own decisions. My destiny might actually be different than what my coaches were choosing for me now. I knew complications could arise from entertaining such bold thoughts, but I smiled inwardly as I gave myself permission to hope. After all, tigers can't be kept down for long. We are often ready to leap at new challenges and strive to land solidly on our feet. But the government was a bigger tiger than I could ever hope to be. I knew if I were to survive her jaws, I'd need to give her a reason to keep me around.

At various tournament invitationals within Jiangsu Province, my teammates and I had the chance to flex our competition muscles. Every four years, professional sports teams from the training camp competed in a tournament between the different regions within Jiangsu Province. The *wushu* team was divided into regional groups. My hometown of Baoying was in the Yangzhou region, and other team members were representatives of other regions. Each group was composed of professional team members born in that area and local *wushu* amateurs who won at their local team trial selections. The teams got together and practiced for one week before the competition. At the competition, locals got the chance to compete against the professionals—as I did in Xuzhou when I won third place as an amateur. This four-year event was also special in another way. The second team had an opportunity to compete against other second team members and, just at this regional tournament, compete against the first team as well.

In the late spring of 1977, the big four-year provincial competition was held in Wuxi. Coach Wang had been pushing me hard in training for this competition. I was the oldest member of the second team and less than two years younger than the youngest first team member, White Flower, who I thought of as stubborn and proud. I knew intuitively that Coach Wang was anxious to see how well I would perform against her because we were competing in the same age category. The pressure on me to do well was intense.

In the competition arena before my events, I tried to calm my nervous energy. I remembered how casually I had competed in Xuzhou four years earlier, but Coach Wang's expectations prevented me from feeling that relaxed again. Before it was my turn to compete, Coach Wang guided me in my warm-ups. "You have one-half hour before you go on. Go outside and run for ten minutes." Then he instructed me to practice a couple of movements, the ones that were my best. This gave me a certain measure of confidence when I competed in my weapons events.

White Flower competed in different weapon categories so that the only event where we went head-to-head was in the longfist. Coach Wang knew how to encourage me to reserve my energy and motivate me to do well. When they called me up next for the longfist, he gave me one of his penetrating looks and calmly said, "Now, don't look around. Simply do your best. Your score doesn't matter." His words helped me relax, and I carried that feeling with me onto the competition carpet.

At the end of my performance, I felt satisfied I hadn't made any major mistakes. When the longfist awards were presented, I successfully captured my second gold medal of the day. I had beaten White Flower, and Coach Wang lit up with happiness like a bright lantern. When I glanced toward the sidelines, I saw White Flower ranting at her coach. Her face was easy to read as she communicated her outrage at having a second team athlete outperform her. That evening I endured her angry looks and cold shoulder. Naively, I didn't let her reaction bother me, assuming she would get over it soon.

Coach Wang rarely hid his feelings. After I won each gold medal, he grinned broadly while nodding his head. *Now, I'm finally close to making the first team.* What I failed to see, however, was how unhappy the first team coach was at my success.

Over the next few months, the decision was made to let me compete at the national competition in the fall as a first team member. Two older first team girls hadn't shown any signs of emerging as top scorers at the nationals and were told to retire. Two of us from the second team were bumped up on a temporary basis to fill their places.

First team girls usually didn't compete as long as the boys. It depended on whether the girl could still work hard and hadn't gained too much weight because of early biological development. *Wushu* athletes needed speed, and excess weight slowed them down, preventing them from executing high jumps. The first team coach, however, was reluctant to let his members go.

To encourage hard work and reward achievement, many benefits were awarded at the training camp for those athletes chosen to compete. As I slipped my arms into my new warm-up jacket, a thrill raced through me. This jacket made me stand out in the camp and signified my new status as a competitor. Very few athletes had attained a higher status or had received jackets indicating they had competed on a national team or won a championship at a national or world level.

Coaches and camp officials wanted athletes to feel pride in their achievements and offered other tangible rewards to competing athletes. Benefits like new uniforms, chocolate bars, and extra milk powder seemed like big advantages when we felt the envy of our teammates who had yet to be elevated to such a level of honor. To keep up our strength for the added evening training session, the cafeteria stayed open to provide an extra meal to competing athletes before they retired for the night. Also, any competing athletes who developed injuries during training were bumped to the front of the waiting line to see doctors at the camp hospital.

Late that summer, an announcement revealed competing athletes would be given one bowl of cold beer to drink. I suspected a story from a Western team—probably a German one who attributed its success to drinking beer—prompted the new policy.

The camp's first refrigerator was purchased from outside China to chill the beer. Never before had athletes been offered something cold to drink, and this became wildly popular in the heat of the late summer. No age limits meant even competing prepubescent gymnasts qualified for bowls of beer. Older athletes approached the younger kids. "You don't drink, but go ask them for your bowl of beer and I'll trade some of my food for your beer." When a couple of my female teammates started giggling and singing songs, I knew they'd had a couple of bowls too much.

Drinking alcohol wasn't new to my male teammates, who often sipped Coach Wang's alcoholic drinks. Sometimes Coach Wang urged one of them by saying, "Come here, boy, and finish this cup." If Coach Wang saw any hesitation, he added, "We're in the tradition of great martial artists. Didn't you read in that famous book, *All Men are Brothers*, how the hero Wusong 武松 used his bare hands to kill the big tiger? He was one of the book's 108 characters. Did you read about anyone in the book who *didn't* drink?"

Coach Wang encouraged them to drink, but they also did it secretly to protect him. Coach Wang's *wushu* teacher was a heavy drinker and passed on the habit to Coach Wang. The boys claimed any alcohol they drank behind Coach Wang's back helped him drink less. Once, they tried adding a little water. Coach Wang took one sip and roared, "You think I'm stupid?"

Another reward for athletes who won medals at competitions was setting up an extra window in the cafeteria for special orders. Food was generally prepared in one big pot for the camp athletes, but at the winners' window, orders could be placed for beef, pork, or fish that would be cooked separately. We called this benefit "small pot-cooked food."

These benefits couldn't be purchased and remained only as long as an athlete continued to be selected to compete. I had no guarantees I would remain a competitor, so I savored each pleasure while it lasted. It helped offset the growing terror that plagued me in the dark hours of the night as I prepared for my first national tournament. In my nightmares, I feared I wasn't good enough, that a mistake would snowball and I would fail. But the biggest fear of all was that I would be sent home in disgrace, to suffer embarrassment in a menial job like my sister. Silently, I closed my eyes and recalled the old astrologer's prediction in an attempt to restore faith in myself.

In White House Rose Garden during 1974 Friendship Tour
(Coach Wang is third from left)

Coach Wang

Coach Wang

Coach Wang   Coach Wang

A CLOSED DOOR
SIGNALS TROUBLE

18

*F*renzied cheering erupted from tens thousand fans packed into the arena, momentarily distracting me from my preparation on the sidelines as I waited to be called as the next competitor. I looked up as a blur of pink silk flashed before my eyes. With a broadsword in each hand, White Flower rapidly slashed and jabbed at an imaginary circle of opponents. Like a whirlwind spinning leaves in a tree from bottom to top, from one branch to another, her twirling swords moved rhythmically around her body acting as a protective shield. After reaching amazing height on a difficult jump kick, White Flower's solid landing signaled the end of a crowd-pleasing performance. As she marched off the performance carpet, her eyes bored into mine while her mouth curled up in a cruel grin.*

As she drew near, her words revealed her contempt, "You'll never top me."

I stood stunned with disbelief that White Flower would antagonize me so openly. An implied code existed at the camp among athletes not to show hostility toward each other, to maintain a polite friendliness. Even with our closest rivals, that façade remained at all times. In an overcrowded country where a sense of privacy was nonexistent, people learned to behave without offending anyone or embarrassing themselves. Only a person's mind was considered personal territory and rarely shared.

White Flower and I were almost two years apart but competed in the same age bracket. She held a coveted place on the first team as its youngest member. I primed myself as the next in line for promotion to join her, and surely she felt me nipping at her heels.

She passed by me but didn't turn around when I called her name— the sound lost in the noise of the spectators. I wanted to tell her she had it all wrong. I thought if I explained I wasn't trying to show superiority over her, she wouldn't see me as a threat. I only wanted to join *her on the first team not* replace *her. Before I could follow her, my name resounded over the loudspeakers.*

Obediently, I assumed my starting position on the competition carpet and brought my right fist up to meet my left open palm in a bow to the five judges. In the back of my mind I tried to dismiss White Flower's attack and concentrate on my performance. Just as I began, however, it occurred to me she planned this stunt to weaken my composure and throw off my score.

From the beginning of my performance, I felt removed from my body's motions. Some other girl who looked like me executed the movements—a punch here, a kick there—but with a slowed-down rhythm. One minute my body bounded up from the splits and the next it jumped and landed with a clumsy thud instead of gracefully like a cat. A kind of body memory spurred me on from one move to the next while my mind seemed clouded and confused. Then something every athlete dreaded happened; my mind went completely blank. For the first time, fear paralyzed me. I heard a smattering of laughter, sounds of the audience clearly enjoying my predicament. After a panicky minute in which blood hammered in my ears, I did the only thing that occurred to me in my state of shame. I bowed hastily to the judges and ran out of the arena as fast as I could with downcast eyes, unable to face disappointment in Coach Wang's eyes.

With heavy breathing, I awoke in a strange place on a strange cot in the middle of a nightmare-induced anxiety attack. My sweaty limbs stuck to the damp bamboo mat as I rolled over to face the window. The faint glow of dawn warned me I was only hours from having to deliver the perfect competition performance I feared Coach Wang expected. I told myself not to worry, that it was all a dream. Deep breaths helped ease the gripping anxiety my dream produced.

Mental anguish prior to competition was the bane of all athletic competitors. Fear, desire, uncertainty, and exhaustion from overtraining fermented together giving rise to panic whenever an athlete faced possible failure. Athletes could find themselves one step closer to their dreams or in a confrontation with an angry coach claiming they didn't deserve further instruction. Only those two extremes existed. Fear became my unwelcome visitor in the dark hours of the night, a time when doubts intensified and action wasn't a viable remedy.

On that cold day in November gray skies outside the dorm window slowly awakened with color, as if bruising in pink- and crimson-colored welts. A girl in the room coughed, and bodies began shifting positions. It was almost time to get up. I grabbed my things and tiptoed out of the room, hoping a light jog outside would calm my nerves before I joined Coach Wang in warm-up routines.

At mid-morning, I entered the competition arena via the women's locker room and glanced around. My fingers absently smoothed out wrinkles in the pearly white silk of my uniform, my favorite one ornamented with Chinese-style filigree on the bodice yoke and belted securely around the waist with a long silk sash tied in a bow. The excitement buzzing in the air added to the nervousness plaguing me since last night's dream. I tried to ignore it and, for a few moments, simply watched the action on the floor.

This was the fall 1978 national competition hosted by the city of Xiangtan 湘潭, located near Chairman Mao's hometown in Hunan 湖南省 Province. In the performance area, three red competition carpets provided the stages for athletic *wushu* routines. Before me, barehanded solo athletes flew through the air with grace and speed while executing incredible jumping and flipping maneuvers occasionally ending in the splits. Each afternoon of the ten-day event, athletes brandishing weapons competed, followed in the evenings by the crowd's favorite, the fighting sets. These duels pitted two or three athletes against one another, with each athlete wielding a different weapon—a spear, a dagger, a broadsword, a straight sword, or a staff—or no weapon at all. Although the audience knew the routines were choreographed, there was a real sense of danger because the movements were so quick with weapons passing within an inch of the opponent's body. Spectators held their breaths, knowing the timing had to be perfectly matched.

As a break from the tediousness of daily life, forty thousand *wushu* fans eagerly gathered for the opportunity to see their idols perform and cheer their provincial teams to victory. Magazine and calendar photos of top professional *wushu* athletes fueled their adoration and became collectors' items. With each daring athletic feat, spectators clapped, hooted, and whistled with enthusiasm, tugging at my confidence.

After my gold medal win the year before at the big four-year provincial competition held in Wuxi, the decision was made to let me compete at this national competition as a first team member. Two older first team girls hadn't shown any signs of emerging as top scorers at the nationals and were forced into early retirement. Two of us from the second team were bumped up on a temporary basis to fill their places. Although excited about my chance, I felt sad about taking the place of one of the girls. It was a relief to learn she became a music teacher in an elementary school even though her skills were self-taught. She had spent her free time learning to play the piano in the gymnastics gymnasium and entertaining us on Sundays.

I turned to the sidelines and caught sight of Coach Wang. Proceeding in his direction through the maze of busy athletes, I tried to compose myself. My dream had rattled me and I couldn't quite shake it, but I didn't want Coach Wang to notice. When he looked at me askew, I knew he was trying to assess my frame of mind.

He put me to work right away in preparation for my turn at competition. My body easily slipped into the familiar warm-up patterns. My greatest anxiety wasn't that I would make a mistake because I had practiced my routines so many times I often found myself performing them in my dreams. My fear was that I couldn't meet Coach Wang's expectations for me because I wasn't really clear what they were. Coach Wang had drilled in us the importance of having a strong mind, saying that what distinguished the winners from everyone else was their mental fortitude. *Could I meet his expectations? Could I steel my mind to give my best performance?* I didn't want Coach Wang to give up on me. I looked to him as a surrogate father. He was the only person at the sports camp who showed any concern for me as a person as well as a competitor. I didn't want to disappoint him.

Gradually, with the help of Coach Wang's attentive guidance, I began to relax into my movements. I could feel his confidence gently coaxing my inner tiger out of the cage where I kept it safely guarded. Amid the noise of the bustling arena, I transformed myself into a young, sleek predator ready to step out on the competition carpet.

My strongest event was the popular longfist, with over one hundred athletes competing in that event alone. With the fears of the night vanquished, I prepared to deliver every ounce of energy possible while performing. Yet, I wasn't the same girl who had once performed so eagerly and carefree in Xuzhou. I knew I would never see that innocent girl again. She had been driven out by all the pressure I was under as an athlete. Tuning out the audience, judges and athletes, I zeroed in on one pair of eyes. I performed for Coach Wang only, mindful of displaying every nuance he emphasized in his teaching. A ribbon-like connection existed between us as I sought to please him with everything I had learned. At the end, I searched the crowd for Coach Wang. When he didn't scowl at me, I knew he was satisfied with my performance.

The tournament boosted my confidence because my scores weren't that much lower than the scores of White Flower on the first team. Just then a magazine photographer approached me. "I want to take your photo for a calendar of future *wushu* stars." Feeling flattered, I agreed to pose for him on the sidelines, but doubts soon entered my mind. I dismissed the idea the photographer selected me because I was exceptionally good or especially pretty. Although I wanted to believe otherwise, I told myself the photographer probably chose me because he knew Coach Wang's reputation.

While I posed for my photo, White Flower watched from the sidelines, scowling at me. I tried not to worry about it because I hadn't done anything to antagonize her.

After we returned to Nanjing, I was surprised when our current team leader, Leader Qian, told me he needed to meet with me privately. He ushered me into the room where we held our weekly forum meetings, turning and shutting the door behind us.

Closed doors signaled trouble in China. Privacy at the sports camp was foreign and taboo for the athletes during the daytime. Even our toilet facilities contained a series of stalls without doors where we squatted over open drains. In the Chinese culture, privacy was a state of mind. With so many people living in close confinement throughout China, physical privacy wasn't possible. If an athlete at the camp tried to close a door— the exception being when the girls were locked in their dorm rooms at night—others saw it as a warning of sickness or a statement of exclusion or conspiracy that caused all sorts of social problems. There was a general paranoia in China of people plotting against others, and the closed door made me uncomfortable and wary.

Leader Qian motioned for me to sit down on one of the bench stools before he began talking. "We're sorry you didn't place at the national competition."

I didn't know they had expected me to place there. I had never heard of anyone placing in the top five out of one hundred competitors at her first national competition.

He continued, "Coach Yin and I feel you would benefit from having him personally train you."

Coach Yin was the head coach of the first team, and I instinctively didn't trust him. To me, his eyes, which he hid behind his black thick-rimmed glasses, were alert, yet deceitful. Like a spitting cobra, he lured his prey into a false sense of security in order to spring forward and strike with venom powerful enough to blind an opponent. I silently called him Coach Cobra.

I knew I didn't want to train with Coach Cobra. He'd never shown me an ounce of friendliness, and besides, it was customary that an athlete's second team coach should remain the athlete's coach even after promotion to the first team. The second team coach had invested his time into training the athletes and knew their strengths and weaknesses. I knew automatically what I wanted to say.

"Coach Wang has been training me for a long time, and I want to keep training with him," I said softly, sitting tall. "But I also want to serve on the first team and compete at the national tournament."

"Well," he said in a sharper tone, "we feel you aren't ready to compete as a first team member and you need the kind of training Coach Yin can give you."

This hurt me, but I refused to show it. "I think I did well at the tournament."

"You did okay, but not good enough."

What is going on? Do they just want me to work harder?

"I have another matter to discuss with you." Leader Qian adjusted himself, his appearance frail but deceiving. "I understand Coach Wang's been mistreating his athletes, hitting them."

I was stunned and sat quietly because I wasn't sure how to

respond.

He continued, "He's also been drinking too much alcohol."

Here he paused, but I remained silent.

"You're the oldest of Coach Wang's students. You have an obligation to speak up for your teammates. What he's doing isn't right. We must correct this problem."

"Coach Wang has never mistreated me," I truthfully told him.

"Have you seen him hit any of your teammates?"

I hesitated, then replied, "I can only speak for myself."

Leader Qian moved closer to me until I felt his hot breath on my face. "Coach Wang may be removed from the coaching staff. If that happens, you'd have many opportunities on the first team. You have to think about your career and what Coach Yin can do for you. All you have to do is write down that you've seen Coach Wang hitting or mistreating students."

I couldn't believe what he was asking me to do. All I could think about was what Baba or NaiNai would tell me to do. In my heart, I couldn't fault Coach Wang. I knew he only wanted us to be good athletes. He always treated me fairly.

"No, I can't do that," I said, quaking inside at the possible consequences.

Leader Qian frowned. "You better think about it."

I left the meeting feeling despondent. Leader Qian's words were all I could think about over the next few days. I didn't dare talk to Coach Wang about it or even to any of my teammates. Training hard had been my focus, and, therefore, I wasn't always observant of the political intrigues taking place in the camp, so this took me by surprise.

The conclusion I reached was Coach Cobra wanted control of Coach Wang's students. Eighty percent of the first team members had been Coach Wang's former students. As a reward for being a successful athlete, Coach Wang had been originally assigned the head coach position. He selected athletes and trained them for several years, building their strength and skill. Just before the athletes reached their competition prime, however, he lost his position. Coach Wang related the story many years later.

"The other coaches wanted the head coaching position," Coach Wang told me. "One day, as I sat in a meeting with the coaching staff, someone mentioned it was more important for an athlete to be Red than skillful to attain his highest level of recognition in China." Being Red meant being a loyal Communist.

"I commented that being skillful was necessary first," Coach Wang said. "The team leader argued with me by saying, 'Remember what Chairman Mao had said, that friendship comes first, then competition. It's the same here. Be Red first, then skillful.'" Athletes were always encouraged to be friendly to their opponents both before and after competing.

"I reminded the coach of the world ping-pong champion, Zhuang Ze Dong 庄则栋, who had received the highest honor bestowed on an athlete. He was invited to sit on the dais at the Gate of Heavenly Peace as Chairman Mao addressed over one million Red Guards. Zhuang Ze Dong had received that invitation because of his skill."

"The team leader and the coaching staff twisted my comment to show that I had a political consciousness problem and needed to learn more from Chairman Mao's red book. They said I wasn't Red enough to hold the head coaching position," Coach Wang said with a fleeting look of sadness before his fighting spirit reappeared. "I was still young, so I decided to start a new team, your team."

Coach Wang had only been in his mid-twenties and couldn't argue on his own behalf to keep his job. The first team belonged to the government. He had to follow the decision handed down because he also belonged to the government. Coach Cobra then took over the first team.

Coach Wang didn't know how to play political games. He gave those first team students a strong foundation in *wushu* basics, and then he was forced to give them up. Some of those boys became winners, and their success was publicly attributed to Coach Cobra, even though he had been training them for a comparatively shorter time. It was like being in the middle of the Cultural Revolution again where everybody was trying to grab power.

The result of my failure to denounce Coach Wang was that two new girls were brought in as first team members. They had been training in Xuzhou under a coach who was an ex-team member of the same generation of athletes as Coaches Wang and Cobra. The girls hadn't been professional team members, but their coach had a good reputation for training excellence. Their older ages put them in a different age bracket than White Flower, something I didn't realize was important at the time. Coach Cobra was protecting his favorite athlete because White Flower couldn't handle being the loser. All I knew was that one of those girls took the place on the first team that should have been mine.

This was a dark time for me, and I felt so alone. I couldn't talk to my coach for two reasons. Coach Wang easily lost his self-control and had on occasion instigated fights. I didn't want to rouse his anger and have him punch Coach Cobra. I was also afraid he would become discouraged with me. I assumed he'd just tell me to work harder and that my time would come. I didn't want to lose his favor because no one else there cared about me.

I didn't have any best friends on the team. Even though Coach Wang encouraged us to be like brothers and sisters when we weren't competing, we never confided in each other about our deepest thoughts and feelings. It wasn't the Chinese way to reveal anything that could be deemed an inner weakness. Also, we had such little free time, and any free time was spent recovering from the fatigue of training. Physical exhaustion was denied for so much of the day that when we had the chance to relax, fatigue consumed us and there was no extra energy for talking or socializing. Instead of basking on the sunny side of a mountain, I endured this gloomy time alone in the chill of the mountain's shadow.

Shortly thereafter, a much-needed boost of camaraderie among all female *wushu* athletes occurred to help me regain my equilibrium. One day after our weekly forum meeting, Clever Treasure asked the girls to remain behind. I was curious as to what this was about. "Some of you are developing," she announced. "You need to wear a bra. We'll show all of you what to do after breakfast on Sunday in my room." My teammates and I looked at each other and giggled. We were excited to be growing up.

On the girls' second team, I was the last one to develop even though I was the oldest. At almost seventeen, my shapeless body with its long coltish legs remained as skinny as a boy's. Some of the girls teased me, "Liu Yu, you're so skinny maybe you really *are* a boy." It made me wonder if there were something wrong with me.

On Sunday, the older girls announced they would teach us how to make a bra from the patterns they had made. The first step was getting measured. I shyly submitted to being measured by Clever Treasure, embarrassed about my lack of development but proud at the same time. The later a girl developed, the better her chances of competing longer. Staying slender allowed me to jump high, something I would need to become a champion.

Clever Treasure whispered encouragement. "Liu Yu, you need to make one, too, because you'll be developing soon. Just pick the smallest pattern."

After purchasing fabric and hooks at the store, the older girls supervised as we cut the fabric and sewed the seams completely by hand. My bra was the first thing I'd ever made.

Several years before, we had also learned other things from the older first team girls. One day, when an older girl looked like she wasn't feeling well, Coach Wang inquired about her problem. She turned red and shook her head. Coach Wang then yelled at her in front of the group. "What are you going to do on competition day if you have your monthly time? You can't say, 'Excuse me, judge, but I can't compete.' No, you still have to perform and you still have to train hard."

As a younger girl, I didn't know about monthly cycles and asked an older teammate to explain it to me. That's how we learned about it. The girls on the first team acted as big sisters to the younger ones. Yet, rivalry and cultural habits sadly prevented us from becoming close friends. And the more we competed, the larger the gap between us and the lonelier we felt.

Often, in the middle of the night when I couldn't sleep, doubts crept into my mind. *Had I made the right decision by refusing to link up with Coach Cobra?* In my heart, I was proud I had remained loyal to Coach Wang, but the possible consequences were scary. I felt lost in a maze with no way out. The walls were closing in on me and suddenly I couldn't breathe.

Liu Yu visiting Beijing
for the Big Games

Coach Wang's publicity photo

 CAUGHT IN THE CROSSFIRE

Every four years, the national tournament turned into a gigantic event in China called the "Big Games," with all Olympic sports, plus *wushu*, convening for the competition. Before this competition, held in the fall of 1979, we hosted visitors for the whole summer, visitors who were the biggest rivals of our Jiangsu Province athletes, especially the men's first team.

Coach Wu Bin 吴彬教练, the head coach of the Beijing Wushu Team, was smart. No having the competitive background Coach Wang had, he looked for ways to give his team a competitive advantage by seeking out *wushu* teachers who could impart the benefit of their experience. Coach Wu headed straight to the coach with the most experience competing, hoping he was also the one who could be most easily manipulated.

The summer was long and hot, but our training didn't slow down like it did most summers. Instead, it went into overdrive. Even when sprinting in warm-ups, everyone pushed hard to beat the other team. The coaches added an extra training session for both teams in the evening, and Coach Wu compelled his athletes to practice secretly at night. He took each athlete aside, pointing out a movement he wanted them to learn from one of our team members. "See that athlete doing the double head spear? I want you to get that difficult martial arts movement and practice it tonight. Tomorrow you'll show our team what you learned." He didn't tell our team about the assigned homework, but we learned about it later.

While training on the carpet, Coach Wu drove his team in competition with us, and we answered the call. Off the carpet, we became good friends with the other team. One of the Beijing team members who stayed in my dorm room later became Jet Li's first wife. She was a complainer who never made it to the first team. Because Coach Wang encouraged our team to feel like a big family, treating each other as brothers and sisters, we were surprised to learn romantic attachments formed on other teams.

Coaches Wang and Wu were extremely friendly, drinking beer together every day. My teammates and I were enlisted as servants, fetching cold beer and food from the kitchen. Usually the kitchen didn't allow any prepared food to leave the cafeteria, but the father of one of my teammates worked a shift in the kitchen. From time to time, we took advantage of this relationship by sneaking into the kitchen to grab a snack. The cooks in the kitchen had watched Coach Wang grow up, and they willingly prepared food for us to take back for Coach Wang's entertainment of Coach Wu.

When I delivered more cold beers and food to the coaches, Coach Wang, in his drunken euphoria, bragged, "*Wushu* people should be like one big family. Coach Wu is my brother. *Wushu* brothers and sisters should share all the best things with each other. You're our witness. See how friendly the Beijing team is? They came all the way from Beijing to train with us."

I answered dutifully, "Yes, Coach Wang." Inside, however, I was sorry for our team and especially for Coach Wang. He was so honest and trusting. I didn't share his idealistic vision of the world. I thought Coach Wu was crafty. His team was gaining all of Coach Wang's best teaching.

Fifteen years later, Coach Wu confided to me in a private conversation about how well he managed his team. "I may not be highly skilled in *wushu*, but I'm a great team manager. I know how to play politics."

During the time the Beijing team spent training with us, all the athletes moved up a notch or two in ability. We traveled together, giving demonstrations in a couple of cities within our province. Our skills improved from watching each other, and I was especially interested in catching an eyeful of Jet Li's powerful movements. As a person, he was polite to everyone and very respectful with Coach Wang. Before returning to Beijing, Jet Li confided to us, "You guys are so lucky to have Coach Wang as your coach. I'm sure you're all going to be great because of him."

My teammates and I learned some things about Coach Wang after our exposure to Coach Wu. Both coaches trained their teams exceptionally hard, but we sensed that Coach Wu's cold manipulative scheming negatively affected how his athletes felt about him. We were beginning to see Coach Wang as a person and appreciate his warm heart. As younger athletes, we feared Coach Wang, but now, as we grew older, he relaxed more with us outside the gymnasium. He felt like more of a father to us, someone who was guiding us to reach our goals in the best way he knew how. This realization made me more determined than ever to make him proud.

Excitement stirred the second team members when Jiangsu government officials announced Coach Wang had been successfully encouraged to compete again as an individual at the Big Games. In 1979, rivalry ran high, and every province wanted to win in as many sports as possible. Coach Wang was enlisted to help beat the successful Beijing Wushu Team.

Although Coach Wang was thirty-three years old, he always remained in shape by training with us. He had retired from competition several years before, but because the boys on the Jiangsu Province first team weren't quite at their peak strength for winning gold medals against Jet Li, he agreed to train again for competition. Since Coach Wang's retirement, Jet Li had been China's All-around *Wushu* Champion each year. The Jiangsu team needed Coach Wang to compete against Jet Li in his last national competition before retiring from the Beijing team.

The sport of *wushu* takes tremendous agility, strength, and speed. Men rarely compete past age thirty. Eventually, one woman in her thirties remained on a *wushu* team as their *taiji* (also known as *taijiquan,* the *pinyin* spelling of *t'ai chi ch'uan*) and *bagua* (or *baguazhang*) competitor. *Taiji* and *bagua* are known as internal martial arts. The energy displayed in their gentle movements develops internally over time as opposed to using external muscle in the faster-paced *wushu*. *Taiji* athletes improve over time and rarely reach their peak at a young age.

The 1979 *wushu* competition was held in the city of Shijiazhuang 石家庄 located in Hebei 河北省 Province. The opening and closing ceremonies, along with events in other sports, were conducted in and around Beijing. I was selected as an alternate for the first team, deeply saddened not to be competing.

We traveled by train, Coach Wang keeping us stretching and moving during the entire trip. "Hurry up, here comes a big station. Get your running shoes on." While passengers and luggage were loading and unloading, we hopped off and ran the length of the train, back and forth, and then performed kicks before we boarded again. Inside the train, we stretched in aisles and doorways and stood still in various *wushu* poses. Everyone had a training program for the trip prepared by Coach Wang. He didn't want anyone's legs to swell from sitting around.

At the opening ceremonies in Beijing, the teams from our camp proudly walked in behind our "Jiangsu Province" sign in new jackets and pants. What an honor it was for us to be there. The air in the huge open arena with 100,000 spectators sizzled with excitement. Brightly colored balloons floated up filling the sky, and then hundreds of pigeons rapidly beat their wings as they escaped from their cages, surging up and out of the stadium. Dancers in colorful costumes entertained us, moving gracefully in rhythm to the toe-tapping music.

At competitions, it's not about how many individual gold medals your team wins that counts. Of course, winning medals was necessary to achieve the highest honor and accumulate the most points for your team. The overall objective of every team, however, was being named the number one team for the year.

Each team member was required to compete in six different event categories, five of which were individual events and the sixth a fighting set. The five individual event categories were (1) empty hand, such as the longfist (*changquan*), Southern style fist (*nanquan*) or *taiji* (*taijiquan*); (2) short weapon (straight sword or broadsword); (3) long weapon (spear or staff); (4) traditional empty hand (*bagua*, *xingyi*, eagle claw, monkey form, etc.); and (5) traditional weapons, which included single weapons (long-handle broadsword, monkey staff, etc.), double weapons (double hooks, double spear, etc.), and flexible weapons (nine sectional whip, three sectional staff, rope, etc.). The traditional weapon contestants competed only against their own weapon category; for example, single weapons didn't compete against double weapons. A longfist winner was highly esteemed because that category wasn't divided compared to the traditional weapons category that would have many winners, one for each subcategory.

My specialties were longfist, straight sword, staff, *bagua*, and double hooks. The fighting sets were between two or three people and included various combinations of weapons, bare hands, and martial arts styles.

My services as an alternate on the team weren't required, and so my eyes were riveted on the action unfolding on the competition carpet. I zealously watched and absorbed all I could from the competitors, especially from Coach Wang.

Coach Wang had received special training from famous older-generation *wushu* masters, and it showed in his movements. A tendency existed among young athletes to copy each other in the execution of their forms. When Coach Wang performed the same form, he displayed more flare and grace with strong and purposeful movements that flowed beautifully with long arm and leg extensions. Sadly, regional differences in the execution of a form were gradually disappearing as everyone sought to imitate their *wushu* idols.

The biggest event, the jewel of the competition, captured the attention of all 80,000 spectators in the arena. Two performance areas were going at once, but all eyes shifted simultaneously to the carpet when the men's fighting sets were called. The Jiangsu team was scheduled to appear toward the end.

When Coach Wang finally marched out to the center of the carpet with his two students, a roar went up in the arena. The audience gasped and applauded at each skillful movement of their empty-handed fighting set. The action was newly choreographed with daring jumps, kicks, and bodies slamming on the carpet as they propelled themselves at each other from all directions.

There I was, watching Coach Wang as he must have been as a young champion. I nearly burst with pride upon hearing the spectators' cries of "well done" and "amazing Jin Bao." The Jiangsu men's fighting team gratified everyone, including the five judges who each gave a 9.5 score. Only the Beijing team remained to compete.

What happened next was the surprise of the tournament. Instead of the traditional two- or three-person fighting team, five Beijing team athletes took command of the center carpet. Even their costumes went against tradition with a sparkly red stripe emblazoned on each shirt that was partially cut away, exposing one bare shoulder and arm.

Jet Li, with his shaggy head of hair, led his four teammates in an outstanding performance that included an extra rendition from the movie Jet Li had just completed called "Shaolin Temple." The movie was soon to become a huge hit in China and would thrust Jet Li into movie star status. An enthusiastic audience welcomed their performance, while I sat feeling sorry for myself.

It was difficult sitting on the sidelines, feeling fired up from the excitement of the crowd, and wanting desperately to be out on the carpet. I knew my skills were as good as many of the competitors but Coach Cobra had taken away my opportunity to compete. Now I felt like I was simply running in place and not getting anywhere. I distracted myself by turning my attention to how the judges would score the men's fighting set event.

The judges took their time conferring, obviously not knowing how to respond. It turned out having a five-man team wasn't against the rules, but no one had thought of going against tradition before. The cunning coach of the Beijing team constantly thought of new ways to give his team a sharper edge toward winning and being the best. The five judges finally held up their score placards with 9.5 all around.

When the scores of the five top team members were averaged, the Jiangsu team tied in points with the Beijing team for first place. Whenever a tie occurred, the rules always furnished a clear way to break the tie. In this case, the judges added the highest and lowest scores and divided that number by two. Whichever answer was closest to the final score of that team's event—whether it was higher or lower didn't matter—resulted in a winner, but not this time. There was still a tie after the high-low average.

Next, the scores of the individual events of the athletes who performed each team's best fighting set were averaged and compared. The average of our three competitors' scores came in lower than the average of the scores for the five Beijing athletes. The gold medal *wushu* team winner of the Fourth China All-Sport Competition was the Beijing team. We won the silver, but placing in the top three was highly respected. Still, Coach Wang wasn't happy, but there was nothing to be done about it.

The next year the rule changed. Three athletes became the upper limit on fighting sets. Two years later, after costumes became elaborately fancy, judges ruled costumes must be traditional.

Each year, we looked forward to the national competition where we watched famous *wushu* athletes from around the country display their forms. If we saw athletes exhibit some unusual movements or a special form we liked, it was common to make an appointment with them at the end of the competition so they could teach us. These athletes felt flattered by this request, and many of us took advantage of the opportunity. During the extra few days we stayed over after the competition, the host team also had the duty of driving all visiting teams around in buses, showing everyone the sights of its city.

Before we returned home, Coach Wang took our team to Chairman Mao's Memorial Hall. We waited in long lines to check our bags and then went through a security check before finally approaching the crystal coffin containing the embalmed body of Chairman Mao. We were ushered through quickly and not allowed to stop and stare. When I saw the rosy cheeks and red lips that were painted on the dead body, I thought how fake they looked. Teammates around me sniffed and suppressed tears in the reverent silence that pervaded the room. My own eyes remained dry, but the unreality of the moment spooked me. When we returned to the camp, one of my teammates bragged about our group being the first one from Nanjing to see such a remarkable sight.

Coach Wang received a lot of attention at the camp for doing well at the Big Games. He was proud of himself, but he didn't know how to show it in a humble way. Even at local demonstrations, Coach Wang was a show-off, always ready to jump on the carpet to demonstrate when he should have shown reserve. His pride produced jealousy among the other coaches. I worried Coach Wang was making trouble for himself and for us.

One day during intensive body conditioning, Coach Wang said he had an announcement. As my teammates and I struggled through the agonizing pain of half an hour of handstands, he told us, "When I heard the Beijing team would be taking its second team to the spring competition, I negotiated to have our team go, too. This is a rare opportunity. You'll be competing with the first team on an equal footing. From now on, we'll be training harder to get ready."

Audible groans never heard under normal circumstances now escaped from several mouths in this time of weakening resolve. We'd already joined the older first team in pre-competition training, which increased our daily seven-hour training time to ten hours, seven days a week. But with Coach Wang on a mission to get us ready to compete, I knew we faced the kind of workouts that would turn my lips white from lack of oxygen.

Yet, competition was the focus of our hard training, and we were eager to see what we could do against the other provincial teams. Our experience in regional competitions only partially prepared us for national competition. I was the oldest athlete on the second team and the only one with any experience competing at a national tournament. We reacted to the announcement by clenching our jaws with determination and enduring the intensive preparation for the upcoming invitational competition.

Every team member suffered from the same sweat-inducing nightmares before a competition. In my dreams, a uniform sash was missing or not packed. It was time to step on the competition carpet and the needed weapons were in another room. At the end of one spiraling movement, my mind suddenly went blank. The pressure on each athlete to deliver a perfect performance produced unhealthy fearfulness. Preparing for the competition, I spent a lot of restless nights filled with panic.

Each spring, one of the provinces hosted an invitational *wushu* competition where all teams who competed at the nationals had a chance to face off in a less formal setting. In May of 1981 at the invitational held in the coastal city of Yantai 烟台 in Shandong 山东省 Province, rivalry between my provincial team and Beijing's was at an all-time high.

Before my performance, Coach Wang took plenty of time to ensure I felt calm in spite of the cheering crowd. He helped me find my inner confidence by having me practice my best moves on the sidelines. He gazed at everything with an intensity of purpose, and I felt his single-minded attention scrutinizing my movements. Instead of making me nervous, his mindfulness communicated a heightened sense of steady awareness, which I quickly adopted as my own.

Although I competed in six events, my strongest was the popular longfist, my bare hand routine. Because males and females didn't compete against each other, my competitors were all female. On each six-person provincial team, five of the girls competed in the longfist. Approximately thirty girls' teams attended the invitational in Yantai with 150 athletes competing in that event.

When the judge called my name, Coach Wang's normal gruff manner softened. He quickly counseled me, "Let go of everything. I don't care about your score. Just do your best." His words infused me with happiness because they acknowledged he cared about me. Though only sixteen years my senior, Coach Wang was my surrogate father. He inspired me to set aside my fears and give my best performance to please him.

I stepped onto the performance carpet and saluted toward the table of imposing judges. A deep, calming breath helped me get in touch with my inner strength, "my tiger energy." As I began my performance, I allowed the rhythm of the movements to take over my body. Despite my shy nature when interacting with others, I had a natural sense of showmanship on the competition carpet. Soaring through the air on high jumps and landing with strong, unshakable stances produced an unparalleled sense of freedom.

Keeping my mind strong and focused generated a sense of power for my moves, one of which was the butterfly twist. In this jump, my body was thrust into a high move parallel to the ground with a half twist in the air before landing in the splits on the ground. Coach Wang also developed a difficult sequence of movements to highlight my exceptional flexibility. It began with a forward-facing flip, known as an aerial walkover, followed by an aerial, which is a no-hands cartwheel going sideways. It ended by swiftly moving from the aerial into a high front jump kick with its sharp slap of the foot and landing in a balanced stance. No one else performed this combination, and it pleased me when I executed my signature movements without a wobble or any under- or over-rotations. The fears haunting me before the competition, particularly in my dreams, didn't come true.

After ending my routine, I ignored the applause of the crowd and the judges' scorecards and searched for Coach Wang's face. Seeing his smile and the slight nod of his head was all the satisfaction I needed.

My performance in the longfist at the Yantai competition wasn't the start of the problems Coach Wang and I shared, but it proved to be an imaginary jab in Coach Cobra's face. To everyone's surprise, and Coach Wang's undisguised pleasure, I was awarded fourth place in the female longfist category. To be among the top ten winners in a competition against other professional athletes spelled success. Difficulty arose, however, because no other girl from our province placed. More specifically, no *first team* girl placed and that included White Flower.

My win threatened the status of Coach Cobra, who was supposed to be superior to a second team coach. Even though my success as a second team athlete caused a loss of face for the first team coach, I wasn't sorry. I'd suspected he was behind the plot to have Coach Wang ousted. What I didn't expect, however, was the nasty controversy my win stirred up that spun a political web around me.

In retaliation against my achievement, Coach Cobra grabbed at an explanation to quell everyone's suspicion about the quality of his coaching. After we returned to camp, I learned from rumors flying around the camp that Coach Cobra and his subordinate coaches had approached the Jiangsu Province high official, arguing I wasn't good enough to have won fourth place. They told the official the reason I won was because Coach Wang had begged a favor. They accused Coach Wang of bribing the judges.

Each province sent two or three professional judges to a competition, and those judges were required to pass a qualifying test for the appropriate competition level—county, province, or national. The judging committee assigned the same group of judges to score every competitor in one event, and competitors knew approximately what day and time they needed to step on the carpet when the competition week began. The longfist judges had the morning to perform their judging duties, and then they took a break while another group of judges took over for some other category. There were five judges and one head judge per event.

The judging rules clearly regulated the scoring. The highest and lowest scores were never used. The three remaining scores were averaged, but the head judge could alter the score based on rulebook situations. If a head judge determined one of the judges consistently scored too low or too high or favored his team in any way, then this judge was removed and suffered humiliation. Plenty of standby judges waited to be called.

In my mind, the likelihood of any foul play on the part of Coach Wang was unthinkable, and I could tell he was hurt by the allegations. I couldn't understand how the other coaches could do this to him. This was surely proof in my mind that Coach Cobra conspired to have Coach Wang removed.

Feeling trapped between the crossfire of the two coaches angered me. The worst was yet to come, however. Coach Cobra acted to prevent me from embarrassing him again. With a heartless ruling, he swiftly and dramatically altered the direction of my life.

The blow came at one of our weekly forum meetings. Any information communicated to athletes was done at these meetings. Nothing was considered too personal or worthy of advance private notice. When someone was retiring or receiving a promotion, everyone learned about it in the meeting.

During this particular session, I observed Coach Wang looking despondent. This immediately put me on alert, stirring up my inner paranoia. He stared straight ahead at the team leader, not making eye contact with anyone. I assumed the other coaches had made trouble for him. As a result, I sensed imminent danger approaching.

At the end of the meeting, Coach Cobra addressed the group, informing us, "A decision has been made about who will be training to become the new *taiji* girl for the team. Liu Yu's new bare hand event will be *taiji*."

A recent national directive required that one team member must compete in *taiji* to keep this style from disappearing. However, no one wanted to be chosen for *taiji* because young people considered it too slow. They thought it didn't show as much athleticism as the faster longfist.

Unable to breathe, I sat quietly, looking down at my hands. This meant I wouldn't be allowed to compete in longfist, my specialty, any longer. Out of all the girls, I was the best at longfist. This was a huge blow for me, but I was careful not to show any anger or tears even though inside I burned. Even if Coach Wang could have convinced any judges to do his bidding or keep quiet about his asking them for a favor, I shouldn't have been punished for it. But, I realized my talent was a threat to the first team coach, and he had to make sure I didn't embarrass him again.

My expectation was always that Coach Wang would protect me while I was away from my family. Now I understood this wouldn't be the case—not because he didn't want to, but because he didn't have enough power to do so. He didn't know how to play political games to keep others from being offended by him, and this was his downfall. As a consequence, I was being taken down with him because I had pledged my allegiance to him.

The *taiji* training I subsequently received from one of the older first team boys felt like punishment—not because I didn't like it, but because Coach Wang and I had put so much effort into my longfist training. My visions of popping up as a *wushu* star diminished. Now I faced my toughest mental challenge—how to survive the shattering of my dreams.

For several days, I was overcome with helplessness and spiraled down toward an abyss of no return. Lying awake in the darkness, listening to the rhythmic breathing of my roommates, I fell deeper into depression. All my defenses dropped away. Reaching down to the foot of my bed, I pulled my quilt closely around me to ease my heartache. When I'd arrived at the sports camp as a young trainee, I kept my homemade blanket—the colorful patchwork one Baba had made especially for me—carefully hidden. I assumed the other girls would have store-bought blankets and didn't want them to see my poverty. Now, this keepsake quilt was my most treasured possession. It was the only thing that gave me comfort.

With my fingers curled around an edge of the quilt, I forced myself to analyze the situation. My dreams had always centered on championship glory in the longfist, yet my mind told my heart to let those hopes go. I needed to face my future. I couldn't afford to lie awake at night and feel sorry for myself. Intuitively, I knew it was dangerous for me to spend even one more moment feeling depressed because I might not get back to where I was before.

Often, athletes were unable to make their own decisions. The protective net of being on a professional team hindered us from learning to think for ourselves. I discovered that allowing others to decide my future when it ran opposite my wishes was against my nature. I would find some way to come out on top while avoiding the cultural taboo of showing too much independence. My sanity required it. I was determined that one day I would think for myself, make my own decisions. Yet, first I had to survive the training.

During this difficult time, I yearned to see my family. Without warning, I thought about my blue socks floating away in the river and NaiNai's words about life going up and down. I saw her in my mind saying with determination, "Everything you have could go away very fast. Today you own this, but maybe tomorrow you won't have it. The most important thing is what's inside you."

NaiNai's life was rarely easy. She lost her husband and financial security while raising her children. Yet, she was never depressed and kept her optimism. I knew I had to follow her example.

Mustering all my tiger energy, I decided not to look back. I wanted to move forward. I had made myself stand out when I was younger by becoming the best at the weapons no one else had wanted to learn. Now, I resolved to focus my energies on my other events, especially my double hooks routine. In the meantime, it would take time, I realized, for the pain to subside. And time was abundant because I had nowhere else to go. I was stuck in a rut of endless training, spinning my wheels and getting nowhere. Gaining more competition experience, something I desperately wanted, was not a guarantee. Instead, the monotony of team life was about to change, but not in the direction I expected.

Yao's Young Warriors movie cast
(Liu Yu second row up second from right; Coach Wang front row third from left; Little Sparrow second row up first on left; Wei Wei back row first on left; Wang Ya Chun back row second from left; Huang Jun front row second from right)

Yao's Young Warriors movie poster

Foreign students studying *wushu* with Coach Wang
(including Roger Tong second from right in second row,
Robin Shou sitting in front row fourth from right, and Paula
sitting in front first from right. Photo by Norm Petredean.)

Liu Yu (left) in movie scene

Liu Yu in movie costume

 20 *SHIVERING ON THE ROOFTOP*

agerly, I packed my bags, saying goodbye to the camp I called home for seven long years. Government officials declared *wushu*, Chinese chess, and the new sport of rhythm gymnastics no longer matched the Olympic flavor of the professional training camp. These three non-Olympic teams moved from the outskirts of Nanjing to the Jiangsu Province Sports Center at the All-Sport Official Headquarters 江苏省体育运动委员会体育中心 in the heart of the city.

My teammates and I were especially thrilled to leave behind the sports camp's dreaded wake-up alarms. Living in the city opened up a new world for us to explore. For the first time—presumably because we had reached the ages of young adulthood—walking unescorted to a few nearby places was allowed, *if* we had any free time.

We had bypassed the age when Coach Wang required half a day of training on Sundays, although he often strategized to make us practice on Sunday anyway. Sometimes he introduced a new, complicated move on Saturday and threw in an element of competition to see who could master the move first. Another scheme was finding fault with us on Saturday and assigning Sunday practice as a punishment. Despite Coach Wang's tricks, we managed to steal away from the sports center whenever possible for some much-needed entertainment.

The nearby university hosted concerts and frequently gave us free tickets. Shopping was within walking distance, and we saw our first indoor movie at a large theater nearby. Jackie Chan 成龙 was our favorite star who staggered across the screen in his drunken form imitation, successfully fighting evil villains. Occasionally, we saw a pirated James Bond movie on tape. Even though we couldn't understand the language, it provided a fascinating glimpse of the Western world.

Up until this time, the only movies we had seen had been projected on a big sheet in the middle of our former camp's soccer field. We used to sit on our little folding army stools while viewing the movies from either side of the makeshift screen. Those early movie tapes pirated from Hong Kong featured our martial artist heroes.

After the Cultural Revolution, Western tourists began trickling into China and aroused the Chinese people's interest in fashion. In the early 1980's, independent vendors started selling clothing on the free market when previously the Communist government owned all businesses. On one of our Sunday excursions we walked to the free market near Nanjing's Confucius Temple. After years of seeing people wearing Mao-style jackets, we were eager to wear something different. We didn't want to be flashy and attract a lot of attention, but we wanted to feel a bit more modern.

One day, I bought some dark beige pants the merchants were calling jeans. They weren't real jeans, but they were made from a thick material and cut very loose. Wearing the comfortable jeans helped fulfill my need for change. Strolling to the cafeteria, I ran into our new team leader, Leader Chen, who was a strict Maoist assigned to our sports team. Her eyes grew large as she looked at me with surprise and said, "Liu Yu, what are you wearing? I didn't think *you'd* be the kind of person to wear those. Why'd you buy them?"

I flushed with embarrassment and couldn't think of anything to say. I couldn't tell her the truth—that I wanted to wear something besides training clothes. She sputtered, shocked that I had worn such pants because I was considered the most mainstream person on the team, the one who never went against tradition or caused trouble. Coach Wang, the team leader, and my parents all thought I would be the last one to do anything wrong. The abuse in the square during the Cultural Revolution had seen to that, silencing me for fear of repercussions. Humiliated by Leader Chen's reproach, I ran back to my dorm and hid the pants away. I never found the courage to wear them again.

My teammates occasionally snuck out of their dorms, meeting boyfriends or girlfriends in unauthorized areas, such as the swimming pool or the roller skating rink. One time, instead of the boys acting rebellious, a disobedient group of girls stole away and encountered some wild boys near the swimming pool at lunchtime. In response to the boys' tauntings, the girls bravely replied, "Stop it, and don't bother us." Things escalated into a near fight with the three girls standing back to back while facing their assailants. Some other athletes passed by and ran to get help from the boys' *wushu* team. When the team arrived, the bullies were holding bricks, threatening to throw them at the girls. My teammates advanced toward them with fighting poses, scaring them away.

Furious, Coach Wang dealt out a harsh punishment that included daily meetings and written promises not to venture away from approved areas. "I told you not to make trouble," he lectured, pacing in front of us. "You were all warned not to enter certain areas of town. We have a reason for these warnings. The government has spent a huge amount of money on you. If you get injured, you waste both money and the training. What would I tell your parents? Your actions disrupt the entire team."

Coach Wang's words reminded me of something NaiNai used to say when she cooked over a small brazier in our courtyard. "When cooking a pot of food, if a bird flies over it and drops something into it, that one drop will ruin the whole pot. Families are like the pot of food. They must stick together and help each other so nothing destroys them." Coach Wang always said our *wushu* team was like a family and our actions affected all of us.

The girls on the team were chosen partly because of their beauty, but this was why they had to be careful. They could attract the attention of the wrong type of people. My lack of bravery saved me. Of all the elements—wood, fire, earth, metal and water—that influence Chinese astrological signs, water was considered the most soothing. As a water tiger, my personality was cautious, and I valued the respect of others. I tried to avoid trouble, but I often got teased for being so guarded. I wasn't going to let anyone disrupt my goal of becoming a champion. Yet, when Coach Cobra went out of his way to tear down my resolve, I found it harder to walk such a virtuous path.

After our move into town, a shake-up occurred on the team. A new coach was hired. He was a former senior athlete who had retired from competition. Coach Wang was told he had too many students and couldn't continue training all twelve athletes. He must give up either the boys or the girls to the new coach.

Coach Wang decided to continue as the boys' coach, but only if he could keep me as well. He argued he had spent a great deal of extra time training me and wasn't finished. Coach Wang said his plan to raise an athlete's abilities to her highest level could take over eight years, and I had only been training with him for seven.

When I heard Coach Wang wanted to keep training me, relief flooded through me. One reason I was grateful to stay with him was because I feared the risk of injury should I change coaches. The new coach wouldn't be familiar with my strengths and weaknesses, and any serious injury could permanently dash my remaining hopes for an athletic future. Coach Wang never let us jump high or try difficult movements until he was certain we were capable of them, and then we had to be adequately warmed up first. Being pushed into greater difficulty too soon could turn an athlete into a shooting star that bursts suddenly on the competition scene and then just as quickly fades away after an injury.

But my main reason for not wanting to change coaches was because I took Coach Wang's preference as a sign I still had a chance at a championship, while I doubted I could reach my full potential with a new coach. I trusted Coach Wang who said it wasn't a fast process to raise a *wushu* star. My dreams of emerging as a star like Coach Wang had been in his younger days hadn't completely died when Coach Cobra forced me to stop competing in my best event, the longfist. Coach Wang had carefully built a strong foundation for me with steady training, and I had no choice but to trust him that my double hooks performance was also worthy of a championship. Once again, I put my faith in Coach Wang.

It didn't occur to me that the real reason Coach Wang kept me was probably because he suspected my fate would be the same as Clever Treasure's. As Coach Wang's favorite, she had received poor treatment under Coach Cobra. Her bright star had faded.

After several months of training with the boys, Coach Wang announced he had arranged for me to pair up with Clever Treasure in a straight sword fighting set. Fighting set partners had to be the same height, and my recent growth brought me to the same height as Clever

Treasure. This was an honor and meant all the extra training I received from Coach Wang had brought me to a level that nearly matched that of my role model.

Clever Treasure's specialty was the straight sword, and no one came close to matching her graceful yet vibrant movements. After training with only boys, I knew Coach Wang wanted me to glean some special qualities from her. And yet, the time I spent training with Clever Treasure awakened more than just my inner strength; it awakened my sense of self, something I had lost all those years ago. Unsheathing my tiger claws to stand up for myself no longer felt like a foreign idea. I borrowed a little of Clever Treasure's boldness and made it my own.

One day, Coach Wang surprised us with an announcement. "Some of you have been chosen to act in a martial arts movie." We all hoped our lucky day had arrived.

A well-known Hong Kong 香港 movie director had scouted at one of the competitions, looking for handsome boys and pretty girls to cast in her new martial arts movie. Inspired by Coach Wang's expertise, she asked him to choreograph. She then selected more than half our boys' team—from both the first team and the second team—and a couple of boys from other teams. Only two girls were needed, and I quivered with excitement to be chosen. Coach Wang negotiated to bring the entire boys' second team to the filming even if all of them wouldn't be acting in the movie.

Before filming began, we had to learn how to ride horses. Due to Coach Wang's naturally overprotective nature, he had prevented us from learning anything that could cause potential injuries, even swimming. Now, he relented, taking us to live at an army cavalry camp in Nanjing. Although the horses intimidated us at first, learning to ride was relatively easy. I even enjoyed those times when my horse took me racing through the fields. We bragged about how quickly we learned to ride, in less than a month. What we didn't know was that the cavalry's horses were well cared for and accustomed to being ridden.

In the movie, the horses we rode were another story. They were wild and difficult to control. One of them stepped on a coach's toe, bruising it and causing the coach to walk with a limp. It turned out Coach

Wang had reason to be cautious with us.

One day, I rode a handsome, chestnut-colored horse for the morning chase scenes. Although the horses were unpredictable, I was able to control this one until the noon lunch bell rang. Then, my horse jerked, bolting off at a gallop as quickly as people rushing toward an open bus door. Zooming at breakneck speed, I hung on tightly with my legs and hands until the horse abruptly turned toward the barn. I lost my grip, and my body flew forward, smashing to the ground. Trying to sit up, I noticed my left arm looked bent. I must have been in shock because I didn't feel any pain. My injured arm felt numb and useless, but it wasn't bleeding.

The team doctor rushed to my aid, ripping off the sleeve of my costume. "I need to take you to the hospital for an x-ray," he said and walked me to the Jeep.

Later, I watched the doctor examine the x-ray without comment. He took hold of my arm and said, "Let me look at that." The next moment he was manipulating my arm. It caused a clicking noise as well as a sharp jab of pain. I gasped, trying not to cry.

"Good," the doctor said. "You didn't break the bone. But, you've torn the tendons and ligaments at your elbow joint. We'll have to put a cast on it to keep it immobile. I'm afraid I have bad news for you. You might not be able to practice your double hooks anymore."

A flood of emotion raced through me. First, the longfist had been taken away from me. At that time, Coach Wang had consoled me by telling me my double hooks performance was also worthy of a championship. Now, I might lose the ability to perform my double hooks. I spent all those years of training without any injury whatsoever and now this. I didn't want to be forced into giving it up. I still wanted my dream.

That night, I telephoned Baba. He advised me, "Don't listen to all of it. Only listen to half. It might not be badly damaged."

I was supposed to keep the cast on for a month but after fifteen days, I panicked when I saw my shrinking muscle. I shocked the doctor by bravely demanding that he cut off the cast. I promised to hold my arm steady and protect it.

During the month my arm was healing, I didn't sleep well. As I lay on my cot, many of my thoughts were about whether or not I wanted to be a movie star. Everybody thinks they want to be a success like Jackie Chan or Jet Li, but those martial arts stars paid a physical price for their fame: broken bones, twisted knees, muscle pulls. I wanted something more.

When I appeared in front of the camera, I didn't feel comfortable. I didn't have enough confidence in myself, especially if I needed to speak with my unfeminine "left voice." I also thought movie stars should be prettier. Out of my sleepless nights emerged a decision. Becoming a movie star wasn't part of my dream.

My injury didn't jeopardize the movie because the movie took more than one year to film. Gradually, with Coach Wang's guidance, I built up the muscle in my arm and regained full usage. Thankfully, Baba had been right; the team doctor had overreacted.

Early filming of the fight scenes was shot in the countryside of Shandong Province where there were no overhead wires. In this isolated place, China pumped its oil. We were happy when the filming took us to more civilized locations because the food in the remote area wasn't good.

My overall impression of the movie business was poor. The actors spent much of their time waiting: waiting for the sun, waiting for rain, waiting for the mud to dry up, and waiting for their characters to be needed. On some days, after our hair had been styled, make-up applied, and costumes put on, they canceled the scene. "Sorry, everyone, not today." Coach Wang then rushed us to change our clothes so we could train for the remainder of the day. He could turn any spare moment into a training session.

Not all the scenes were filmed in remote locations. Many took place in Yangzhou's beautiful Slender West Lake area and the historical *Ge Yuan* Gardens 个园 with its opulent mansion.

In one nighttime scene at the gardens, the director wanted two of us girls to jump off the entry roof of a two-story building with nothing below to break our fall. We climbed up cautiously onto the roof with its curved roofline, slippery from the winter's snow and ice. When the director called out for us to jump, I balked. It looked incredibly risky.

From my lofty perch on the roof, I looked down at the expectant faces in the garden below. An eerie vision of Morning Glow standing on the towering chair over the tabletops above the Red Guards flashed across my mind. Her defiance that day brought her a lifetime of misery. Ever since then, I had avoided trouble with my passive behavior, believing it was better to give in than to incur embarrassment, disgrace, or other people's anger. This time, however, the risk of not standing up for myself seemed much higher.

I panicked. *What should I do?* I had already endured an injured arm during filming, and I certainly didn't want to damage my legs and my future over a small role in a movie. I looked around futilely for Coach Wang to help me. *Where is he?*

I glanced at the girl standing beside me, noting that she showed no signs of moving either. Then I knew I had to make my own decision. When the director instructed us once again to jump, I summoned my courage.

"No," I said as firmly as I could with my heart racing, "I won't jump."

"Well," the director responded, "we'll wait for you."

Even though I was freezing up on the roof in my light silk costume and clutching a cold metal sword, I was determined to protect my body from injury. I stood defiantly on the rooftop without moving.

"You waste everybody's time and money," the director said impatiently as she tried to reason with me.

"I don't care. I won't jump," I stubbornly declared. As soon as the words left my mouth, I noticed a well of strength open up deep inside me. It gave me newfound confidence to stand my ground.

The director, who was a smart woman, tried a new approach, "I thought you were a nice girl."

She also tried to convince the other girl on the roof with me to jump. "You jump and show us it's easy." She wouldn't jump either, which was lucky for me. I think she knew even if she did jump, she would have to do it again because the director wanted the scene with both of us jumping at the same time with our swords raised in the air.

The director balled up her fists in anger. "If you'd acted like this at the beginning of the movie, you would've been gone," she uttered in frustration.

We were near the end of filming the movie, and I knew she couldn't switch me now. I responded again uncharacteristically, "Well, I don't care."

I felt like a different person, someone I didn't recognize, although this girl was someone I wanted to be. Realistically, I knew the consequences of acting this brave during training would only lead to trouble. I could admire this daring side of myself in this situation only.

Finally, after more than an hour of cajoling, the director asked, "If we get some cardboard boxes for you to jump onto, then will you jump?"

I thought about it and then reluctantly agreed.

Although I was still scared, we jumped. The director wasn't pleased because we didn't raise our swords high enough, but she was smart enough not to ask for a retake. I was very relieved I didn't get injured.

The movie, "Yao's Young Warriors," was due to be released in 1983, and several of the boys on our team were the movie's stars. My part was non-speaking. Only four girls were in the movie, and two of us were acting as companions to the main actress. We also acted as extras in many of the scenes, donning different costumes all the time. Often we dressed as boys in headdresses wielding swords in the fighting scenes or lay on the ground for a long time pretending to be dead. Many of the scenes were filmed in the dark after midnight, which we didn't like. The metal cuffs we wore as part of our costumes scratched our wrists with each twisting motion of our swords. Waiting around for perfect conditions in which to film was barely tolerable. I had my taste of movies, and I didn't jump at the chance to do it again, although several opportunities later came my way.

As China opened its doors, foreign martial artists became interested in *wushu*. Coach Wang was the most famous *wushu* athlete of his generation in China, and it didn't take foreigners long to seek him out. After his comeback competition in 1979, a Chinese American named Anthony Chen came to train with him. In the early 1980's, Anthony Chen 陈继光 from San Francisco and another Chinese American, Roger Tong 董培德, from Los Angeles, brought groups separately to China for about a month of training. Later, martial artists from Japan and Canada also trained with our team.

Coach Wang's philosophy was, "If they want to learn, then why not?" He accepted them, even though they didn't come from a friendship country. Because of the Korean War, China was still wary of America.

About twelve foreigners came in each group and generally stayed one month. Coach Wang and everyone on our team felt honored to have them. We were amused when, after the first day of training with our team, the foreigners were so sore the next day they could hardly walk. They didn't have a comparable training background, and many of them were older than our team members.

My teammates and I liked having the Americans with us. They provided a welcome break from the years of rigorous training and enlivened our lives. Sometimes they made us laugh, like the first time we saw them wearing colorful Hawaiian shirts. We whispered to each other, "I thought only women wore clothes with flowers on them. Those shirts look like women's underpants." We didn't think they were very manly.

When foreigners trained with us, Coach Wang slacked off on our own training. Instead of repeating each jump one hundred times, it was reduced to ten times so the foreigners could keep up with us. We spent time each day teaching them forms. I taught double hooks, a beginning *taiji* form, and the longfist.

When the coach came by one day to see how the teaching was going, I commented, "The foreigners are slow. They can't remember the movements." After the coach departed, one American said to me in Chinese, "I understood that." My face turned bright red. I didn't think he knew Chinese.

The foreigners presented some problems for the team. The Chinese people weren't used to seeing Caucasians whom they called "big noses." Uncontrollable crowds quickly developed around the foreigners whenever they appeared in the streets. Chinese officials announced they didn't want the Americans roaming around freely, viewing the country's poverty and backwardness. To remedy these problems, Sunday tours were instituted. Coach Wang, one or two other team members, and I led the outings to visit temples and historical sites.

At first no athletes were allowed to mix with any foreigners at meals or during free time. After a couple of groups came and went, the rules against fraternizing relaxed. When the foreigners weren't huddled in Coach Wang's room to hear his stories translated—which was often— they spent their free time with the boys on our team. Coach Wang was careful with me and forbid me from going into town with the foreigners, despite the fact that some of them were girls. Even if I wanted to go with them, I felt Coach Cobra was waiting for me to make a mistake so he could dole out a harsh punishment.

Before the first group left, we had a farewell party. In the center of the room, the sequined surface of a spinning disco sphere reflected dazzling jets of light everywhere. In total contrast to the spirited mood the light created, dignified ballroom dance music played over the loudspeakers.

Giggling with excitement, I sat in a corner with the other girls Coach Wang used to train. The boys congregated near the table of food. No one danced. Then, I saw the team leader and the foreign department official stand up in the center of the room.

"Come on, everyone, dance. Why are you so shy?" they asked. "It's a party. Go on, dance. Show Chinese friendship with the Americans."

Coach Wang stood up, pushing all the boys onto the dance floor. We girls had never seen ballroom dancing before. Before us, the *wushu* boys paired up and began dancing with each other while holding hands and the shoulder or the waist of the other. Behind them, the Americans looked briefly stunned before bursting out in laughter. That did it. The laughing was contagious. We girls couldn't control ourselves, especially when the boys danced by, making faces at us.

The Americans' team leader motioned to his team. "You guys go on and show them how to dance."

When we saw the Americans crossing the room toward us, we girls tried to hide behind the backs of each other. Somehow, I was pushed out in front at the last minute.

A handsome Chinese American approached me. "May I dance with you?"

I shyly admitted, "I don't know how to dance."

"That's okay," he said, "I'll show you."

I stood up and tried it. After stepping on my partner's feet a few times, I was finally dancing. This was the first time a boy held my hand, and it felt special. My partner, Robin Shou, later became a movie star in Hong Kong. His most well-known movie was "Mortal Kombat."

As going-away gifts, the Americans made presents of their tee shirts to the boys on the team. They also gave us small gifts like pencils. One of the Americans named Norm Petredean brought a bouquet of fresh flowers and handed one to each girl. Flowers were rarely seen and made a special gift. We girls ran to find cups to hold our flowers.

Coach Wang received some nice wine purchased at one of the four-star hotels. He was always good about sharing his gifts, but when the boys tasted it, they grimaced. Then they got the bright idea of adding some sugar to make it taste sweeter, like Chinese wine.

Soon the foreigners learned they couldn't give us anything expensive. We had to hand over gifts like watches to the higher officials. Any gift that was too good was taken away. We never knew where these gifts ended up.

The weather conditions were difficult for the foreigners. They weren't used to training in the severe summer heat of Nanjing. One American, Kenny Perez, came back to train for the whole winter. He didn't know it would be so bitterly cold and that we wouldn't have heat. Our winters in Nanjing were much colder than in Beijing even though Nanjing was farther south. The hotel gave him two extra thick cotton blankets, but the American still wore all of his clothes to bed to keep warm. We also gave him a rubber hot water bottle. He wrapped himself in every blanket he could find and slept sitting in a ball instead of on the bed. He now lives in Arizona.

After a couple of years, the government officials decided too many groups were coming over and distracting the team. They announced Coach Wang couldn't train foreigners anymore. The foreigners could come, but they had to train with another coach. After this, the number and size of the groups dwindled.

I missed the foreigners' visits and having the monotony of training broken up while I waited impatiently for the coaches to say I was ready for serious competition. Meanwhile, Coach Cobra showed no signs he wanted to use me as a competitor. He passed me over when he selected his team for the 1982 national competition. I could only wait and believe Coach Wang when he said developing a champion took time. After all these years of training, it was becoming almost impossible to remain patient. Fortunately, another diversion came along to distract me temporarily. I found myself in the middle of an unusual situation that piqued my curiosity and transformed my outlook on China and myself.

Liu Yu (right) on Canadian roller coaster

 ## WUSHU STARS IN CANADA

The announcement came at our weekly meeting. Coach Wang's eyes sparkled as he stood before us, a sure sign he had something exciting to say. "Because of our team's reputation worldwide," he began, "we've been invited for a performance tour in Canada."

All around the room, eyes grew big and hands covered gaping mouths. Turning to the person next to me, I saw my own excitement and disbelief mirrored in her face. We laughed, bouncing in our seats. Some people clapped.

Coach Wang put up his hands for us to listen. "Only a limited number of athletes can go. They will be selected for the trip based on the number of forms they can perform."

Immediately, the excitement diminished and was replaced by uncertainty and a sense of rivalry. Once again, Coach Wang had fired up our competitive spirits. Everyone wanted the honor of being selected. If given a choice, however, I preferred staying and preparing for competition.

Besides *wushu* athletes, the acrobatic gymnastics team was invited, along with coaches, team leaders, and a government representative.

We soon learned that high government officials at the Jiangsu Sports Headquarters bumped up the number of officials going to three because being part of a foreign delegation improved the equation used to determine their retirement benefits. This was an increased hardship for the host country, as they had to provide higher-class travel and accommodations for the officials, in addition to special diets. The number of athletes chosen had to be cut to compensate.

The *wushu* program consisted of a variety of individual forms and group fighting sets. I was selected to perform six different routines.

One of my younger teammates received the news she couldn't go on the trip. Little Sparrow and I had been the first members of the second team to compete with the first team. Her trouble began when we made the movie. At age seventeen, she was discovered sneaking away from the movie set with one of our male teammates. Of course, Coach Wang and our team leader were furious. They had made it very clear romance between teammates was forbidden. When they decided which athletes would go on the Canadian trip, the girl was barred, but not the boy. Justification for this decision was that male athletes had better futures because they could compete longer. In addition, the girl came from a local opera family where she learned to be more open and flashy, always concerned with looking attractive. The officials believed the boy had been trapped by her showiness, even if it wasn't intentional on the girl's part. Little Sparrow's wings had been broken. This reinforced my determination not to make any mistakes.

Specialists were brought in to help us with our trip preparations. Although a hairstylist gave us instructions on special hair arrangements, I liked the simplicity of wearing my hair in one long braid.

Music was never used at competitions. For our performances in Canada, however, a professional symphony orchestra analyzed the rhythm and timing of each performance for several weeks. Special individual musical pieces were then developed to match each form using classical Chinese music recorded by an orchestra of twenty musicians.

I loved my double hooks music, which was based on a famous Chinese classical piece called "Moonlight on Spring Water." Practicing with this music, I felt liberated. Music had never touched me so personally before. I learned how little exposure I'd had to music and how much I enjoyed listening to it. Music became a favorite pastime, along with reading and drawing.

A famous costume designer who worked for the Beijing opera came to live with us for a short time. She designed an outfit for each routine we performed. From a myriad of choices, my teammates and I selected colors for our new silk uniforms. My straight sword group chose hot pink for our demonstration. *Taiji* performers usually wore white, and a beautiful traditional-style uniform with shoulder and side closures was created with gold and red trim. In all, five new outfits were designed for me. Instead of a sixth costume, I elected to wear my most treasured gift, something Clever Treasure gave me.

My mentor was retiring from the team soon and therefore unable to join us in Canada. One evening, she deeply touched me when she came to my dorm room holding a silken bundle.

"Liu Yu, I am giving you my favorite uniform," she said as she presented me with the gift.

I saw that it was the costume I most admired, the pale pink silk outfit with graduated color on the bottom of the pants that went from hot pink at the edge blending upward to pale pink like the sunset in a watercolor wash. It had the unique addition of a clear ballet skirt that sparkled all over. It had been made especially for Clever Treasure in her early days when she was often chosen to represent China on trips out of the country. She always looked like a princess when she wore it.

"I don't know what to say. Are you sure you want to give me this? Aren't you allowed to keep it?" I asked.

"I've thought about it and decided to pass it on to you. You tried to help me."

When Clever Treasure first faced retirement, she set her eyes on a coaching position. Most athletes thought becoming a professional team coach was the ideal job with the most prestige, yet no woman had ever been selected to be a coach or a coach's assistant. Clever Treasure decided a two-year college program would help her win the coveted placement.

Although Clever Treasure wasn't required to pass a college entrance examination before enrolling in a two-year college program, she did need some basic skills. She had joined the team at a young age, and her formal schooling was limited to finishing second grade. In addition, the educational focus for first team athletes was inferior to the schooling offered to the second team. Generally, coaches and athletes alike cared very little about education. Training required maximum concentration, and many viewed education as a waste of time.

One day Coach Wang had pulled me aside, asking me to help Clever Treasure with mathematics. Yet when I tried to teach her how to add fractions, she only got frustrated. It surprised me to learn she couldn't comprehend even the simplest mathematics at a first-grade level. At first she believed if she worked hard at it like she had worked in athletics, she could learn it. When she discovered her effort didn't help, she blurted out, "Forget this. I won't go to school. That'll just give me more wrinkles." She was such a pretty girl, but she missed out when it came to education. Even though her gold medals made her college entrance equation higher, it turned out it wasn't enough.

As Clever Treasure's retirement approached, Coach Wang and the other three coaches had the power to name the new coaching staff. Unfortunately, the three coaches often opposed Coach Wang, and it wasn't surprising that one of Coach Wang's favorite former students failed to be chosen as a coach.

Clever Treasure was upset with Coach Wang because he didn't have the power to help her stay on the team, but she understood his predicament. As a result, her talent and open heart would be underutilized in her new job at the Nanjing youth recreation center. She didn't give up, however, and eventually obtained several leaves of absence from her job to make movies, her most famous one called "The South Shaolin Master." Any income she received from making the movies went to the government in exchange for keeping her job. She also became involved in judging *wushu* competitions but never found a way to become as successful after retiring as she desired.

Draping her pink costume over my arm, Clever Treasure said, "You take it with you to Canada. It's yours now."

"Thank you. I'll treasure it," I said, noticing sadness in Clever Treasure's moon face.

Like a deflating balloon, she suddenly sat down with a whoosh on the edge of the bed. I joined her, masking my curiosity. Never one to hold anything back, she readily admitted, "I miss being a youth champion, being a special guest of President Nixon at the White House." With a sigh, she said, "I've gone backwards since then, having to train under the wing of another coach. You're lucky! You're still Coach Wang's student."

Instead of acting jealous, Clever Treasure was encouraging me. I could tell she still loved Coach Wang like a father. It made me feel sad for her.

Clever Treasure had known for a few years she didn't have a chance at accomplishing anything further. Even though she had pushed herself with an extra practice session, she learned she couldn't do it on her own. Hard work must be coupled with guidance. Coach Cobra resented Clever Treasure too much to give her any special instruction. And because she was no longer Coach Wang's student, he wasn't allowed to give her any further instruction. This hurt both of them.

While Jet Li had climbed higher after becoming the national youth champion, Clever Treasure hit the skids after sharing that championship with him. I blamed Coach Cobra. He wasn't a great teacher and didn't know how to motivate his athletes. Plus he treated White Flower with favoritism. It was hard for Clever Treasure to take.

I thought about how Clever Treasure's success affected others. To me, she was an inspiration. To Coach Cobra, she was a source of shame. In Jiangsu Province, only Coach Wang and Clever Treasure had been chosen as members of the national *wushu* team representing China on the 1974 friendship tour to the United States. Coach Cobra resented the success she achieved under another coach, and he wasn't willing to promote an athlete who had been the favorite of his rival.

Now, Clever Treasure gave the uniform on my arm a little pat, leaving me wishing I could do something for her but feeling helpless. Then, like the sunshine returning after a rainstorm, her face broke out in a contagious grin. "Don't worry about me. I will find my stage," she said before leaving the room.

Holding the costume under my chin, I allowed it to cascade down in silky waves against my body. At that moment, I felt like Clever Treasure had passed the baton to me to become the next women's champion from Jiangsu Province. At least, that's what I hoped.

For several weeks special meetings were scheduled, informing us of the rules for the trip to Canada. At each meeting, we received variations on the speech about being representatives of our country and how we must carefully act in a proper manner. The biggest rules were not talking to any strangers and never going anywhere alone. Even in the hotel, we must be accompanied by at least one other person from our group at all times.

In each city there would be Canadian hosts, but we weren't allowed to accept invitations to dine at their houses. If we passed a Chinese restaurant, we were forbidden to enter because Taiwanese probably ran it, and China wasn't on friendly terms with Taiwan. We were made to think we wouldn't be safe in Canada. A few Americans and Canadians who had trained with Coach Wang were invited to travel with us as escorts. These were the only people our government deemed worthy.

Coach Wang told us about his first trips outside the country to Czechoslovakia and Cambodia when he was a younger man. These were political trips instead of athletic events. Representatives from education, religion, sports, and culture—Chinese dancing and music—accompanied the government and military leaders. Even though the common people didn't enjoy full freedom of religion, the Chinese government showed its respect for religions by including representatives of Buddhist, Taoist, and Muslim religions along with representatives from each minority group, such as Tibetans and Mongolians.

While in Cambodia, Coach Wang performed his famous monkey staff form. Afterwards, Zhou Enlai rubbed the top of his head saying, "Keep working hard for your country." In preparation for those trips, Coach Wang had attended many meetings over a two-month period, having his brain "washed" to avoid the temptation of defection.

Preparing for our trip, we were told not to tell people we were a professional team. "Say you're just part of the youth program at the sports institute," they told us. Even though *wushu* wasn't an Olympic sport, China didn't want outsiders to know how highly structured its professional sports programs were. China modeled its government-sponsored sports programs after Russia, with one national team and each province training its own professional teams who were national team hopefuls.

When each of us received a suitcase, we immediately reacted by saying, "We don't even know what kind of clothes we should pack to wear."

Our government travel liaison then informed us, "Everyone has to wear nice clothes. You'll all be fitted for one suit with a matching vest. Each boy will receive an extra pair of slacks and each girl an extra skirt. Boys must wear ties with their suits."

Color selection for our clothing was left up to us. Without thinking, I chose dark brown for the suit and white for the skirt and vest. No one chose any bright colors for our suits because we were unaccustomed to seeing anyone wear them. On impulse, however, I bought a bright red shirt at the free market and paired it with my white skirt and vest. It became my favorite outfit on the trip and I felt fashionable each time wearing it.

Even though they measured us for the clothes, the finished products weren't shapely and looked baggy. The idea was that as we grew older, we would get wider. The jackets had built-in shoulder pads making them appear to hang from our large athletic shoulders. The youngest gymnast attending the trip was ten years old and very skinny. When she dressed up in her gray suit, she looked like she was wearing a frumpy old lady's suit. After the trip, I gave the clothes to Mama, and they fit her perfectly.

We were also given a little extra money and taken to a government store reserved only for people traveling outside the country. I used my money to purchase a necklace carved out of animal bone. This was the first piece of jewelry I ever owned.

Each person traveling received a package of make-up, even the boys who would need it for their performances. We were told to practice putting it on. I excitedly tried the bright red lipstick, black eyebrow pencil, white face powder, and powdered pink rouge. We helped each other apply fine lines and rosy cheeks. We girls looked like pretty flowers, although some girls put on too much make-up, applying black lines along their eyelashes. We all laughed, calling them panda eyes.

One evening, everyone was told to apply their make-up and attend a meeting with our team leaders so they could judge our progress. When the boys entered the room, we girls couldn't believe our eyes and erupted into uncontrollable laughter. The team leaders and coaches smiled, even though they were familiar with exaggerated Chinese opera face painting. The boys sported bright red lips, white faces with a round dot of pink on their cheeks, and very black eyebrows looking like two black silkworms hanging on their faces.

"You guys look so weird," we said, giggling.

They defended themselves by saying, "Our coach said doing this is part of our job."

Coach Wang then waved his arms and said, "Who cares what you look like. People are paying to see how good your *wushu* skills are."

Finally, our day of departure in the summer of 1983 arrived. Excitement buzzed among the athletes lucky enough to be traveling outside country to perform. While sitting in the surprisingly large airplane during takeoff, I was amazed at the sensations swirling in my stomach. With my eyes glued to the disappearing landscape, I decided I loved flying and feeling the thrill of adventure.

During our month in Canada, we visited large cities, such as

Toronto, Montreal, Vancouver, Victoria, and many smaller cities and towns, such as Yellowknife in the Northwest Territories. Everywhere, parties or banquets were given in our honor. Hosts of the local areas took us on tours to snowy mountains, alpine hot springs, or Indian history museums. The abundance of fresh flowers adorning Victoria's gardens took our breath away. We delighted in the cinematography and sound effects of the new "Star Wars" movie, even though we couldn't understand the words.

Wherever we went, we always dressed up in our fancy suits, even when we went to the amusement park. Buttoned up in our dark suits, we rode the roller coaster and other dizzying rides in the hot summer sun while the Canadians dressed in loose, comfortable clothing.

Our evening performances began with a traditional Chinese lion and dragon dance used for all celebrations. Each *wushu* boy wore a separate piece of a dragon draped over his body. When the lights were turned out, the light bulbs inside the dragon sections lit up the enormous golden dragon undulating and leaping to the rhythm of the deafening drums and cymbals. The acrobatic gymnasts wore lion dance outfits, with the youngest girl dressed as a baby lion. Spectators watched as lions playfully danced with a friendly dragon.

Instead of the anxiety we normally felt at competitions, my teammates and I experienced pride in our accomplishments and our country. The girls' routines added grace and elegance to the shows. The *wushu* boys performed a monkey king routine from a famous story. They dressed in their flowered outfits with fake rabbit trim. Their pink cheeks made them look like French puppets. Unfortunately, while they moved in monkey-like fashion, the monkey hats they wore on the tops of their heads kept slipping into their eyes, making them appear more comical than manly.

Following our demonstrations, one of my male teammates, who performed the drunken sword form routine, and I became the sought-after idols of a group of excited fans vying for our autographs. We never dreamed we would find ourselves in this position. In Canada, Chinese officials encouraged us to give autographs and take photographs with fans because these were seen as promoting friendly relations between China and Canada.

Our team leaders carefully monitored us on our trip; however, they weren't always able to watch us every moment. At one of our hotels, an athlete discovered that a special channel, paid for by a previous guest, hadn't been turned off in his room. We called it a "yellow film"—pornography. Word spread quickly, and everyone on both the *wushu* and gymnastics teams arranged to meet in that room at midnight to satisfy their curiosities. I was curious, too, but I chose to stay in my hotel room. It wasn't because I thought of myself as too pure, but if we were caught, Coach Cobra would use it as a reason to get rid of me. I couldn't take the chance.

One of my female teammates who had felt unlucky to be sharing a room with our team leader instead of a teammate approached me with disappointment clouding her features and asked, "Liu Yu, can I ask a favor of you? I heard you aren't going to watch the yellow film. Could I switch rooms with you just for tonight?" She looked sad to be left out of the special viewing.

"I don't mind," I said.

The next day, I heard everyone had crowded together in the room and watched the restricted channel. I noticed the girls acting sheepish and quiet. They told me the yellow film was worse than they expected and embarrassing to watch with the boys. I was glad I didn't go.

In a couple of cities, Coach Wang received an invitation for him and two athletes to dine at a restaurant. He asked my teammate who performed the drunken sword solo routine and me to accompany him. Of course, we had to bring our team leaders with us, also. While sitting in nice restaurants with such friendly people, I thought about how lucky I was to catch these extra glimpses of Canada and its people.

At one of the dinners, one young man of Chinese heritage asked through a translator if he could have my address. Before we left China, a pack of business cards was printed for our group, and I handed him one. Then he asked, "Could we become friends?"

I tried to make light of the situation by saying, "Oh, everybody's our friend."

It shouldn't have surprised me that after the trip the man I met at dinner wrote me a friendly letter about how much he enjoyed our performances. I wrote back to thank him and he replied again. With his third letter, he included a cassette tape a lady made for him in Mandarin Chinese because he only spoke Cantonese. She explained he wished he could talk to me and get to know me better. My roommates and I always shared our letters with each other. When they listened to the tape with me, they started teasing me. I quickly made it known I wasn't answering his letter. A couple of weeks later, I received a fat envelope from Canada. I could feel pictures in the envelope and decided it could cause me trouble. On the team, if you receive any letters from outside the country, it's the right of the team officials to investigate. Nothing can be hidden from them. Close friendships with the opposite sex were strictly prohibited. I made a point of announcing to my teammates I was sending it back unopened. I took the envelope and put it into a larger mailer and sent it back. It was the only thing I could do to avoid problems. I never heard from him again.

One of our host ladies at another dinner offered to take us to a shopping mall. Inside the large department stores, I was shocked by the amount of merchandise. She encouraged us to look around when we entered the clothing section. I lingered a little too long beside a well-made cream-colored raincoat. The lady asked me to try it on. I refused because in China when you shop, you can't touch anything, but she insisted it was just for fun. She tried to get me to select something to buy, but I declined, saying I didn't want anything. Seeing the opulence at the shopping mall with no lines and no people fighting their way through it to purchase something was amazing enough.

At the airport as we were leaving the city—now I can't remember if it was in Montreal or Vancouver—my host handed me a bag. "This is a little gift for you," she said. I tried to refuse, but she insisted I take it. When I got on the plane and opened the bag, I already knew it would be the raincoat. There was no such thing as privacy on the team, and my teammates took a look. They were surprised and jealous. I couldn't explain to the lady that I wouldn't be able to wear it in China. It was too special looking. In the early 1980's, China didn't have quality clothing, and all the coats were dark-colored and worn for function rather than style. My new raincoat simply wouldn't fit the Chinese lifestyle at that time. I didn't want to appear too fancy. If you're the one sitting on top of the fence for any reason, people will try to knock you down. I packed the raincoat away when I returned home.

The girls on my team and I carefully observed Canadian fashion and hairstyles. When one teammate envied the job of our host's hairstylist and make-up artist, she took the team member to her beauty shop. Afterward my teammate told us, "I don't want to be an athlete or a coach. I want to work in a beauty shop." That seed of desire became planted on her trip to Canada. Later, she fulfilled her dream by becoming a hairstylist in Los Angeles.

Some of the Americans who had trained with us in China joined us for parts of our tour. When they departed, they gave us small gifts. In China, all gifts given to the team were the same, but foreigners liked to give different gifts to each person. I received a box of colored pencils because everyone knew I liked to draw. Another girl received a prism to hang in the sun to make rainbows. I envied that gift.

One of the girls who had trained with us named Paula was Canadian. She handed Coach Wang a very large gift wrapped in colorful wrapping paper. My teammates and I were anxious to find out what was in such a big gift. Coach Wang said, "Okay, Liu Yu is going to open it. Maybe everyone can share it." When I opened it up, I found it was a colorful quilt. One insensitive teammate whispered quietly, "It's just a blanket. What's so special about that?"

We learned that Paula had made the quilt herself. In China, only poor people had to make quilts out of scraps. Everyone else could afford blankets. We then discovered that quilting was considered an artistic expression.

Coach Wang handled it well by saying, "Thank you. It's very nice."

Canada impressed me with its cleanliness and open space. At first, the friendliness we encountered made us feel suspicious about what the people might want in return. However, we soon learned to admire and appreciate the warmhearted people we met. I began to connect the carefree spirit of the Canadians with the freedom I witnessed, which was opposite to the oppression I felt in China. In contrast with China, the Canadians could travel, apply to colleges of their choice, select their own careers, change jobs, and even relocate to other towns if they desired. They were free to date anyone and speak up about their government. I marveled at their independence. I thought about what it would be like living in such a place and admitted to myself that I wouldn't mind it at all. I gained a new perspective on China, one that wasn't flattering.

On our way home from Canada, we stopped in Hong Kong to give demonstrations, which the CNC International Film Corporation used to promote the upcoming release of our movie. To show their appreciation for what Coach Wang and all of the actors did for the movie, they wanted to give us a gift.

They asked us, "What can we give you?" We knew if they gave us anything good, we wouldn't be allowed to keep it. The government officials felt because we were cared for by the government, any gifts we received should go to the government. Gifts were passed up the line and no one knew where they stopped.

The new thing in China was color television, so Coach Wang mentioned that as a possibility. Upon hearing that, our eyes bulged.

Before we left for Canada, each person traveling was given the equivalent of thirty Canadian dollars—a sum equal to ten times a regular person's monthly salary—to spend on the trip with the provision that it could only be spent in Hong Kong and not in Canada. When the movie directors heard that, they said they had an idea to help us. They would combine our money with their contribution and buy a Japanese-made color television for each person who helped in the movie. They reasoned that the televisions would be purchased partly with our own money and therefore weren't strictly gifts.

The team leaders and government officials traveling with us were quick to object to the plan. The movie personnel, however, refused to give up. They wined and dined the leaders and officials until finally, in a drunken haze, they agreed.

At the time, only one large electronic gift could be brought into China per person without having to pay a huge tax. Televisions, VCR's, and refrigerators were rarely sold in China.

When we returned to our province, Coach Wang told us to go directly home to our families for a visit, taking our televisions with us. "Don't even go to your rooms first," he insisted. Coach Wang was smart in not letting us go into the sports center with the televisions, but he suffered for that decision.

To the delight of my family and the disappointment of Coach Dai, Mama and Baba became the first family in Baoying to own a color television. Coach Dai's wife made it known that she and her husband should have received the television because I wouldn't have achieved professional status without Coach Dai's training. I was later embarrassed because of my social ignorance. At the time, I only wanted to make my family happy with my gift. When I was approached about it later, I said, "If I'd received two televisions, I would have given the second one to Coach Dai."

While on our trip, my teammates and I were told we could take the little soaps and shampoos from our hotel rooms. The shampoo bottles were so cute, and everything smelled so good, unlike similar items in China. We used these as gifts to give to friends and family. My parents enjoyed these, but wouldn't use them, keeping them displayed on a shelf. I also saved chocolates and my airplane snacks, bags of peanuts and packages of cheese and crackers, and only ate the perishable fruit. One girl kept her empty milk container, which she later discovered smelled up everything in her bag.

One of the male acrobats took metal forks from the airplane and set off the metal detector in the airport as we prepared to leave Canada. When his luggage was checked, they found a hotel blanket. My teammates and I felt sorry for him when we noticed his face turning red from embarrassment. In the early 1980's China was so poor that anything with a foreign label was a precious gift.

While on my trip, my raincoat made my teammates jealous. When I returned to China, I hid it so hopefully my team leader wouldn't find it.

As a result of all the flattering attention in Canada, I gained more confidence upon my return. The audiences loved the fighting set routine I performed with two young men. When I demonstrated with my double hooks in Clever Treasure's sparkling pink outfit, I enjoyed the adoration of the audience as I swayed and leapt to the music that accompanied the performance. At twenty years old, I felt like a young woman for the first time. *Maybe I'm pretty after all.* It made me all the more eager to test my competition abilities.

The only thing that stood between me and my dream was Coach Cobra. I tried to think of ways to melt his anger toward me, like playing with his young daughter, but things only got worse. More darkness was waiting to descend. Political maneuvering was about to trip up Coach Wang while I watched helplessly from the sidelines.

Canada trip group photo (Liu Yu is third from left in the front row,
Coach Wang is standing second from left, Little Spring is second from left in front)

Group *taiji* performance in Canada
(Liu Yu front left)

Liu Yu in Clever Treasure's
pink outfit in smoke-from-
burning-incense-rises-to-heaven pose

Coach Wang

LOCKED ON THE GROUND

When executives from CNC International Film Corporation in Hong Kong invited Coach Wang and the five main male actors to the film's premiere, Coach Cobra intervened, commandeering Coach Wang's spot. Coach Cobra and the boys then traveled by train to Beijing, joining the movie's director and producer, who would escort them on a flight to Hong Kong.

The director and producer were fond of Coach Wang, having developed a friendship during the filming. Coach Wang's reputation in the film industry began when he was the first person in China to choreograph a martial arts movie and train a famous movie actress, Liu Xiao Qing 刘晓庆, in her martial arts movements, tasks he also carried out for our movie. When the women saw Coach Cobra, they asked, "Where's Coach Wang?"

"Oh, he had something else to do and couldn't make it," he told them. "I'll represent him."

The two strong businesswomen looked at each other but didn't say anything. They knew how things worked in China and guessed what had happened.

The next day before the flight to Hong Kong, they told Coach Cobra the event in Hong Kong had been cancelled. A sullen Coach Cobra hauled the actors back to Nanjing.

One afternoon shortly thereafter, I left the shower area of the locker room and overheard a girl gloating over someone being lost. Chinese called it "being locked on the ground and unable to get up."

"Liu Yu," she said as I came into view, "have you heard about Coach Wang? He was told to leave his job."

The words hit me in the pit of my stomach, turning it sour.

I discovered the athletes who had gone to Canada, but who weren't in the movie, had reacted with jealousy when they didn't receive televisions, too. They complained to the other coaches and the high officials at the sports center. I suspected this wasn't the only reason.

Coach Wang had made too many enemies among the other coaches from his generation, and a competitive athletic spirit still boiled in their blood. Coach Wang incurred others' jealousy because of his fame as a young athlete, and each time he excelled or received recognition, his peers burned with envy. The spotlight often fell on him because he had been a national champion for many years and was the first person in Jiangsu Province to go outside the country—to Czechoslovakia, Cambodia, and the United States.

Coach Wang was a natural showoff, but he never tried to act superior or make anyone jealous. He simply overflowed with enthusiasm. He'd say, "I'm good at some things, but I don't try to beat people down. I do the best I can without feeling I have to apologize for my talent."

Roosters born under the wood element are hard workers and sociable. They have a gift for telling stories and appear to strut their stuff. As a rooster, Coach Wang felt he didn't have to tone down his cocky behavior. He simply tried to be the best at what he did at every moment, something I personally admired.

Coach Wang's birth fell on the last day of the year of the rooster, and he claimed the qualities of the year of the dog strongly affected him. Dogs—especially dogs born under the fire element—exhibited the traits of a born leader: charm, dynamism, adventurousness, self-assurance, faithfulness, and integrity. Unfortunately, dogs forcefully take over situations without waiting to be asked. The Chinese say playing politics is like riding a horse. If you aren't good at politics, then you fall off your horse and there's no way to get back on.

After being forced to leave the team, Coach Wang moved to Yangzhou and worked at the city sports center as a *wushu* coach, which was one position below his job as our team coach. We athletes heard the news via the grapevine.

Coach Wang never said goodbye, but it didn't surprise me. People were afraid to show sympathy for the person stepping down, fearing their enemies would believe they supported the opposition. During the Cultural Revolution, it was customary for wives and children to leave their husbands and fathers if party leaders even hinted at any disapproval. As a result, a protective Coach Wang slipped away without a word before anyone could be seen talking to him.

Coach Wang had fallen off his horse, and I was crushed hearing he was gone. His departure affected me deeply. My dream—the dream Coach Wang had carefully fashioned from my innocent and steady determination—was ripped from me, leaving an emotional scar. I didn't know how much my career could be salvaged or if I even had the energy to do so. I lived within a cloud of sadness and doubt, fearing what my life would be like under Coach Cobra's command. Not that he would hurt me physically, but I was afraid I would be further ostracized from my peers and every shred of control I had ever had over my future gone.

The first afternoon practice session after Coach Wang's departure foretold my future. Coach Cobra pointed to the end of the practice carpet and commanded, "Line up for tornado kick jumping drills."

I watched my teammates take off one by one across the carpet in spinning jumps, slapping their feet midair, and landing in seating stances with their legs curled around their bodies. With a fiery voice, Coach Cobra prodded and encouraged the whirling athletes. "Faster, faster. Good height!"

When it was my turn, I put all my energy into my highest jump and strove for excellent form, hoping to earn the coach's approval. Upon landing, I glanced in Coach Cobra's direction, only to find his back turned away from me. Demoralized, I walked to the back of the line while several teammates smirked, delighting in my predicament. Each smug look stabbed at my heart like a thrusted spear. When another unpopular athlete took off, I saw Coach Cobra deliberately ignore the jump. It was obvious which students had caved in to the team leader's pressure and had written letters against Coach Wang. They were being groomed for competition, while I was being punished. A colorless future loomed before me.

As a favored student of Coach Wang's, I was now unpopular by association. My teammates said hurtful things to me. I could feel them pulling further away, not that any deep friendship ever existed between us. Instinctively, I avoided trouble by ignoring their offensive behavior. When someone wanted to take my place in a fighting set routine, I stepped aside. When new clothing was being distributed, I let others select their sizes first. Even at the cafeteria, I allowed them to jump ahead of me in line. I thought of NaiNai who would have asked why I would fight with someone over something so inconsequential when to do so would disrupt my real goal. Fighting with teammates would only give Coach Cobra the excuse he needed to drop me. My tactic was to bend with the wind.

With Coach Wang gone, my teammates and I hoped the other four coaches and our team leader would work together to raise our team's skill level. They had always worked well together—albeit in unison against Coach Wang—but soon competition drove them to jockey for new positions of power. As their infighting grew, less attention was given to training.

The other coaches heard foreign groups sought training from Coach Wang in Yangzhou. They didn't understand Coach Wang was a magnet for the groups not only because he was famous, but also because he was recognized for his excellent coaching. It was too bad the coaches and government officials didn't realize they could make money from the foreign students who paid to train with Coach Wang. Then, as the reputation of the Jiangsu team dropped, teams from other provinces stopped coming to train with us. Life became very dull at the sports center.

The boys, however, managed to spice things up when they started imitating their movie idols. They began growing out their hair and parting it in the middle until they resembled the fashionable shaggy headed stars on the movie screen. As a result, Team Leader Chen dragged us into a meeting. She pulled on their hair. "Look at your hair. It's over a Chinese inch. That's too long. You don't look like girls. You don't look like boys. What're you boys doing?"

Week after week, we had meetings that went on and on. In the meantime, the length of the boys' hair grew to six or seven inches. Leader Chen tried her best to persuade the boys to get haircuts, but they refused. She argued, "You're professional athletes. You shouldn't have the kind of hair that straight boys wear." Straight, outspoken boys were rebellious teenagers who didn't listen to their parents and formed antisocial groups, although they weren't considered gangsters.

We girls grew very impatient with all these long meetings, sitting on our backless stools and hating the boys for being so obstinate. Finally, the boys did something about it. At the next meeting they walked in with shaved heads. We waited to see the team leader's reaction.

She looked at them and said, "First, you refuse to cut your hair. Then, you shave your heads. You did this because you don't agree with what I say. You'll be punished and we need to have several more meetings until you understand your wrong thinking." My female teammates and I groaned at the prospect of more meetings even though we knew the team leader was simply doing her job.

The truth was the coaches didn't know how to motivate the athletes and earn their respect. Even though Coach Wang had trained us hard, we respected him because his motivation was to see us become the best we could be. He put our training first, to the exclusion of the needs of his own family. He was so passionate about *wushu* and teaching it that he made *wushu* the most important thing in his life. When his daughter was born in Yangzhou, Coach Wang didn't go home right away to be with his wife and baby. This taught the team that nothing was as important as our training, especially right before a tournament.

Coach Wang had always lived with the team, unlike the other coaches. Part of the reason was because his wife held a job in a pharmacy in nearby Yangzhou. Her job was attached to the local government. It didn't match the high level jobs Coach Wang or we athletes held. Coach Wang preferred living at the camp because he loved his job and wanted nothing more than to personally coach China's next national champion.

Three levels of jobs existed in China, each with its own set of retirement benefits. The highest level included government officials, military personnel, athletes, coaches, and anyone with a national government-supported position. The middle group was called the Big Group and included local companies. It was funded by local rents paid to city governments. Within the lowest group—run by districts with no city support—were small jobs with low pay, such as Da Jie's job stringing firecrackers.

Government residency regulations were restrictive. Workers had to remain in their hometown unless their move met a government need, like joining the Army, going to college, or becoming a professional athlete, musician, or dancer. If husbands and wives worked in different cities, they could only visit each other on holidays. Children were permanently attached to the city of the parent with the lower desirable place of residence.

These residency restrictions arose in Chinese history when high officials were chosen to work for the emperor away from their hometowns. Wives weren't allowed to accompany them, so these officials supported concubines in their places of work, a tradition that changed with the new China under Chairman Mao.

My teammates and I felt sad for Coach Wang's daughter. She didn't have a daddy around when she was growing up because he was always taking care of us. To ease her sorrow, we brought her little gifts whenever we visited Yangzhou.

Because Coach Wang had worked hard for us and had given up so much to be with us, we never wanted to let him down. We wanted him to be proud of us. When the boys started smoking cigarettes, I knew they would never have done that if Coach Wang were still their coach.

Yet some of Coach Wang's students had gone against him, either in writing or orally. I think they blamed him for his inability when dealing with political pressures and enemies. Although we should have realized it, no one considered that his young age was a factor.

Even though Coach Wang had the skill and drive to train us to be champions, he couldn't give us any guarantees. My teammates witnessed the unfavorable treatment I was receiving because I had been Coach Wang's favorite student, and they feared their careers would suffer if they remained aligned with him or with me. They grabbed the opportunity to compete on the first team, but I think it made them feel guilty.

Life on the team became intolerable. Most of my teammates shunned me, and my coaches ignored me. All my hopes of becoming a *wushu* star fizzled with Coach Wang's banishment. I couldn't go home, and even my dorm room failed to be a place of solace.

One of my new roommates was trying out for the *wushu* team. This young girl had the worst possible hygiene, and I silently nicknamed her Stinky Socks. On more than one occasion I caught her putting on dirty socks for practice. One Sunday, I told her that her dirty laundry smelled up the dorm room, and she reluctantly agreed to wash her clothes. Later, at the long sinks where we washed our clothes, I laughed when I saw her. With her fingertips, she pinched the very end of a pair of underpants and gently dipped it in and out of the water. She complained that the water was too cold for her hands. In her defense, this nine-year-old girl was too young to live away from home. I tried to show her how to wash her clothes properly, but I could see she resisted learning. "Okay," I told her, "I'll wash your clothes for you." I decided to follow NaiNai's example of being kind to those in need.

My life changed dramatically after Coach Wang's departure and not just because of Stinky Socks. In daily practice, Coach Cobra continued ignoring my presence. Like Clever Treasure, I received no instruction to improve my skills. Coach Cobra's reputation in *taiji* was good, and yet he took away my best skill when he changed my specialty from longfist to *taiji* and then refused to teach me. The message was loud and clear. Coach Cobra didn't think I was worthy of his attention.

As my confidence plummeted, it was replaced by cold fear. I knew Coach Cobra hoped to trip me up and pounce on me. I had to step carefully. Showing anything less than full enthusiasm for my training would land me back in Baoying in disgrace. It took enormous self-control to fake an eagerness to train and appear unaffected by my dismal future. I dreaded attending practice where I felt phony and excluded by everyone.

Out of the six girls who had been my original teammates on the second team, only three remained. Little White Bunny left the team after becoming bulimic and suffering an emotional breakdown. Little Sparrow fell out of favor following a friendship with a male teammate and was sent home before the trip to Canada. Another, Delicate Iris, was dismissed after three years because the coaches didn't feel she had progressed rapidly enough.

Three young girls were brought in to replace those departing second team girls, including the one I called Stinky Socks. Unfortunately, they developed injuries to the tendons in their knees or Achilles' heels that prevented them from continuing on the team. Although reparable to some extent, the coaches believed they would never be as good as before. In a flash, their whole lives changed because an inexperienced coach pushed the girls too rapidly toward competition. Coach Pong didn't know how to build an early training program. Only one of the girls under his care escaped major injury.

Now, just three of us girls remained with enough experience to compete and who were healthy enough to do so. As slots opened up on the first team, Coach Cobra had no choice but to use me for competition, but it was difficult to muster the same enthusiasm I had felt under Coach

Wang's direction. Even though Coach Cobra decided to let me represent Jiangsu Province at future competitions, no announcement was ever made to indicate my promotion to the first team. The same thing happened with the rest of the second team members. We would always be known as members of the second team simply because we were part of the second group of *wushu* athletes at the camp.

Out of all of Coach Wang's students, only two of us stayed loyal to him and suffered when he left. The other person was a male teammate named Wei Wei 魏巍. He was like me in many ways, with a strong work ethic, unwavering loyalty to Coach Wang, and a disinterest in unauthorized diversions during his free time. He also came from a family with no political connections. Both he and I kept a low profile and tried to avoid drawing attention to ourselves. With dreaded certainty, we doubted we could convince Coach Cobra of our value to the team when Clever Treasure never could. We silently endured Coach Cobra's contempt.

Political connections or *guanxi* weren't something you could buy. If you had them, then you had *kaoshan*, which meant "a big mountain supported your back," making everything in life much easier. If you had a relative who was a high official, he could ask for favors on your behalf. The other party might not want to fulfill those requests but someday he might get trapped if he didn't, so he usually complied. In a country with a history of obligatory loyalty to the ruling classes and frequent political coercion, petitioning for political favors happened far too often. Unfortunately, in China, success rarely occurred without political connections. For the first time in my life, I felt the full impact of being powerless. Not even an anthill supported my back.

I missed Coach Wang and having a mentor who cared about me at the camp. I began to lose hope and even thought being sent home would be a relief, but I remained stubborn. I didn't want my family and friends viewing me as a failure. Even though inside I felt more and more like a trapped animal, during the day I wore a mask of indifference. I tried to hang on and hoped my false look of unconcern fooled Coach Cobra.

Whenever anyone on the team suffered an emotional breakdown, it was because of politics. We learned to endure the toughest training, even when we were tired and over our limit. It was the unfair rules and judgments that hurt us the most and caused mental and emotional anguish.

One of the happiest girls on our team had been Little White Bunny.

Just before our trip to Canada, she became obsessed about her appearance and began wearing white face powder and blackening her eyelashes. I suspected she secretly liked one of the *wushu* boys, but I didn't know which one. When she grew quiet and depressed after the trip, I figured she probably felt torn between following team rules and her attraction to boys.

One day, the janitor complained that one of the girls had been repeatedly vomiting in the gymnasium toilet. It wasn't difficult to guess the offender, as keeping secrets at the camp was impossible. Little White Bunny had been vomiting her food to make her muscular body appear thinner. Through hard work she had developed good body conditioning, but after her exposure to Western-style fashion she became self-conscious about her heavier body type. Soon, she couldn't stop herself from vomiting and ended up in the hospital, followed by dismissal from the team.

One evening at our weekly forum, Little White Bunny's mother barged in, disrupting our meeting. With a red face, she yelled at the team leader and coaches. "You took her for all those years and then you gave her back. Her health is ruined. She can't do anything because she's too sick to work. What should we do with her? Her life's going to be all messed up from this moment forward. It's your fault. You could've turned her out earlier."

Then, the mother turned to my teammates and me and said, "What do you think of all this? Do you realize you have no control over your lives? Why do you let the team leaders and coaches make all your decisions? They don't care about you. Why do you work hard for them? How can you put your future in the hands of these cold-blooded people?" My teammates and I were shocked and felt sad for the family.

Later, when I visited Little White Bunny, her mother looked at me with sorrowful eyes, saying, "I wish my girl was like you. You'll have a good future. Not my girl. I have to watch her every minute. She breaks things. She cries and becomes wild. She screams at me and yells ugly words. She can't control herself. She can't work. Just look at her. Her teeth are all yellow from the medication, and some of them are loose. Her skin's so wrinkled she looks like an old lady."

Within that unfortunate family, a brother had a liver problem and Little White Bunny's younger sister was disabled. The dreams of her father, who was a *wushu* coach, and of all her family were attached to Little While Bunny's success.

It broke my heart to see what had happened to her. Her mother was understandably upset. "I'll always have to take care of my girl. She can't take care of herself."

Another sad outcome happened to a former basketball athlete named Blue Spring Flower. Someone told me she got pregnant while still an athlete. The camp officials tried to send her home to her parents, but they rejected her. When her baby was born, the officials took it away with the result that she went crazy. Despite that, she received no guidance. Camp officials gave her a tiny room and a janitorial job, but she remained ostracized and neglected. No one cared about her.

My "big sisters" warned me not to get close to Blue Spring Flower because she was unpredictable. Curious, I took notice of her whenever she was around. Although she acted withdrawn, I saw no indication of instability unless people were deliberately rude to her and then she yelled at them. Men tried to take advantage of her. Occasionally, we heard her yelling late at night, "Get out of here, you stinky man." I felt sorry for her, especially when I saw how lovingly she looked at the little gymnasts, reminding her of her missing child.

One teammate was very muscular and a little heavier than the rest of us. Her childhood nickname had been Little Chubby Girl, which she took as a compliment because it meant she had more food to eat. Her real name meant Wise Beauty, which was opposite of the rude and foolhardy way she behaved. One day she suddenly snapped, and from that day forward she was a different person. Her first explosion occurred during training and was directed toward Coach Cobra. "You're not being fair," she yelled, taking us all by surprise. No one had ever shown any disrespect to a coach, and I immediately became fearful the entire team would be punished for her outburst. She continued ranting. "You give all your attention to White Flower. You never watch me. You must be sleeping with her."

White Flower was clearly Coach Cobra's favorite, but every athlete recoiled at Wise Beauty's accusation. We watched the blood in Coach Cobra's face boil. When he turned away without doling out the harsh reprimand everyone expected, we couldn't believe our eyes. She was saying what all of us were scared to say and nothing happened to her.

In the cafeteria that evening, we stared with open mouths when Wise Beauty picked up a bowl and threw it at Coach Cobra's table while screaming, "I hate you. You're a mean person." Again, Coach Cobra did nothing.

I turned to one of the older teammates with a quizzical expression. She leaned in close to me, saying, "Wise Beauty has a relative who is a high official. She's not afraid she'll be sent away because Coach Cobra has no power to get rid of her."

Coach Cobra had a weak spot. He had to bow to the wishes of his superior and endure Wise Beauty's outbursts, something he did for nearly two years.

Predictably, Wise Beauty never found happiness and had no skill for managing her life. She later married a man we called a "honey mouth" and had a child. When their marriage broke up, she went crazy. Her relative arranged a tiny room for her at the sports camp next to the public showers. She lived a lonely existence, dying within a few years.

I wished the older generation would keep their politics among themselves. We children weren't prepared to handle their mental games and flagrant favoritism.

Baba had feared I would be dismissed from the team and unable to catch up with my classmates in school. I don't think he ever worried I would have a mental breakdown because I never told him about the mental hardships I faced at the camp. I also knew my parents would never argue with my coaches or team officials on my behalf.

Powerlessness was slowly killing me. In the isolation of the night, I thrashed about in my bed, unable to escape the tears that burned my eyes. I sank deeper into an abyss of darkness and nearly surrendered to depression.

One lonely Sunday afternoon while lying on my bed in the emptiness of my dorm room, I buried my troubles in a book. Suddenly, without warning, a crash sounded next door like the breaking of a large water ewer. An angry screech followed. "I HATE EVERYONE!"

I set aside my book and listened to the sobs of the girl next door and the murmurs of a woman trying to pacify her. Outside, the gloomy quiet of a deserted campus echoed the loneliness I felt inside. The shattering of the ewer left my jangled nerves raw. Just then, a thought surfaced that had fearfully lurked in my mind. It was time to realize my dreams had been shattered beyond repair.

Lying on my bed, I stared at a photograph I had pasted on the wall at the foot of my bunk. There I was at my first national competition, my face alight with innocence and hope. In that instant, I knew I didn't want to practice on the training carpet any longer. For twelve years I had loved *wushu* with a burning passion. Now the time spent in training brought me heartache and suffering. I was afraid to make any kind of mistake that would be ridiculed. Girls were out of control, throwing weapons and acting crazy. Coach Cobra didn't know how to guide them. He simply waved his arm in disgust, saying, "That girl's crazy."

I closed my eyes to my empty room. Ten years on the team—half of my life—stretched out behind me. I had survived those years of intense discipline with only Coach Wang's inspiration and faith in myself to pull me through. With my dream destroyed, all that remained was loneliness.

I worried if I stayed on the team any longer, I would go crazy. My reputation was being smeared and I felt powerless to stop it. It bothered me that people could make up things about me and spread them just like during Cultural Revolution. I cared too much about being treated with respect. By acting honorably, I always thought I could hold my head up and avoid trouble.

Tears now threatened my eyes while dueling desires for survival and integrity battled it out in my mind. I knew, however, that staying with the team and playing the game Coach Cobra's way by denouncing Coach Wang was too distasteful. I discovered I had a limit to how low I could go before I might break.

What saved me from drowning in despair was recalling the hardships my family had suffered. Not only did they endure problems much worse than my own, they didn't let it eat away at their determination to survive. I thought about Mama's prison-like job that kept her from being with her loved ones. I thought about NaiNai's endless chores performed with her aching, deformed feet, and yet she never complained. My family had pulled together during the famine and endured near starvation, and even then NaiNai had shared our food with my uncle's family. My family wouldn't understand if I gave up. Slowly, I derived a small measure of comfort from following their example.

Holding onto my remaining shred of self-respect, I refused to allow myself to go crazy just to escape the team and the daily torment I faced. Something inside me wouldn't give up. A spark of hope still burned in some small corner of my being. The only acceptable outcome was to keep my self-respect and give up my dream. Now, I just had to figure out if anything was within my control or whether I was doomed to be at Coach Cobra's mercy forever.

What new dream could I fashion? I had lived my life by always succumbing meekly and playing it safe. To find a new dream meant to risk everything, including my enviable status as a professional athlete and my family's dignity, to honor myself and grow as a person. It was easy for coaches to kick out athletes, but athletes were owned by the government and not allowed to leave of their own will. That's why some of my teammates had gone crazy. I didn't want to go crazy just to get a ticket out of the team. The question I faced was where could I go? Could I find the courage to rise up against China's cultural tide and discover a way to leave the team with my self-respect intact? And, would my courage take me where I wanted to go? All I had were questions with no one to confide in or to receive guidance from.

While stretched out on my bed listening to the cries of an athlete who refused to be comforted, I dreamt of escape. Remembering the freedom the Canadians used to forge their lives, I longed to find some way to gain control over my destiny even though I knew total freedom to be impossible in China. Methodically, I began weighing my options.

My position as a team member guaranteed me a lifelong job. In China, this was called *tiefanwan,* which meant "having an iron bowl that would never be empty." The government job could be as prestigious as a team coach or as inconsequential as selling tickets at a recreation center. With my personality, I had no aspirations to become a coach who must act tough with her students, and a menial job was distasteful. Another option was going to a small city in China, establishing a recreation center and offering classes to the community. Athletes, however, had no choice over where they were sent. Consequently, it sounded like a dead end to me with the possibility of being stuck in an undesirable place. A select few pursued roles in movies. I had already tried acting and knew that wasn't for me.

College was another choice, but only good students were approved. Various universities had recently developed a special two-year program they offered to professional athletes, which was considerably less rigorous than their usual curriculum. If team members completed two years of college, they still retained their benefits and received guaranteed jobs upon graduation that were better than most, but they also remained under the control of the team.

The youngest girl on the first team was Coach Cobra's favorite student. White Flower was almost two years older than me and had been with the team three years longer. She and I were often competitors because our close ages put us in the same category at competitions. White Flower didn't go out of her way to be friendly with me, and she worked hard to make sure nobody could surpass her in competitions. Looking back on my earlier competitions, I realized Coach Wang had measured me against White Flower. He desperately wanted me to outperform Coach Cobra's favorite.

Instead of joining the team on our trip to Canada—much to my relief—Coach Cobra took White Flower with him to Japan and Mexico to teach. When White Flower retired from the team, Coach Cobra arranged for her to become the first athlete from the team to gain a distinguished referral for a two-year college athletic program at the Nanjing Physical Education Institute. Coach Cobra provided many special benefits for her while she attended college, including full salary and an arrangement for her to continue eating in the athletes' cafeteria even though it was against the sports center rules.

After college, White Flower joined the coaching staff, but after two years she left the job when she married. She decided coaching was too hard and switched to a job at the Jiangsu Wushu Research Institute so she could have a family and raise a child.

Each province supported a Wushu Research Institute, and the easy jobs consisted mainly of reading newspapers. This institute attracted many team retirees who had enough of hard work. Although coaching was a desirable position, not everyone wanted to continue getting up early with the team and spend energy pushing athletes to perform.

Another first team member was so burned out from *wushu* training that she vowed she would never perform *wushu* again in her life. Uninterested in maintaining any link with the team, she used her family's connections to obtain an invitation offered to professional athletes to attend the two-year program at the Beijing University of Physical Education.

This first team athlete always hated her name, which meant Little Spring. Every time she made a mistake in practice, she complained, "My brain doesn't work. It's my parents' fault. They gave me the wrong name growing up. I don't know why they gave me that name. Little, little. I was never little. They should have given that name to my younger sister. Instead, they gave her the name Jade Spring. I like that name better." We suppressed smiles when Little Spring let loose with a tirade.

I remembered the secret dream I cherished as a young child. I dreamt about becoming a teacher, which would mean a better job and choice of locations. Teachers, however, were required to complete four years of college.

Because I knew instinctively I needed to escape the control of the team and had no family connections to rely on, two years of college wasn't a consideration for me. It occurred to me no one I knew had tried for a four-year college program. All team benefits, including a lifelong job, ended with the four-year program and no one wanted to lose those except Little Spring. I felt, however, it was worth the price of my freedom. I wanted to sever all ties to the team, and I didn't want anyone to tell me where I could go to school or what job I would have when I graduated.

At that moment, I remembered the old fortuneteller's prophesy. My destiny was to receive a college education. The deep longing I'd suppressed for so many years abruptly spiraled to the surface with the intensity of a tightly wound coil. I realized my only desirable option was applying for a four-year college degree.

Qualifying for a four-year degree program meant passing the national college entrance exam like any other high school student in China. I worried the quality of my education on the team wasn't equal to that of a regular high school and the entrance exam would prove to be too difficult. I decided, however, I would worry about that later. First, I needed Coach Cobra's permission to take the entrance test, but I didn't know what it would take to get it.

Liu Yu

Liu Yu

Liu Yu competing at Yinchuan tournament

 ## PLANNING AN ESCAPE

Instead of making disloyal comments about Coach Wang, as many of my teammates had done, I tried other tactics to win Coach Cobra's acceptance. When being friendly, showing an eagerness to train, and graciously accepting Coach Cobra's decrees without argument didn't work, I resorted to the typical Chinese method of acquiring favor. On several occasions I brought Coach Cobra and his wife gifts. However, their feelings for me didn't change, and now it seemed insufferable living with the team any longer.

When I finally approached Coach Cobra about retiring from the team and attending college, he adamantly responded, "You don't need college. Besides, the team needs you right now." He then turned abruptly away, ending the discussion. I expected this, but I refused to give up easily.

Over the next couple of months I gathered up my courage to talk with Coach Cobra again. One evening, I arrived at his apartment outside the athletes' living area. He reluctantly let me in, offering me a seat at the dining table next to his wife. I had already decided I wouldn't get anywhere unless I tried starting with a different, less direct tactic.

Back straight and hands clasped in my lap, I summoned my courage and asked, "Coach Yin, I would like to know if you think I am satisfactorily contributing to the team and following all of its rules?"

He nodded his head slightly, peering at me suspiciously.

I continued. "I know you and Coach Wang didn't get along well, but I hope you don't think any of that was my fault."

Although my heart throbbed rapidly, I forced myself to appear calm. Upon hearing my words, his expression softened slightly. "No," he admitted, "you haven't done anything wrong."

I swallowed hard. "I would also like to ask you to reconsider my request for college."

Now the softness disappeared. "My mind hasn't changed on that matter. I want you to stay. Soon I will need you to compete with the team."

Even the prospect of future competition didn't dim the strong desire I now had to leave the team for good. Very gently I said, "I can't stay and compete with the team forever. I need to think about my future."

Coach Cobra glanced at his wife through his black-rimmed glasses, not in a nervous way, but to allow him a moment to prepare his words. "Stay two more years with the team and then you can go to the two-year college here in the city."

I anticipated this. "My dream is to go to a four-year college and get a degree in physical education. I would like to go to Shanghai."

Only five collegiate *wushu* teams could compete against professional teams at national competitions. By attending Shanghai, I could combine my desire for higher education with the ability to continue competing, fulfilling a lingering desire to explore my potential. However, Coach Cobra might view my possible future success with trepidation and try to disrupt my plans.

"No," he disagreed, "I can't give you permission to go to Shanghai by myself. I need to let the team leader and high officials know. We'll need to hold a meeting to discuss it."

When someone said they had to discuss a matter with others, it either meant a long wait or was just an excuse for saying no. Nevertheless, I decided it would be wise to drop the matter at this time, but I wasn't going to back down. I was, after all, molded to be a champion. Dropping a sword during a performance didn't interfere with my next routine so why should I let this stop me? I would continue to ask for permission to take the admission test required to enter a four-year college.

Two months later, I surprised Coach Cobra when I competed at the national competition held in Shandong Province's capital city of Jinan 济南. My *taiji* performance won sixth place, surprising me, too.

The quality of the *taiji* instruction for professional athletes was mediocre because *taiji* didn't carry the prestige of *wushu*. Five out of six members of each team vied with each other to be the best at longfist where they could showcase their athleticism. The sixth member competed in *taiji* to fulfill a national requirement that *taiji* be kept alive in the minds of the people. *Taiji*'s popularity remained low because the slow movements weren't as exciting as the more dynamic *wushu*. When I won sixth place, it didn't carry the same weight in the coach's mind as a comparable win in *wushu*, but it boosted the team's overall score.

I hoped Coach Cobra would see me as more of an asset to the team, but he seemed threatened by my win. Shortly after the Jinan competition, I took the opportunity to repeat my request for permission to take the college entrance exam, adding, "Let me try. I'll work hard to prepare for the next national competition. I just want the chance to take the test."

My offer to put my best competitive foot forward was made to help him save face in the negotiation. Of course, I was supposed to do my best at all competitions, but I knew he needed me to compete and do well because two first team girls were new and didn't have enough competition experience.

"I want you to stay until the younger girls get stronger. You should serve the team a little bit longer," he said.

In my mind I was already gone, but I decided to show some modesty by saying, "I don't even think I'll be accepted at Shanghai. How about letting me take the exam? If you let me try, then I'll have a sense of the exam's difficulty. It's been a long time since I went to a regular school. I don't even know if I can pass the exam."

Coach Cobra's eyes squinted behind his glasses, which I took as a bad sign. With my breath caught in my lungs, I braced myself.

"So, you want to go to college. That means you want to leave the team when the team needs you to compete." He paused briefly and then said, "Okay, you can take the exam in six months. But if you don't pass the test, you lose your place on the team and you'll be sent back to your hometown. Don't think I'm being difficult. This is your choice, your responsibility. If you don't make it, it's not because of me."

I saw what he was doing, making the penalty severe enough that I would think twice and relent. He assumed no one would throw away a secure future and take such a big risk. As a shy girl who had received minimal schooling at the sports camp and had no political connections whatsoever, I no doubt appeared to be an unlikely candidate to pass the college entrance examination and gain admittance to college. However, I was so disenchanted with my life on the team that I vowed to leave at any cost. *He expects me to fail,* I thought, *but I'll show him I can do it.*

I simply nodded to Coach Cobra that I understood and walked away. He could have been ugly and refused me once again, but my persistence and caution had paid off. Coach Cobra underestimated me, though. Armed with permission to take the exam, I celebrated being one step closer to my goal.

The exam was scheduled for the week following the national competition. With triple workouts for several months prior to the competition, there wasn't much time left for studying. Secretly, I hired a tutor with my own money and began the formidable task of cramming everything in my head I thought I needed to know. If Coach Cobra didn't think I could pass the exam, then he didn't know me very well. "Choose your goal and accomplish that one thing, and then everything else will be easy." These were the words Coach Wang always told us.

For the next few months I focused on passing the entrance exam. I repeated to myself, "I can do it. I know I can." After passing the exam, I would worry about obtaining permission to attend the college in Shanghai.

☯

Our team accepted a demonstration invitation, traveling to Japan in springtime at its loveliest. We almost didn't go because team officials worried about whether the trip would negatively affect us at the national tournament coming up several weeks later.

Knowing the Japanese were more cultured and fashion-conscious than the Chinese, I slipped my fancy Canadian raincoat into my luggage for the trip. I wanted to wear it once, and I found my opportunity during an afternoon of sightseeing. My heart and feet felt light as I enjoyed the decadence of dressing stylishly instead of in my usual dowdy clothing.

While in Japan, we encountered budding trees, serene temples, busy city streets, and screaming girls. The Japanese girls acted like crazed fans, following the boys on our team everywhere. Perhaps they had seen our movie, but I heard it was because they practiced *wushu* and thought the boys on our team were handsome.

At restaurants—where I was one of the few Chinese to enjoy eating Japanese food—the girls came in soon after us, seating themselves at nearby tables. They giggled endlessly and shrieked whenever one of the boys looked their way. We never thought Japanese girls would behave in such a frenzied manner. In my mind, I had pictured them as traditional Japanese ladies. The boys seem flattered, of course, to have such ardent admirers and whispered to each other about the attributes of each girl. In comparison, we Chinese girls appeared demure.

The adoration the boys received made me scrutinize their appearances. I had lived with them for over ten years, but this was the first time I really thought about how handsome they were. The boys didn't consider my female teammates and me special. Growing up in that environment, I never thought of myself as pretty until I went to Canada.

Whether the boys tried to sneak around and go out with the girls, I never knew, but one Japanese girl later married one of the boys on our team. She made several visits to Nanjing after our trip to Japan, and the boy spent some time in Japan as part of a teaching exchange program. Being the most cautious girl on our team, however, meant I was always the last one to learn what was going on.

Although I knew my teammates were thinking about relationships, I blocked the idea from my mind. I never gave anyone who approached me a chance because I was too afraid of being dismissed for violating team rules.

Once when I got sick with the flu, one of my male teammates had brought me some sugar. Sugar was precious and many of my teammates saved their sugar rationing tickets for their families. I immediately became suspicious. "Why did you bring me that? I don't want it. Take it back," I said rudely.

Although I was sorry to embarrass him, I didn't want any trouble to start. The girls were always the first ones to be punished. Several wayward girls thought they were smart enough to avoid trouble, but eventually they got caught.

A female gymnast became involved with an athlete who had just been promoted to substitute coach. When she got pregnant, they didn't do anything to the man, but the girl's parents were asked to take her home.

I found if I spoke clearly and directly about my disinterest, nobody would bother me. My teammates accused me of being too straight-laced like Coach Wang.

The 1985 competition was held in Yinchuan 银川, Ningxia 宁夏省 Province, in the northwest part of China. Instead of being held during the usual competition week in the fall—a time when the weather in the northwest would be bitterly cold—the competition was changed to the summer. Traveling for three days by train to and from the predominantly Moslem region bordering Mongolia was tiring and I tried to eke out every moment possible for studying. Despite enduring travel fatigue, I experienced a performance breakthrough at the competition.

At earlier competitions when Coach Wang was still training me, he expected me never to make a mistake, increasing the pressure I felt to please him. I remembered one day while on the performance carpet, my mind suddenly went blank in the middle of my *bagua* form. I panicked but was smart enough to keep walking with my *bagua* step until I recalled my routine. Fortunately, my form wasn't a standard form with a ritualized sequence of movements. At the end of the form, I glanced at Coach Wang. He didn't look upset, so I thought he hadn't noticed my error. I decided I wouldn't tell him what had happened.

The pressure to be perfect wasn't there in 1985. For the first time as a team member, I was more relaxed during our competitions. My teammates and I didn't feel our usual competition anxiety, and I knew it was because we lacked respect for our coaches. When I finished my competition performances, I was surprised by how much I enjoyed myself. This was a remarkable discovery for me, and it made me more eager to continue competing while attending college.

The competition level for *taiji* was much higher than during the previous year. Team coaches had finally realized a gold medal in *taiji* was still a gold medal. They began inviting *taiji* masters to teach at their camps.

Prior to the competition, Coach Cobra brought in an old *taiji* master who gave instruction to all the athletes, even the ones who didn't compete in *taiji*. Unfortunately, we didn't take it seriously. Every time the master advised us to "slow down, slow down" in his soft, drawn-out voice, we giggled. Behind his back we mimicked him. We thought *taiji* was just a slowed-down version of *wushu*. I should have used that opportunity to try to comprehend how different *taiji* was as a martial art from, but I felt too jaded to care anymore.

Later, I realized Coach Cobra had helped the deprived master by giving him a temporary job with a salary. Coach Cobra could see the old master was very good, but we were just too young to appreciate it. Our behavior should have embarrassed us. I could have benefited from that instruction and earned better placement at the competition.

At the end of the competition week, I approached one of the judges who worked as a *wushu* professor at the Shanghai Physical Education Institute. After we talked for a short while, I dared to tell him, "I'm taking the national college entrance exam next week. If I pass, is there any possibility I could go to your school?"

He quickly responded, "Why not? It would be good for our school team to have someone from the professional team."

Although there was no guarantee I would be accepted, I was pleased to have made this connection, while at the same time fear quickly overwhelmed me. My exam was only a week away. On the long train ride home, I used every possible minute cramming in last-minute information while hoping I wasn't forgetting some important category of knowledge. I tried not to dwell on the thought that passing this exam was my only acceptable chance to escape.

The boys and girls on my team parted company in Beijing. The boys headed north for a sightseeing tour, and the three of us girls who had competed caught the train back to Nanjing.

When I took my seat on the train with my two teammates, I was surprised to see one of the Americans who had traveled to watch the competition take a seat a short distance away. He smiled and waved at us, and I immediately became concerned he was trying to get my attention.

The name of the dark-haired American was Norm Petredean. He had trained with Coach Wang in the summers of 1982 and 1984 and accompanied the team on our 1983 Canadian tour. Just before this 1985 competition, I received a note from him translated by a high school English teacher who spoke Mandarin Chinese. The note said he heard I was planning to leave the team. He asked to see me after I got to college, so he could get to know me better. I immediately sought out my friend on the chess team who had a reputation for being a smart lady. I explained about the note. "He wants to get to know me better. What do I do?" I asked.

"Well, what do you want to happen?" she asked.

"I just want to go to college. I'm not interested in dating anybody and especially not a foreigner," I admitted.

"Then you have to make it clear to him you aren't interested," she said. "I'll help you write a letter back."

When I saw him on the train, I suspected he searched me out after receiving my response. Traditionally in China, girls remained segregated from males as much as possible to protect them. In addition, I always took the greatest care to avoid situations Coach Cobra could twist around and use to criticize me, and this included talking to foreigners visiting our team. Although we had spent a lot of time in close proximity, it had always been under the supervision of Coach Wang. We never had a private conversation, even when I'd taught him a *taiji* form, because he couldn't converse in Chinese. However, I had noticed him staring at me on several occasions. Fearful of what my coaches would say if they knew, I nonchalantly ignored his gazes.

At one point during the long journey, my two teammates left me sitting alone. Norm took the opportunity to approach me. After exchanging greetings, he asked bluntly in Chinese—the words coming out like he had memorized them—about the possibility of our getting married. I learned later that he had admired me the entire time we were training together and had tried on several occasions to approach me, but the coaches had stood in his way. He knew the only way he would ever be allowed to see me was if he made his intentions clear. After watching me and getting to know me from the way I handled myself—the sweetness and integrity he said he saw in me—he had decided to take the risk, no matter how implausible it might seem to me or to anyone hearing his tale.

But at that moment, I blushed and a smile escaped my lips. His proposal took me by surprise as did his ability to speak in broken Chinese. While some girls might jump at the chance to leave China as the bride of an American, I was facing the prospect of attending college. That was the freedom I longed for and I didn't want anything to stand in my way. Although I didn't know how to handle the situation and whether to take him seriously or not, my usual knee-jerk reaction kicked in. I responded by saying, "I haven't thought about it."

He smiled before saying, "Can you…think about it now?"

I squirmed in embarrassment because everyone in the train car seemed to be staring at us. To make my feelings clear, I told him, "I want to focus on college."

"You…should go to college," he hesitated, no doubt translating the language in his mind, "and I'll visit you there."

Before I could disagree, our conversation ended with the return of my roommates. For several minutes I sat wondering if all Americans were so direct and knew what they wanted. Having lived such a sheltered life, I certainly didn't know what I wanted and felt emotionally closer to fifteen than to my twenty-four years. Instead of puzzling any further over what just happened, I picked up my study notes. My exam was only a week away and I needed to be prepared. Still, I couldn't help but wonder what such a relationship would be like.

Liu Yu with her double hooks

24   *A CHANCE ENCOUNTER*

The process of selecting high school students for colleges was intended to be made anonymously by each college's recruiter. College recruiters weren't supposed to meet students before they selected them. Instead, selections were to be made from each province's list of students who passed the college entrance exam. Recruiters, however, didn't always follow the rules.

In addition, high school students weren't supposed to chose their own college. In fact, they didn't complete an application for college until after the college entrance examination had been graded and they had received notice that a college had already selected them. The problem with this system was that it gave almost all the control to the schools and its representatives. Sometimes, this allowed for untraceable favors and bribes. Fortunately, not all recruiters made deals under the table; at least that was my experience.

The week before the scheduled exam, recruiters from various colleges were staying at the sports center's rooming house. The *wushu* professor at the Shanghai Physical Education Institute 上海体育学院 had passed my name on to the college's recruiter, who then sought me out.

He confirmed my desire to attend college in Shanghai and relayed that his school was interested in me. His friendliness impressed me.

At breakfast a couple of mornings later, a coincidental meeting unveiled a new option for me to consider. As sunlight and fresh air streamed in through the open window near our table, I casually began talking with a businessman seated at my table. He explained he was from Beijing, and our conversation centered on the city he was visiting followed by questions he asked about my team and me. "How many *wushu* athletes are training here? How many years have you been on the team?"

I rarely had the opportunity to talk with someone I didn't know. Instead of feeling uncomfortable with a stranger, the conversation was relaxing. Conversing with this older, thin-haired man with his gentle voice reminded me of Baba talking to his patients. To soothe his nervous patients, Baba calmly asked them about their families until they forgot about their immediate problems. Occasionally, I accompanied Baba to the hospital and was allowed to sit nearby while Baba met with patients. He always had a long line of patients who waited for him. Baba tried to encourage them to seek treatment from Dr. Yu because he was better educated and held a higher position in their department, but the country patients preferred waiting for Baba rather than seeing his conceited boss. When Baba talked to his patients, they knew they could trust him.

"What are your plans after you retire from the team?" the man asked with a kind voice as he sipped from his teacup.

I explained I was about to take the college entrance exam and wanted to attend the sports college in Shanghai. He then revealed the purpose of his visit.

"I'm actually in town to talk to athletes who might be interested in attending college in Beijing," he said, explaining that he was a volleyball coach who was interested in athletes of all different types of sports.

I inquired, "Oh, which college do you represent?"

"I'm a recruiter for the Beijing University of Physical Education 北京体育大学, which used to be known as the Beijing Sports Institute 北京体育学院. As you probably know, we're one of only two universities in China with a separate *wushu* department. Most schools have a combined sports department, usually gymnastics and *wushu*. This is how the program is structured in Shanghai. We believe we have the best instructors and are able to recruit top athletes from the professional teams to become members of our collegiate *wushu* team. Our team does extremely well in the national collegiate *wushu* competitions," he explained.

"Your *wushu* team also competes in the nationals against the professional teams," I added.

"Yes, only five colleges can compete against the professional teams at the national competitions."

I reached for the teapot and refilled his cup while he asked, "What are your reasons for wanting to go to Shanghai?"

"My coach would like me to go to a two-year college and stay close by. I want a four-year degree, so I chose Shanghai as the closest one."

"Do you think there's another way, a better school?" he inquired with a sweet smile crinkling his eyes. When I looked back at him with a puzzled expression, he continued. "How would you feel about going to school in Beijing?"

"Well," I admitted, "it's far away and I don't have any connections. I thought the Beijing University of Physical Education would be very hard to get into."

"That's true, but there's a chance. We'll be asking one, maybe two, people from each professional team. We can take only nine students from all over China this year for the *wushu* department. What I look for is a top athlete with academic ability, as shown by passing the entrance exam, and one which—how shall I say it—doesn't have his head in the clouds," he said as he waved his hand over his head. "Some of the professional team members have such big egos they aren't interested in talking to ordinary people. We don't want someone like this. But we've been talking here for half an hour, and I'm very impressed with you. You're down-to-earth and have a friendly personality. I would like you to think about coming to Beijing."

I blushed at the compliment. "I don't think I can convince my coach to let me go," I informed him.

He waved his hand aside. "Just don't tell him about it now."

"Also, the Shanghai school already expects me to apply there," I admitted.

"That shouldn't be a problem," he said. "I can talk to the recruiter at Shanghai. We often set up student exchanges between the two schools."

Instinctively, I trusted this man whose personality was the opposite of the aggressive coaches I was used to dealing with. I was confident he wasn't playing games with me. "Well," I replied, "I'll certainly think about it."

He smiled and said, "I'll be in touch with you. Good luck on the exam."

I thanked him and told him I enjoyed talking with him. My steps out of the cafeteria were lighter than usual as intriguing thoughts of Beijing buzzed in my head.

The college entrance examination tested us in five categories: mathematics, Chinese language, physics, chemistry, and politics. Questions on Communism and its history made up the politics section and required a lot of memorization. A regular high school prepared their students for that part of the exam. Our team school introduced us to all these subjects, but because not many students were interested in learning, we didn't progress very far. Over fifty percent of the material I had to learn on my own.

After taking the lengthy exam, I kept a low profile. If anyone asked me about it, I told them I probably didn't pass. This wasn't true, however, because I actually thought I did well enough to pass. Fearing my eyes would give me away and not wanting to arouse suspicion, I consciously avoided happy thoughts when I was around anyone else. When alone, smiles and positive thoughts reigned free. Uncertainty still existed, but I clung to my hope because the alternative was too dark to face.

Ten days after taking the exam, the loudspeaker at the dorm blared out, "Liu Yu, you have a telephone call. Please come to the front."

Lucky for me I was in my dorm room at the time and heard the page. I raced to the lobby, picking up the phone with a shaky hand. "Hello, this is Liu Yu."

"This is the recruiter for the Beijing University of Physical Education. I have just received the list of students who passed the college entrance exam, and your name is on it. Congratulations."

"It is? Great!" I covered my mouth with my hand before I broke out in a big smile. My policy was to avoid arousing suspicion and having to answer unwanted questions. Glancing around the lobby, I determined no one had been watching me.

"I'm not supposed to be calling students. All the recruiters are meeting together to select students for their schools. A couple of us snuck out, and we came across the street to use the public telephone. I hope you've been thinking hard about coming to school in Beijing because we have a place for you here."

For weeks I thought about nothing else. It was an incredible opportunity. Shanghai was a good school, but Beijing was better with famous professors. I thought living in the capital city would be exciting. My strongest motivation to go to Beijing, however, was severing my ties with the team and putting as much distance as possible between us.

"Yes," I admitted, "I've been thinking a lot about Beijing. However, I'm concerned the school in Shanghai is holding a place for me. It'll make me feel uncomfortable to back out on them when I'd already made the connection and asked to go there."

"Well," he confessed, "my roommate here just happens to be the recruiter for Shanghai, and we were talking about you. He's right here. I'll put him on the line."

"Okay," I said with increased trepidation.

"Hello, this is the recruiter for the Shanghai Physical Education Institute. Congratulations on passing the exam."

"Thank you."

"You're very popular. Both universities in Beijing and Shanghai would like to have you as a student. Do you know where you would like to go? We'd like you to have the final say. It could go either way."

"Well, I'm not one hundred percent sure. I feel some obligation to you because I contacted you first," I said truthfully.

"Don't feel guilty. If I were you—and this would be my personal choice, of course—I would choose Beijing," he admitted.

Suddenly, I felt ten pounds lighter, as though a weight had been lifted from my shoulders. He was so nice to say this. In a single moment, I knew what I wanted to do. "Okay, I'll go to Beijing."

"Good. Don't worry about your decision. It's a good one."

When the Beijing recruiter came back on the line and I told him I wanted to go to Beijing, he said, "Well, you got it."

I was overjoyed. "Wonderful. *Xie xie*. Thank you very much."

He cautioned me before we ended the call, "Don't tell anyone yet until you receive the official letter in the mail. I'll see you in Beijing."

Of course I was ecstatic, but I cautioned myself to wait, to make sure nothing went wrong. When the official letter finally came in the mail, I raced across the campus, showing it to Coach Cobra right away. Official test results still hadn't been released yet, so he knew nothing.

The words coming out of mouth tasted so sweet. "Coach Cobra, I've passed the college entrance exam and here is my letter of acceptance into the Beijing University of Physical Education."

When I saw Coach Cobra's shocked reaction, I knew he had not only expected me to fail, but had never dreamed I would gain placement at such a prestigious university…and all without his help. I wouldn't have to owe Coach Cobra any favors.

With my letter clutched safely in my hand, I ran back to my dorm and began packing my belongings. I would leave on the first bus in the morning to avoid wasting any more time on the team.

That evening, Coach Cobra arranged a special meeting and announced my departure. He gave a little speech and presented me with a blue notebook and a pen. This was quite an honor because to my knowledge no one had ever been given a farewell tribute. I wasn't flattered, however, because I knew Coach Cobra hadn't changed his mind about me in just a couple of hours. He knew after college there was a possibility I could come back one day and be his boss.

After piling all my belongings into a pedicab for the ride to the bus station, I glanced back briefly at the university where we trained. I wasn't the same girl who began life on the team with such high hopes. Yet, for the second time in my life, I felt like a Chinese princess, a warrior princess.

I had survived eleven years of grueling training, but I knew I didn't regret them even though things didn't work out as I had hoped. The biggest benefit was that I escaped a hard life of retraining in some faraway province. Also, my health had improved as a result of the generous quantity of high quality food available to me at the sports camp.

Yet, a few fears lurked in the back of my mind. Would I fit in with the other students when I was twenty-two and they were nineteen? Would my lack of formal education hinder me in keeping up with my peers? And what about boys and dating? I still had so much to learn, but I was eager to begin.

As the pedicab rounded a busy corner, we passed an old woman walking on the street with her granddaughter. I thought about my beloved

NaiNai, who had taught me never to give up and to find dignity in being respectful and friendly. With a pain in my heart, I recognized how much I missed her and how grateful I was for her guidance. And I was thankful to have this new beginning.

On my way to my hometown, I stopped in Yangzhou to see Coach Wang and share my news. He was genuinely happy for me. Neither of us spoke about his new job. Instead, I shared the news about the team. Even though he never said this in words, I knew he worried about the futures of his former students. Now, I was one less worry.

I purposely hadn't told my parents about my plans to leave the team because I didn't want them to fret over my future. I wanted to choose my own college without their input. It was much easier to tell them what had already been decided. I reasoned they had relinquished their power over me the day I left Baoying. In this way, I was more modern than most Chinese girls, but I had been independent of my family for a long time. When I arrived in the evening at my parents' apartment, I had far too many bags to pretend this was an ordinary visit.

"What's all this?" Mama said to me as Baba appeared in the entry room doorway. His eyes took in all the bundles on the floor.

"I passed my college entrance exam and have been accepted to begin college at the Beijing University of Physical Education," I told them.

"Beijing!" they both repeated in astonishment.

Mama showed immediate concern. "You'll have a much harder life up north in Beijing. They don't get all the good vegetables and fresh-water fish, and they don't get enough rice there."

"Mama," I said calmly, "I don't care about vegetables. I want to study *wushu* with the best teachers and be part of a top collegiate team. Besides, things are better in Beijing now. There aren't any shortages."

Baba stared for a moment and then said, "This is a surprise, but it's good news. Why didn't I hear anything about this before today?"

"I didn't want to worry you," I answered.

"You're an independent girl, and I mean that in a good way," Baba said. "Jian Guo took the college entrance exam this year, too, but he didn't pass it. I wish your brother was more like you."

"How long will you be here?" Mama inquired.

I smiled. "I have one week to convince you this is a very good move for me."

飛虎

庚申年

一旺

Part Three

Beijing 北京, China 中国

1985 - 1990

飛虎

虐心筆

一旺

Hiking group, Liu Yu is third from left in rear

FREE AS A BIRD

Habits can't be changed overnight. After years of being guarded in relationships, squelching impulses, and enduring Coach Cobra's undue scrutiny, I needed time to adjust to my new life at college. Even though my cautionary instincts prevailed, each discovery confirmed my difficult years were behind me.

The first students I met traveled with me from Nanjing to the Beijing University of Physical Education. Travel arrangements were coordinated with five other students from my province. Two of them were rhythm gymnasts from my training camp.

Traveling alone was unthinkable for several reasons. Reserving seats wasn't possible, and almost always more tickets were sold than train seats existed, leaving surplus travelers standing in the train's aisles. The lucky ones grabbing seats can't use the toilet unless friends or family come along, fighting off anyone trying to claim the empty seats. Group travel also prevented belongings from being pilfered during the long ride.

Boarding the train turned into a shoving match, but our little group managed to stay together, finding companion seating in the hard seat section. We rode the cheapest—and therefore the slowest—train, stopping at every town along the way during the eleven-hour trip from Nanjing. Excitement prevented us from sleeping.

One of the boys in our group entertained us with his guitar. The rhythmic music calmed the chickens, ducks, and roosters in our car and lulled passengers to sleep. It took my mind off my fatigue and the unpleasant odors emanating from the animals and the unwashed floor used as a toilet by traveling children wearing split pants over their bare bottoms instead of diapers. The gentle strumming soothed my fears about the unknown.

We talked during the night about the adventure we faced, giving me a glimpse of possibilities open to me. After years of compliance to rules, I finally had the chance to discover myself and explore the notion of independence. Opportunities abounded to try new sports like swimming, roller skating, and ice skating previously prohibited by coaches who feared injuries. Most of all, I yearned to develop close friendships. Too much competition among teammates and other athletes at the training camp, combined with chronic fatigue, lack of social activities, and fear of punishment for stepping even slightly out of line hindered intimacy. We simply never learned to trust each other, believing that anything we said or did could turn up in someone else's daily journal read faithfully by our coach.

NaiNai cautioned me as a young girl by saying, "Don't talk. Just listen. Be smart. No talking, talking, talking. Instead, listen, watch, look, and think. Your mouth is the source of all misfortune. You can get sick through your mouth and trouble can arise from what comes out."

The very nature of Chinese culture had always been to think while refraining from speaking our true feelings. At a young age, we learned never to complain to our parents. Words can get a person into trouble in China. I took NaiNai's instruction to heart at the camp, but I longed to find friendship, a greater sense of closeness with others. However, I knew it would take time to adapt to a new way of life.

My college roommates welcomed me right away. "Oh, finally, we have more girls."

One of my roommates explained. "Each year, only two *wushu* department girls have been admitted compared to a dozen or more boys. But this year, there are eight new girls and fewer new boys."

Two other new students and I were assigned to share Room 222 with four girls who had started at the college one or two years prior. The rest of the new girls bunked together across the hall. Standing in a room full of smart, athletic, and modern girls, I had high hopes for making friends.

Everyone exchanged names and home provinces. One other new girl introduced herself with a touch of pride. "I was a professional team athlete." The other girls grew wide-eyed in amazement when they recognized her name. I knew her because she was a national longfist champion and the protégé of a close friend of Coach Wang's.

The Chinese say two tigers born in the same year cannot share the same mountain peak. Right away, I sensed my roommate, who was also a tiger, was wildly territorial and possibly spoiled. Even though she was out of her normal team milieu, she still acted like she deserved to sit on top of the mountain. It didn't bother me because I was starting over in life and wanted to explore a new side of myself. My roommate, however, had some life lessons to learn. Tiger Princess seemed a fitting name for her.

"Liu Yu was also on a professional team. From Jiangsu Province," Tiger Princess added.

I quickly countered by saying, "But I wasn't famous." I wanted to fit in with everyone and avoid having my roommates fawn over me in any way because my professional background impressed them. Then and there I made up my mind to sidestep any deference.

Even though Tiger Princess and I were older than the average first-year students, we fit in well with our seasoned roommates who were in their second and third years. One girl in particular made me feel the most comfortable. Her name was Xie Han 谢涵 and she immediately made us new girls feel at home by orienting us to the room. "New students sleep on the upper bunks. You can put your suitcases and extra belongings on the empty bunk here," she said pointing to a top bunk near the door. "The rest of us use the storage room under our beds."

Room 222 contained four bunk beds for seven girls, two bunk beds arranged end-to-end along each side wall. A single shelf at the head of each bed was used for book storage. For privacy, blue curtains with bamboo designs could be drawn along the sides of our bunks. In the middle of the rectangular room, chairs surrounded a long, slender table with drawers where we stored our bowls, chopsticks, and other miscellaneous belongings. This served as an area for studying and eating. A radiator squatted in front of our only window at the end of the room. Metal extension bars hung outside the window for drying our wash. The unpleasant-smelling squat toilet and open shower facilities to which we were accustomed were situated down the hall.

After settling into my new room, I was ready to embark on my new life on campus. However, new students couldn't start classes until they had fulfilled an obligation to their country.

Upon arrival in Beijing, I began a month of mandatory service with the Chinese Army where we drilled for days on end, marching with our firearms and practicing for battle. Afterward, I attended a required meeting with the campus Communist Youth Party, whose affiliates weren't members of the Communist Party but could apply after college for membership. During the meeting, every new student's personal file—the one that followed an individual for life and contained all personal records, including political, legal, and family history—was examined. During an interview, I answered questions such as whether I had ever been jailed or punished while on the professional team.

Joining certain political groups or parties in China was automatic at each stage of a person's life and kept all doors open for the future. My application for the professional team would have been rejected had I not followed the required political path. In elementary school during the Cultural Revolution, I wore a red scarf like the rest of my Young Pioneers classmates. It signified my promise to be considered one of Chairman Mao's children, giving my heart to Communism. For a part of each school day, elementary school teachers drilled students on political ideology and demanded recitation of its principles. We wanted to be obedient and love our new country.

Many adults, including my parents, took the path of least resistance politically, trying to fulfill their duties while remaining inconspicuous. Burned into everyone's memory was Chairman Mao's campaign to find snakes hiding in their holes, which led to the Cultural Revolution.

In 1957, a youthful Communism encouraged people to suggest how the government could change from an old, stagnant country into a better place for everyone. People were told that speaking out and not hiding anything meant their hearts were very close to the Communist party, close to Chairman Mao. Scholars and educated people had more ideas than the general populace and were the first to give their opinions.

Before too long, however, criticism of a shaky government became out of control. Then, Chairman Mao said it was time to guide snakes out of the holes where they remained hidden.

Snakes weren't considered to be good astrological signs in China. Cold and sneaky by nature, they lived underground and not outside in the sun. Everyone who criticized the government had to be pulled out of his or her snake holes. From this, people learned the government could change its position at any time, causing them to adopt careful attitudes and heed the recommendations of their political leaders when no other choice existed.

At the end of my first Communist Youth Party meeting, several of us older students were chosen to become captains of our class, providing a link between students and teachers. We helped teachers pass around information and organize meetings. As the second oldest student who also had a clean personal history file, I was chosen as vice monitor and Communist Youth Party leader for my class. One of my duties was conducting the weekly Communist Youth Party meetings. This honor made me feel proud and nervous at the same time. While on the professional team, I was always the last person to speak, and now I found myself in charge. Learning to meet the challenge of speaking as a meeting leader, however, slowly boosted my self-confidence. It also gave me some snippets of hope I could improve my social status.

While at the training camp, I remained under a shadow with Coach Wang as the cloud. It didn't matter to Coach Cobra, who considered Coach Wang his enemy, whether my longfist abilities could some day bring honor to the team. Coach Cobra had the attitude that if he helped me to become a top challenger, he would be promoting his enemy's student, something that was distasteful to him. I hoped I was finally free of those prejudices and petty animosities.

The aspect of college life I found most difficult in the beginning was sitting for so many hours during the day. Our classes began at 8:00 each morning, stopped for lunch, and ended at 5:30 in the afternoon, Monday through Saturday, with seven classes per semester. We followed a set program of classes in athletics, political systems, and the sciences of anatomy, physiology, and psychology.

My athletic classes didn't require a lot of sitting except in the study of the sport's theory but required a certain level of physical skill to pass the course. Whether running, jumping, lifting weights, playing basketball, or training in judo or gymnastics, I found my former body conditioning gave me an advantage. Although my skill wasn't as good in a particular sport as the students who majored in that sport, my placement scores remained high. I appreciated the excellent foundation of strength, flexibility, and agility my *wushu* training had given me. It helped me do well in every other sport.

We could elect to take some sports for fun, and I chose to learn how to swim. I also wanted to take ice skating, but it wasn't allowed. The college administration's frame of mind was that the university trained teachers. No ice skating facilities existed south of Beijing and students generally went back to serve their home province. Only Northern provinces would benefit by having their student representatives improve their ice skating abilities.

Learning new forms in the *wushu* classes was a breeze. Other students coming from a traditional high school spent an enormous amount of time learning these routines. Their level upon graduation had to be good enough to qualify as teachers or coaches.

Not all students with *wushu* as their major competed as members of the university's *wushu* team. I was among the first professional *wushu* team athletes nationally to attend a four-year university degree program. We professional athletes strengthened the college *wushu* team.

The team's two *wushu* coaches, who came from college-trained backgrounds with no professional team training, held coveted positions in their department. Right away the other professional *wushu* athletes and I noticed one of the *wushu* team coaches, Coach Shi, acted nervous around us. He seemed self-conscious, probably because his *wushu* level was lower than that of a professional athlete, although he seemed like a good teacher. I sympathized with his position and made every attempt to appear courteous and communicative. Later, after becoming friends, he confided to us he had felt intimidated because he expected the professional athletes to have large egos and be difficult to handle. But our friendliness and respectfulness made him feel comfortable.

Scheduled team practices to prepare for competitions began at 4:00 in the afternoon and lasted only one or two hours—way too easy. My team practices ended later than my roommates' classes, making me late for dinner and miss the better quality food—even then it failed to come close to the superior food provided at the training camp. To remedy two problems, I came up with a plan to help my warmhearted roommate,

Xie Han, and me at the same time.

The cafeteria building, located next to our dormitory, held limited seating, so some of my roommates and I ate in our rooms. Everyone purchased their own food, and I noticed right away Xie Han always came back with the cheapest selections. I worried she wasn't getting enough food to eat and the quality of her food provided less nutrition. I wanted to help her, but if I offered my help, she would be embarrassed and resist.

I presented part of my plan to her. "Xie Han, I'd like to ask for your help. Because my training schedule runs late, I can't get to the cafeteria before the better food runs out. Would you buy food for me ahead of time, so I can get a better selection?" Of course, she kindly consented.

Sometimes, I gathered a couple of my other roommates together, including Xie Han, and said, "I was wondering if we could put our meal coupons together and share our dinners. This way we can eat more variety." They didn't hesitate to agree.

Money wasn't a problem for me, but it was scarce for some of my roommates. Many families in China had bright children who could do well in college, but often their families didn't have enough money to support them while there. Luck shined on me when I left the team because a short window of time existed in which anyone leaving the team was given a retirement settlement based on the number of years of service to the government. I received 3,000 Chinese *Yuan* for being on the team for over ten years. This was a lot of money when I compared it to my mother's monthly salary of 38 Chinese *Yuan*. When I tried to give the money to my mother, she wouldn't take it. I then put it away in a bank to use for my college expenses. I didn't have to pay college tuition or housing expenses, but each student had to pay for books and food.

A benefit of being on the university's *wushu* team was receiving one Chinese *Yuan* a day in food coupons. It wasn't much, but it helped me buy extra food I could share with my roommates.

Whenever I had a problem with my class assignment or wasn't sure what to study for a test, I went to Xie Han. She graduated at the top of her class in high school and received a good educational foundation, unlike me. In return for her valuable help, I was happy I played a small role in getting her more food to eat. While helping each other, we slowly became friends.

The more I got to know Xie Han, however, the more I felt her name didn't fit her. *Xie* meant being appreciative or thanking someone and *Han* meant being humble and excited about learning things. It was the humble part I had trouble matching to her personality. Instead of acting humbly, she expressed her feelings in a straightforward manner, just like the dragon that she was. Yet, she was also sensitive. The combination of her liveliness and her traits as a dragon reminded me of spicy Hunan food. The name of Spicy Dragon seemed to suit her better.

One day, a pleasant surprise came my way and reinforced my feeling that I had chosen the correct school. I remembered the treasured poster that hung on the wall in my Baoying home with *wushu* athletes demonstrating various poses. Many of the athletes, including Jet Li, had become first string Beijing team members I got to know. One of the *wushu* girls in the poster had greatly inspired me in my childhood with her flexibility and fame. At the national competitions I had attended, I always tried to watch her demonstrations. Now, in college, I had the good fortune of having her as a teammate while she attended the two-year college program. Finding myself performing on the same stage with her at college thrilled me.

The two-year college program for professional athletes enhanced the college's competition strength in *wushu*. Top *wushu* athletes ready to retire from their professional team were offered placement in the program. No entrance exam was required—many of the athletes would probably flunk it if it existed. Gold medal winners in team competitions were given favored entry into this college's special program. Armed with a two-year college degree, these athletes were then awarded more prestigious jobs.

Athletes of all sports attended college under the two-year program. My biggest childhood idol was the world championship gymnast whose poster at the Baoying sports center had fueled my dreams. At college, a casual introduction brought me face-to-face with the famous gymnast. She had retired from professional competition and was attending the two-year athletic program. Right away, she shot down my naïve image of famous people acting snobbish and important. Instead, this down-to-earth girl made me laugh with her incredible sense of humor. I should have told her how much she inspired me when I was younger, but I couldn't summon the courage. As I stood on the same patch of ground and talked with her, gratitude welled up within me for my good fortune of being in

Beijing and meeting the elite athlete I had idolized as a child. Beijing was where I also formed the beginnings of my first real friendships.

A first team *wushu* athlete from my province had used her friend's connections over two years earlier to attend my college as a two-year athlete. Little Spring and I arranged to meet for lunch one day. She waved at me from one of the corner tables in the busy cafeteria. Joining her, I noticed how vibrant and strong she looked. As one of the tallest female athletes in *wushu* at our training camp, her long legs and broad shoulders combined with her exceptional skill to make her an impressive performer.

After we greeted each other, she said, "I can't believe you want to major in *wushu*."

"I wanted to get away from the team, but I still like *wushu*. What are you doing now?"

"After my two years of college were over, I got a job in the registrar's office. It isn't much, but I'm happy staying here."

"What did you study?" I asked.

"Everything except *wushu*. I like dancing and aerobics. And I made a movie over the summer using my bodybuilding skills. The school gave me the time off, but I had to pay them the money I earned from making the movie," she added, bitterness lacing her words.

Now I knew why she looked so fit.

I wanted to verify what I had heard. "Didn't you take *any wushu* classes?"

"No, I'm through with *wushu*. I'll never do it again."

I sympathized with her desire to change her life. She admitted people asked her to teach them *wushu*, but she continually refused. This was such a waste of talent because she had such a strong root in *wushu*—something only developed by beginning the training at a young age—and she had a lot to offer as a *wushu* teacher. While on the team, we had a distant friendship, which meant we were good friends but not too close. I hoped our shared training backgrounds, however, might bring us together in Beijing, creating a deeper, more open friendship.

After class exams in mid-January, the school doors opened and everyone fluttered home free as birds for the one-month Chinese

New Year vacation. Eagerly, I awaited the year of the tiger to begin on February 9, 1986. When a person's birth sign returns every twelve years, luck is magnified, resulting in either double calamity or double prosperity. Believing my hardships were behind me, I sensed a fortuitous year ahead.

Chinese New Year was the most important holiday of the year, and for the first time in over ten years, I would be spending it with my family. Memories raced through my mind of past celebrations our family shared. My mouth watered at the thought of the homemade treats lavished on the family during the holiday.

Mama greeted me warmly, saying, "Oh, good, you can help me make sticky round sweets this year."

How I missed my family's cooking! In the northern part of China, boiled potstickers were popular instead of the sticky rice specialties I loved as a child. The kitchen at the training camp served sticky rice facsimiles that never came close to the homemade ones lovingly prepared by NaiNai. I had over ten years of deprivation to remedy.

For the first time in my life while at home with my family, I felt grown up. Helping my parents by doing things for them made me happier on a home visit than I'd been in a long time. Together, we swept and washed everything, making the entire house clean to welcome the New Year. Purchasing new household items was the ideal but not many people could afford it. Instead, most people cleaned everything. Mama gave me cooking instructions, and I worked closely with her, preparing the foods I had fantasized about for so long. While indulging in these heavenly treats, I vowed to spend Chinese New Year with my family every year.

My parents no longer lived in my childhood home. After the Cultural Revolution, homes once divided into segments for various family groups to occupy were returned to their original owners. This set off a wave of panic as people scrambled for scarce accommodations. Finally, to my parents' relief, the hospital agreed to provide housing for its doctors. They moved into a simple, three-room apartment with running water, electricity, and shared basic toilet facilities located in a small building behind the apartments. Two years later, they qualified for a larger place. After living in our original tiny, dark apartment that had only one small window in the main room and where we used smoky oil lamps for light, my parents marveled at their new bright third-floor apartment with its large windows and private toilet.

Da Jie, now married, lived with her husband's family. No longer a child, I began calling my sister by her name, Liu Jing. I had become her equal and we no longer felt any age difference between us.

Liu Jing's job situation had greatly improved. When she worked for Mama's company as a seamstress aide, my parents brainstormed to find her another job. Mama knew how hard the employees of her company worked and didn't want that kind of job for her daughter. So, Liu Jing switched jobs, working for a factory making parts for radio connections. Meanwhile, Baba hatched a plan to raise Liu Jing's job marketability. Taking her under his wing, Baba taught her much of what he knew about medicine. After the threat of re-education in the countryside subsided, Liu Jing completed her high school education and the equivalent of a two-year college degree via correspondence courses. Eventually, a manufacturing company making parts for the Army—readying itself to fight its Korean and American enemies if need be—hired Liu Jing as a nurse practitioner. In preparation, she was sent to receive further medical training. Liu Jing felt lucky for the first time.

Baba always hoped his children would choose to be educated as doctors. Before I left for the professional team, Baba occasionally invited us children to visit the hospital. My brother always answered this with a question, "Can we spend the night?" If the answer was no, then Jian Guo made a face and said he didn't like the smell. Even Liu Jing would rather play with her friends than go there. I was the only one who liked visiting the busy hospital.

When children came to the hospital with their parents who worked there, the parents never worried the children would catch the flu or any other disease. Children were considered healthy and tough. Medical personnel were too busy to worry about us. We learned how to stay out of the way and watch.

Once my brother and I stood behind a little window and watched Baba perform an operation. Oh, how my brother hated to see blood and said he would never come again. Baba's slumped shoulders and sad eyes showed his disappointment.

Jian Guo was willing to come if we could spend the night while Baba worked the emergency shift. If an ill person couldn't come to the hospital, then Baba traveled to the patient's house, even in the middle of the night. With no telephones, messengers arrived at the hospital to guide him. Sometimes, if the situation wasn't too serious or time-consuming, we were allowed to tag along.

Baba gave up hope of Jian Guo becoming a doctor, but Baba held on to his dream of his son attending college. Now, while at home during my college break, family members expressed their concern about Jian Guo passing the college entrance exam on his second try.

Jian Guo had gone through a rebellious patch in high school. During his first year in high school, he shaved his head and neglected his studies. The next year, Baba arranged for him to be sent to a high school in the countryside. He lived in a dormitory with other students who came from rural villages.

The poverty of the village students surprised Jian Guo. In the school cafeteria, each student received a bowl of rice. For the equivalent of five cents, a serving of cooked vegetables could be purchased. The village students couldn't even afford that. Either jars of homemade food were brought to school or a little broth to flavor the rice was purchased for one cent.

When Jian Guo told Baba about the poverty, Baba said, "See, that's what I wanted you to learn from being in the countryside."

Jian Guo stayed at that high school a couple of years. He admitted the experience taught him to appreciate his life. He learned not to act too spoiled.

Now, the family brainstormed about improving my brother's chances of getting into college the next year. Baba directed his comments to me when he said, "Jian Guo wants to study to become a teacher. The college in Yangzhou requires an interview. We aren't sure if he'll be accepted."

Jian Guo squirmed in his seat at the dining table. Since childhood, he had grown quieter—though some would say the right word was sneaky, in keeping with the qualities of a snake.

"Can you think of any way to help?" Baba asked me.

I looked at Jian Guo and said, "You could say you have a background in *wushu*. It'll make you stand out."

He looked at his hands while slouching in his chair. "What if they ask me to show them something in the interview? Besides, I'm not even sure I want to go to college."

"Don't throw away this chance," I said. "At college, you can prove yourself, have a chance at a good future. I can teach you a *wushu* form for the interview. We'll start now and when I come back in the summer, we'll polish it."

Jian Guo reluctantly agreed. Although unenthusiastic, Jian Guo proved to be an able athlete who performed well during the interview and won college acceptance.

My visit in Baoying for the Chinese New Year celebration coincided with the wedding of Young Soldier, my childhood *wushu* rival. I accepted the invitation to attend the wedding banquet where I sat at a table with my neighbor, Liu Zheng Qiang, whom I had called Da Liu and who had acted as intermediary to my childhood trainer, Coach Dai.

One of Liu Zheng Qiang's friends sitting across the table from me was drinking heavily. Midway through the sumptuous meal, he turned to my former neighbor and blurted out, "How do you know Liu Yu?"

Professional team members were held in high esteem in Baoying, and I was considered famous. My name was listed in the town's history book along with a professional soccer player from Baoying. My neighbor's friend was surprised to see us chatting freely. I sensed jealousy in the air.

Liu Zheng Qiang's face reddened as he stumbled over his words. "It's hard to explain." If someone has done something good in life, that person isn't supposed to mention it to other people.

I decided I would speak for him and simply tell the truth. "Da Liu was my childhood neighbor and provided my introduction to Coach Dai. If not for him, I wouldn't have been on the team."

Da Liu's face beamed with pleasure.

Another fellow at the table had led Coach Dai's students in stretching and basic movement drills. His face flushed when he heard my words and some confusion arose about who was the first one to teach me *wushu*. I decided to clarify, "Well, Da Liu, you did teach my brother and me first before we went to the park."

Later, Da Liu went to my mother's house and told her what happened. "Xiao Yu, she's so nice. She's very mature now. You raised a good daughter."

Mama questioned me when she got the chance. "You did that for him?"

"Well, I didn't think I was doing him a favor. I just told the truth about what he did." Sometimes, my forthrightness got me into trouble, but in this case, it gave considerable face to Da Liu. It felt good to help him.

During my visits to Baoying over the years, I witnessed the slow modernization of the burgeoning town. One example was when electric grinders replaced the slow grinding stone variety, making holiday meal preparation easier. Not everyone owned one but it could easily be borrowed. In addition, fewer people obtained their drinking water from the river as more water pipes were installed around the city. Bicycle ownership also grew with residents' incomes.

Not everything improved the quality of life, however. River barges were increasingly becoming motorized, fouling the water and causing noise pollution. Additional factories dumped their waste in the city's canals or allowed it to defile the air. Safety and thievery were issues. Children could no longer walk in the dark unescorted as I did to and from my *wushu* classes as a child. As optimism replaced fear in daily life, however, people appeared happier.

While riding the train back to Beijing in the middle of the night, I made a decision about my future. Somewhere in between a baby crying, old men snoring, and conversations with my schoolmates, it occurred to me that becoming a teacher would give me a more flexible work schedule, one with time to enjoy two long vacations each year.

I giggled to myself. The old fortuneteller was right after all. Teaching could be in my future. In first and second grade, I admired Teacher Li's ability to stand in front of the class and share her knowledge. She inspired me to learn. I never thought I could get past my shyness and speak in front of other people, but I had already accomplished that this year in college. Feeling the respect of my classmates gave me the confidence I needed to overcome my fears.

In my first semester at college, I discovered professors didn't work any harder than elementary school teachers. Plus, they earned more salary and benefits. Now, I knew what I wanted to do in life. I longed to become a college *wushu* professor.

Chairman Mao had said women hold up half the sky. In my generation, women were now equal with men. Opportunities existed for me if I worked hard. Politics was the only unknown factor, but I felt confident I could cultivate the goodwill of my professors. Setting my sights on this goal suddenly brought everything into perspective for me.

The New Year began auspiciously. I considered it my lucky year of the tigress because, as a female tiger, I was becoming a woman who could finally select a life of her own choosing. My spirits danced, my hands trembled, and I itched to try my wings, to discover myself. I didn't want to hold back any longer. It was time to take the leap.

During my first semester at school, teachers guided students in organizing social events. Now we were on our own, and my classmates and I took up the challenge. We reserved the gymnasium, planned our event, chose music, rolled up the carpet, and decorated the room. Our party was more of a performance, with students acting and singing different parts. Having a poor singing voice no longer mattered. I learned to laugh at myself. Everyone sang for fun and enjoyed playing certain characters. It helped me that the group was mostly composed of girls.

As the weather improved, we loaded up our bags with food and drinks and bicycled to parks for picnic lunches. Many friendships deepened on these excursions, and this happened to Spicy Dragon and me. She was the first person with whom I let down my guard. I admired her friendliness and sincerity and tried to return it.

Students at the college came from all corners of China. Spicy Dragon and I liked to observe the different clothing the students brought with them. A few bold imported fashions contrasted mightily with my plain-colored team-approved attire. Daring to be brave, I bought a pink shirt, which in my mind signified my rebellion against former team rules. Not yet overly courageous, however, I stuck to middle-of-the-road fashions, never wanting to be considered too fancy. I wore my pink shirt often as my personal sign of independence.

As long as students kept up on their studies, teachers were unconcerned about how we spent our free time. While on the professional team, I felt like a trapped mouse with eyes watching me all the time. The novelty of freedom at college was heady and I never failed to appreciate it.

Eventually, my friends and I took boldness to a new height. One day, someone said, "Let's go get haircuts."

Putting any misgivings aside, we rushed to the beauty salon. As our long hair dropped away, we laughed as if emerging from a cocoon to find plucky faces framed by wispy layers of coifed black hair.

One girl carried her bravery further. In a corner of the beauty salon, she had her ears pierced. While we stood around admiring her courage and her earrings, we inquired about how much it hurt. On our next visit, Spicy Dragon and I copied her.

To celebrate our new appearances, we ventured to Tiananmen Square to eat at Beijing's first American fast food restaurant, Kentucky Fried Chicken. The line to get in was long, but we waited for our turn to try it. For ten Chinese *Yuan*, we ordered one of the most expensive meals, which we shared between us. It was delicious.

On another day, we arranged to go to a newly opened California beef noodle shop. One trip to each new place was enough as we had to take a complicated series of buses for over an hour to get downtown. Whenever we felt adventurous and hungry for something new, we enjoyed trying a trendy restaurant.

Although getting a haircut was fun, after a sweaty workout my hair looked flat and unappealing. I decided short hair was not such a good idea for me. I begrudgingly conceded there were some good rules while on the team. The team officials had prohibited girls from cutting their long braided hair.

In everything, some things are good and some are bad. I benefited from spending all those years on the team, but I didn't want to admit its overall worth. I couldn't forget the cruel oppression thrust upon my teammates and me at such tender ages when we weren't equipped to handle it. I was about to find out, however, just how much good I had derived from my *wushu* training. And once again, something good led to something bad.

Liu Yu (right) with classmate

New *wushu* students at Beijing University of Physical
Education (Liu Yu is fourth from left)

During my college breaks I visited Coach
Wang in Yangzhou, where he insisted on
continuing my training.

Biking fun at Beijing University of Physical Education
(Liu Yu with a peace sign)

Liu Yu posing with wooden staff

Beijing University of Physical Education
wushu team on Tibet tour
(Liu Yu is third from left in front)

Liu Yu on the cover of
Chinese Wushu magazine

SECRET PRACTICE

"Congratulations, Liu Yu," Spicy Dragon whispered from the seat next to me.

Still in shock, feeling my cheeks glow like red plums, I muttered, "I never expected to win."

In the campus-wide student assembly marking the end of my first year, the university's president had just stood before everyone announcing the results of the award for best student of the year. Each department had submitted the names of its three highest honor students for a college-wide vote. All students at the university then voted for the most deserving student who exhibited the highest levels of academic ability: respectfulness, friendliness, morality, and political integrity. To my amazement, I won the distinction.

I didn't mind being recognized for my hard work, but not in front of my classmates. It made me stand out. Now I was fair game for criticism, murmurs that I thought I was better than everyone else.

My desire to work hard in school fulfilled an inner need to explore my potential. Unfortunately, I was afraid that my classmates, especially the two former professional athletes, wouldn't view it that way. Team members held weird views about competition. They took wins and losses personally. It was in our blood, though I tried to save my competitive spirit for the performance carpet.

While I took school seriously, many of my classmates didn't. Although students who had received a high school diploma had a strong foundation in education and could have easily outperformed me on written tests, they suffered from burnout and made socializing a priority in college. They didn't care about doing well as long as they passed their classes. In contrast, I remembered how satisfying it was to do well in elementary school through the fifth grade and was eager to test myself academically again. That desire along with utilizing my talent to easily memorize details—something I didn't know I had until I studied for my college entrance examination—helped me ace my college tests.

When I compared myself to other former professional athletes, I noticed our training backgrounds gave us an advantage on performance tests in various sports. On written tests, however, their substandard schooling generally caused them to struggle just to keep their heads above water. My five solid years in elementary school before becoming a professional athlete saved me. Joining the professional team at an older age, as I did, was the exception rather than the rule.

After the assembly, my freshman classmates left quietly while upper classmen and teachers offered their compliments. This worried me. To minimize my peers' potential jealousy, I devised a plan. The award came with a scholarship prize equivalent to $40—not much, but an honor all the same and something my poorer classmates would envy. I played it smart by inviting my classmates to help me celebrate. I spent all the money buying treats for my department and taking a few roommates out to a local restaurant for dinner. These gestures headed off problems and showed my classmates I wasn't after the money. I had smoothed their ruffled feathers.

After a six-week summer break, the new school year started on a high note. Liu Yu Ping 刘玉萍老师, my female *wushu* team coach at the college, detained me after practice in the gymnasium. "Liu Yu, would you be interested in attending an early morning *taiji* practice? I think it'd be helpful in preparing you for next year's collegiate tournament. It isn't a class, just a small private practice with one of the graduate professors, a few of his graduate students, and a couple of teachers. Although undergraduate students aren't supposed to participate, I'm hoping the professor will make an exception at my request. It starts at 5:30 every morning. Should I try to arrange it with Professor Men?"

I'm always pleased when someone offers to help me. Generally, students don't receive extra instruction outside class, making this a special opportunity. "It sounds like an honor."

"We hold the practice outside campus because it isn't part of the curriculum. We call it our secret practice," my coach added, encouraging me to keep it confidential.

She didn't have to explain further by saying she didn't want the other *wushu* department professors, who didn't get along with each other, to find out. The three of us could find ourselves in trouble for disobeying the custom of not interfering with someone else's student. Although I didn't want to be marked as a favorite student like I had been on the team, I was curious enough to risk political repercussions by attending. And Liu Yu Ping wanted accolades for being the coach of a winner at the collegiate tournament.

During the last few years of my professional career, I specialized in *taiji*. Even though at one time I considered myself to be the best on the second team at longfist, it was too late to pick back up where I left off after easing up on that training for several years. I continued practicing my longfist forms but not with the same level of intensity. *Taiji* remained my specialty for the college team.

Coach Liu Yu Ping and I met at dawn a few days later and walked toward the railroad tracks running behind the campus. In a small clearing secluded by overgrown trees and bushes, three people were bending and stretching as part of their warm-up routine. Copying my coach, I bowed to a man with a bushy head of gray hair and followed the group's movements. Several moments later, everyone assumed standing postures with eyes closed and arms held in a circle as though hugging a round ball in front of their abdomen. Professor Men, whose full name was Men Hui Feng 门惠丰教授, motioned for me to do the same. I attempted to copy the position, feet shoulder width apart and knees slightly bent.

For quite some time, I stood there feeling silly because I didn't know what I was supposed to be doing. What was the purpose of assuming this position and then standing still? Coach Wang had made my teammates and me hold various positions for a long time because the hard work made our legs burn, which strengthened our muscles, and trained our young bodies and muscles to develop a sense of memory related to our postures. This practice allowed Coach Wang to make adjustments to our postures, although sometimes he used it as punishment. I assumed this was also some kind of posture training, but I didn't know where I should focus my thoughts.

After some time passed, Professor Men instructed us to lower our arms and slowly open our eyes. When I looked up, he told me to stay in a standing posture. I closed my eyes again and took a deep breath. Eventually, I heard footsteps behind me and felt a hand running lightly along my spine, encouraging me to keep it straight. Hands placed outside my hips guided my lower back and my pelvis to slightly sink down and gently tuck. When the discomfort became apparent in my legs or back, I discovered that by relaxing my muscles and making slight adjustments to how my body lined, the pain disappeared.

By the end of our secret practice, all I had done was assume the standing posture. Professor Men didn't offer any explanation about its purpose and I knew it wouldn't be proper to ask. During the walk back to campus, however, I gained a few insights from my coach.

"Professor Men teaches in the traditional way like the old *taiji* masters. They decide what you need to learn. Students need to have patience," Coach Liu Yu Ping offered. Patience was a skill I had learned well and would use now.

In the traditional way of teaching *taiji*, students had to prove themselves worthy of receiving instruction from the master. Stories existed of masters testing their students' sincerity and patience. The Communists, who encouraged more openness, frowned on traditional ways of teaching *taiji*, saying any teacher-disciple relationships had religious connotations.

Professor Men's teaching wasn't totally traditional because he didn't require allegiances and didn't receive students' services in return for his instruction. If my attendance were discovered, the consequences for Professor Men and Coach Liu Yu Ping would be political in nature, possibly affecting their teaching records but most certainly in the form of hardships doled out by the other professors. I knew all too well how much one could suffer by having every political advantage removed from life, and I could be facing a repeat scenario. It made me apprehensive, but I decided to stick it out a while longer to find out if it was worth the gamble.

After a week of standing meditation—as I learned it was called—

Professor Men asked me to show him the opening step to my *taiji* form. All forms begin with feet together, followed by bending the knees, emptying the weight off the left foot, taking a step to the side until feet are shoulder width apart, and shifting the weight to evenly stand on both feet again. After watching my movements, he instructed me to practice them slowly for the rest of the session.

Glad to have something new to do, I carefully practiced the simple movements over and over again. I assumed it was a test to figure out what Professor Men wanted me to learn from each exercise. I tried to use the insights I'd derived so far from my standing meditation: the importance of keeping a correct *taiji* posture and relaxing deeply, especially in the abdominal area just below the navel called the *dantian*.

Over the next few months, Professor Men's small corrections to my *taiji* forms gradually conveyed a sense of how different *taiji* was from *wushu*. My old *taiji* could be called *wushu taiji*. I learned it by duplication, thinking I had mastered the forms. I took each movement and made it look pretty, but now I laughed at how my flowery hands had flopped around on my wrists and my movements were so rushed. For the first time, I understood why *taiji* was considered an internal martial art while *wushu* was external.

Taiji required internal preparation to achieve softness with all movements maintaining a strong connection to the center of the body. A *taiji* practitioner cultivated energy within the abdominal area just below the navel called the *dantian* and used the whole body as one cohesive unit. *Wushu*, on the other hand, utilized muscular energy with straight legs, a puffed up chest, and limbs working independently of the body. In contrast with *taiji*'s softness and its rounded arm movements, *wushu* used a direct and quick fighting style based on the principle that faster movements will beat out slower ones.

I spent all those years on the team without anyone pointing out to me the subtleties of *taiji*. I could have been a *taiji* champion for the team. Coach Cobra's specialty was internal martial arts. He could have shown me how *wushu* and *taiji* postures were different. I dismissed the idea he didn't know the difference, assuming he held it back from me because I wasn't his favored student. What a relief to put those years behind me.

Despite the danger of discovery, each morning I looked forward to sneaking out of my room for practice. Each small revelation opened my eyes wider. Without corrections and an insight into the essence of *taiji*,

I would have been stuck at the same skill level for twenty years. I knew Professor Men could correct many of my movements, but he didn't give away his secrets easily. A belief existed that students will value something more if they work hard to attain it.

As the competition drew closer, Professor Men watched sections of my competition form and made slight corrections to my posture. I gained confidence my *taiji* form wouldn't show any big mistakes.

The competition took place near the end of my second school year. Chengdu Physical Education Institute 成都体育学院 in Sichuan 四川省 Province hosted China's collegiate championships, an event held every two years. Just like the *wushu* nationals, each competitor entered six events.

To avoid having everyone on our team compete in the double weapons category, I agreed to forego competing in my double hooks form. Instead, I learned a traditional single weapon form using the long tasseled straight sword. A professor at the college taught me this beautifully flowing form that used alternating left and right hands to hold the weapon as it weaved this way and that way in a spirited fight with an imaginary opponent. He encouraged me to show dramatic flair with my arms and body, and to practice using my eyes to add much needed emotion to the event. I captured a second place win with my new sword form at the competitions. As expected, my former professional team roommate, Tiger Princess, did well at the competitions with her double straight swords in the double weapons category, garnering a higher score overall.

The *taiji* event captured most of my interest. Scanning my early competitors, I noticed how stiff they appeared. The ability to discern this deficiency made me smile. The corrections Professor Men had given me had seemed slight, but now, for the first time, I realized how my *taiji* practice had given me a whole new look. With confidence, I attempted to intertwine the qualities of calmness, buoyancy, and fluidity into my movements while I performed. It worked; the first place scores were mine.

I felt a glow of satisfaction. Although my collegiate gold medal wasn't as distinguished as a gold medal at the *wushu* nationals, it represented a personal triumph. This win fulfilled a need I had carried around for many years: recognition for being the best and a reward for all those years of brutal training while everything else in my life had been put on hold.

Coach Liu Yu Ping showed her happiness at my win with a satisfied grin. Without her help in getting me secret instruction, I would never have won. As my coach of record, she earned benefits for my first place win rather than Professor Men.

My college teammates couldn't conceal their surprise at my becoming China's collegiate *taiji* champion. With her hands on her hips, one girl said, "I didn't know you were that good. Who's been teaching you?"

I tensed at her line of questioning, worried about where it might lead. Instead, I simply answered, "I've just been practicing every day." I should have noticed the dark clouds starting to circle around me. The Chinese were fond of tearing down whoever was on top, especially when the person thought there might be a chance to replace the fallen star.

My popularity with my classmates dropped further when my photo appeared on the cover of *Chinese Wushu* magazine. In China's *wushu* world, this was a big deal. I imagined Coach Cobra's reaction. When Chairman Mao spoke about dealing with enemies, he advocated killing or crushing them at the right moment. He explained that if you let a tender bud or young sprout blossom fully, it's too late. "Catch them early," he said. Although Coach Cobra did his best to suppress my potential, he hadn't fully vanquished me. Now he knew that I hadn't allowed his domination to stop me. I never gave up.

After the competition, my classmates watched me carefully. They had ignored my early wake-up before but now seemed nosy. I knew my acceptance into the secret practice group had been conditional, only to help me prepare for the competition. Now that it was over, I felt less welcome, even though no one said anything outright. I didn't want to make trouble for Professor Men, who was giving favored guidance to another professor's student, so I reluctantly quit going.

Before the school year ended, my studiousness again earned me the distinction of being named the best student on campus. Once again, I sat in the meeting hall while our campus president embarrassed me with his announcement. "In addition to winning a second time," he said, "Liu Yu has earned a higher honor. She has been named as the top university student for the entire City of Beijing. She has set an outstanding example and we're proud to have her at our school. If she continues to make such excellent grades, she'll receive automatic approval to enter a Master's degree program."

Even though I tried to appear modest about my accomplishments, I couldn't escape the rising jealousy. Even spending my prize money on my classmates didn't help. Tiger Princess gave me the cold shoulder. With our similar backgrounds, she probably expected me to be an unsuccessful student—especially when she labored in her own coursework. She felt she deserved the most attention because she was more famous.

Tiger Princess's popularity in our dorm room sank because she didn't know how to show respect. She held that against me. At the beginning of the first year, my roommates treated Tiger Princess and me well because they were impressed with our status as professional team members. I refused their offers to do chores for me, but Tiger Princess accepted their overtures and soon took for granted that she didn't have to do anything.

The members of our dorm room drew up a schedule of cleaning and sweeping chores for everyone. When Tiger Princess saw her roommates growing tired of doing her chores, she came up with excuses why she couldn't do them, complaining of a sore back or faking illnesses. She accepted others' kindnesses but didn't know how to return them. After a while, the others resented her. Eventually, she and one roommate stopped speaking to each other. As a result, Tiger Princess began spending most of her time with her new boyfriend, a young faculty member, and stayed away from the room as much as possible.

Little Mouse was the other professional athlete who entered college at the same time as Tiger Princess and I. She bunked in the dorm room across the hall and was my close friend our first two years. With her tiny eyes like a mouse, she seemed to sense things around her. I admired her ability to negotiate for what she wanted while not caring what people around her thought. When she began pulling away after my recent recognition, this hurt me.

Little Mouse's comments had been supportive in the past but now were suddenly critical. "Liu Yu, you waste your talent studying too hard. You can get what you want by using ten percent of your effort, like me. Just ask people to help you. You're too shy." She resented my success.

I began to feel defensive even though I stubbornly believed I hadn't done anything wrong. Unfortunately, I didn't know what else to do to remedy the problem. Maybe the upcoming trip would ease the tensions between us.

Due to our success at the collegiate championships, our team received the honor of representing China on a trip to Tibet. Usually the government chose a group composed of athletes from different provinces to make up a temporary national *wushu* team for a trip outside the country, but this time the government decided to take our entire team instead.

After rehearsals in the heat of the early summer, we spent a week in Sichuan Province to accustom ourselves to a medium altitude. While we were there, a doctor friend of Professor Men's taught us *qigong* exercises every day.

Qigong combined simple movements with deep breathing and focused visualizations in different parts of the body. Its purpose was to remove blockages of *qi* (life-force energy) within the body. *Qi* was described as inherent but latent oxygen in the blood that, if stimulated, produced heat and provided stamina and vitality. Stagnant *qi* or an imbalance of energy flow created fatigue in the body and paved the way for illness. In Chinese medicine, the only cause of sickness was congestion of *qi*. *Qigong* practitioners claimed it reduced stress, helped relieve pain, and promoted healing when sick.

The 11,500-foot elevation in Lhasa 拉萨, Tibet's 西藏 capital city, took its toll on our bodies. We could barely walk the first few days and couldn't exercise at all. One girl huddled in bed the entire first week. Our qigong instructor traveled with us and continued our *qigong* exercises to help us become accustomed to the high elevation.

A *wushu* performance was scheduled for our second week in Lhasa. However, the amount of time needed for us to adjust to the altitude was misjudged. Many athletes could only perform half of their routines before their lips turned purple from lack of oxygen and they fainted. The audience, however, didn't mind waiting for the performers to recharge on the oxygen tanks provided in the back of the gymnasium before resuming their demonstrations. I fared better than many of the athletes. My body was already accustomed to living with a low level of oxygen in my blood due to my childhood anemia.

A Tibetan girl who had graduated from my college and worked in Lhasa bubbled with excitement to see us. She escorted us throughout the city—as much as our bodies permitted—to see amazing sights. Gazing with wonder at the majestic Potala Palace 布达拉宫, a fortress rooted in the earth with its lofty penthouse in the heavens, I experienced mixed emotions, viewing myself as an ant in the world while feeling inspired by man's homage to religion. Growing up with only the remnants of

Taoism and Confucianism left me with curiosity, though the weight of Communism's indoctrination in freedom from religious oppression hung heavily in my mind and wasn't to be quickly shaken.

Once inside the Potala Palace, we encountered dozens of dark rooms filled with old Buddhist statues and a horrible yak butter smell that made breathing as difficult as if the air were thick with chalk dust. The oppressiveness of the place made me feel a connection to the Dalai Lama as a young boy. His training to become the leader of the country must have put enormous pressure on him as my team training did on me. When I visited the summer palace, however, I was happy to discover beautiful gardens and light-filled rooms, a playful place where the young boy could relax and enjoy himself.

In those gardens called Jewel Park the Tibetans were celebrating their New Year by dressing up in national clothing, singing, dancing, and drinking from their Tibetan bowls. When my classmates and I admired the colorful costumes of Tibetan dancers performing for a special celebration, our former college mate arranged for us to dress up in Tibetan clothes and have our picture taken before the backdrop of the mountainous palace. We girls chose traditional Tibetan dresses with colorful stripes on the bodice but were quickly counseled by the photographer, "You girls aren't married and can't wear those dresses. You must choose the plain ones."

We giggled and responded, "We don't care. This is for fun. We like the color." With all the enthusiasm of putting on one of our musical performances, we struck high-spirited poses to amuse each other followed by dignified ones for our families.

My happiness was marred, however, by Little Mouse and Tiger Princess huddling together for the photos and deliberately snubbing me, as they had done throughout the trip every chance they got. It hurt me and I longed for the company of Spicy Dragon, who wasn't a member of my college team.

In Barkhor, Lhasa's old market, merchants hawked their colorful jewelry. I ignored the unfriendliness of my teammates as we tried on the Indian-style bracelets, rings, and earrings. Then the make-up stalls drew our attention because cosmetics were rarely sold in China. I patted my pocket where I stored my new purchases: a few bright bangles and a tube of lipstick, souvenirs to take home. The last stop was a visit to a Tibetan temple where I copied reverent Buddhists by giving a little push to the prayer wheel to show my respect.

On our return trip, we stopped in Sichuan to acclimate ourselves to a medium altitude. Our school representative arranged for us to take a two-day hike up Emeishan 峨眉山, a Buddhist holy mountain containing several temples. Either because they weren't physically strong enough or because they didn't want to do anything with me, the other girls on the trip dropped out halfway up, and I made the rest of the 10,000-foot climb with the boys.

The climb took tremendous energy and strength of mind, especially for the steepest passages that were steps carved out of rock. Many times on the narrow stairs we flattened ourselves up against the rock to make room for workers with bulging packs on their backs made out of bamboo and nets. This was the only way food and supplies could be delivered to the temples.

The Buddhist temple at the top of the mountain hosted the climbers. After the day's exertion we slept soundly on floor mats in two rooms, a big one for the men and a smaller one for the women. We were awakened early for the ritual of watching the sunrise.

While brushing my teeth before going outside, I heard familiar sounds coming from a nearby courtyard. The grunts, stomps, and metallic clanging noises were coming from a young monk practicing his broadsword. Far away from civilization on a lonely mountaintop, I was surprised to see such a sight. My teammates joined me and we whispered to each other about the attributes of the monk's technique. His self-discipline impressed me.

Shivering in the early morning cold, everyone seated themselves on the rocky summit to await the sunrise. With the temple behind me and the first ray of light poking through the clouds, I felt myself melt into the profound silence. Slowly the light grew bolder as the clouds turned from pink to red. The sun finally rose over the top of the clouds as if floating out of an ocean.

The experience of watching something so beautiful filled me with happiness. Suddenly, I didn't care that the other girls had made a clear line of separation between us. I realized that life wasn't about pleasing everyone, nor was it about luck or having my destiny drop out of the sky at my feet. Instead, life was hard work and had to be taken step by step, just like the climb up the mountain. The important thing was to have a goal and make progress toward that goal. I set my goal to become a college professor and in the meantime I wanted to take advantage of opportunities at school that allowed me to grow as a person.

While making the long climb down the mountain, I thought about how I threatened my classmates' competitive confidence. They had underestimated me because I hadn't been a winner during my professional team years. Now I was seen as a successful student who had won a gold medal and achieved academic honors. I was shedding my shy persona and becoming more popular on campus with students, and especially boys. I was proud of my accomplishments, although I tried to appear humble because I didn't want to make any enemies. I was learning, however, that fulfilling my aspirations meant I could no longer play it safe by taking a middle-of-the-road direction. The consequences of discovering my potential were that it wasn't possible to stay on everyone's good side all the time. After escaping the tyranny of team life, the promise of freedom and friendships in college wasn't unfolding as I had imagined. Winning was a double-edged sword with disappointments to face and choices to make.

As I stepped carefully down the stone stairs, I thought about another area of my life in which I had attempted to play it safe. During these past two years, I had tried to avoid romantic entanglements. I now realized I was losing that battle.

Liu Yu with Zhang Wenguang, who was a member of the
Chinese Wushu Team sent to the Berlin Olympics in 1936.

Liu Yu

27 *MATCHMAKERS*

I never thought about being pretty until I went to Canada. My professional teammates and I were selected mostly for our athletic potential, but also partly because Coach Wang favored our appearances. Yet we were all in the same boat, so we took our looks for granted, rarely giving it much thought. At home, my sister was considered the beauty in the family, while I assumed the athletic role.

When I discovered college boys eyeing me with interest, I automatically deflected their attentions in an off-hand manner. When dealing with others, the indirect approach was largely preferred in China. Rather than declaring inner feelings and having them rejected face-to-face, emissaries were recruited to scope out possibilities or speak on one's behalf. Avoiding direct embarrassment saved face, which meant saving one's sense of honor and dignity.

Usually, a girl approached me asking what I thought about a particular boy. Right away, I would become suspicious and answer, "We're friends but nothing more." Changing the subject afterwards got the point across.

Sometimes, they pressed further by revealing, "He'd like to get to know you better."

I would counter by explaining, "I don't want to think about that right now. I just want to study and have fun, have a good time." This wasn't seen as a rejection and usually avoided hurt feelings.

My priorities at college involved exploring my educational potential and developing friendships. I didn't want the complications of dating, which in my opinion led too quickly to expectations of marriage. There's a saying in China: make one thousand friends, but don't make one enemy. I made it a point to be friendly with everyone. Sometimes, however, I didn't catch on right away to people's motivations for wanting a friendship.

One day, one of my roommates told me about an invitation she received for us to have dinner with a local family. The husband came from my province and wanted to hear news from home in a familiar dialect. My roommate and I delighted in our good fortune, eager to eat a home-cooked meal instead of the humdrum cafeteria specials. This quickly became a regular weekly visit. After a while, however, my roommate wasn't invited anymore, and I went alone. Then, after my arrival one Sunday evening, I was introduced to their son. Right away, I knew they wanted me to pair up with him. I sat politely through the dinner and declined their invitations after that.

Another experience occurred with a basketball coach at the university and his wife. I explained that their connection with my home province wasn't enough for me to be more than friends with their son. My revelation produced a grim, tight-lipped expression on the wife's face.

As an older student, I was closer in age to younger faculty members than to other students. This caused me to tiptoe my way around some situations with single teachers. When an assistant teacher of anatomy introduced me to his mother and sister who were visiting from Yangzhou—where Coach Wang lived—a warning light went on in my head. The sister, who wasn't shy like her brother, pulled me aside to tell me the usual, that her brother wanted to get to know me better.

With a surprised expression on my face, I replied, "Oh, I'm so sorry, but I hadn't considered that."

Later, a male friend of the teacher said to me, "He's a very nice man. Do you know how much he likes you? Why do you want to hurt him?"

"I'm sorry. I can't be more than friends with him just because he likes me." As a result, I could tell the friend harbored some anger toward me. If embarrassment was avoided, I managed to remain on good terms after these exchanges. The anatomy teacher, however, became extremely withdrawn, and our friendship quickly evaporated.

Throughout Chinese history, if people didn't get what they desired, resentment and anger resulted. If the boy's parents asked the girl's parents to allow an arranged marriage for their children and the answer was no, then those two families feuded with each other for many generations. Indirectness had its benefits.

I tried to handle matchmaking situations delicately, not wanting to create enemies. Generally, I thought I handled it well. Sometimes, however, I wondered if I were too quick to close the door and keep boys at a distance.

When one of my teachers spoke on behalf of a classmate who was a friend of Spicy Dragon's and a former professional athlete, I responded by saying, "I thought the policy at the university is for students not to have close boyfriend-girlfriend relationships. I don't want to make trouble for myself."

This teacher acted more like my friend than a teacher and said, "That rule was made to keep the younger students from doing anything serious. You're a special case because you're older. I don't think there will be any trouble if you break this rule."

I was twenty-six at the time, while most students were ages eighteen to twenty-two. I still refused, however, saying I just wanted to be friends.

Much later, Spicy Dragon informed me her friend had confided his disappointment. She chastised me by saying, "You were terrible to him. He complained you blocked him whenever he tried to talk with you."

"Well," I admitted, "he seems like a good person, but I don't think he's the right person for me. I don't want to marry a professional athlete."

While growing up in the isolation of the professional team, we athletes missed out on learning daily life skills. We always had people doing everything for us so we could focus on training. We never learned how to do ordinary things, like buying tickets, obtaining treatment at a hospital, or purchasing and cooking food. I was afraid if two people with the same background married, they wouldn't make a good couple. My cautiousness with men worked well in avoiding complications, except in one case where the rules were a mystery to me.

One evening in the late autumn of my second year at college, I answered a knock on my dorm room door and recognized the familiar Caucasian face smiling at me. The last time I saw Norm Petredean was on the train after my last professional team competition when he courageously asked me to marry him rather than using a go-between like the Chinese. Even though I had turned Norm down, I admired his straightforward approach. Now, he inquired if he could talk to me.

I looked over at two of my roommates who stared in amazement at my visitor. I introduced him, saying he had trained many times with my team coach. Turning back to face him, I answered for the benefit of my roommates, "Yes, I could take a few minutes to talk to you and show you around the campus, though you won't be able to see much in the dark."

Outside, we walked along the main campus street toward the *wushu* gymnasium, chatting about Coach Wang and members of the team. He asked me about my college program. At one point, I steered him toward the shadows when other students walked in our direction. I wanted to avoid being peppered with too many questions if anyone saw me in the company of a foreigner.

Norm took it as a hopeful sign and teased me, using a combination of his improved Chinese vocabulary and hand signals. "You like me. Can I see you tomorrow?"

Watching the other students move away down the road, I urged Norm to continue walking, then said, "Oh, I can't. It's a school day."

"When? I want help to buy dragon kites," he said, faltering on the pronunciation.

"Kites? For who? For you or for kids?" I asked.

"For me and for gifts."

"Kites are for children, not adults," I said to discourage him while puzzling over the idea of an adult who would have time to play with kites. Young people in China are too busy studying, working, and fulfilling their responsibilities. They don't have time to play. Right then, I wondered if Americans were different. I tried to explain further. "When I was a child, I never had any toys bought from a store. Everyone made his or her own toys, even kites. Maybe rich people can buy kites somewhere, but I don't know where."

"We could…" he said, searching his mind for the right word before continuing, "…hunt for old *wushu* books. And I want to buy an *erhu* for a friend," he added as he pretended to strum a musical instrument. "Coach Wang would want you to help me."

"Okay, I'll meet you on Sunday," I said, wondering whether it was a good idea.

Norm grinned with happiness while we made arrangements to meet away from campus. His transparent emotions were easy to read and a source of curiosity for me.

Spending time with Norm on Sunday turned out to be fun and yet frustrating. I welcomed the change of activity but felt uncomfortable with ethnocentric Chinese staring at *Da Bizi*—the pet name adopted by Chinese for Caucasians, literally translated as big nose. Norm's large nose, a product of his Romanian ancestry, contrasted greatly with the smaller nose of my countrymen.

Riding on the back of Norm's bicycle on the busy city streets, I scanned the traffic for policemen. A new law prohibited riding double, though it was largely ignored. If I spotted a policeman, I shouted to Norm to slow down quickly so I could jump off.

While exploring antique booths and booksellers' stalls in an old market, I found myself looking curiously at Norm from time to time. I didn't know it would be such fun to be in his company. His undiminished belief we were destined to be together became the theme of the day. It seemed he didn't mind hearing me say no over and over again. Maybe because he made me laugh so much, we didn't take each other seriously.

A few weeks after we parted company, I received my first letter from him. One of my former teammates must have given him my address. The writing was simple, like a five-year-old child. I put the letter aside, deciding to answer it when I could give it more attention.

I didn't see Norm again until the next summer when I arrived in Yangzhou to visit Coach Wang. Meal preparations were underway in the tiny kitchen, after which a sumptuous feast would be served on tables set outside in the yard. With a beer in his hand, Norm watched Coach Wang cleave a whole chicken. Coach Wang's wife stood alongside a boiling pot on the stove.

I had just returned from Tibet and hadn't visited Coach Wang since I won my *taiji* championship title. Coach Wang stood with knife in hand as he watched me come in through the front door and enter the kitchen. We didn't exchange any words, but I knew the dark look crossing his face meant he wasn't pleased with me. He reached over and grabbed a heavy slab of pork, which he then slammed down on a chopping block. "Take the hairs off that," he ordered in a gruff voice. I didn't like it, nor did I understand why he was so angry, but I obeyed, grumbling to myself because I knew he did it to put me in my place.

Norm obviously knew why Coach Wang was so angry. He tried not to laugh when we spoke together that evening, but his eyes twinkled in amusement. Even though his Chinese had improved over his last visit, Norm used hand motions and his translation book to communicate his impressions of what had upset Coach Wang. "You walk in looking very… outgoing, the… confident college student wearing pants..." His hand made a cutting motion at the knee to indicate my shorts. "…that I never see anyone here wear. Coach Wang looked at them, and then his face…" Norm's face screwed up into an imitation of Coach Wang's irritated one, making me smile in spite of my embarrassment. Then, he added, "Nice legs," embarrassing me further.

Norm secretly flirted with me throughout my stay in Yangzhou, though we were often distracted by some of my former teammates, recruited by Coach Wang to help train visitors. Everyone was accustomed to seeing Norm each year and friendships had developed. Early attempts at segregation and chaperoning established at the training camp in Nanjing slowly fizzled out and were nonexistent in the relaxed atmosphere of Yangzhou. Regular late evening talks with a group of athletes—who were interested in exchanging information about each other's lives—occurred while we sat around one of the rooms in Coach Wang's house eating watermelon and drinking tea.

Over the next few weeks, I came to know Norm better. Much of what I discovered about him I learned by hearing him talk to others. In some ways, he reminded me of Coach Wang. The most significant thing they had in common was they both dealt with others in a straightforward manner. I found this especially comforting while among my teammates whose polite demeanors camouflaged their true emotions. At least I had always known where I stood with Coach Wang.

When I left Yangzhou for a visit with my family in Baoying, Norm returned briefly to the United States. He would be assisting a tour group of American foundry owners, his brother included, who arranged to visit comparable metal casting factories in China. He would be back in China within two weeks.

After school started again, Norm showed up in the *wushu*

gymnasium during practice. He attracted so much attention that I decided it was time to have a talk with him.

As we walked toward my dormitory, I said, "You can't show up here in front of everyone."

"Why not?" he asked, not making this easy.

"Everyone will talk about me."

"What will they say?"

"That we're boyfriend and girlfriend."

"What's wrong with that?"

"They'll think I'm looking to be rich, find a millionaire boyfriend," I shyly admitted.

After I helped him look up the words rich and millionaire in his translation book, he laughed. "I'm not rich."

During those evening gatherings in Yangzhou, with everyone firing questions at Norm about his life in America, I had learned Norm came from the northern state of Michigan. His family owned a foundry and lived in the country. Norm worked for them part of the year when he wasn't leading tours or traveling. He had recently hooked up with the Asia Society as a tour manager for a group of Chinese musicians performing in the United States—twelve cities in two months. Part of his time in Beijing was spent visiting the musicians he had escorted.

"I know you aren't rich, but they don't. They'll think I want an easy life and don't want to work hard, that I can't do anything for myself. It's against Communist principles."

"Who…cares what they think?"

"What they think affects my life here at school. It affects how people treat me. I don't think you understand," I said in frustration.

"Well, hike with me Sunday and tell me more."

I shied away from our going to remote areas alone. Instead, I agreed to lunch downtown.

On Sunday morning, Norm chained his bike to a tree on campus. After hearing we needed to take three buses to go downtown, he urged me to take a taxi. He didn't understand the look of shock on my face.

"A taxi is…quicker," Norm said.

I tried to explain how much the difference in price might be.

"Our time is…worth money," he said.

I shrugged my shoulders, not understanding what he meant. "It does take time to ride the bus, but I would never spend the money to ride a taxi."

"It's my money, not yours."

"No," I said firmly, "I won't ride in a taxi."

"Okay. We'll take a bus."

We hopped aboard the number 366 downtown-bound bus to reach our destination, a busy vendor-filled street. We browsed the stalls with Norm looking for old-fashioned goods while I steered myself to tables with more modern-looking clothing. We worked our way toward the restaurant and took seats at a small table in the back room.

"What would you like to eat," Norm asked me.

"Oh, anything," I answered.

"Speak up and tell me what you want."

"I would like to eat anything. What do you want and we can order it?"

Frustration was beginning to show on Norm's face. "I don't understand it. When my Chinese friends eat with me, it's the same thing. They don't want to say what they want to eat."

I found myself in the position of trying to explain something never talked about. "It's a cultural thing. It's my background, the way I was raised. I can't ask for anything, even if I'm thirsty."

"That's...confusing."

It embarrassed me to reveal cultural customs that might be seen as peculiar to outsiders, but I forged ahead. "We can accept something that's offered, but only after saying no at least three times. Otherwise, people will say we aren't trained properly and didn't receive good family education."

"Three times? Why didn't someone tell me this before? I know I've... offered food to your teammates and was refused. One time I offered watermelon on this really hot day. I couldn't believe they didn't want any."

I giggled. "I heard about that. They said they couldn't believe you ate the watermelon in front of them and didn't offer it to them again."

"Well, it's their...fault for not being...honest with me. Now, what do you want to eat?"

"I'll eat anything."

"Okay," he said with a big sigh, "just order us some potstickers and whatever else you think I would like."

As we finished our meal, I requested again that he not appear at gatherings on campus. "Because of your visit in the gym, I've already received requests to have you change money and buy things at the foreign store."

China produced two types of currency until sometime in the 1990's: Chinese currency and one for foreigners to use at stores catering to their needs with imported foods and goods unavailable at Chinese markets. Possessing foreign *Yuan* allowed anyone to use it at the foreign store.

"Besides," I added, "I feel uncomfortable when people talk about me."

We finally agreed to pass messages through a male classmate after introductions were made.

While waiting for the bus, Norm said, "I almost forgot to tell you. I found a... calendar today with your picture on it. It was a photo similar to the one on the cover of *Chinese Wushu* magazine except you were using double hooks instead of the straight sword. I'm going to bring it home with me to...remember you."

"I didn't know they used one of my pictures for a calendar." Having photos taken was considered an honor. No permission was required before using the photos and I didn't receive any money or even a copy of the calendar. These things changed later so that China was more like the West.

When the bus arrived, it was a free-for-all to get on as people shoved toward the door and stuffed themselves on. When Norm hesitated, I grabbed his hand in the confusion to keep us together. Somehow, as we stood crushed against each other, we managed to secretly continue holding hands. Memories swirled through my mind of the times long ago when Baba gently washed my little hands and when Mama clasped my hand in hers on the way to the bus station the day I left Baoying for my new life at the team. It felt strangely comforting to be holding the hand of this foreigner, and our friendship took a baby step in a new direction.

During Norm's stay in China, I slipped away on most Sundays to spend time with him. He recounted his week of bicycling adventures on progressively narrower rural roads leading away from Beijing.

"The other day, I bicycled to the...hills," he began. "I ran into a...military base. The...guards at the lonely...outpost looked...startled to see me coming. They told me, 'you can't be here.' When I answered them in Chinese, they were...shocked. We had a friendly conversation. They were bored and wanted a break in the...monotony of their jobs."

Norm took me shopping and we dined at restaurants. I accompanied him as he visited many historical sites in Beijing. Near the end of his visit, Norm pushed again for my promise to marry him.

I responded by saying, "It's my dream to finish college and become a college teacher. Marriage doesn't fit into my dream right now."

"You should finish college. After that, there are many… opportunities for you in America to become a teacher. We have a good time together. Won't you think about it while I'm gone?"

I finally agreed to think about it, but I honestly didn't hold out much hope that I would move to America with him.

I always thought of myself as mature in many ways, but the ways of the world still baffled me. How could I think about getting married when I had such limited experience with men? I was more inclined to make my own way in the world first.

The idea of leaving China intrigued me, however. One day I had an idea. The German language wasn't popular in China. After one year of studying it, I saw an opportunity to use it. Although no formal exchange program existed between China and Germany, the university in Cologne sent one student each year to study in the master's degree program at our school. I began thinking about applying for a master's degree exchange to Cologne. It had never been done, but I liked a challenge. As a top student who performed well on German tests, I sensed the university might agree to let me go there. I reasoned it was worth pursuing even if it was a long shot. I could always change my mind about it later.

A couple of days later, I confessed to my German studies professor, "I don't feel confident speaking German. Do you have any suggestions on how I can improve?"

He introduced me to Susan, a girl attending a nearby university. We agreed to meet every weekend. She would help me with my German pronunciation and conversation, and I would teach her *taiji*.

During this time, I was surprised to find myself in a dilemma as my days at college became less carefree and jealous classmates unsheathed their claws. College ceased to be a place of fun and possibilities. My lucky year of the tigress was definitely over and I needed to start looking in new directions. But where?

Liu Yu (left) with Spicy Dragon

Liu Yu

28   *DEFENDING A TIGER'S HONOR*

While leading a meeting at school during my junior year, I squirmed when one of my classmates heckled me, interrupting me for the third time with his rude remarks. A group of four girls sitting with him, Tiger Princess and Little Mouse included, laughed boldly at my predicament. Color rose to my face though I tried to appear calm. This wasn't the first meeting in which he had taunted me, and I was determined to put a stop to it.

After the meeting, I boldly went up to the boy and asked to speak with him. "I don't appreciate your rudeness," I told him. "I don't want to be spoken to in that disrespectful manner. Don't do it again." He tried to act nonchalant as he left, and I couldn't tell what effect my words carried. As I walked back to my dorm, I mulled the situation over in my head.

A lesson I failed to learn thoroughly on the team was that others will try to pull down anyone who shows them up and they feel justified in doing so. Coach Cobra had acted to have Coach Wang dismissed because he didn't fit in with the norm and had stood out. His peers then hammered him down to keep him even with everyone else. At college, I was so busy developing my independence and pursuing knowledge that discovering my jealous classmates were eager to crush me took me by surprise. They didn't want to look bad when we vied for jobs upon graduation.

Many of my classmates stayed up late at night playing mahjong and gambling with the young faculty. This led to inappropriate relationships with teachers. Instead of studying, they looked for ways to circumvent the system. In addition, Spicy Dragon, another roommate, and I soon noticed signs of cheating—classmates' knowing questions or answers for tests ahead of time, although their inability to memorize well kept them from getting top scores. I suspected Tiger Princess's young faculty companion, who was now her fiancé, was helping her cheat. She, in turn, was probably being used by other friends who conned her into helping them.

Shortly thereafter, a suspicion I had held about Little Mouse was confirmed. She and a professor were seen coming and going from each other's rooms at odd times during the day. Although no one wanted to think about a young girl having an affair with a professor in his fifties, too many signs pointed in that direction.

The professor in question could have been called *hua hua gonzi*, loosely translated as a strutting peacock—a playboy. He tried to attract everyone's attention by dressing vainly in a tailored suit, a colorful tie, and shiny dress shoes. Stylish glasses and slicked back oily hair accented his chubby face. Long after he recovered from a slight stroke that caused him to use a cane, he sported the cane to maintain his look as an English gentleman. For these reasons, I thought of him as Professor Peacock.

One evening, a couple of my roommates and I answered a loud knocking at our door. When the door was opened, several classmates from across the hall flew into the room.

"We don't have anywhere to go. Can we stay here for a while? One of the girls is having a male visitor in the room."

My eyebrows went up. I questioned the girls and found out that Little Mouse was indeed entertaining Professor Peacock alone in her room and that it had been going on for some time. It made me disgusted to think about it.

"I don't understand why school officials let him get away with this. They must know," I said. "The two of them don't appear to be hiding it."

Everything seemed so mixed up. Students were dating teachers. They spent their time having fun instead of studying. I felt like an outcast.

Suddenly fearful of losing my friendships, I tried to determine what changes I could make to keep them. During this frustrating time, I failed to study for an important test. Maybe subconsciously I wanted my friends to accept me.

I was outraged, however, when my test report was returned with a failing grade. Although I had not fully prepared for the test, I didn't believe I deserved such a low mark. When I found out that Tiger Princess and her clique, including the heckler who was a poor student, had done well on the test, I bristled with rage. In a bold move, I clutched my test report and, with all the dignity I could muster, entered my teacher's office.

"I think there's been a mistake on my grade," I said bravely, though inside I trembled.

Lines erupted on my teacher's forehead as he replied, "No, no mistake."

I distrusted the teacher, who was one of the regular mahjong players, so I continued, "I want to see my test."

"Well," the teacher said in an officious tone, "I can't do that."

"And I want to see the tests of my classmates," I announced, daring him.

My remark hit a nerve and he snapped. "That's not possible. I can't show other students' tests to you."

"I want you to know," I said with a show of strength that usually appeared only on the competition carpet, "that my tests need to be fairly graded or I'll ask for an investigation."

"I assure you that will not be necessary," he answered with a touch of condescension.

Feeling I got my point across, I turned to leave. Outside the door, I became a pile of nerves, but I knew I had to take a stand or suffer further injustice.

Late that evening in the cluttered hallway outside our dorm room, I was feeling low when I ran into Spicy Dragon. "I feel like I don't want to learn anymore."

"You've done everything so well; don't fall apart now. Keep up on your studies," she encouraged.

I had to admit that having my grade drop in my class made me feel worse and I knew it really wouldn't improve my failing friendships.

"You're right. I need to study hard and get my grade back up. I would go study right now, but the library will be closing soon."

"I have the key to my friend's room across the hall," Spicy Dragon confided as she pointed out the room. Her friend held a job as an assistant teacher that entitled him to a room he shared with only one other person. "He and his roommate are both on work trips out of town," she said. "You can study there. I'll leave our door unlocked so you can slip back in when you're finished."

It was after midnight and after curfew when I tiptoed quietly across the hallway toward my room. When the doorknob wouldn't turn, I panicked. I didn't know what to do. Very quietly, I tapped on the door. I was surprised to hear a tussle on the other side.

I heard Tiger Princess's angry voice saying, "She's too late. She can't come in."

Spicy Dragon answered, "She was only studying. I left the door unlocked for her."

"Well, I locked it after you went to sleep."

The scuffling continued until finally Spicy Dragon managed to unlock the door and wrench it open.

I tried to explain calmly about studying in an empty room.

"No," Tiger Princess said accusingly, "you were out late with a boyfriend or whatever and now you want to sneak back inside."

A door opened behind me and several classmates, hearing the commotion, spilled out into the hallway.

Uncharacteristically, my anger rose. In a trembling but calm voice I said, "*I'm* not the one who goes out with boyfriends all night and never comes back to the room."

Tiger Princess, now bolstered by a larger audience, said mockingly, "You're a country girl. You don't know how to play city games."

"Well, I like it that way," I said with dignity. "And, I don't cheat."

Tiger Princess smiled with arrogance. "I'll report you for being out late."

"I didn't do anything wrong," I said in defiance.

Spicy Dragon and our other roommates finally got all of us in our beds, and I snapped my curtain shut.

The next day, my roommates and I were summoned to appear together before our respective advisors. In much calmer voices, we explained what occurred the previous night. The teachers agreed to check my story.

Later, my advisor spoke to me privately. "We investigated your story and have learned it was true. I personally don't feel you did anything seriously wrong. And I totally understand your side. Your roommate is trying to make this a big deal. It's up to you if you want us to pursue this further and give you a clean slate."

I suspected immediately some teachers wanted me to blow this up. They secretly wanted the chance to confront a spoiled Tiger Princess. I sensed danger. I didn't want the teachers to use me to get back at her, a typical Cultural Revolution tactic. They hoped I would tell them about how Tiger Princess stayed out all night with her young faculty boyfriend and that someone was probably doing her homework for her. My experience of living with teammates, however, taught me not to let problems escalate.

"As long as you and the other teachers know I did nothing wrong, I'm satisfied," I said.

My fight with my roommate left a bitter taste in my mouth. Changing my personality or feeling embarrassed and guilty for going against what was socially acceptable didn't feel right to me. I questioned whether I fit in with China's culture, a culture in which students weren't punished for cheating, teachers could alter anyone's grades on a whim, and people took advantage of each other to get ahead. It made me doubt the wisdom of my goal to become a college professor. There were no guarantees that, as a successful student, I could even win a teaching position against an opponent who simply had connections. Did I really want to work in this kind of unfair environment? Although disheartened, I reacted stubbornly. I buried myself in my studies, not willing to waste the opportunity of learning as much as I could. Defying the accepted norm, however, left me with a sense of foreboding. A young coach I met a few weeks later added to my feelings of uncertainty, especially about relationships.

The year was 1988, and China's doors were opening for students who then jumped at the chance to travel to other countries where they could continue their education. Students nearing graduation who had plans to leave China contacted me to teach them *taiji* before departing. Word traveled that foreigners delighted in seeing *taiji* demonstrated. This enabled Chinese students to meet more people and make friends easier. Also, being able to teach *taiji* in another country was a source of extra income, even if their level of *taiji* was barely adequate. I taught several seniors the basic twenty-four movement form as a favor and didn't receive any compensation. In return, I enjoyed getting to know other students. Having a few of my own students who were learning *taiji* from scratch provided a great learning experience for me.

In addition to graduating seniors, a young coach contacted me to teach him *taiji* before departing for Australia at the end of the summer. He coached the equestrian part of the training for athletes on China's Olympic pentathlon team who competed in five events: a 5000-meter cross-country horseback ride, 4000-meter cross-country run, 300-meter swim, foil fencing, and pistol shooting. We met every day outside on the campus grounds.

One day, the coach explained that although he was from Mongolia 内蒙古, he was born in Shaanxi 陕西省Province, north of Xian 西安. Moving to Mongolia usually meant political exile, and I was curious about it.

"Why did you move?" I asked.

"My family was banished from Shaanxi after my uncle died. He got caught in unfair politics between Chairman Mao, Chairman Liu, and Zhou Enlai. During Mao's long march, my uncle befriended Mao, who lived with our family. When my uncle got caught in a political web and lost Mao's favor, the whole family suffered."

I found it interesting to listen to the smooth talk of this tall, handsome coach. I wished I could talk to other people this easily.

Before long, something unexpected happened. When this young coach, whose age was close to mine, was halfway through learning the *taiji* form, I realized we were attracted to each other. We then started seeing each other outside the lessons. Because his departure for Australia was approaching, our relationship progressed faster than it would have otherwise. By the time he had learned the *taiji* twenty-four form, the coach and I were talking about how we could get to know each other better. He wanted me to commit to waiting for his return.

Everything became hugely complicated when Norm arrived back in Beijing announcing his plan to stay in China for six to eight months. Seeing Norm again left me confused about what I really wanted to do.

Spicy Dragon was my confidante. I told her everything and trusted her judgment. She didn't sugar coat her observations, speaking the truth even if it wasn't what I wanted to hear. I appreciated her wisdom because my sheltered upbringing left me naïve about dealing with relationships.

While alone in our dorm room, I explained the situation to Spicy

Dragon. "The coach is hard to get to know. He talks a lot but he doesn't reveal much about what he's really thinking. Norm, on the other hand, is like an open book. I like that better. I sense Norm is more sure of himself, though maybe stubborn. Sometimes I think I just don't have enough experience to make a decision. Both men are pushing me to choose."

She looked at me in disbelief. "You told each of them about the other? You're brave. How did they take it?"

"They hate each other," I said.

"And how long is the coach going to be gone to Australia?" she asked.

"He doesn't know," I admitted.

"I thought my own life was complicated, but this is worse." Spicy Dragon was engaged to a foreign-exchange student from France. They wanted to marry after they graduated, but it was against Chinese law. The problem wasn't that he was a foreigner; it was that he was only twenty-three. The purpose of the law was to prevent young marriages in a country trying to reduce its birthrate and therefore women were forbidden to marry before the age of twenty-two and men before the age of twenty-four. Spicy Dragon's boyfriend got mad, ranting against the injustice of having to follow Chinese law when he wasn't Chinese.

Spicy Dragon and I agreed to have her meet the coach. She had already met Norm. After our meeting in the cafeteria over lunch, Spicy Dragon and I walked back to our dorm.

"Well," Spicy Dragon said, "I'll tell you frankly that I don't like the coach."

This surprised me. I waited for her to continue.

"He doesn't know how long he'll be gone. Waiting for him for an unknown period of time is ridiculous. I think he's taking advantage of you. If he really cared about you, he would cancel his plans and make you the most important thing in his life. I don't think he's the right guy for you."

What Spicy Dragon said rang true to me, but I hadn't realized it before now. I wasn't sure if I had only been facing my natural reluctance to commit myself, wanting to play it safe and keep people at a distance. I was hesitant to be involved with a foreigner and the complications it would bring. It made me especially uncomfortable to think about people gossiping about me and drawing false conclusions about my relationship with Norm. Yet I didn't feel totally comfortable with the secretive coach either. I said sadly, "You're right. I couldn't see it because he and Norm are both pushing me to make a decision between them."

Spicy Dragon surprised me by saying, "I like Norm. I feel you can trust him."

"I'm beginning to think so, too. But I still feel uncertain about committing myself."

I finished up my third year with our usual end-of-the-year *wushu* exams, not as a competitor but acting as one of the ten judges. At the beginning and end of the finals each day, we judges marched around the performance carpet while spirited Chinese marching music played over the loudspeaker. Then we seated ourselves at a long table. While we were judging the younger *wushu* athletes on their skills, a table of coaches and teachers were judging us and our scoring abilities.

The *wushu* gymnasium was bright and airy with large windows allowing the sunlight to spill over the wooden parquet floors and the two green performance carpets. The ceiling fans blew at a fast clip, ruffling the tan banners pinned above the mirrored portion of the wall. The black lettering reminded us that people who practice martial arts should respect others and have pure hearts.

The atmosphere was brimming with excitement. Students brought in stools to sit on while cheering for their classmates. Fighting set and solo routines unfurled before us as weapons clanked and thudded amid the dynamic contests of agility and muscle power.

The occasion was marred for me because of the sadness I felt over Spicy Dragon's upcoming graduation. She and her fiancé had been invited to live with her parents until either her fiancé was old enough to marry in China or Spicy Dragon received a visa to travel to France to marry. She was delighted because she wanted her family to get to know her fiancé better. Spicy Dragon was like a little revolutionary because she had such a stubborn, independent, and strong personality. I, on the other hand, always did what people expected of me. I would miss Spicy Dragon and didn't look forward to a new roommate taking the place of my best friend in the dorm.

When summer break began, I spent the first part of it in Beijing with my parents, who were thrilled to be visiting while staying in my roommates' empty bunks. Norm had gone to Tibet, saying before he left, "I'll be gone for six weeks. I hope during that time you'll get the coach out of your system and make a decision to be with me. I can't imagine that he cares more about you than I do." We parted under uneasy terms with Norm's frustration making me feel anxious and guilty. I didn't want to hurt his feelings.

I continued to meet with the coach for *taiji* lessons while my parents were napping but refused to see him outside our class time together. As the time neared for me to head to Yangzhou to help Coach Wang, I knew I had to finally decide about the coach.

Late one afternoon after our lesson, the coach and I walked back toward my dormitory. We stood next to the gymnasium where a sheet was being strung out on a line for an evening movie showing. When he asked me again if I had made a decision about waiting for him, I asked, "Do you really need to go to Australia? I know everyone wants to travel outside China to help them qualify for a better job, but you're already a coach."

"It took me a long time to get this chance to travel." Then he turned to look at me and said, "I could take you to Australia."

I looked at him quizzically. "How can you promise that?"

"I can't promise, but maybe it could happen."

Suddenly I felt skeptical. I realized I had been waiting for some signal, however small, to push me over the edge toward making a decision. The coach's offhand remark seemed more like an appeasement than an indication he really cared about me. I took a deep breath and said, "We haven't had enough time to really get to know each other. I understand you're looking for a change in your life by going to Australia. It's your choice whether you decide to go or stay and get to know me better. If you do go, I'll be fine, but I can't promise to wait." My words were meant to let him down easily and keep his self-respect intact.

In the end, he chose to leave. I found I didn't feel hurt by it, only relieved. Before he left, he asked me for a favor. He claimed to have nowhere to keep his belongings and I reluctantly agreed to hold them for him.

I then nervously headed to Coach Wang's house in Yangzhou, where I expected to face an angry Norm. I needed to tell him the coach was gone, that he wasn't the right person for me.

After the long train ride, I stayed in Nanjing for two nights with a friend who was the daughter of a tennis coach at the training camp. She lived outside the grounds of the camp, and we spent part of our day together making a trip inside the gated facility to seek out mutual friends who now held coveted coaching positions.

We checked in with the uniformed guards at the roomy gatehouse and walked down the shady, tree-lined avenue. We headed toward the huge open-air track arena, passing the tennis and outdoor basketball courts where I spent years in agonized training. Just walking along the camp's main road exhumed all those fearful and unhappy feelings buried deep in my psyche. I tried not to dwell on my old feelings of unhappiness while living at the camp, but now I saw clearly the contrast between the emptiness of my former life and the lightness and sense of liberation I experienced at college. I purposefully shook off the eerie sensation of my old protective shell and replaced it with a rush of gratefulness. I had escaped without becoming mentally or emotionally crippled.

Thankfully, I managed to avoid Coach Cobra. Instead, as we ambled around the arena toward the various sports buildings, I bumped into White Flower, my former rival. She greeted me with the old familiarity of a competitor. When I asked how she was doing, she boasted, "I'm now coaching the girls' team. With my college degree, I'm qualified to be a coach."

As soon as the words left her mouth, a shadow quickly darkened her face. I sensed a realization dawning that her two-year college degree would be superseded by my four years. She asked nervously, "What are you planning after you graduate?"

"Don't worry," I said. "I don't think I'm coming back here." Two truths existed as to why I would never return. In all honesty, no one would welcome me back. Also, I clung to my desire to leave this prison behind me forever.

To my great relief, my friend suggested we cut our visit to the camp short and return to her apartment. Before leaving Nanjing, my friend's mother, the tennis coach, surprised me by asking, "Do you want to come back to the team? I could help you." She and Coach Wang had been good friends during the many years she worked at the training camp. She implied I was the only one who could rectify some wrongs on the team and fight back against Coach Cobra. With my college degree, I would outrank him. This made me squirm. I didn't doubt that her vast connections reached like a spider web and could pull me back to a lofty position. She didn't know me well enough, however, to understand how I detested politics and using power to force others to obey my will.

My response to her was, "I don't know, but I don't think I'm interested. Thank you, though." Although I liked to be definitive in my answers, sometimes it hurt people's feelings when they were doing something nice. I thought it was better to let her believe I would think about it but was leaning against it.

My former teammate, Wei Wei, and I hooked up to travel to Yangzhou together. On the bus, we talked like a brother and sister who'd been apart too long, raising our voices to compensate for the driver's constant horn blasts as he bullied his way down the middle of the narrow road, forcing carts and trucks to the side.

It saddened me to hear of the vindictive treatment my teammate continued to receive from Coach Cobra, all because Wei Wei had refused to write the grievance paper against Coach Wang many years ago. Wei Wei was never given the chance to show his immense talent, and yet he wasn't free to leave either. Athletes belonged to their team with no rights to quit. That may be why some suffered mental breakdowns; consciously or subconsciously, it was the only way they saw to get out.

Forced to hang around the team, Wei Wei faced gloomy prospects for bettering his life. A menial job selling tickets and a shared room in which to stay were his probable fate.

Wei Wei admitted, "I would like to be a team coach, but I haven't been able to change Coach Cobra's prejudicial feelings toward me. I fear I'll never move up."

I looked at Wei Wei and shuddered with the deep realization this could have been me. Life on the team had brought us a level of prosperity unheard of during China's upheaval, but we also suffered from some of the same corruption that existed during the Cultural Revolution. At the training camp, people with power controlled everyone else, just like in our government. With no mountain at our back—no one to support us—we floundered like fish out of water.

When I joined the team, I believed I'd escaped going to the countryside and the dismal employment prospects Mama had endured. I didn't realize I would discover greater oppression as a professional athlete. Now that I had tasted freedom at college, I trembled to realize how narrowly I had escaped a life of permanent tyranny. Naively, I thought that was all behind me, though I couldn't shake the creeping doubts that arose each time I encountered unfair treatment from my peers and professors.

When Wei Wei and I arrived in Yangzhou, I discovered Norm wasn't there yet. After a quick greeting, Coach Wang put us to work.

Each summer, Coach Wang ordered some of my former teammates

and me to help him with visiting athletes who came to Yangzhou to train with him. This summer was no exception.

A few days after my arrival in Yangzhou as I guided a spunky American teenager in the intricacies of the straight sword, Norm popped up beside me. At his look of wonderment, I melted inside. Our relationship had practically limped to a halt over my aversion to being pushed to make a decision between two suitors.

Once we were able to break free of the group without raising eyebrows, Norm talked about his visit to Tibet to meet with a Tibetan folk music group interested in hiring him as a tour manager. With a wounded expression, he confided he unsuccessfully tried to forget about me. I breathed a sigh of relief to see him again and realized I didn't want our relationship to be over.

"What… happened with the other guy?" Norm asked with a mixture of panic and uncertainty materializing in his eyes.

"He's gone. I won't be waiting for him to come back," I said.

We then found ourselves smiling at each other and knew we didn't want our connection to be broken. In spite of that, however, I still clung to my hesitation to commit to marriage.

Lu Yong Ling 吕永玲, Coach Wang's wife, and I became closer after I started college. We felt like sisters, even though her husband was a father figure for me. She was only slightly younger in age than Coach Wang but much younger in heart.

Lu Yong Ling delighted in the upcoming birth of her second child, who would be born under the auspicious sign of the dragon. She came from a large family with seven siblings. The Communists changed the rule in China to allow only one child for each couple with few exceptions. Peasant farmers could have two children if the first one was a girl. Also, after a lengthy application process, any person who was an only child with only one child born in the two closest antecedent generations could receive government permission to have two children. Coach Wang fell into the second category. His older daughter would be twelve years older than her new sibling.

One afternoon, I took the opportunity to direct my conversation with Lu Yong Ling toward the subject of Chinese men. I confided in her, "I had a boyfriend for a short while, but he left to study in Australia." After further discussion about him, I said, "I couldn't tell what he was thinking, so I didn't really get to know him."

Lu Yong Ling stroked her plump belly and said, "Men never let you see inside them. I think they're afraid to show any softness. Even my husband, who usually is too outspoken, keeps part of himself hidden."

Naïve about the nature of relationships in my culture, I found the subject fascinating. I took other opportunities to explore it further with my sister and married friends. They admitted some problems were more than a lack of communication. How the husbands spent their time away from the family and how much money they spent were taboo subjects. Energy wasted just trying to figure out what was on a husband's mind left wives feeling tired and upset.

I had grown comfortable with my independence and abhorred the idea of having a relationship with someone who dictated orders and never shared his thoughts. My confidence rose with the realization that I had made the right decision to let the coach go. Norm, on the other hand, didn't play games. Yes, he was persistent, but he knew what he wanted. He wasn't afraid to say what was on his mind. This gave me the feeling I knew where I stood with him. I was flattered by his attention and believed he saw special qualities in me. Slowly, I opened the door to thinking more seriously about what it would be like to marry Norm. The prospect of eventually having to tell my parents about Norm, however, filled me with dread and uncertainty.

Liu Yu with Norm Petredean

Lu Yong Ling (Coach Wang's wife) and daughters

Dueling swords between Liu Yu (left) and Spicy Dragon

Liu Yu and Norm Petredean

29   *BABA'S ANGUISH*

One Sunday evening during the beginning of my senior year, I lingered with Norm in the safety of darkness before returning to my dorm room, a room now less inviting without Spicy Dragon's presence. As Norm gently caressed my shoulders, he whispered, "I don't get to see you enough."

I sighed. "I can't get away as often now that I'm teaching."

A high demand existed for *taiji* instructors at various colleges in Beijing. To fill teaching requests, my department head analyzed which students had the skill and maturity to teach at our school and recommended me for the prestigious job.

Despite taking time away from my visits with Norm, I was pleased to have my first job outside the team. A fellow student and I rode our bikes for over thirty minutes to the countryside to reach the special Communist school that educated government leaders. When we arrived, we were shown great respect as someone brought us water to wash our faces and a pot of freshly brewed tea. Sometimes, a chocolate bar was served with the tea. The students, who were older government officials, called me Little Teacher.

My classmate and I taught the twenty-four movement *taiji* form and a straight sword routine to our class of about one hundred students. After two days, we lost our voices trying to make sure everyone could hear us. Our *wushu* department professors were helpful, giving us suggestions on how to project our voices by using our *qi* energy, where to stand so everyone could see us, and how to make beginning students comfortable with the pace of learning.

As compensation for teaching the class, I received ten *Yuan* but had to give half to the *wushu* department. Though five *Yuan*—about $1.25—wasn't much money, my classmate and I felt it was worth the effort. I appreciated my professors' encouragement, thinking about how it contrasted with life on the team where Coach Cobra and others tried to pull me down and prevent me from displaying my skills.

A couple of weeks later, a young teacher at my school approached me. "I heard you've been teaching *taiji* around campus to students leaving China. I wonder if you'd be interested in making some extra money. I know of some Chinese-speaking foreigners who live at the former Russian compound. They want to learn *taiji* and will pay ten *Yuan* for a one-hour lesson. Are you interested in teaching them?"

I didn't hesitate because that was where Norm was staying. The Russian compound used to house high-ranking Russian Communists after it was built in the 1950's. It was now Beijing's Friendship Hotel 北京友谊宾馆, with buildings containing hotel rooms or apartments that housed foreigners. Norm liked the squeaky wooden floors and combination Chinese-Russian style architecture.

Businessmen and their wives, originally from Japan, Hong Kong, and the U.S., who were now living in Beijing for a few years, became my students. One American, who was born in Taiwan and educated in the U.S., worked in IBM's Beijing division. Twice a week, I rode my bicycle in the morning for forty-five minutes to teach my students in the lovely Chinese garden on the hotel grounds.

My students paid me in the Chinese currency issued for foreigners. I received ten *Yuan* from each of my six students. Every day after teaching, I hustled over to the hotel's store to buy nuts and a heavenly loaf of fresh sweet bread. Even with all the bicycle riding, I gained weight, my face getting chubby and round.

Teaching at the Friendship Hotel was unauthorized by the university, making secrecy necessary. Young teachers and sports injury specialists who served as team doctors made extra money giving massages and chiropractic treatments to foreigners at the Friendship Hotel. A Japanese couple asked them for a referral to a *taiji* teacher, and that was how I got the job.

Norm was happy about my teaching at the hotel because we could see each other more often. We spent time together sitting in an out-of-the-way area on the tree-filled grounds of the hotel. While huddled together on a bench, Norm tried to help me learn some English by translating lyrics of popular Dolly Parton songs.

One day I listened to Norm engage in a lively conversation in English with someone at the hotel. It surprised and relieved me to hear him speak so fluently in his own language. I had naïvely believed that Norm might not be highly intelligent because he failed to speak Chinese well—though he improved with each trip and was taking Chinese classes in the U.S. between visits. This misconception about foreigners being less intelligent was rampant among Chinese. From a young age, we were told our culture was the greatest on earth. The country was closed off from the world for several decades, so Chinese people had little exposure to other cultures and we had nothing to use as a comparison. Even though I had studied German, I really had no idea how difficult it was to communicate with someone in another language or how hard Chinese was to learn for an English-speaking person. I looked at Norm differently after that.

Sundays were our adventure days. We hiked along stretches of the Great Wall meandering under the richness of blue skies before pollution changed the color to a permanent dingy gray. We visited popular historical sites, cooed at the animals in the zoo, attended a trade show of Russian goods in the Russian Pavilion, stuffed ourselves on meaty potstickers and roasted duck, drank tea in underground coffee shops, and watched amusing Chinese martial arts films as well as an occasional English movie.

One night we ate dinner at a popular hot spot where I knew the owner. We joined a throng of my classmates, which meant Norm and I acted like we were merely acquaintances. After dinner, everyone took turns singing songs or reciting poems. As one fellow began his poetic recitation, "Blue on blue, heartache on heartache, blue on blue now that we are through…" I saw Norm biting his lip in an attempt not to laugh, especially when we heard the words, "Night after lonely night, we meet in my dreams, as I run to your side, you wait with open arms…" Only later did I hear these were the words to a song not a poem and Norm thought they sounded very funny spoken in a serious voice by a Chinese man. Norm hadn't taught me those lyrics, so I couldn't understand the English words and failed to fully appreciate the humor.

When the weather turned bitterly cold, Norm pulled a ski mask over his head, making it easier for us to be together in public without raising eyebrows. Everyone could tell my beau was foreign from his clothes but probably assumed he was of Chinese ancestry.

Not all the time we spent together was harmonious. The drawback to having a boyfriend who spoke honestly was hearing things that made me uncomfortable or even hurt my feelings. When a cultural difference loomed between us, we attempted to explain our sides of the situation, sometimes not fully appreciating the other's point of view.

One time, Norm presented me with a lovely pink Patagonia jacket and several pairs of thick cushiony socks to replace the miserably thin ones I always wore. The next week he questioned me about why I wasn't wearing the socks. It was difficult to explain that several people had raved over the socks and I felt compelled to give each of them a pair. I could never feel comfortable wearing them if it meant other people would interpret it as my showing superiority over them. It was much better for me to give them away. Norm fumed in anger.

As December approached and Norm faced his last month in China, our talks turned more seriously toward marriage. Norm showed me photos of his large family, of their country home in Michigan, and of his travels in the U.S. and abroad. It was reassuring to see Norm's family wasn't wealthy because I was sensitive about what my family and friends would think. Escaping to a rich life was looked down upon.

Norm asked me if I had heard the story of Cinderella. I knew the story about the poor girl marrying the prince. I explained to him, "I'm not the type of person to marry for money." Chinese girls who married foreigners were accused of marrying millionaires. The thought of being accused of that made me uneasy.

If Norm had talked about America being such a big and special country, it would have been the wrong thing to say to me. I had been to Canada and imagined the U.S. to be similar. But many Chinese people envisioned the U.S. as a country of contradictions. An elite Hollywood glamour sector contrasted with a stratum of society predisposed to guns and violence, where black people suffered from prejudice and poverty. My parents probably thought about the latter. I knew from my trip to

Canada, however, a large middle class existed. It was possible to have a good life in America.

More and more, I realized I wanted to marry a man who would be a good husband and father. Norm's honesty suited me, though he claimed being transparent was probably a more accurate description. According to Chinese astrology, Norm was born an ox—though this sign is sometimes referred to as a water buffalo. Notorious for their strong will and straightforward manner, oxen exhibit a stubborn bullish refusal to budge and are prone to becoming defensive if they lose confidence and domineering if angered. Curious, nature-oriented, and innately organized, oxen strive for perfection in their lives. These tender-hearted creatures stick firmly by their family commitments, and this quality endeared me to Norm.

Although tigers and oxen are drawn to each other, a clash of temperaments may cause strife. Our relationship went through many ups and downs as one might expect between individuals of two disparate cultures. Chinese husbands are often much older than their wives, so the age difference of thirteen years between us didn't bother me. When I found out, however, that Norm had been briefly married before, this temporarily saddened me.

With each trip Norm made to China to see me, he came closer to winning my heart. His desire to stay for an extended period of time on this trip made me feel I was important to him. I doubted I would find anyone who cared about me more. I used to feel surprised that I felt more connected to Norm than to men of my own country. As we grew closer, I believed more and more that it was possible for two people from different cultures to be happy together.

Norm spent some of his time teaching English to a couple of desk clerks at his hotel. In return, they kindly allowed us to slip past them on our way to Norm's room. Ordinarily, they were required to telephone the authorities but made an exception in our case. A few stolen hours away from prying eyes bound us closer together. When I finally consented to marry Norm, we held each other tightly trying to freeze the moment in time.

We agreed I should finish college before marrying. The next step, Norm insisted, was to inform my parents and Coach Wang before Norm's upcoming departure from China. This prospect overwhelmed me with anxiety that quickly escalated to a state of full-fledged terror.

Norm preceded me to Yangzhou, and I uneasily made my way there as soon as my school schedule allowed. We would test the waters by breaking the news to Coach Wang and his wife first.

Horrified by our revelation, Coach Wang thundered, "NO! NO WAY!" He made small stabbing and slicing motions with his pointed finger as he continued to yell. "Liu Yu's a precious flower and you, Norm, are like a raw apple. This can't be."

Lu Yong Ling surprised us by saying to her husband, "I think it's more important that the man cares about the woman. Liu Yu isn't a little girl anymore either. She isn't your daughter. She's twenty-seven years old and can make her own decision."

My heart went out to Lu Yong Ling at that moment. I admired this pretty lady who should have had a husband who had been more of a companion. Her older brother had coached the Yangzhou Wushu Team and introduced the famous Wang Jin Bao to his sister. Coach Wang's mother forced her hesitant son to marry. The implication was he needed to move on after his relationship with the gymnast was cut short. Lu Yong Ling was only twenty-one when she married a man whose first love was the team and who spent most of the year living away from her. Upon hearing his wife's words, Coach Wang's intensity softened slightly.

Coach Wang was fond of Norm but took this opportunity to tell him, "You're trying to crawl into a bull's horn." A bull's horn is wide at one end and closed at the other. Crawling into the wide end meant going nowhere. In a typical offhand manner, Coach Wang was saying he didn't have a lot of faith in the marriage of the two of us with our dissimilar cultures, yet in a way he admired Norm's persistence.

I had telephoned my sister and asked her to bring the family to Yangzhou to discuss my future. Meeting them on neutral territory at Coach Wang's house would protect my parents from needing explanations about a visiting foreigner in their home. Prior to the meeting, I sat nervously across from Norm in a concrete teahouse shaped like a dragon boat resting on the shore of Slender West Lake 瘦西湖. Norm, all spiffed up in his best clothes and with his shoes shined, tried to calm me down. I don't think he fully appreciated the situation and how strongly my father was likely to react to our news.

"What kind of strategy should we take? How should we…pitch this to them?" he asked.

My foot nervously shook under the table and I could feel myself biting my lower lip. "I really don't know," I admitted. "The only thing I'm sure of is that you must not ask them a question that allows them to say no. You can say you wish to marry me, but don't ask them for their permission. We'll have to give them some time to think about this and not pressure them for a response right away." I sighed, feeling my stomach bunching up in a knot. "My parents are old-fashioned. They arranged the marriage for my sister. I don't think they'll react favorably."

Norm insisted he speak to my family without me in the room. My sister would translate as Norm wouldn't be able to understand the Baoying dialect. I agreed to baby-sit Wang Miao-王淼, the Wangs' new baby daughter, in the bedroom. Coach Wang and his wife would wait politely in the courtyard in case they were needed.

When we entered Coach Wang's house, the tension was palpable. After greeting my parents, sister, and brother, I took Wang Miao from her mother's arms and excused myself. A few minutes later I cringed with embarrassment as my father's raised voice barreled through the walls. After things quieted down, Lu Yong Ling came in shaking her head and saying, "Your father isn't well. Go see him."

Baba lay curled up on the living room bed, his face white and pinched and his body shaking all over. Norm was nowhere to be seen.

"Baba, are you all right?" I asked as I bent over him.

"You would be too far away for us to protect you," he murmured with a wounded stare. "I never thought you would be the girl to hold on to a foreigner, to go against your own culture." His words cut through me and pierced my heart.

My family was ashamed of me. How could I marry Norm? What was I thinking? This wounded man had done so much to ensure the success of each of his children. I was mortified that I had hurt him. Maybe I wasn't ready to marry Norm after all. Yet, even though I was less than one hundred percent sure about marrying at this moment, something inside me didn't want to say the words to make my father feel better. Deep down I resented not being able to make my own choice. I had played it safe for many years, always doing what others expected of me. I wasn't ready to give up my newly won independence or my sense of control over my destiny.

After escorting my family back to Baoying, I suddenly realized how stuck I felt in this situation. Not wanting to stay in Baoying any longer—which would give my family the opportunity to try to convince me to change my mind—I went in search of Norm. I headed to Shanghai where he would soon be catching a plane for the U.S. and where he might be visiting my former teammate and his close friend, Wang Yia Chun, who attended the Shanghai Institute of Physical Education.

It was evening when I stepped off the bus feeling weary and alone. A man greeted the group of arrivals, saying, "Do you need an inexpensive place to stay? Board my bus and I'll take you there." He herded us onto his bus. We felt some safety in numbers.

After traveling more than twenty minutes, I became alarmed at my stupidity in boarding an unknown bus. How far away was he taking us? We soon pulled up next to a warehouse. With fearful expressions, my fellow travelers and I entered a building converted to curtained sleeping areas with a central toilet facility. My anxiety level dropped after wearily climbing into bed.

The next day, I called Wang Ya Chun 王亚春, only to find out he hadn't heard from Norm. "Tell Norm I'm in Shanghai when you hear from him," I said. Meanwhile, I fled to the university and took a room at the visitor's dormitory. I spent my time walking while anxious thoughts haunted me.

Two days later, Norm arrived in Shanghai. I was called to the lobby of my building. From there, Norm and I escaped to a small arboretum on campus away form prying eyes.

"I'm glad you tried to find me," Norm said as he took my hand. Feeling relieved to see him, I grasped his hand tightly.

I still didn't know what had happened in the room between Baba and Norm. I had been reluctant to ask my family about it and face Baba's full-blown anger again. "Tell me what happened," I asked.

Norm admitted, "I wasn't prepared for your father's explosive reaction. He yelled about how Chairman Mao had ordered anyone with relatives in the West to be held in contempt. He kept yelling, '*zuo feiji, zuo feiji,*' as he stood in the flying-like-an-airplane position."

As I listened, a knot developed in the pit of my stomach. "When I was four years old, my father took me to see the punished aristocrats in the town square who were walking bent forward with their arms raised behind their backs. Anyone with connections to China's enemies received harsh treatment. He's afraid it will happen to my family."

Norm's voice developed an edge of aggravation. "He asked me what would happen if a second Cultural Revolution occurred. How am I supposed to control that? I told him I couldn't do anything about it, that it was his country, not mine. Then he collapsed on the bed."

"Oh, Norm, you said that? No wonder he was upset. Even though what you said was true, it was disrespectful. You should have said you felt some concern for my parents."

"I do feel badly he got so upset. Everyone rushed to him to see if he was okay and then they all turned to stare at me like I had tried to kill him. I didn't know what to say after that, so I left."

My mind reeled with compassion for Baba. "I'm putting my family in jeopardy. Maybe we should call off this marriage," I said in frustration.

"No way! When I left Yangzhou, I admit I was hot-tempered, but after I cooled down, I had to come find you. I knew I shouldn't have acted like I did in front of your family. I went to Nanjing but turned around and returned to Yangzhou. They told me you had gone to Baoying. I asked Coach Wang to call me a cab. He looked horrified and tried to talk me out of it, saying it would stir up everyone in Baoying."

That was an understatement. Only rich people rode in cabs. My parents would be the talk of the town. I didn't comment, however, and just continued to sit there listening to Norm's story, feeling stunned by what had transpired.

"Lu Yong Ling said not to force the issue with your parents because then they would be compelled to keep you a prisoner in Baoying. Coach Wang dragged his feet a bit but finally found me a ride to Baoying in the back of a dump truck. I had a lot of time to think while watching the river traffic next to the road. And I really appreciate Lu Yong Ling's help. She's a sweetie."

I nodded and walked over to a nearby bench and took a seat. Norm sat next to me. "I wore my ski mask on the street and finally found your parents' house from directions Coach Wang gave me. I crouched in an alleyway across the street for a while, but didn't see anyone coming or going. I couldn't wait, so I went over and knocked on the door. Your sister answered the door, saying, 'She's gone, she's gone.' Your father wasn't home, and your mother was so excited I couldn't understand what she was saying. Liu Jing translated for me, 'She went to Shanghai.' I'm glad you tried to look for me."

"What are we going to do, Norm?"

"I'm not letting someone else make our decisions. And I'm not giving up because you're afraid for your family. I want to marry you. Look, the hard part is over. We've told your parents. You aren't going anywhere until after graduation. Let's let everything cool down."

A jumble of emotions battled within me—anxiety over my family's reaction and relief that Norm hadn't given up on me. He cared about me so much he was willing to fight for me. It took great courage on Norm's part to stand before my father and speak his mind. I hadn't been brought up with that sense of freedom, but I admired that Norm wasn't afraid. I hoped I could learn to stand up for myself more and not keep my feelings so hidden.

I took Norm's hand. "Now that we've told my parents, I feel more committed. There's no going back."

"YES! That's what I want to hear," he said as he clasped my hand in both of his. "I only have a few days left before returning to the U.S. Let's go to town and have some fun together. We won't feel like everyone is spying on us in Shanghai."

Beijing was the political capital of China, but in Shanghai, known as the economic center of China, attitudes towards foreigners were more relaxed. Norm got us rooms at the Sheraton Hotel, and we spent our days sampling the restaurants and comfortably enjoying each other's company.

Those few days in Shanghai bound us closer together. When it was time for me to return to Beijing, I suddenly realized I didn't want to go back. I was ready to move to the U.S. at that very moment.

"You need to finish school," Norm insisted as his arm reached out to caress me. "You're so close now. It won't be long before we're together again. I'm planning to lead some Americans on a bicycle tour around China. If everything goes right, I'll be back at the end of May."

After a sad farewell, I returned to Beijing in low spirits. Shortly thereafter, an unusual opportunity came my way that stirred up my life in unimaginable ways. Even more startling, I never would have predicted my reaction.

Liu Yu (center rear) with her students at Shaolin Temple

 HUNTING DOWN THE TIGER

A week before the Chinese New Year vacation, Liu Yu Ping, my *wushu* coach, asked to speak with me privately.

"Liu Yu, I have a message for you from Professor Men," she said as we warmed ourselves in the sunshine pouring through the large gymnasium window. "He wanted you to check out the possibility of attending a unique *taiji* seminar organized by the Chinese Wushu Research Institute. Famous *taiji* masters will be attending, as well as professors and *taiji* instructors from all over China. Professor Men mentioned you should find a way to attend this seminar."

Professor Men couldn't extend a personal invitation to me; although having been through the Cultural Revolution, he knew how to surreptitiously accomplish things. Unfortunately, my *wushu* coach had no authority in this situation and, therefore, I was on my own regarding gaining entrance to the seminar.

Liu Yu Ping advised, "You might be allowed to attend if you show up and pay your own tuition, room, and board. Don't you know a lady who works at the Wushu Research Institute? I think she's from your province. She's one of the organizers for the seminar."

I thought for a moment, fingertips pressed to my forehead, and then looked up with sudden realization. "That's right. I've known her for many years." Slowly, a smile crept across my face.

As she filled me in on the details, I nearly shook with excitement. Training with Professor Men had whetted my appetite for a deeper understanding of *taiji*. Knowing there were *taiji* secrets I might uncover at the seminar filled me with a yearning to attend. The chance to meet and examine *taiji* masters was an incredible opportunity.

Eight of the ten days of the seminar coincided with the last week of my New Year vacation, and for that I was grateful. I made up my mind on the spot to end my holiday visit with my family early. The seminar costs could be paid for from my team retirement funds.

During the train ride home, I worried about what pressure my family would apply toward ending my relationship with Norm. Surprisingly, they acted like nothing had happened and his name was never mentioned. Instead, they fawned over me in the hopes I would be tacitly persuaded to change my mind. A kind of stubbornness seized me, however, and before I left I refused to say the words they were dying to hear.

My early return to Beijing for the *taiji* seminar meant a lonely ride without anyone to accompany me. Instead of taking the cheapest and longest train back, I splurged and took a faster train with fewer stops. While staring out at the passing scenery, I thought about my family. Their obedient girl who had always catered to everyone's wishes and expectations was now a woman developing a mind of her own, a dangerous thing in China. I disliked being the wayward daughter, but I found putting my life's desires second and succumbing to the will of others left an unpleasant taste in my mouth. I longed to be courageous and stand up for myself without fearing the consequences. This meant, however, I no longer fit in anywhere, not at home, not in school, and now not even in China.

The day after my return to school, I rode my bicycle two hours to attend the *taiji* seminar. It was held in the countryside at a chicken farm, an unusual place for so many famous people to go. The strange location was probably chosen to keep uninvited people from finding it. Upon arrival, and with some trepidation, I filled out the paperwork and submitted it for entry. When they took my forms and money, I breathed a sigh of relief.

The purpose of the seminar was to refine and polish standard forms for four of the five styles of *taiji*—Chen 陈, Yang 扬, Wu 吴, and Sun 孙. The Wu/Hao 武/郝 family and its disciples weren't interested in designing a standard form for the fifth style of *taiji*. This family came from a long line of wealthy scholars who never taught their style for a living, preferring to keep it a secret. Therefore, knowledge of this style wasn't widespread and it didn't have profound influence. No one outside the family and its disciples knew it well enough to develop a standard form.

Professors at my school had developed the standard forms: Professor Men designed the Sun-style standard form, and his wife, Professor Kan Guixiang 阚桂香教授, developed a standard form for the Chen style of *taiji*. Professor Zhang Wenguang 张文广教授, who was the oldest and most well respected professor at my school, began his *wushu* career in 1936 when, as a boy, he demonstrated *wushu* at the Berlin Olympics. He was the principal creator of the Yang-style 42 standard form.

Many *taiji* masters were "invited"—although in truth they were ordered by the government to attend—and asked to examine the standard forms that had been created. Masters representing their own styles included Master Chen Xiaowang 陈小旺大师, a direct 19th-generation descendant of the famous Chen *taiji* family, and Master Yang Zhen Dou 杨振铎, a 4th-generation descendant of the well-known Yang family. Other attendees were professors and two fortunate *taiji* instructors selected from each province to bring the standard forms to their area.

The seminar workshops split the participants into separate groups for each *taiji* style. I selected two styles to focus on at the seminar: Yang because that was the style I knew and Chen because it was the source of the Yang style. At the workshops held in the chilly outdoors, the creators of the standard forms demonstrated the movements. The *taiji* masters were asked to comment on whether the movements were true and correct for that style.

At this point, I was an observer. When the *taiji* masters took turns demonstrating their subtle renditions of each movement, I savored the different nuances they brought to the same piece. These masters had never come together before, and I couldn't believe my good fortune to be present.

For everyone to agree on the standard forms was remarkable considering all the different personalities and egos present. After final approval, these forms were then taught to seminar attendees. We practiced them all day and on our own at the conclusion of each day's group instruction before retiring to nearby dormitories.

On day six, one of my professors hunted me down to bring me a message from Professor Peacock. "The professor found out that you're here and he's not happy about it. He said students aren't supposed to be here. You better get back to school right away."

I nodded my head like I agreed, but I had no intention of leaving yet. School still wouldn't start for three more days.

Before seminar attendees could teach the standard forms in their home provinces, they were required to pass a test of their abilities. The tests would be given on day nine of the ten-day seminar with certificates awarded on day ten. Now I had to make a decision. Should I stay and face the consequences at school for arriving late for classes or forego this unbelievable opportunity? Within minutes I convinced myself that I already knew the Chen and Yang forms and I wanted to take the test. I wasn't going to leave and I would deal with any problems that arose later.

On day eight, Coach Liu Yu Ping approached me. "I heard from your professor and he's surprised you're still here. You better go back. You're going to be in trouble."

All my life I had succumbed to the pressure to be obedient and stay out of trouble. NaiNai always cautioned me not to make trouble over things that really didn't matter. But, suddenly, I knew this seminar mattered to me. I didn't want to miss any part of it. In an unusual show of bravery, I told Coach Liu Yu Ping, "I know I should go back, but I really want to finish the seminar."

"How about going back after you take the test tomorrow?" she said. "I'll pick up your certificate for you the next day before I leave."

"Okay," I said with relief. "And thank you." She smiled in understanding.

On day nine I took my test, then hopped on my bicycle and raced back to campus. I only missed one day of classes and hoped my absence hadn't caused a big problem. I was wrong.

The next afternoon all students and faculty gathered together for a *wushu* departmental meeting. A fuming Professor Peacock stood up and vented his outrage. "I want to tell everyone about a fourth-year student who came to school one day late. The student attended a prestigious *taiji* seminar that was intended only for teachers. That's against the school rules and *everyone* is supposed to follow the rules. All you freshmen, be warned. N*ever* do anything like this." As he spoke, his eyes bored into mine so that everyone knew who he was talking about without having to give my name. All heads turned to look at me.

I heard Little Mouse nearby say under her breath, "Yeah, we know who that was." My composure was momentarily thrown off because I had never been pointed out as doing something wrong before.

But then I began thinking, why should I be in trouble for using my passion and my own money to increase my knowledge? Wasn't that what school was about? After all, I wasn't cheating.

For years I hid from others. I had believed flaunting one's abilities only brought trouble just like it had for Coach Wang, and the more I remained inconspicuous, the better. College life, on the other hand, allowed me the freedom to grow and become a more independent thinker.

I was tired of hiding my feelings and avoiding trouble by always rushing to cooperate. And I wasn't sorry I was late for class. I felt like there was a revolution going on inside me to change my old way of thinking. The younger me would have been scared to death in this situation, but following my heart had given me some confidence. I learned I didn't have to please everyone. If I tried, I knew I would never be able to do what *I* wanted in my life. As I walked out of the meeting room, I remained surprisingly calm despite my belief that trouble would rear its head somehow. I braced myself for what lay ahead.

Rumors circulated that Professor Peacock tried to rally support from the other professors to punish me for attending the seminar. I learned he failed because he wasn't that popular. Several times he confronted me about the seminar, trying to incite me to fight with him so he could drum up some support for his side. Each time I carefully sidestepped the issue. We called it "playing *taiji*" where he tried to move toward me, and I deflected him and backed off. *Taiji* practitioners never tried to muscle an opponent if they went head-to-head. They learned the art of leverage and the principles of optimal timing. I was glad I didn't have to stick around and watch things escalate.

Shortly after the seminar, I prepared to fulfill my three-month student teaching requirement before graduation. I looked forward to leaving behind the aggravation of campus in-fighting. Before I left, however,

Professor Peacock cornered me in the gymnasium. His fingernails tapped the end of his walking cane while he hovered over me. I stepped back to put a safer distance between us. "Before you leave for your student teaching assignment," he began with an air of superiority, "I need to let you know I'll be your evaluator. Toward the end of your assignment, I'll be visiting you and discussing your work with the local teachers."

Inside I flinched but managed to gaze back at Professor Peacock with all the innocence I could muster. The last thing I wanted was to be thrown uncomfortably together with him in a remote location. I worried about getting a fair evaluation and staying out of his slimy grasp.

"I hope my teaching meets with your approval," I replied and hurried out of the building at my first opportunity. I was careful not to say something I would regret.

Accompanied by four other classmates, I headed to the lovely Songshan Mountains 嵩山 in Henan 河南省 Province and the prestigious Shaolin Temple 少林寺, known as the birthplace of Chinese *wushu*. I looked forward to finding out how much knowledge I had gained after more than three years of college. I was also anxious to develop my skills as a *wushu* coach because I hoped to put them to use in the future.

According to legend, a monk named Bodhidharma traveled from India to China and founded Zen Buddhism at the Shaolin Temple in the sixth century A.D. When Bodhidharma discovered the monks at the temple could not stay awake during his meditation instruction, he developed exercises to make the monks stronger physically and spiritually. These special body positions and movements were derived from Bodhidharma's observations of the hunting and defensive motions of animals. Along with the addition of breathing exercises, the monks practiced standing meditation for one hour at a time in a horse stance position—so called because the person appeared to be riding an imaginary horse. The monks soon found their strong legs and good balance helped them stay on their feet when attacked by bandits. Over the years, the monks' fighting techniques were refined and a code of honor, loyalty, respect, and honesty developed ensuring fighting skills would be used only for self-defense against injustice and not for personal gain. The underlying philosophy of the Shaolin Temple became that martial arts was a means for developing physically, mentally, and spiritually, and not merely a fighting method to defeat enemies.

In the early 1980's, Jet Li visited the abandoned and crumbling temple prior to making the movie blockbuster "Shaolin Temple." The movie commemorated the temple's famous legend of thirteen Tang Dynasty Shaolin monks who used *wushu* to rescue a Tang Emperor from an evil warlord. Inspired by Jet Li's character, thousands of Chinese boys and girls flocked to the temple, eager to become martial artists.

When I arrived in 1989, the Shaolin Temple was flourishing. More than twenty-two *wushu* academies surrounded the temple where ten thousand *wushu* students received instruction from hundreds of teachers.

Local officials puffed up with pride as they escorted my classmates and me on a tour of a few of the biggest schools. The sign over the largest one read "Dengfeng Shaolin Temple Wushu School 登封少林武术学校 and Beijing University of Physical Education, a jointly organized vocational school." My university had recently agreed to sponsor the school, causing its popularity to surge. One of its teachers who was in charge of all the *wushu* schools in the area had studied at my university during the past summer, receiving a special coveted training certificate.

"A lot of these kids are troubled kids from the countryside and towns, and they didn't do well in school," one of the regular teachers told us. "Many of them were headed for a hard life. This is their last chance to learn a useful skill and avoid a life of poverty or incarceration."

Parents were required to pay tuition for their children to train at a Shaolin Temple school. Private schools were a new thing in the 1980's and families recognized the opportunities they presented for their children. Parents signed three-year contracts, hoping their children would learn a skill to improve their future job prospects.

Many families scraped together tuition money from low-paying jobs, selling farm animals, or by receiving assistance from a relative, which would have to be paid back in the future. These families earned a meager living as farmers, waiting all year before finding out how much their share of the harvest was worth. After dividing up the profits based on earned work points, farmers collected their earnings only once a year and never knew in advance how much to expect. It made it hard to meet their financial obligations.

We watched the children moving purposefully in unison through their daily drills when one official bragged to us, "These children can take hard work. You can drive them like slaves. They don't have any choice. They have to take orders."

I watched as the teacher walked over to one of the boys wearing a filthy misshapen shirt and pants he'd outgrown. In an angry voice, the teacher yelled at the boy, "Work harder," and abruptly slapped him hard across the face. The teacher sauntered toward us with a proud expression as though he had put on an entertaining show for us. I cringed inside, feeling sorry for the boy whose eyes brimmed with tears and cheeks burned in embarrassment.

Seeing the boy slapped sickened me, but it didn't shock me. I had witnessed that scene many times while on the team, although Coach Wang only did it when he felt it necessary to motivate the athlete. My team coaches were convinced that striking students helped them to improve. Directing and disciplining children in that fashion was common in the Chinese culture, even with parents. If children complained to their parents about their treatment at school, it would fall on deaf ears. Their parents would say, "Good. That's part of the training. You have to take it. This is your only opportunity to better yourself." Poor peasant parents from the countryside wanted better futures for their children than to become farmers like themselves. As a result, the teachers felt it was their obligation to provide the most difficult training that would yield the highest benefit.

Henan Province, where the Shaolin Temple was located, had a history of being the poorest province in China. The parched land made it difficult to grow things and the inhabitants constantly endured floods from the Yellow River. They were known for suffering any hardship without complaint. Martial arts played a big part in their lives. When people were starving, as happened frequently in such a harsh environment, they reacted by starting a revolution. They believed fighting was better than starving to death. These tough country people offered their children no sympathy and expected hard work would make them stronger.

I looked from the boy in tears to the teacher who slapped him, anger roiling inside me. After spitting on the floor, the teacher turned to us and said, "If you don't drive them hard, they won't listen and obey."

But then my anger immediately turned to panic. Hitting students was something I could never do. It went against my nature. I was afraid I would stand out because I would be the only one who couldn't dispense bodily punishment. With a sinking feeling, I realized I didn't fit in. I worried that my inability to be like everyone else would affect my student teaching evaluation and give Professor Peacock ammunition to use against me, and yet I couldn't beat a student.

Out of five in my college group, one girl was told she would be teaching at this school. The two boys with us were split up and placed in different schools to teach Chinese *wushu* kickboxing called *shanshou*. The remaining girl and I learned we would be working together to assist in training the county's demonstration team of the thirty best young athletes chosen from among all the schools at the temple.

A teacher of the county demo team introduced us to the children, whose ages ranged from seven to fifteen. All pairs of eyes stared at us, the children wondering what kind of teachers we would be. I smiled back, my bravery deserting me. Teachers here were ruthless and I had no experience teaching troubled youths. I was terribly nervous, knowing I didn't have it in me to be tough.

We started work by asking the team what forms and styles of *wushu* they knew. After discovering the demo team's repertoire lacked a broad range of entertaining styles, I taught the students various fighting sets, such as the three-person broadsword against two spears, a sword fighting set between two girls, and a three-person barehanded fighting set that Coach Wang had devised especially for me to fight off two boys. The students were eager to learn, and passing down my knowledge made me feel happy to help these needy children.

Many *wushu* styles had regional origins, and the "monkey staff form," popular in Jiangsu and Sichuan Provinces, wasn't taught at the temple. Coach Wang and Xiao Yingpeng 肖应鹏 from those respective provinces were nationally known as the famous Monkey Kings. Although monkey staff was never one of my specialties, I devised a form based on many years of watching my teammates and coach perform that style. One boy eagerly became the sole monkey staff performer.

During the lessons my classmate and I taught, the regular instructors stood by with sticks in their hands, occasionally lashing out to smack the kids on the backs of their legs. My classmate followed the other teachers and adopted a strict voice when talking to the students.

Unable to play the role of a tough disciplinarian, I decided to treat the children with respect and kindness. I encouraged and complimented them on their work. Slowly, after they felt safer with me, the children responded with enthusiasm. I was relieved when no adults raised their eyebrows at my approach or challenged me on my methods.

As I got to know the kids, I grew to like them. Their friendliness blossomed along with their excitement about learning new things. They had a sense of maturity about them that didn't correlate with their young ages. I worked them hard, but they responded to having someone show them respect by practicing diligently. They recognized the value of my teaching and appreciated it.

When my classmates and I first arrived at the temple, we were given simple and inexpensive motel lodgings like regular teachers, which consisted of a shared room with five other roommates, including strangers, but no bathroom. After we began teaching, however, the officials moved me and the girl teaching with me to the best accommodations, Shaolin Hotel, saying our teaching skills were vital to the demo team. Instead of eating the mundane food at the cafeteria, we enjoyed higher quality food at the hotel.

One day, the kids that my classmate and I taught invited us to see their dormitory. We were shocked at their living conditions. The two dark windowless rooms reeked of unwashed bodies and stinky shoes. Instead of the bunk beds I had while on the team, one giant brick bed called a *kang* filled up each room. Over twenty boys slept together on the straw-topped *kang* without the benefit of mosquito netting. The crumbling walls were made from a mixture of mud and straw. Each child had dug out a small hole in the wall where they crammed their bowls, chopsticks, a change of clothing, and other personal items. Their toilet was an outdoor hut with a revolting pit in the ground that swarmed with flies. For years, I had thought about how difficult my life had been on the team. Seeing the barest living conditions at the Shaolin schools, however, made me feel thankful for the good treatment I'd received. I wished these students had fared better.

Once a week when my classmates and I weren't teaching, the local sports officials and teachers took us around to visit different schools in the area. We always seemed to arrive at mealtime, usually dinnertime. The officials told us the school administrators were honored to host banquets for us, but those administrators were forced to offer that we dine with them. The sports officials used us as an excuse to get free meals and attend banquets.

Drinking alcohol at the banquets was customary and something I never felt comfortable doing. It took very little alcohol to make my face feel flushed. I disliked the sensation alcohol provided and wanted to avoid it. If I drank one drink, I'd have to match my hosts and drink ten. As the oldest of the group of five from our school, I told the officials we girls were supposed to limit our drinking. I also lied by saying that alcohol made my skin break out in a rash and exempted myself from drinking anything other than tea. Out of a sense of honor and to ensure a good written report to Professor Peacock, the two boys couldn't refuse. The empty cups were placed in a tight circle and the alcohol was poured from a teapot into the cups in one continuous flow. When the cups were distributed, the boys felt compelled to match the officials drink for drink otherwise the boys would be accused of not liking the officials enough to drink with them. With effort, we three girls managed to lead the drunken boys back to the hotel on those nights, and we served tea to sober them.

After several banquets, the schools' officials and teachers thought of us college students as their friends and equals. One official casually remarked about the death of a student just a couple of weeks before our arrival. With a total lack of concern, he related that one teacher had whipped an undisciplined student to death with a bamboo stick. With pride, he bragged that the parents couldn't do anything about it. They had signed a contract and had no rights to sue the school.

My eyes stung with tears when I heard the shocking story. With sadness, I thought of the enthusiasm the students gained from watching Jet Li movies and how proud they must have been to train at the Shaolin Temple, only to have their zealousness turn to terror because of mistreatment. My heart hurt for the child's parents who had pinned their hopes for the future on their child bettering himself. Instead, the parents would receive only a little money in return for their child's life.

Teaching these underprivileged children was an experience I would never forget, though it wasn't a job I would ever choose to do for an extended period of time. It didn't fit my sensitive personality and I felt powerless to stop the abuse. Then and there, I vowed never to get stuck in a job that required me to compromise my integrity. I wasn't sure about the specifics of what I would do with my life, but I knew I could never become the type of person I wanted to be if I remained in China, always having to bow before those with seniority and look the other way when I encountered corruption and brutality. More than ever, I wanted to leave China's unjust system behind and start over again in a place that valued freedom, a place where a poverty-stricken child was viewed as having potential instead of being seen as worthless and replaceable.

One child especially captured my heart, the oldest boy, whom I tagged the team captain. He kept me informed about school rules, routines, and interesting tidbits about other students. "See this boy here?" the team captain said as he patted a boy on the back. "His father's so clever. He makes a big pottery full of green pea sprouts every day. He knows how to make the best ones. Each morning, he sells them all. That family has lots of money." The boy whose face was all smudged and dirty beamed with pride.

These kids responded well to any kindness. Each morning, they squatted in front of our hotel and waited for us to come out and lead their morning jog. The older girls offered to wash clothes for us, which I politely declined.

As the last month of my stay rolled around, I began looking around nervously for Professor Peacock to show up. One day, as my classmate and I dined in the hotel, the professor made his entrance with local officials. His eyes opened in surprise when he saw us eating dinner in the hotel. After sauntering over to greet us, he fumbled through his briefcase.

"For you, Liu Yu." Professor Peacock extended his hand. "I'm sure this letter will tell you what's been going on in Beijing. Students are protesting in Tiananmen Square, asking for democracy. I hope you two won't be involved in it when you get back."

The hotel where my classmate and I stayed had a television. We had already seen a couple of news broadcasts and were surprised to hear about the protest. In one of the broadcasts, Premier Li Peng 李鹏 met with student representatives who questioned him about the future of China. The students, joined by a professor, tried to convince Li Peng that the people wanted greater democracy. A flustered Li Peng responded by saying students were supposed to return to school "The government will decide where the country is going." At one point, Li Peng answered a question with, "I'm not supposed to answer that question."

Although having the premier talk to protest leaders in this fashion was unprecedented in China and might indicate the country could be headed for a change, I sensed danger. The premier appeared embarrassed by not having an official response to the question directed at him, and I was sure he disliked being questioned by intelligent protesters. Li Peng would find a way to recover his lost face, and that spelled trouble.

After Professor Peacock left, I ripped open my mail. The letter was from my former teammate, Little Spring, the bodybuilder who worked on campus. She wrote about all the excitement I was missing, about how our government was ready for change and about to move forward. A million people—students and residents of Beijing joined by students from around the country—were protesting the weak government, with over 100,000 of them camping out in Tiananmen Square. Little Spring wrote about a company in Hong Kong donating tents, which were then adorned with colorful banners to proclaim university allegiance.

I wasn't surprised to hear this gullible girl was caught up in something so dramatic. Generally, athletes with inferior education never learned to be deep thinkers. My classmate and I agreed that China wasn't going to change dramatically just because of a serious protest. Even though people wanted change, China's history showed the government was unlikely to give in to demands and give up power. A few times Chairman Mao had played tricks on people, allowing them opportunities to speak their minds before changing his tactics and making examples of them as traitors. As a result, I had little faith the students' protests could affect much change and they were surely putting themselves at risk. I became anxious to return to Beijing and see what was really going on. But first, I needed to focus on something more pressing. Was Professor Peacock going to make my life difficult in any way?

The next day, Professor Peacock chatted with my supervisor while I self-consciously taught my students. More than once I caught the children gawking at Professor Peacock's fancy clothes and peculiar mannerisms.

That evening at a banquet, Professor Peacock successfully ambushed me when my classmate wasn't with me. "Tell me, Liu Yu," he said, his expressive opera hands stirring the air, "what are you planning after you graduate?"

"I don't actually know," I responded, feeling reluctant to discuss anything personal with him.

"I'm your teacher," he purred. "I can help you if you trust me." His eyebrows moved up and down as he spoke and soon little bubbles appeared at the corners of his mouth that he wiped away with a flourish. "Do you want to stay in school?" he asked, "perhaps as a graduate student or on the faculty? Or are you planning something else?" His narrowing eyes belied his casual tone.

Although I felt a twinge of fear, I held my ground. I assumed Little Mouse had told him about the American who visited me often, and Professor Peacock probably itched to hear about it personally. However, my reluctance to confide in him was too strong, so I answered, "I want to keep my options open right now."

At that moment one of my classmates approached, and I carefully drew him into the conversation before quietly slipping away. The topic of my lack of ability to discipline the students hadn't come up. When Professor Peacock left the next day, I breathed a sigh of temporary relief. I hadn't been fooled by him.

The same feeling of persecution I had when I lived under Coach Cobra's control now haunted me, and I couldn't shake it. I worried Professor Peacock was trying to unearth my plans so he could foil them. With only a little over two months left until graduation, I hoped to be slippery enough not to let him entrap me. Each time I thought about facing a battle with him after I returned to school, however, my heart sank. I knew at that moment that as long as I remained in China, someone would always try to control me, just as Coach Cobra had done and just as the local officials were doing to these powerless children.

On our last Sunday, the children begged to take my classmate and me on an excursion. As we hiked a dusty yellow path through green hills to a tranquil water pond, I listened to the children rattle off information about the beautiful area. The children thought I was rich because I owned a camera, and I took several rolls of film while they posed in various *wushu* postures.

My last day arrived, and the students showed their appreciation by scraping together a little money they used to buy me a photo album. Everyone wrote their names on it. It meant a lot to them to give me this gift. It was such a sweet moment that brought tears to my eyes.

My inquiries about what opportunities existed for the children convinced me they faced difficult lives. Not much attention was placed on school work at the temple. At least I had some hope when I first went to the sports camp that my hard work would be rewarded with some kind of permanent job. Any future these kids had was one they managed to scrape together on their own.

Teaching the kids took hard work, but being able to use the knowledge from my team training and college experience to teach these higher level students who were intent on learning as much as possible gave my life meaning. I tasted the best part of being a coach without having to resort to the type of discipline expected at that school. Discovering I had the talent to be a good teacher gave me confidence that one day I would be able to use my experience to teach *wushu* athletes in the U.S., but first I knew I had to learn English and establish a new life for myself as Norm's wife.

Thinking about Norm made me realize how much I missed him. We hadn't been able to communicate much in this remote location, but I knew I would be seeing him in a week. I could hardly wait.

It was near the end of May when I returned to Beijing, and I was shocked to find that the city wasn't the same as before. In my absence, everything had turned upside down. The unreal situation made me extremely apprehensive. I suddenly realized that if things worsened, any hope of leaving China might be gone.

Taiji seminar (Liu Yu third from right and Master Chen Xiaowang fourth from right)

北京體育學院武術系八五級畢業留念 1989.6

1989 graduating class of Beijing University of Physical Education
Wushu Department (LiuYu is seventh from right in middle row,
Professor Men Huifeng is second from left in front row)

Fitting in a performance at Coach Wang's hometown in 1988

Liu Yu is second from the right and
Fang Zheng is third from the right

FEAR OF HISTORY
REPEATING ITSELF

After securing my luggage in my room, I headed for the cafeteria where I found students wearing makeshift headbands sporting the words "hunger striker." I stared in confusion when Little Spring came rushing toward me.

"You're back! Come sit with us over there," she said pointing to her table where a few of the militant students sat.

"Little Spring, what's going on? Why are students wearing headbands with 'hunger striker' written on them and yet eating food?" I asked.

"They just came back from the protest. Students are going on hunger strikes like Mahatma Gandhi to show the government how serious they are about democracy. I tease them about eating. They defend themselves by saying they don't eat while they're at Tiananmen Square. Some of the students go on three-day hunger strikes and then they rotate, but many of them eat at the beginning and end of the day. Grab your food and come over."

During dinner the students filled me in on what had transpired while I was gone. On April 15, 1989, former Communist Party secretary Hu

Yaobang 胡耀邦 died. Using his death as an excuse, a million Beijingers gathered for a spontaneous anti-government rally. During my lifetime the only precedent for such a demonstration had occurred in January 1976 when Premier Zhou Enlai died, but many students were too young to have heard about an event the government had covered up. As when Zhou Enlai died, protesters mourned a senior Communist official, an action intentionally criticizing the ruling dictators. In the 1976 incident, the protest was against Chairman Mao and the Gang of Four. It ended with 4,000 arrests, hundreds beaten, and sixty protesters secretly beheaded.

Thirteen years later, students were once again protesting against government corruption and repression. They demanded economic reforms to curb inflation and unemployment, changes Hu Yaobang had promoted. On April 21, 1989, the day before the state funeral, overnight camping began in Tiananmen Square. When the government sealed the square and the police advanced, protesters peacefully chanted. Even though some students were beaten by policemen, the protesters refused to leave. Student leaders drew up a list of demands that included the resignation of Premier Li Peng. A power struggle was going on within the ruling Politburo and they were radically split about how to proceed. Meanwhile, foreign media arrived for the upcoming Sino-Russian summit scheduled to begin May 15. The students responded by beginning their hunger strike to play up to the media.

When Mikhail Gorbachev arrived in Beijing, the people greeted him as a hero. A million people flooded the streets causing major traffic jams and extreme embarrassment to the Chinese government. On May 20, martial law was declared and the Chinese government dispatched a fleet of Army tanks from the northwest side of Beijing. They were moving toward the center of the city and had to pass through our campus on their way. With an organized agenda, students took to the streets and blocked the Army tanks from advancing. This had been going on for a few days when I arrived back in Beijing.

"Isn't the university prohibiting students from going to Tiananmen Square?" I asked.

Little Spring said, "No. Many young teachers are involved, too."

Several students at the table related how exciting it was at the Square. "Each school has a tent for its headquarters with flags we made from strips of cloth ripped from old tee shirts. That's what our headbands are made from, too. The Beijing University student leader has organized every school department with schedules for when we march and when we work on security. It's very peaceful, almost like a party. We also need volunteers to take shifts to stop the Army tanks from reaching the square. Would you like to volunteer?"

Before I could answer, Little Spring chimed in, "I've been over there twice to lie down in front of the tanks. Liu Yu, you can come with me tonight."

For a moment I sat just looking at these enthusiastic students. Their young hearts were filled with passion. They didn't see themselves as doing anything illegal that would have huge repercussions. Instead, they hoped their peaceful protests would impress the government to institute changes. I admired the protesters' sincerity and their efforts not to give the government an excuse to fight back. Their cause was worthy, especially after seeing how those poor children lived at Shaolin Temple compared to the comfortable lives of the teachers and officials, yet something held me back. It didn't make sense to me that the government could be so easily persuaded. Suddenly, I felt older. My heart was no longer young. I couldn't bring myself to share in their hope.

We had finished eating, so I casually said to Little Spring, "Please come outside with me." I stood up to go. Little Spring looked at me questioningly but followed.

When we were outside, I turned toward her and blurted, "I'm not going to lie down in front of the Army tanks and you shouldn't either."

"Why not?"

"Don't you remember what it was like after the Gang of Four were arrested?"

"Sure, we had all those meetings and didn't have to train," she answered.

"But after that, there was a revolution. The loudspeakers blared with the news of officials being attacked because they had supported the Gang of Four. The camp leaders were split into two groups. The people who thought they had always done the right thing found themselves in trouble and were denounced. Right now it's scary to take sides because you don't know who's going to end up on top."

"I know you're right," Little Spring said, "but everybody's participating."

I recalled what had happened to Morning Glow, my mother's co-worker and friend, all those years ago, and I felt a chill work its way down my spine. "That's because the students are too young to remember the first Cultural Revolution and how awful it was. Besides," I added, "there are too many people. Even though they have good hearts, the traffic jam will cause people to get hurt. I won't go."

Little Spring scoffed, thinking I wasn't brave. I watched her walk away.

The freedom to dissent arose because China adopted more relaxed policies in the 1980's. To qualify people for certain benefits, the government no longer checked three generations backwards and forwards. Entire families would no longer suffer for the wrongdoing of one relative.

During the Cultural Revolution, Chairman Mao checked as many as nine generations back before labeling a family as Red or Black with Black signifying the enemy. Students couldn't relate to the widespread fear that had contaminated the lives of older generations in which innocent people lost their jobs, were sent to jail, toiled in the countryside, or lost their lives for being related to troublemakers.

My decision to avoid the demonstrations wasn't cowardly; it was wise. Having read many books on China's history, I saw patterns replaying themselves—a split in the government coupled with population unrest would force the military-backed government officials to squelch insurgence and implement tighter controls using military force. The more I learned about the protest, the more I suspected Zhao Ziyang 赵紫阳, a leading liberal who advocated negotiations with protesting students, of using students and intellectuals to try to gain power. Zhao Ziyang tried to copy Chairman Mao who had rallied the young Red Guards, but Zhao Ziyang didn't have the military backing him, something that was crucial to every leader in China's history. When he openly opposed the use of violence against the protesters, he was politically ostracized and lost all hope of ever gaining the power he sought. As more and more disgruntled workers joined university students in nationwide protests, however, the government would be forced to act against this enormous threat to their power. Retribution would be coming soon.

Leaving my dormitory the next day, I worried about Norm's upcoming visit. Would the government refuse him entry? As much as I wanted to see him again, I hoped for his safety he wouldn't be allowed into the country.

I heard my name called out and turned around. My former roommate who was now a graduate student greeted me. "You came back just in time to get involved in changing our government. I'm on my way to Beijing University to hear the latest news. Come with me and I'll show you the posters at the democracy wall."

It surprised me that this girl, who was usually so calm and cautious, seemed so caught up in the political excitement. "I'm not interested in going there," I told her. "The first Cultural Revolution started there. It could happen again. You could be in the wrong place at the wrong time. I advise you not to go either."

"This isn't the same as the Cultural Revolution. I guess you can't understand because you weren't here to witness the excitement of people coming together and finally taking a stand to show the government how serious we are. We can make a difference in China," she said with passion.

"I'm just not interested in stirring things up," I said.

"Well, if you won't go with me, then come by my room some time and listen to the student radio broadcast in the evenings." With a shrug of her shoulders, she went on her way.

A few days later, amid all the dissension, Norm arrived in Beijing leading a group of Americans on a bicycle tour of China. Thinking it would put me in the spotlight if he came to my campus, I met him and his tour group for lunch near his hotel, only a few blocks from Tiananmen Square.

Being introduced as Norm's fiancée gave me a thrill. As I scanned the friendly faces of the Americans, I felt a sense of freedom in not having to hide that part of my life. Slowly, some of my anxiety about my future dissolved. While holding hands with Norm under the table, Norm translated the conversation that centered on the protest.

Tour members spoke about meandering through the sea of tents neatly pitched in rows in Tiananmen Square. The Goddess of Freedom, a tall plastic statue fashioned after America's Statue of Liberty, presided over the square as the students' symbol of liberty. The Americans in Norm's group remarked on the friendliness of the student demonstrators.

In the middle of our meal in the noisy restaurant, Norm leaned closer to me with a look of concern in his eyes. "A lot of students are visiting Tiananmen Square just for fun. Have you been over there?" I was aware of the festive atmosphere in the Square, especially at night. Word circulated among the students on campus that the Taiwanese singer and songwriter, Hou Dejian 侯德建, and the first Chinese rock star, Cui Jian

崔健, had joined the protesters and sang while many danced. However, it wasn't enough to entice me to go.

"No, I don't want anything to do with it. It makes me nervous," I declared.

"That's good. I hope you don't go. Even though the protesters are friendly, you never know what the government will decide to do about it," Norm warned. "I'm worried about my group being there. To them it seems like another American-style sit-in. They don't realize how volatile this situation could get. We're leaving Beijing tomorrow. I hope things calm down and we can spend more time together when I return here at the end of the tour."

"I'm sorry I can't get away to spend more time with you right now," I said.

"I understand. I'm pretty busy organizing this tour, anyway."

Suddenly feeling apprehensive, I squeezed Norm's hand. "Be careful. No one seems to be worried about this situation getting out of hand but us. Everyone tells me how good it is that a government official and student representatives are talking and negotiating. The students feel a false sense of security because the situation has been going on for so long without the government forcing them to leave. But the government has declared martial law. This can't go on forever. I'm worried the students will get boxed in and the government won't give them a graceful way out."

At the end of the meal, I said goodbye to Norm, thinking I would see him in a few weeks, and wished everyone a good trip. I slipped out of the restaurant first so I wouldn't be seen walking on the streets with foreigners. Maybe I was being silly and paranoid, but my instinct for self-protection was operating in high gear.

The next day, June 3, Norm and his group flew to Xian to continue their tour. That evening, I headed toward Little Spring's apartment on the north side of campus but got waylaid along the way. I heard angry student voices broadcasting the latest news from a loudspeaker set atop the North No. 1 dormitory that housed the students who were earning master's degrees. The exhaustive political rallying had turned the campus into a hot pot of unrest. Worried, I decided to visit my former roommate and hear what she had to say.

My friend's room was packed with people, all passionately discussing the situation. I didn't see her among the bevy of people, so I sat on the edge of the bed to listen.

Someone was arguing that China had changed since the Cultural Revolution. "Mao's gone. The government has a different leader. The students need to make the leaders understand it's time for a change. We want more freedom." At that point, someone turned on a radio broadcast, which reported clashes between troops and students in the streets near Tiananmen Square. The government representative on the radio warned people not to go to the square because if the conflict escalated, troops with guns would fire on the people.

A student reacted to the broadcast by saying, "No way! They wouldn't dare kill students. We're all Chinese and many of us are Communists. All we want is for the country to move forward. They just want to scare us. Even Mao sent the Red Guards to the countryside rather than resort to violence against them."

An older student confronted everyone by saying, "What if it's true? What do we do then?"

Many students in the room expressed doubts that the government was doing anything other than using scare tactics. "They won't hurt us," someone argued. "We talked to some of the troops. They're nice. They're young, our age. They smiled at us. We gave them food."

"I agree," another person added. "They're people just like us. They understand we won't do anything violent. We aren't trying to fight with them. We even told them they should be standing on our side."

Then, the older student cautioned, "Remember the Chinese saying, 'Even if you prepare for 10,000 things, the one thing you didn't prepare for could cause everything to fall apart and go wrong.' We have to consider all possibilities and be prepared. We can think of 10,000 reasons why they won't kill any of the students, but what if one part fails? What if we're being too naïve and idealistic?" Silence hung in the room, leaving everyone nervous.

Between the jumble of bodies, I caught a glimpse of my friend. Normally a mature person, today her blood showed all hot and fresh in her face. I decided not to bother trying to talk to her and left the room.

"Have you heard the news?" I asked when I arrived at Little Spring's apartment. "There's trouble near Tiananmen Square."

"Yes, and I'm worried about my boyfriend. He went there today."

"Can I stay here with you in the extra bed?" I asked my friend.

Little Spring's absentee roommate had married and moved away, yet didn't want to give up the use of the apartment in case she would need it.

"Sure, I'd like the company."

Sleep was impossible during the night. We heard people running around the campus and knocking on doors. Sometime after midnight, someone shouted outside the building, "Let's go. Take all the weapons we can carry. We have to give our support. We have to fight."

"Something's going on," Little Spring said in the darkness. "Let's go see what's happening."

"No," I said forcefully, "I won't let you go out there. Let's stay in the room." We tried our best to go back to sleep.

In the blackness of the early morning, we heard boom, boom, boom in the distance. We gave up on sleep at that point but stayed in our beds talking. I tried to reassure her that her boyfriend would be okay.

It was still dark outside when someone abruptly banged on our door. I froze. Little Spring opened the door and her boyfriend burst into the room out of breath, his eyes wild and fearful. In between heavy gulps of air, he tried to talk, but nothing came out. His face was all white, and we feared he was in shock. We made him lay down on the bed, and I boiled water for tea.

After a little time, he managed to say a few words, "Shot. Shot."

"What do you mean by shot?" we asked. Little Spring checked his body to see if he was hurt.

"Real shots," was all he managed to say. We waited for him to calm down.

I set cups of tea on the table. Slowly, he started to describe what had happened. "They were shooting. The tanks were using real guns. They were shooting at us."

We stood there, unable to comprehend the enormity of his words.

"How did you get away?" Little Spring asked.

"When the guns started, I ran, dodging tanks and dead bodies. I escaped down a *hutang*." As a local Beijing boy, he knew the maze of narrow alleyways that seemed to go on forever as they cut through the city. To avoid any Army tanks, which blocked all the major roads, he slipped down one of the alleyways and ran eight miles back to our campus. "I only went because I was curious," he added sadly.

Little Spring looked in my eyes and said, "I didn't feel afraid when I went to lie in front of the tanks to block them, but now I'm scared."

Over cups of steaming tea, we pondered the situation. "What do we do next? Should we go back to Nanjing?" Little Spring asked.

I held my cup tightly to capture its warmth. "The roads are probably a mess. I remember reading that during World War II many people who tried to escape the cities died on their way to the countryside. I don't think we should go anywhere," I said and my friend agreed.

We soon discovered escape wasn't possible anyway except on foot. The buses weren't running and my bicycle had been stolen. The thief probably wanted transportation to the train station. Outside, students had cut down trees and used them to block the perimeter streets of the campus so the tanks couldn't get in. I had my doubts about whether the trees could stop the tanks.

I offered a suggestion to my Little Spring. "Every time China has a war, there isn't enough food. You have a refrigerator and a gas stove. What do you think about going to the campus store and buying a lot of canned food in case things get worse? I'm scared and don't want to starve." She agreed.

On our way to the market, Little Spring and I noticed a cluster of people looking at something beside the road. As we approached, we saw a rope had been strung between two trees and on it hung bloody clothes and shoes. My heart filled with sadness thinking about the students who had worn them during last night's horror. We recognized students and teachers with pinched lips silently walking around a large poster board. I caught a glimpse of the photos that were taken during the massacre with bodies lying dead on the ground. I didn't feel brave enough to look closely.

"Hurry up, Little Spring." I pulled on her sleeve and she came along quietly with her hand over her mouth. I knew she was thinking about her boyfriend and how easily he could have died.

A long line of people stood outside the doors of the store. We joined the line and waited for our turn to stockpile as much nonperishable food as we thought we needed.

News traveled slowly. We had no idea how many students had been killed, though later reports of deaths indicated they ranged from 300—by Chinese government estimates—to over 6,000—by foreign reporters. Estimates of the numbers of students and soldiers injured ranged from 7,000 to 30,000. At the last minute, soldiers from the countryside had been brought in to do the fighting. They had been secluded and brainwashed with no grasp of the situation. These indoctrinated soldiers simply followed orders.

Shortly after the massacre, seemingly endless meetings began for senior students and young teachers. "Everyone has to tell us who went to Tiananmen Square and who didn't," the meeting leader insisted over and over again. Although the university students were the ones protesting, we heard the government was zeroing in on young college instructors and other intellectuals as the instigators. The atmosphere at the university changed into a hotbed of investigation.

Large mailboxes appeared around campus overnight. We were encouraged to write anonymous letters naming the guilty. Suddenly, the prospect of a second Cultural Revolution loomed over us. Anyone could write a letter saying anything. Your worst enemy could lie and turn your name over to the authorities. All those feelings of disbelief, uncertainty, and fear I had experienced as a young girl came rushing back to sicken me. I worried someone saw me go downtown the day before the massacre when I visited Norm at the restaurant, even though I never went to Tiananmen Square. An icy chill traveled down my spine to think that someone could mark me as a subversive for having foreign connections. The situation seemed like a nightmare that had suddenly become real.

For three days after the massacre, we couldn't make phone calls. The phone lines had been cut off on campus because the government wanted to shut down the spread of news to places outside Beijing. I knew my parents would worry about me, but, most of all, I fretted about Norm. Had he made it safely out of the country? My only hope was that the provinces didn't know what had happened in Beijing. After all, the government controlled the media.

At our next meeting, party officials informed us the government had regained control. Everyone would be allowed to make one telephone call at the central telephone station on campus the next day, which was the fourth day following the incident. We were advised to keep our calls short and not say anything except that we were okay. Somebody would be listening to our calls.

We lined up early in the morning, shivering before the sunshine brought us some warmth. The line snaked across campus, and every student waited a couple of hours to make one call. When I reached the station, I was handed the telephone through a square hole. The operator dialed the number I gave her for my sister's office.

"Liu Jing, let our parents know that I'm okay and still at school."

Her voice at the other end sounded relieved. "Oh, good, you're still alive."

"I didn't go anywhere or have any trouble," I said.

"I'm glad you didn't go. Baba and Mama were worried about you."

That was all I was allowed to say, so we said goodbye and hung up.

Much later, I learned my parents had heard that students tried to start a revolution by attacking and killing Army troops. They tried to burn up the tanks. My parents believed the news reports that the government didn't do anything to retaliate.

Paranoia permeated the campus and the area known as "university town," the northwest district of Beijing in which our campus was located. Army troops guarded every street. Friends whispered to each other, "Spies are everywhere. The security police are posing as students. We have to stay quiet, zip our mouths and listen. Don't trust anyone."

One evening at dinnertime outside the cafeteria, some friends motioned me aside. "Fang Zheng 方正 has been moved to our university hospital. A few of us are going to sneak over there tonight and visit him. Do you want to go?"

Fang Zheng was a fellow student who lived down the hall from me in my dormitory and was tragically injured at the riot. I hesitated for only a moment and then agreed to go.

At the arranged time, we made our way to the campus hospital but stayed in the shadows. Anyone reporting our visit could create a huge problem for us.

The hospital was nearly empty and unguarded. One of my friends had been to see our classmate before and already knew how to enter the hospital without being seen. We tiptoed down the hall to the right room and quietly closed the door behind us.

Fang Zheng was awake and perked up when he saw us. We immediately expressed our sorrow about his accident. He waved his hands in dismissal, not wanting to hear our pity. Instead, he spoke as the proud hero everyone thought he was.

"I went to Tiananmen Square with my friend's girlfriend. We thought it was a nice, sunny day to be outdoors among friends, and we were looking forward to a fun evening. First, tear gas clouded the square." Fang Zheng's expression mimed the uncertainty everyone at the square must have felt. "The soldiers expected everyone to leave after that, but we thought they were just trying to scare us," he said with a show of confidence returning. "I don't think anyone anticipated what was coming. When no one budged after the smoke cleared, Army tanks rolled in. We started to panic then. I remember pushing someone out of the path of a tank when I got hit by one from behind." A brief flicker of disbelief shot across his face before he quickly masked it again.

He pulled back the bedcovers to display his stubby legs, amputated after being crushed by the tank. Tears stung my eyes and my heart ached for him. Hearing about the suffering the protesters incurred was difficult enough, but actually seeing something so horrific deeply rattled me.

Fang Zheng tried to hide his emotions, but the barest hint of sorrow and regret registered in his eyes. He continued, "After my surgery, the government questioned me. I told them I only went for fun. I was glad they decided not to arrest me. Maybe they thought I already had enough problems. Then the university arranged to have me transferred here for my protection."

As our friend spoke those last words, a shimmer of hope burned in everyone standing in the room. Our university officials had acted aggressively to protect a student. We'd already heard rumors that the university administration had denied any student or faculty involvement in the direct planning or recruiting of the protest. Campus officials delayed their reports to the police and only admitted to a few students attending the riots out of curiosity—those whose photos were being handed around for identification. Until that moment, I joined everyone who feared the approach of a second Cultural Revolution. Now, standing within this cocoon of camaraderie, I sensed people had changed. They were willing to step out of line to help each other. This was a good sign.

The injured student was the only son of a poor family. I heard his disfigurement broke his mother's heart. This handsome boy, who had been one of the tallest students in the sports theory department—a major that attracted the smartest students—fought to maintain his dignity and refused to be demoralized.

Many students donated money to have him fitted with artificial legs. When the doctors determined he was not a good candidate for prosthesis, we bought him a wheelchair instead. Determined to be self-sufficient, he later used his wheelchair to get around his hometown and sell cigarettes for a living.

I read in the book *Red China Blues* by Jan Wong that he continued to improve himself by lifting weights and competing in discus, shot put, and javelin competitions. Although he became China's national disabled discus champion, he was barred at the last minute by China's Sports Commission from competing in the 1994 Far East and South Pacific Disabled Games when foreign reporters asked to hear stories from athletes injured in Tiananmen Square. When I learned that, I felt a special connection to Fang Zheng because politics had stood in the way of both of us achieving our dreams. I lost track of him after that until I learned of his immigration to the U.S. in 2009.

Each day after the riot, my classmates and I watched the repetitious propaganda on the television news. We had difficulty stomaching the lies.

Rumors circulated about student protesters receiving asylum at the U.S. Embassy and being rushed to America. Many years later I met a friend who had graduated a few years before me and who had been working in western China at the time of the Tiananmen Square tragedy. When she heard about protesters traveling to the U.S., she immediately traveled across China to the U.S. Embassy in Beijing and ended up in America. She hadn't even been involved in the protests.

I feared that because America was coming to the aid of the protesters, it pushed my chances of going there further away at a time when I was more anxious than ever to leave. I knew I couldn't go to the U.S. Embassy and lie about being involved just to escape. Besides, I didn't know what had happened to Norm. After the massacre, foreigners had been urged by their governments to leave China in the event civil war broke out, so I knew Norm wouldn't have tried to come back to Beijing. I felt frantic about whether I would ever see him again. The scenario of borders closing to outsiders again and my being trapped in a hard-fisted China forever loomed large in my mind. I longed to hear from Norm and yet feared it, too. All communication was being monitored and any letter from him was sure to arouse suspicion. And I had no idea how to contact him by telephone.

A few weeks later, Norm accomplished the impossible. After the phone lines were reconnected, he got a call through and persuaded someone to find me. We surreptitiously talked to each other, confirming the other was okay. It was so wonderful to hear from him; I felt a load lift off my shoulders. Norm related his experiences.

He told me a couple of days before the Beijing massacre, a small demonstration in Xian had erupted killing less than a dozen people. It was very hush-hush. Norm and his group only heard a scrap of news about the Xian incident two days later from an off-hand remark made by a taxi driver. The group then continued on their journey by flying to Nanjing. Through a government oversight, the international news coverage hadn't been turned off in their hotel, and Norm's group was shocked by the reports from Beijing.

Norm hustled his group to the top of a hilly cemetery when hundreds of protesting marchers flooded the streets. Several demonstrators held mobile loudspeakers amplifying the taped voice of an impassioned woman who had rallied the mob in Beijing with her moving speech. Her powerful words, broadcast over the scratchy medium, fueled the frenzy in the streets and brought tears to the eyes of many marchers. Before long, they witnessed soldiers converging on the area, producing a wave of panic. As protesters ran, many people went down and were trampled.

Warnings of a possible civil war prompted the group to follow embassy recommendations for a swift departure from China. Norm elected to forego the quick route through the densely populated area of Shanghai where, if the political climate changed and the populace was encouraged to make things difficult for foreigners, the group could be trapped and find it harder to move around. Instead, Norm opted for a flight to Canton, which was further away from Beijing, followed by a train to Hong Kong. I was relieved he escaped safely.

Finally, we got around to discussing the future. I stood outside in the dark with my forehead leaning against the cold wall of the cafeteria building. "Oh, Norm," I confessed with a sinking feeling in my gut, "I don't know how I'm going to get out of here. There are new restrictions on traveling and obtaining passports. I'm scared. What should I do?"

Liu Yu (left) with Little Spring during team years

32 STRUGGLING TO KEEP MY SELF-RESPECT

My inquiries about obtaining a passport weren't encouraging. The Tiananmen Square incident now made the process slow to nonexistent so all applicants could be screened regarding their involvement in the protests. I was told my first step was to apply in the area where I legally resided. As a student, I was on temporary leave in Beijing. My actual residence was Jiangsu Province. Suddenly, I was faced with a dilemma. Graduation was coming up in a few weeks. I panicked at the thought of returning to Jiangsu Province without a job because Coach Cobra could claim I was still under his jurisdiction. As a member of my work unit, he could prevent my application for a passport from being approved. In desperation, I began to strategize about finding a job in Beijing that would change my residency from Jiangsu to Beijing.

In a typical last-minute decision, the university's *wushu* department announced that four students would be selected from this year's graduating class to become assistant professors. I jumped for joy. With my high grades and team experience, I thought I was a good candidate. In one instant, I had the answer to my problem. Unfortunately, the job openings ratcheted up the level of competition among students.

The *wushu* department chair didn't have a professional athletic background and was originally nervous about professional athletes joining the *wushu* program. We won him over, however, and he even helped me secure my first teaching job at the Communist Cadre School 中央党校. When I approached him about the open positions, he spoke first. "Team athletes have had a reputation for doing poorly in academics and therefore have made inferior choices for four-year college students. You've set a good example for athletes everywhere. I'm entering your name on the list of four candidates to be chosen as new assistant professors."

I sighed with relief. With this new job prospect on the horizon, my buried dreams of becoming a teacher resurfaced. The more I thought about it, however, the more I felt pulled in opposite directions. The idea of becoming a professor, even for a short while, enticed me. At the same time, I fretted over taking such a prestigious position and then leaving it after only a short time. Part of me always worried how my friends and acquaintances would react to my going to the U.S. The *wushu* network extended beyond China's boundaries, and I knew future interaction among *wushu* athletes was inevitable. If I took such a position for an unreasonably short period of time, I would never be able to hold up my head again. I trembled just thinking about defending that decision. The alternative, however, was delaying my move to be with Norm just to conform to the unfair system I wanted to escape. That certainly didn't make sense. I finally decided that I would pursue the position even if I had to leave early.

Lost in my thoughts as I walked to the cafeteria, I almost collided with someone I never expected to see in Beijing. In town for a conference, I came face-to-face with Coach Cobra. He surprised me by being friendly, and I sensed he was trying to make amends when he said, "I wish you would forget what happened when you were on the team. Things were complicated then. Now you have a good future ahead of you."

Although I would never forget what he had done to Wei Wei and me, I chose my words carefully. I assured him I had put the past behind me. However, Coach Cobra was capable of striking at any time and to forget that lesson could be dangerous.

The selection process for choosing the new assistant professors included a private departmental meeting. On the way into the meeting, my name was on the list of four candidates. When the list came out, my name was missing. To my surprise, I wasn't being recommended for one of the positions. Something had happened during the meeting, and my name had been switched for another one.

Resentment and anger smoldered within me, but most of all I felt stupid for not seeing this coming. I struggled to find a reasonable explanation. Instead, I found several.

The female candidates were now Little Mouse and Tiger Princess, two women with excellent *wushu* skills but below average grades. Tiger Princess and I failed to get along and strictly avoided each other after our midnight quarrel a year ago. Little Mouse had been my friend for almost two years until she pulled away from me. I let our friendship slip away because I didn't approve of her illicit behavior with Professor Peacock.

Professor Peacock's friendliness two years earlier when he taught me his long tassled straight sword routine had soured because I defied his direct request to leave the *taiji* seminar. I also knew he didn't back me in my bid for the job because Little Mouse had cultivated his loyalty. Another factor came to light during my last talk with Spicy Dragon. She was visiting in Beijing after spending a year with her fiancé in the welcome arms of her family. I thought how lucky she was that her family came from a big city and was open-minded about her engagement to a foreigner.

Spicy Dragon came to say goodbye before leaving for France to get married. We sat together in her old dorm room puzzling about my bad luck. When Spicy Dragon said, "I think you have a coach who doesn't get along with Professor Peacock," a light flashed on in my head.

As a young man, Professor Peacock competed against Coach Wang at national competitions, with Coach Wang always winning. Professor Peacock joined Coach Wang later to choreograph martial arts fighting scenes for a movie. During the filming, the two hard-nosed athletes had a falling out.

Spicy Dragon connected Coach Cobra's recent visit into the jumble. "It's possible Professor Peacock found out from your visiting coach that you were Coach Wang's favorite pupil."

"I think you're right. I did see Professor Peacock and Coach Cobra together. They must have discussed me," I said with worry and frustration knotting my brow.

Spicy Dragon always seemed so observant and worldly to me and showed it when she said sadly, "You have to carry on the burden of the older generation." I agreed it looked like the old system of people being judged based on their parents, their mentors, and where they came from would never disappear in China. This was something from which I couldn't wait to escape.

Actions from Coach Wang's earlier days now came back to bite me. For instance, when he and Professor Peacock trained the movie actress Liu Xiao Qing, a seed was planted. This famous lady, who won best supporting actress at the first Hundred Flower Awards—China's version of the Oscars—became close friends with Coach Wang.

I remembered hearing someone ask Coach Wang if he was the one who had trained Liu Xiao Qing in martial arts. He grinned, saying, "Yeah, we're good friends."

After the completion of the movie, Liu Xiao Qing had bad-mouthed Professor Peacock. I had admired this actress and now she was indirectly influencing my life. Professor Peacock's jealousy over Coach Wang's friendship with the actress may have eventually caused Professor Peacock to want to get even with my coach by punishing me.

"During your first two years here, you always brought Professor Peacock gifts of tea after your visits home. He probably noticed when you stopped."

I had stopped after I found out he was taking advantage of his position by romancing Little Mouse.

Spicy Dragon then encouraged me to bow to Professor Peacock. "Take him a gift. Be polite to him," Spicy Dragon urged.

"No, I can't do that. I've always greeted him with respect. I tried my best as a college student and didn't do anything wrong. I can't go knocking on his door with a gift. I want that position, but I won't buy it from him."

With sadness, I said goodbye to Spicy Dragon, wishing her much good luck and happiness in France. We vowed to remain friends for life.

Much later, it occurred to me that many of the college professors obtained their jobs at the university after the Cultural Revolution changed the rules. Instead of accepting the best students from high school to attend college, Chairman Mao wanted the people who served in the Army, grew up in the countryside, or were workers in factories to become college students and later professors. The gist of Chairman Mao's philosophy was, "If their families are on the Red side, give them an education. They don't need to take an entrance test. Don't give education to people whose families are already educated; send them to the countryside instead."

Many of my college professors were from poor families and didn't receive much education prior to college. They acted defensively around talented students, afraid these students would give them a hard time. I felt sorry for them and always tried to be courteous. I realized, however, they weren't likely to select a new assistant professor who could show them up. It seemed unfair.

Inwardly, I fumed about being caught in an undesirable situation once again. I thought I had started over when I left the team, that the past couldn't touch me. How wrong I was. My ties to the team could never truly be severed. When I started college I naively believed if I studied hard, I would be rewarded fairly with a good job. It seemed I needed to learn another life lesson. Political manipulation was everywhere in China, not just on the team.

I was disgusted with China's system of getting ahead based on connections. I didn't know how to play the game, and I didn't want to. Once again, I felt like I didn't fit in. More than ever, I wanted to start over again in a new country, as far away from the unfairness of China's corrupt system as possible.

The uncertainty surrounding my departure to join Norm in America filled me with frustration and longing. At the same time, a fear lodged in the back of my mind. *What if something else happened in China to prevent me from ever leaving?* I needed to weigh my alternatives carefully. Meanwhile, competition among classmates reached a fever pitch. With graduation only a week away, students hunted for options, not caring who got shot down in their paths.

Up until a year ago, I wanted to continue in school and obtain a master's degree. That was still possible, but I was no longer interested in staying at this university, even for a short duration until I could leave China. Master's degrees seemed like a sham. My former roommate who was completing her master's degree didn't get selected as an assistant professor either. She was an honor student with a lot of self-discipline. In a fair system, she and I would have been top candidates for professors.

The perfect job for her would be at the Wushu Research Institute where her strong research skills would be utilized. She didn't get that job either. It went to a classmate who barely passed his tests. He got the job because he had a friend working there. Before receiving that job assignment, I had asked him about his plans. He said he was going back to his hometown, but he had lied. I abhorred two-faced people. My friend finally ended up with a job no better than she would have received without her bachelor's degree.

Although thinking about it made me uncomfortable, I forced myself to analyze what connections I had for jobs. Immediately, Professor Cai Longyun came to my mind. He was one of Coach Wang's former teachers and also instrumental in developing the Wushu Research Institute, a post he held for many years before returning to Shanghai as a professor at the Shanghai Institute of Physical Education. This traditional *wushu* master was a scholar with books overflowing the shelves in his personal library and a man for whom I held the highest esteem. One time I visited him in his temporary dwelling, a tiny studio apartment in the back of Beijing's Capital Indoor Stadium. He played the *guzheng*, a 2,300-year-old musical instrument the size of a petite piano or organ but more closely related to a harp. The beautiful music captivated me as he plucked the strings with his long fingers. I remembered that whenever he visited Coach Wang, my former coach showed him the utmost respect, even to the point of not drinking too much in his presence. Several times Professor Cai had invited me and another person, a graduate of my university from Zhejiang Province near Shanghai, to dine with him. He generously treated us to a meal at a JiangZhe-style restaurant in Beijing where they specialized in the wonderful cuisine of Eastern China that we missed so much. Yet because I admired Professor Cai deeply, I couldn't bring myself to ask him for a personal favor. After all, I didn't know how long I would be holding the job.

I narrowed down my choices. A job at the Wushu Research Institute was out of the question because I didn't want to lower myself before someone who exemplified such high integrity and was a model for the kind of person I wanted to be. I had rejected a master's degree in Germany after I became engaged. If I were the type of person to seek a position of power, my university degree would open doors for me in Jiangsu Province. But that wasn't my personality. Going back to Jiangsu Province was my least-favored option.

If I didn't find a job on my own soon, one would be assigned to me and I would be trapped into taking it. The government had spent its money to educate me and I owed it a debt. In essence, I still belonged to the government just like when I was on the professional team.

The government matched student graduates with job openings from all over China. The first match-up would be to send students back to their home provinces, but if a position needed to be filled in a remote location, technically any student could be assigned to fill that job. To refuse a position ascribed to me would put a black mark on my record and jeopardize any chance I had of finding decent employment. Officials would defend themselves by saying that was where the government needed me. I would be forced to take the position and to try to find a way out of it after I got there, if that were even possible. Quitting a job was difficult without incurring the risk of becoming unemployable in the eyes of the government. A person's history followed them from place to place and there was no escape.

The possibility existed that I could be sent to a small town within Jiangsu Province where my talents would be wasted and where I would live a life cut off from everyone I knew. In small towns everywhere in China, local officials acted like emperors of their domain. The idea of being forced to work in a small town where my future was at the mercy of selfish local officials was distasteful. For this reason, I had to appear friendly to Professor Peacock. I didn't know who had the power to send me back to teach in my home province or, worse, to a position in a backward area of another province. My biggest fear was that I would be placed within reach of Coach Cobra again. I would do anything to avoid that fate. I had slipped beyond his grasp once, but this vengeful man wouldn't make the same mistake twice.

I finally decided to seek a teaching position at another university in Beijing so that I would be able to switch my residency. When three job offers came in through independent channels, I should have been overjoyed. Instead, a complication arose as a result of the Tiananmen Square incident. To lock young teachers into their jobs, curtail their exodus from the country, and ensure that new graduates serve their country for a significant period of time, universities began demanding that everyone sign five-year teaching contracts. I didn't know how I could get around that requirement.

Two offers were for teaching positions and one was to become a second team coach for the Beijing Wushu Team.

Coach Wu honored me with his coaching offer, although he had to secure final approval from the team leader, whom he took me to meet. Lucky for me, the practice of athletes and coaches staying in their home provinces had been abandoned. However, I had to think carefully about the position because Coaches Wu and Cobra were friends. At one time,

I wished I had been under Coach Wu's wing because he successfully guided several athletes, Jet Li, Li Xia 李霞, and Hao Zhihua 郝致华, toward national championships. Rather than playing favorites, this crafty businessman and aggressive team manager figured out how to make use of others' talents. I sensed he recognized my potential and ability to work hard, and I had confidence I could do a good job in the position. However, my intuition held me back. I didn't really know Coach Wu that well. I wondered whether Coach Cobra could sour Coach Wu's feelings toward me, although my impression was that Coach Wu wasn't easily swayed by other people. I didn't want to feel trapped in a situation where my life would become difficult because I had been Coach Wang's student. Making a five-year commitment was undesirable and I didn't want to let Coach Wu down for giving me a chance at a job so many athletes had their eye on. So I stalled by asking for time to think about it.

Of the two teaching offers, the one I preferred was made from a well-respected and centrally located college to work in their physical education department. It was obtained through my limited connections. Professor Men's friend, Dr. Li, who had accompanied our team to Tibet, recommended me to his wife, who worked in the same department where an opening existed. I had met her at the *taiji* seminar, and she was eager for me to get the job. This nice couple told the university I was a good teaching prospect. I cringed, however, at the thought of signing a five-year contract when I had secret plans to leave the country. I hated being deceitful, but more than anything I wanted to leave China. Yet until things calmed down, until I was able to leave the country, I had limited options. If possible, I wanted to honor the contract if I signed it and not hurt nice people who tried to help me.

The other job offer was to teach at Beijing University of Agriculture 北京农业大学, located outside the city limits in the countryside. The wife of one of my professors worked at the college and was anxious to leave her job. When I told my professor I didn't want to sign a contract, he said, "Let me handle all the negotiations. You don't need to say anything. Let me deal with them."

The agriculture college agreed to hire me and release the professor's wife from her job. I told Dr. Li's wife I was sorry I couldn't guarantee I would stay for five years and turned down the coaching position as well. I accepted the job the professor arranged for me because it seemed like the easiest one to leave.

After I started working at my new job, my department supervisor handed me some papers, "Here's your contract. Please read it over and sign at the bottom."

I took the papers without comment, but inside I bristled, thinking, oh no, what did the professor promise them? I had no intention of signing the next five years of my life away and decided to drag my feet as long as possible. When anyone asked where my contract was, I told them I was still thinking about it. I wanted to wait until my residency file—the one that followed a person for life and contained all her personal citizenship and political information—had been transferred from the college where I graduated.

Upon learning after almost two months that my residency file still hadn't arrived, I decided to visit my former university. I was hoping to avoid this step because it meant I might have to let my former professors know about my desire to leave China. The Chinese harbor a deep reluctance to let other people know their personal business, and I was no exception.

My former department head explained to me the delay in the transfer of my file. "A residency file transfer ordinarily takes no more than a couple of months. After the Tiananmen Square incident, however, all student files are being scrutinized carefully to make sure the government catches all students involved. What's your hurry?"

When I grudgingly explained my situation, he reacted arrogantly to my revelation, probably now happy I wasn't chosen to work there after all. The rumor I heard on the way to his office helped soften my embarrassment, however. Apparently, Tiger Princess's abilities as a teacher left something to be desired. I heard she couldn't control her students, and one incident in particular had left her in tears.

"I'll need to set up a meeting about your case before sending your file over," the department head said in dismissal.

Cheerlessly, I returned to my job, a job that I discovered wasn't as fulfilling as I'd hoped. I taught physical education classes in all sports, not just *wushu*. The students, who were studying to become farmers, had no *wushu* basics, and my skills were definitely underutilized. I was beginning to feel stuck in a job I could never envision being committed to for five years.

The mood in Beijing bordered between cautionary and paranoid. No one knew in which direction the country was headed. Long and boring weekly meetings continued in the post-massacre months, only now I attended them at my new college without my friends around. Everyone walked around feeling depressed. To break the monotony, I rode my bicycle each weekend to stay with Little Spring.

Norm's letters and phone calls were filled with the same question, "Have you started the procedure to get your passport?" I explained about my residency file being stuck at my former university and how I needed it to be transferred before I could ask for authorization to obtain a passport. We were frustrated about how slow things could be in China.

Jobs controlled where a person could live and who received passports. During the Cultural Revolution, permission was required from your job to relocate or even travel on a train. Now, employers controlled whether you could fly out of the country on a plane.

When I was called into my department head's office one day, I dreaded having to tell him once again I hadn't signed my contract. Instead of questioning me, he informed me my residency file had finally been transferred. It had taken almost four months.

He then said, "I don't understand why you've been stalling to turn in your signed contract, but I must have it now."

Trying to subdue my hammering heart, I said, "I have the opportunity for further study in America. I would like to obtain the university's approval to get my passport." I didn't want to tell the university about Norm if I could help it. The reaction to that news would be extremely embarrassing. As it was, I knew how negatively America was viewed in China. Anyone wanting to go there was viewed as a traitor.

The look of disdain I received made me cringe. "You have only been here a few months. How can you just leave? Your professor gave you a good recommendation, telling us, 'We'll send a nice young lady to work for you.' He promised us you would stay for five years."

"I'm sorry about this, but my professor never told me I would have to sign a contract."

"We will have to discuss this issue at our next meeting and decide whether to let you go or not. I will get back to you." He turned away abruptly in dismissal.

A mixture of nausea and shame swirled in my stomach as I left the room, and it stuck with me most of the day. I hated shirking my obligations and having people look down on me. I knew the professor who recommended me would receive a telephone call, but I hoped any repercussions falling on him because of my early departure would be offset in his mind by his wife getting out of her job. His primary motive in placing me was to help his wife. He got his side of the deal. Now it was my turn.

The next day my teaching schedule was light. I set out to take the next step by going to downtown Beijing for the proper forms to present to my employer. After three bus transfers, I arrived only to wait in a long line listening to horror stories of other people trying to accomplish the same thing.

I heard complaints about not receiving full information on all requirements at the beginning of the application process. Instead, it was doled out piece by piece. One young man spoke about his difficulties in obtaining all the proper ink stamps for his application from his employer. Several people tried to talk at once in low voices about having to offer bribes to get the needed stamps. Each complaint stirred up doubt and discouragement in my mind about successfully accomplishing my goal.

When I finally reached the proper official, he handed me some paperwork and explained about gathering stamps from various departments of my university indicating they would release me of my job obligations. Instead of collecting Western-style signatures, I needed inked stamps from everyone's chop, a cylinder or square of jade carved at the bottom with the person's name. After all the rumors I had heard while waiting in line, I dreaded the process of revealing my desires to university officials and asking for their stamps.

Another week went by before my current department head called me to his office. I went immediately and stood nervously waiting to hear what he had to say.

"We had a meeting about your request," he said as he shuffled some files on his desk. "It wasn't approved."

Why couldn't this be easy? At each step, I longed to run and hide, but I knew I wouldn't be happy staying in China. Wearily, I went forward. "Well, I'm sorry I didn't tell you the whole situation. I want to go to America to study but also to marry."

I stood there and suffered through his look of disgust. I knew I wasn't one of those girls who was attracted to everything Western, but that was how I would be viewed. In other people's minds, only a girl with no sense of dignity and honor would condescend to marry a foreigner. A gold digger, they would say.

"We need to hold another meeting about this," he said, his faced pinched with displeasure.

That evening, the university telephone operator tracked me down in my room and handed me a message to call Norm. Since the Tiananmen Square incident, the telephones at the end of each building didn't work, so I walked to the campus phone station to call him.

"What's going on?" he asked. "How come I haven't heard about any progress?"

"Oh, Norm, everything's so difficult." I explained the situation to him, feeling hopeless as the words tumbled out of my mouth.

"Why don't you quit your job?"

"I can't do that. I need to keep my job to get the stamps. I don't want to be sent back to Jiangsu."

"Okay, take one step at a time. I miss you is all." A sob caught in my throat at hearing the tenderness in his voice.

"I'm so lonely here without you," I whispered. "Sometimes I feel so trapped."

He tried to encourage me. "If you have a plan, then stick with it. Something is bound to change soon."

Several days later, when my department chair finally got back to me, he said, "Your request has been denied. We can't give our approval for you to get a passport."

Feeling downhearted, I was ready to beg. "Is there something I can do to change this situation?"

He replied without sympathy, "The only thing you can do is sign the contract or quit your job. I have prepared your exit paperwork for you." He handed me what felt like a death sentence.

I bee lined it into the city for Little Spring's apartment, spilling out my news but withholding my threatening tears.

"Just quit your job," she advised after listening to my outpouring of emotion. "You can live here with me while we figure out what to do."

"But if I quit my job," I argued, "then I might have to go back to Jiangsu. I need my residency to be in Beijing."

"Let me talk to my boyfriend about it."

I didn't want to begin the process of developing connections, which was the Chinese way of getting things done, but I knew I had no alternative. Establishing *guanxi* almost always helped make everything go smoother and faster, but I dreaded asking other people for favors. It meant endlessly buying gifts and owing favors. Meanwhile, I dragged my feet at my job, fearing if I quit I would be floating in a stormy sea without an anchor.

A few days later, Little Spring greeted me with a smile. "Good news. Through some friends, we've found a connection for you at the police department. It's someone who knows you, a former student from our college who now teaches combat *wushu* to new recruits. He has an idea that can help you. We've arranged to meet him tonight."

Liu Yu's Beijing University of Physical
Education student card

BRIBING MY WAY OUT

That evening, I met the stocky fellow from the police department's training academy. I remembered him instantly from my first year of school, which was his last year. He had expressed interest in me before he graduated. I had let him down easy, explaining I wasn't looking for anything other than friendship. He appreciated that I hadn't hurt his feelings. When I explained my current situation, I was surprised to hear he also wanted to leave China.

"I worked hard in school and was the top student in kickboxing," he informed me, "but I lost out in competitions against the nephew of one of the professors. He wasn't even that good, but he had connections." He shook his head and sighed.

The discussion turned to my problem. "I have a friend who might be willing to help you," he suggested. "I want to take you to see this police officer I know and talk about the possibility."

A few days later, we met a police officer who was the friend of my former college mate. He smiled and said, "I've heard about your situation, and I have an idea for you. You could become part of a local family. You could lock your name onto their family book as a daughter.

If you can find a family in my district that is willing to accept you as part of its family records, I can arrange the paperwork to make that change. Then I have the authority to write a letter giving you permission to apply for a passport."

"How do I find such a family?" I asked.

"Start by asking your friends if they know of anyone whose family lives in my district."

I thanked the police officer and handed him a small gift, knowing I would owe him more than that if this plan progressed.

It didn't take long to find a possible family. Little Spring's boyfriend had a friend in his music group who worked in the cafeteria of my former school. We went to see him after his work shift. He kindly agreed to take me to meet his family that evening after he finished his shift.

I followed the cafeteria worker on my bicycle along a dark and bumpy road. Little Spring agreed to accompany us, and I was grateful for her support. When we reached the village where the family lived, we found it in total darkness. The power had been shut off for the evening by the government to save energy.

In the eerie blackness, I questioned why I was taking this chance. How had my life become so complicated? What would Norm think if he knew what I was doing at this very moment? I knew I couldn't tell him because it would violate his sense of integrity. As I peered around me to identify the vague outlines of houses and trees, I decided my only option was to move forward. There was no way out of this jumble.

Inside the small home, an oil lamp flickered in the living room. I met the cafeteria worker's family and explained my request. The mother smiled at me and said, "I have a daughter like you. You're both very brave." She sat silently, thinking for a moment. "Since you already have the backing of the district police and as long as this won't create any problems for our family, I agree to help you. You can join our family in the record book as our daughter."

"Thank you so much," I said in relief. I proffered a monetary gift, not because I was buying her help, but because she honored me by helping me.

With a plan now in motion, my next step was to quit my job.

Back in my room and feeling at a turning point in my life, I spent a lot of time thinking. I thought about my team years and my quest for a championship. I wondered if my woes were just due to bad luck. But I knew, of course, that wasn't totally true.

Sometimes, a dream of becoming something will fail to materialize not because the effort wasn't put in but because a necessary skill was lacking. It's a very lost feeling to know you're missing something you need. Coach Wang's talent for teaching athletes, building a good physical foundation, and inspiring them to achieve their highest potential made him an excellent coach, but he was missing one key ingredient. He failed at politics.

I thought about Tiger Princess, who had worked hard for her championship. In an unusual move, her coaches had gotten rid of their first team all at once. They said if the first team didn't win any titles after four or five years, then they would stop spending money on them. It was considered a very cold move on the coaches' part. The second team, Tiger Princess included, was groomed with several years of intense competition, something necessary to move an athlete to a higher level. Yet, as a professor she was failing. Tiger Princess had to learn a life lesson that she couldn't be a champion at everything.

In my heart, I knew if I had been given the same chance as Tiger Princess, I could have won a first place title just like she had. But you lose something and gain something else. I lost a championship but gained my self-respect because I refused to compromise my values. In the end, I was proud of that.

I thought about Morning Glow and the bad luck she had encountered all those years ago during the Cultural Revolution. But she had made it worse for herself by acting defiantly in the face of the Red Guards. She shouldn't have shown her real feelings. And the people around her didn't dare to speak up for her even though some of them knew her treatment wasn't right. I had taken those lessons to heart without realizing that what was necessary during the Cultural Revolution might not be true forever.

The qualities I appreciated in both Coach Wang and Norm were their abilities to be honest and stand up for themselves regardless of the consequences. Coach Wang never apologized for his talent and never let himself be bought. Norm had been willing to stand up to my father because he loved me. Too many times, I realized, I had been afraid to stand up for myself because in China that meant you opened yourself up to criticism, rejection, and isolation. Or worse. I knew the time had come for me to make a change.

With a lighter step, I entered my department head's office. Here was the moment that had played out over and over again under so many different circumstances. Before, I had always bowed under pressure, did what I was told. No more. Regardless of the consequences, I needed to take a stand now like I did at the *taiji* seminar.

"Are you here to deliver your signed contract papers?"

Swallowing hard and standing tall, I decided it was time I used what I had been taught in *wushu*. I would stand up for myself against my opponent. My greatest weapon was a smile, which I gladly turned on the department head.

"I won't sign the contract papers."

He looked at me in surprise. "In that case, I must ask for your resignation."

I handed him my signed exit papers and faced his look of contempt.

"In order to be released from your job, you have to go to each department head at the university and explain your request."

I knew it wasn't going to be easy, but I didn't get depressed when I heard about this new hurdle, even though explaining my situation was something I had always dreaded.

I started right away by contacting all the people who had to sign off on my exit papers. A couple of them were nice and gave me the stamp authorizing my release right away. The others reacted with pained expressions and mumbled something about needing to discuss my situation within the department.

On my next visit with Little Spring, I asked her advice.

"Now is the time for you to do something under the table by offering bribes to those reluctant department heads at the university. Go get some imported wine and cigarettes at the foreign store and offer it to them," she encouraged.

"Oh, it makes me sick to think about it, but I'll do it," I told her. Accomplishing this step would be learning another one of life's lessons. I would have to compromise my values by bribing people in order to reach my higher goal. It made me want more than ever to live somewhere where this type of thing wasn't necessary.

My job at the university left me with enough free time that I was able to continue giving a few private lessons at the Friendship Hotel. For months, I had been diligently saving all my foreign money, foregoing the purchase of sweet breads at the hotel store. I knew, however, I didn't have enough money.

Naively, I had loaned a large part of my retirement savings to a friend over two years ago. She and her boyfriend were starting a business and looking for funding. I'd known her for over ten years. She had been a professional athlete on another provincial *wushu* team. I thought I was being generous by loaning it to them and didn't know I would need it.

Little Spring used her connections at the university to help me track the girl down. When I showed up at her apartment, she looked nervous to see me.

"Do you remember the money I loaned you?" I said. "I need to have it back. It's important."

She squirmed and said, "Well, my boyfriend and I broke up. His business didn't go well. We're sorry, but we don't have the money to pay you back."

I felt stupid for loaning the money out in the first place. "Can you pay me back anything?"

"No, sorry. I don't have any money."

What could I do about it? I never thought she would cheat me. Here was another one of life's lessons I needed to learn.

Little Spring then advised me to start with smaller bribes, making them bigger only if necessary.

After quietly making inquiries about where the department heads lived and armed with a bag of foreign gifts, I reluctantly approached my first door and knocked. A man I barely knew answered.

Although I was terrified, somehow the words rolled out of my mouth. "Good evening. I'm not sure if I'm correct in coming to you for help. As you are aware, I'm trying to obtain a passport to travel to America to study and marry. The university can't grant my request, so I must get everyone's permission to be released from my job. Could I offer you something to thank you for your help?" I reached into my bag and pulled out a carton of cigarettes.

The man looked down and without hesitation held out his hand to take the carton. With a mixture of relief and anxiety, I proffered my job release form for him to stamp. He went back inside and came out with his personal jade chop, which he dipped in his tiny saucer of red ink and then stamped my paper. Without another word, he turned around and shut the door.

Even though the scheme was successful, I felt humiliated. Doing this was so contrary to my personality but I was determined.

At the next door, the woman looked offended at my offer. All I could say was, "I'm so sorry. I just don't know what to do about this. Does this mean you won't stamp my form?"

After a tense moment, she left and returned with her chop, grudgingly giving me the needed stamp. I felt so grateful and yet worthless at the same time.

I approached each door with dread, not knowing if my bribes were appropriate. When I ran out of gifts, I stopped for the night until I could save enough money to buy some more.

I didn't feel comfortable asking Norm for money. I wanted to save a shred of my pride for our marriage. Thankfully, Little Spring helped me financially.

That evening, the university telephone operator brought me another message to call Norm. I thanked her for being so nice in searching me out. Norm said she did it because she was caught up in the romance of our situation. I appreciated knowing not everyone was judgmental and unsympathetic.

I rushed to make the call. But to my surprise Norm said, with irritation in his voice, "I don't understand why you're still there!"

"You don't understand what it's like here," I countered, explaining what steps I had been through trying to bribe the department heads but leaving out the illegal scheme to join another family, which Norm would have abhorred. "It was so embarrassing. I just want this whole thing to be over soon."

"So do I."

A couple of department heads made me wait another two weeks before giving me the final stamps I needed. Although I felt extremely anxious about quitting my job, I knew I had no choice. I decided to look at it optimistically. Even though things hadn't been easy, I was closer to achieving my goal. Once this was over, I would never have to bend my will to greedy government workers again.

Nervously, I approached my department head and said, "I've obtained the stamps from all the departments on campus. Can I get a letter from the university saying I belong to this school and have permission to leave?"

His face tightened into a scowl. "How can we give our approval when you want to leave?" I watched his lips pinch together as I handed over my exit paperwork without comment. Reluctantly, he agreed to prepare the letter.

After leaving the university and moving in with Little Spring, I carried my precious application form and my work release form with its twelve red stamps to the police officer who had agreed to help me join the local family. He said he would contact me after my personal residency file arrived in his office. My fate now rested entirely in his hands. If anything fell apart, I no longer had a job.

The next week, I watched the police officer shuffle through the papers of my personal residency file that he had just received from the agriculture college. I asked him if I could take a look at it. I'd been curious all my life about what was in there. He pulled out a report detailing where I came from. All my family members were listed, including my uncles, along with their years of birth and addresses. Details from my elementary school revealed the honors I'd received. My team service included my trips outside China. My college honors were detailed. There were no black marks on my record.

"You have a clean file, no problems here," he said. "It'll take several minutes for me to make the needed changes to your file to indicate your new family affiliation."

I took several deep breaths to calm myself as I waited. Having a permanent change made to my personal file left me feeling nervous and scared.

The police officer returned and I managed a smile. He said, "It looks like you have everything you need to go to the passport office. Can you go there now?"

"Yes, I can."

"Okay, I'll seal your personal residency file with wax and a stamp. You can't open it. If you open it, they'll know right away, and nothing in it will count anymore."

"I understand."

"I should be sending this over by carrier, but I know I can trust you." He handed me the packet and the official letter I needed to obtain my passport. I thanked him for his help and turned over a sack containing several cartons of cigarettes to show my appreciation. Before leaving, we made arrangements to meet our friend who taught combat *wushu* for an obligatory banquet dinner.

At the passport agency, I worried my plan would somehow

backfire and I'd end up back in Jiangsu Province or worse, in jail. An older man with greasy hair looked at my papers and announced, "Before we can process your passport application, you need to get a stamp from the political officer at Beijing University of Physical Education indicating you didn't go to Tiananmen Square." Once again, my hopes were crushed.

Disappointed that I wasn't finished yet, I requested the stamp from my former university. The lady in charge said she needed to meet with others in her section. Oh, so many extra steps.

The next week, I followed up on my anti-protester stamp. When I finally secured it after another delay, I returned to the government passport office. A nice lady looked over my documents and said, "It looks like everything's here." I couldn't believe my ears.

She asked me for money to pay for the passport, which I'd scraped together. Then I was told to turn over my Chinese identification card, something I'd carried my whole life. It felt strange to let go of it. Next, photos were taken and I was handed my Chinese passport. After all I'd been through, these few pages of paper bound in a red vinyl cover were worth more than their weight in gold. It had been five months since I started working at my teaching job and a month since I officially quit. Finally, I was over the passport hurdle. I couldn't celebrate yet, however; I still had to obtain my visa.

When I called Norm, he was as happy as I knew he would be. He explained he had already started the paperwork to obtain my visa from the U.S. Embassy. I would have a ninety-day fiancée visa, meaning we had ninety days to get married. If I didn't like it in the U.S., however, I could turn around and return to China before my visa expired. Norm encouraged me to go to the Embassy right away, making me think I had another long, drawn-out process to get the visa.

At the American Embassy, I was directed to a Chinese lady because I couldn't speak English. She had me fill out my visa application while she looked for the paperwork Norm had started on his end. After inspecting my application, she said, "You didn't fill out the reverse side in English."

"Oh, I can't speak English. I need someone to help me."

"Well, you're supposed to hire someone to help you." She looked at my dejected face and kindly said, "I'll do it for you." She graciously took the time to help me fill it out. Relief flooded through me to know I had avoided another setback.

Suddenly, I realized the waiting was over. The visa came through sooner than expected, and I panicked. I wasn't sure I was completely ready to go. One part of me still felt attached to my former life, like I was leaving something incomplete. I worried I wasn't ready to marry, that all those helpless years on the team had stunted my emotional maturity. We were taught to think about our country, our province, and our team, but never about ourselves. I allowed these feelings their due and then reminded myself why I decided to leave and what I would gain.

I recalled the feeling I had in Xuzhou when I won my first medal at the age of ten. I had never felt so light and free and yet grounded at the same time. I expected college life to be as liberating. Now I knew my search for a place in the world must take me away from China and its unfair and repressive culture. Instead of looking behind me, I faced my destiny. Norm and all the unknowns of living in a new country were my future. A calm feeling settled over me and my confidence slowly returned.

With trembling fingers, I dialed the telephone, asking for my sister at her place of work.

"*Nihao*, hello," my sister finally answered.

"Liu Jing, my passport finally came through. I'm leaving China in a couple of days."

"Oh, my," was all she managed to say.

"Do you think the family would like to travel here tomorrow so we can say goodbye? I don't have enough time to go there. Besides, I gave up my Chinese identification card."

"I'll ask them. Someone will be coming."

"Can you carry some things back home for me, some photos and books?"

"Sure."

My sister and her husband were the only ones who came. She didn't volunteer any information about my parents' reactions to my leaving, and I, in turn, ignored the topic. I'd made all the major decisions in my life by myself—joining the professional team and attending college. I knew my parents didn't approve of my decision to leave China and marry a foreigner, but they must have recognized they had no power to change my mind. I loved and respected my family, but after seventeen years of being on my own, I felt I knew what was best for me.

Norm purchased my United Air Lines tickets to Chicago and had them wired to me in Beijing. He made arrangements for friends I knew who had trained with Coach Wang to meet me in Los Angeles and help me change planes.

I packed my weapons, my colorful silk uniforms, my clothes, and some books to read that Norm suggested I buy. Another pile went into a box to be sent home to Baoying with my sister. A third pile contained the belongings of my old boyfriend who went to Australia. My sister helped by contacting his cousin and sending them to her. Only one thing remained that didn't fit in any category. I turned to Little Spring who was chatting with my sister over cups of tea.

"I have a gift for you, something you've always liked," I said as I presented Little Spring with the raincoat I received so long ago on our trip to Canada. I wanted her to have something special in gratitude for her friendship and her help.

"Oh, thank you, Liu Yu," she said with tears in her eyes.

At the airport the next day, as I said goodbye to my sister, I realized somewhere along the way we had become equals. Even though we had lived apart, I felt close to her. I think she trusted the decision I made.

"Remember, the number one thing is for you to take care of yourself," she called out as I waved goodbye.

After the plane took off and China slipped away, I allowed myself a few moments of reflection. I felt myself connecting to earlier times in my life, special times that shaped me into becoming the person I wanted to be.

As a young girl, I had spent a lot of time staring at the poster of Liu Ya Jun, the famous gymnast, that hung at the Baoying sports center. While looking dreamily at my famous idol who had accomplished something special for herself and China, my hopes were to become great at *wushu* and teach school. The seeds of desire began that day, but I had to wait for heaven, earth, and people to help me achieve that dream. Now I knew I would never fulfill my dreams without using the valuable lesson I had struggled for so long to learn: to stand up for myself and be willing to fight for what I wanted. I had finally developed my inner strength and was gaining the freedom I had desperately craved while a prisoner at the sports camp.

I had lived through the golden age of *wushu* when one hundred thousand people filled the Beijing Workers' Stadium and eagerly applauded *wushu* stars. Ten thousand people used to jam the Nanjing arena just to watch their idols, the Jiangsu Province professional *wushu* team athletes. And somewhere a young girl with dreams of winning a national championship had waited on the sidelines for her chance to set her body free. Now I hoped that when Norm and I had a child that he or she would never have to compromise personal values to achieve his or her dreams.

I fondly remembered the freedom and happiness I enjoyed at the beginning of my college life, particularly during the year of the tigress, when I developed meaningful friendships and acquired the independence to finally be myself. I pursued my education like a hungry tiger, but it turned sour in the end.

I didn't want to live in China anymore. To me, China was a place of narrow viewpoints, of climbing the ladder to success on the backs of people you knew and the connections your family had fostered. It was a place where a young professional athlete never felt like a real person, someone who was entitled to fulfill her dreams by her own hard work and accomplishment.

The old Taoist astrologer's prediction held deep meaning. I would indeed be living far away from my family, much farther away than I ever imagined possible.

I liked new beginnings, new challenges. Despite moving to a country where I didn't know the language—except for Dolly Parton lyrics—and despite becoming a wife who didn't know how to cook, I remained upbeat about starting over and exploring the possibilities open to me. I knew with complete conviction that because I'd handled the intense pressure of mind-numbing training and saved myself from plummeting down a depressing pit of darkness, I could handle anything life brought my way. I was a water tigress, and the water element allowed a person to change into a different shape, to be open to new places, and to enjoy all kinds of food and people.

However, within hours, I faced my first obstacle in my new country. All I could understand was that my flight would not be landing in Los Angeles. Instead, the plane was diverted to San Francisco. I never found out why. I greeted my new challenge without anxiety.

After vacating the plane and while walking the long hallways of the airport with unreadable signs posted everywhere, I spied an Asian-looking janitor sweeping the floor. After explaining my situation, he kindly led me to the reservation desk where I passed over Norm's telephone numbers I had scrawled on a piece of paper. Armed with tickets for a new flight to Chicago, I followed a guide to the departure gate.

Weary and nervous, I scanned the crowd upon arrival in Chicago. Norm saw me first and approached with a huge grin and dancing eyes. Everyone was hugging each other openly, and we did the same, a contrast to my departure from China where my sister and I merely offered friendly words.

Norm smoothed the hair out of my eyes with his fingers. "Until I received the phone call from San Francisco, I was never totally sure you were coming. It felt like a dream. Welcome to your new country," he said proudly. "I have so much to show you."

Liu Yu with daughter, Han Ling, and husband, Norm, 2010

EPILOGUE

My attempts at learning English since my arrival in the U.S. in January, 1990, enlightened me about how hard Norm struggled with my language. I managed enough English my first year to teach *taiji* to a handful of students in Madison, Wisconsin and appear as a lead dancer in the dance opera, "Phoenix of the Reddening Sky."

Norm encouraged me to introduce *wushu* in the Midwest, and I traveled to large U.S. Karate tournaments, asking officials for a few moments to demonstrate the uniqueness of Chinese martial arts. Their reactions were skeptical at first but turned to amazement after the demonstrations.

Norm and I accepted an offer to move to Los Angeles, California, where *wushu* was gaining popularity among the Asian population. Eventually, however, we decided to start our own school in a more family-oriented location. We moved up the coast to San Luis Obispo in 1992 and started the Wushu Taichi Center.

Even before I left China, I carried the hope of finding a simple place in which to live, a place where people opened their hearts to one another and didn't play political games. The Chinese say small town residents have narrow minds. This is not true of San Luis Obispo, a city teeming with a variety of talented people who inspire me and enrich my life. I feel I belong here. I'm more comfortable here than anywhere I've lived before.

Our daughter, Han Ling, was born in San Luis Obispo in October, 1993. Her name honors two important people I have admired in my life, Spicy Dragon, whose real name was Xie Han, and Lu Yong Ling, Coach Wang's wife, whose nickname growing up was Xiao Ling. While pregnant, I heard stories of painful childbirths; however, I found thirty-six hours of labor pain to be manageable. There was no comparison between the pain of labor and giving birth and the physical torment I endured while training on the *wushu* team. Giving birth was tremendously easier because I knew there was an end to it; on the team we never knew when or if our torment would be over.

Since Han Ling's birth, Mama has visited me for extended periods in San Luis Obispo. We got to know one another for the first time. One result of those visits was that my daughter, at the age of five, acted as the translator between Mama and Norm, who couldn't fully understand the Baoying dialect.

My brother works as a high school physical education instructor in Baoying. His wife teaches high school government and politics. My sister recently retired from her position as a medical practitioner when her company became a private enterprise deciding to cut costs. After thirty years on the job, she received 20,000 *Yuan*, or $2,500, as her sole retirement benefit. She was too young to retire and many people near her age suffered the same fate. Thankfully, her husband, a high school principal, didn't work for a company that became privatized. Both my sister and my brother have one child each, both boys. The single-child rule in China means that these children receive complete attention and support from their parents. They have a better life than their parents with more emphasis placed on education. The dream of Chinese parents is for their child to graduate from college with a good job.

I don't miss living in China, although I enjoy visiting there. In the United States, I can read all sorts of books with different viewpoints, books from Hong Kong, China, and Taiwan. I experiment with dance and music. I play the guitar, something I never thought possible while living in China because musical instruments were expensive in China in the 1970's and 80's and considered a pastime only rich families enjoyed. During my professional years, I focused on my training, disallowing energy or time for hobbies.

My *taiji* students make my life joyful. They are my extended family. Several times I've hosted tours of China for groups of my American students. They reported their favorite place on each trip was Baoying, my hometown, which has grown from about 60,000 when I lived there to 190,000 today. The people of Baoying graciously honored my students and me with a parade, a fireworks display, banquets, local dance performances, and visits to elementary schools, high schools, the hospital, and businesses. My students, in turn, performed *taiji* for audiences interested in seeing how skillful Caucasians were at performing a Chinese form of exercise. Regional news stations broadcasted our visits.

I love teaching *taiji*. When I attended the national *taiji* seminar while in college, I witnessed great *taiji* masters displaying their fine art. I felt a strong connection to *taiji* that I wanted to keep forever. Those masters inspired me to want to study the art deeply, though I had to be patient and wait for the chance for in-depth instruction. In 1996, I used my connections to entice Master Chen Xiaowang to visit my school. My wish for unreserved, deep *taiji* instruction has been fulfilled each year since that time when my regular visitor, Master Chen Xiaowang, brings his amazing knowledge to share with me and my students.

In 2005, I traveled to Beijing to study *bagua* with Master Liu Jingru 刘敬儒. Some of my friends in China, including the *wushu* professors, acted surprised. "Why do you want to study more martial arts? You've already learned a lot and have trained for over thirty years. You can just buy a DVD and learn any form you want. Well, I guess we don't understand you." It seems few people in China are interested in seriously learning the deeper aspects of internal types of *wushu*, such as *taiji* and *bagua*. They don't realize how valuable it is and how much knowledge and skill is about to disappear forever. They prefer Western sports.

Master Liu Jingru has worried about his art being lost. He wants to pass down his knowledge before he's gone. Masters used to take a long time in testing students' dedication and then carefully parcel out their teaching in small increments. Now they are afraid there is no one to carry on the knowledge for future generations. Many masters find fulfillment in bringing their knowledge and art to other countries where they are more appreciated.

Master Liu Jingru's top student recently stopped practicing *bagua* regularly. The disheartened student had lost his day job when a factory closed. He was part of a lost generation whose education was cut short by the Cultural Revolution. Facing near-poverty situations, that generation lost their spirit to better themselves.

Master Liu Jingru didn't test me too long. When I visited his house for a delicious dumpling dinner, his wife took a liking to me and said to her husband, "She came so far just to train with you and she's hungry to learn." To me, she said, "Inspired students, the kind who are willing to leave families and businesses to learn *bagua*, are disappearing in China. I'm sure Master Liu will teach you well." For the next month, I trained with him every day. It was like eating and eating until I couldn't eat anymore. During our training sessions I learned rapidly how to protect myself because, even at the age of about seventy-two, his quick finger jabs at my mouth drew blood and he nearly poked out my eye. I feel lucky to have been in the right place at the right time.

The Wushu Taichi Center has hosted special visits and seminars with Coach Wang and Professor Men. We sponsored my former teammate, Wei Wei, pulling him out of a near-poverty situation to become an assistant to Professor Men while he studied English, *taiji*, and *bagua* in Beijing before moving to San Luis Obispo in 2003. He then moved to Los Angeles to take advantage of more opportunities there.

My other teammates have settled in many parts of the world, living in Los Angeles, Boston, Las Vegas, England, and Japan. Norm's friend and my former teammate, Wang Yia Chun, is the girls' first team coach in Nanjing. Other teammates also obtained coaching or other government positions in Nanjing and Canton.

When the Jiangsu Province Wushu Team lost its competitive edge, Coach Wang was recruited once again in 1993 to become the boys' first team *wushu* coach in Nanjing, though he is now retired. He expresses disappointment with the trend toward standardization of the *wushu* forms because the individuality and traditional aspects are disappearing. It's becoming more like gymnastics and losing its Chinese flavor, its connection to the spiritual energy of the Chinese culture and the true meaning behind the art and its movements.

I enjoy seeing my Baoying teammates when I visit China. Pretty Green Snake retired from the Chinese opera and teaches kindergarten in Baoying. Little Sweetie is married and lives in Nanjing. Young Soldier's competitive spirit never died. For twenty-nine years he focused on obtaining college degrees. With a newly-earned Ph.D., he works at the Shanghai Institute of Physical Education and is the proud parent of twins, a sign of great luck in China. I continue to honor his father, Coach Dai, each time I visit Baoying.

Spicy Dragon, my closest friend at college, lives in Paris with her husband and two children. Little Spring recently left China and lives in the U.S. Little Mouse continues as an assistant teacher at the Beijing University of Physical Education. Tiger Princess quit her job before her five-year contract expired, married, and moved to Japan.

On one recent visit to my college, I rudely questioned my retired department head in front of a table of former classmates. I couldn't hold back my curiosity any longer. "What happened that time when I lost out on becoming an assistant professor? Why was my name taken off the recommendation list?" Everyone looked shocked at my direct question. Embarrassed, the department head fumbled with an answer about who had more support and power. Then, to comfort me, he said, "Look at how independent and successful you are now. Three times you've been the U.S. team coach. You're an international judge." They were envious of the opportunities I've had. In response to my bold question, they also said, "You've changed." I'm more American now and I wish I had changed earlier. I was too shy then to stand up for myself.

My career in the *wushu* world brought me some satisfying accomplishments. Woody Wong, who trained with me from 1991 to 1995, won silver and bronze medals at the Third World Wushu Championships in Baltimore, Maryland (1995). In 1997, I became the coach of the U.S. Wushu Team, attending international tournaments in Rome, Italy (1997), Hong Kong (1999), and at the Wushu Pan American Games in Toronto, Canada (1998). Mae Hsu, a member of the U.S. Wushu Team, won third place in the spear in Hong Kong, and I was one of her coaches.

I am an internationally qualified *wushu* judge, certified by the International Wushu Federation, and ranked as an international teacher and expert of *wushu* and *taiji*. I received the Seventh Degree Dan of Wushu by the Chinese Wushu Federation in 1999. In honor of my worldwide contributions promoting *wushu,* I received the "Martial Arts Contribution Award" in 1999 from the International Wushu Federation. Acting in the capacity of head judge, I presided over tournaments such as the World Wushu Championships in Baltimore, Maryland (1995), U.S. *wushu* team trials (1991-1999), Canadian *wushu* team trials (1999), and at annual regional tournaments in Berkeley, California (1992-2010) and Vancouver, British Columbia (1995-2002).

I've simplified my life since I worked on the U.S. national *wushu* scene. Now, I spend my time teaching at my school, conducting a tour of China every two or three years, and training with *wushu* or *taiji* masters once a year. In 2008, I became a disciple of Grandmaster Chen Xiaowang, attending the related ceremony in his hometown.

Life moves in circles, enabling me to make contact with many people who were instrumental in my life. Sometimes, I didn't take advantage of all opportunities presented to me. While in Rome, Italy, in 1997, I recognized Coach Fong, who had coached the Shanghai Youth Wushu Team and from whom I learned those fancy weapon forms at a young age. My busy schedule as the U.S. Wushu Team coach was my excuse, but really my natural shyness prevented me from approaching him and telling him who I was and how much I appreciated his teaching. To rectify that, I hope to host a banquet in China some day, bringing together Professor Cai and Coaches Fong, Dai, and Wang. On a recent trip I had the opportunity of enjoying the company of Professor Cai and Coach Wang as my guests for dinner in Shanghai, but Coaches Fong and Dai were not in Shanghai at that time.

The mystery surrounding my lost position as an assistant professor at Beijing University of Physical Education eventually came to light. During that same trip to Rome, Italy for the International Wushu Tournament in 1997, my former college mate, Little Mouse, shared my room for a few days.

"I want to apologize to you," Little Mouse said to me, "for taking your place. That assistant professor position was supposed to be yours. I'm sorry I took it. Everyone wanted that position."

I appreciated her honesty and apology. "That's okay," I said. "It was eight years ago. It's over." Then, I asked her, "Will you tell me what happened?"

"You know, after that first year, we took turns following you for several nights. Your life was so boring. You always went to the library and sat there until closing time with no monkey butt." We labeled anyone who squirmed in his seat in a classroom as having a wiggly monkey butt.

"We followed you because we couldn't understand how you got such good grades," she admitted.

I had been a professional team athlete just like Little Mouse and Tiger Princess, so they assumed they should be able to get the same grades I did. What they didn't understand, however, was what a good student I was before joining the team. Many *wushu* team athletes started at a younger age than me. I received distinguished honors from first to fifth grades. That excellent foundation served me well. Then, while living at the sports camp, I took my academic classes seriously and also self-studied all high school courses in preparation for my college entrance examination.

"Well, we tried studying as hard as you did, but we couldn't get the same high grades. So, we had to look for another way to pass our classes. After our first year, one young teacher became Tiger Princess's boyfriend. He helped her pass her tests, and she helped me."

"I'm curious about you and Professor Peacock," I said bravely.

"Well, I used him. And he used me, too. Professor Peacock had a lot of power at the national competitions. I had never earned a gold medal before. When I asked for his help, I didn't know it would be so complicated. When I tied with a professional team girl, Professor Peacock used his influence as the chief judge during the meeting to determine the winner. He organized the group of judges each year and they were afraid of losing their positions if they didn't do Professor Peacock the favor he requested. The other girl's coach protested the ruling and the two argued over the outcome. But he did it. I won."

I remembered her gold medal win in the double straight sword. This win gave her the credentials she needed to be considered for the position of assistant teacher. I also remembered she received mistreatment while on the professional team. In desperation, she wanted to win to show her former team coach she had achieved her potential.

"Let me tell you," she continued. "Every few years Professor Peacock picked out a new favorite girl. When he died, his daughter came to me with a box. She told me they found this locked safety box of his. I'm sure they were hoping for some money or a treasure. They were disappointed to find it only contained pictures of girls. All his favorite girls. She asked me if I could track down the girls and give them back their pictures. I said, sure, I can help."

I stared in disbelief as I heard the story. It took me back to all the times I was disgusted seeing Professor Peacock coming out of her room. She was only twenty-three while he was in his fifties. And no one ever said a word against him. I don't know how he got away with it.

"Anyway, I'm sorry. I did buy Professor Peacock's help to take your place."

"I forgive you," I said honestly. Truly, I have never been one to harbor grudges if the person is honest with me about it and makes an apology. Sometimes, people like Coach Cobra pretended to be sorry, but I suspected they were saying it as a political ploy. Little Mouse surprised me with how much she shared with me. It made me feel better about that time in my life.

When I left China in 1990, I didn't know when I would see my parents again or how they would react. I have traveled to China every two or three years since then. Each time, Baba was reserved but welcomed me. When I attended my brother's wedding, I went alone because Norm's presence would have created too much controversy. Mama has visited me in California, but Baba never wanted to come. His heart melted, however, when he met Han Ling for the first time. He went out on his own and bought a beautiful red dress for her, a touching gesture of forgiveness. When Norm made a trip to China in 2004, my parents welcomed him openly in their home. Since Han Ling's birth, my parents and I talk regularly on the telephone. All wounds have healed. Norm and I joined my sister and her husband to help my parents purchase their own home, something that gave them and me enormous happiness.

Without my family's early support and encouragement, I would never have dared to dream. I realize the worth of the words and values my grandmother gave me to live by. Sadly, no one is alive today who remembers NaiNai's first name. Not even my mother. Traditionally, when a woman married in China's earlier years, her name became her husband's last name followed by her father's last name and then *Shi* (Mrs.) was added. NaiNai became known as Xu Feng Shi, but her first name was lost. She will never be forgotten, however, as she lives strongly in my family members' hearts.

One thing I know for sure, despite all the pain, despair, and uncertainty in my life, I have come to terms with it. I can see the good that came out of everything that happened. If I could do it all over again, I wouldn't change my life. Well, maybe a few small things here and there, but I appreciate the lessons life has given me. And the opportunities. I believe I have made the most out of my life, and I am proud to be a tigress who fought against all odds to control my destiny.

Reunion of Beijing University of Physical Education graduates
at the 1995 Third World Wushu Championships in Baltimore, MD
(Liu Yu is fourth from the right in the middle row)

U.S. Wushu Team at the 1997 Fourth World Wushu Championships in
Rome, Italy (Liu Yu, team coach, is second from left in front)

Reunion of Beijing University of Physical Education graduates
at the 1997 Fourth World Wushu Championships in Rome, Italy
(Liu Yu is second from right in the back row;
Beijing Team coach, Wu Bin, is third from left in front)

U.S. Wushu Team at the 1999 Fifth World
Wushu Championships in Hong Kong
(Liu Yu, team coach, is third from left in the back)

Photo courtesy of photographer Marilyn Zahm

Dawn Cerf and Liu Yu

ACKNOWLEDGMENTS

Although I wasn't famous, I, Liu Yu, was a witness to that unique period of time in the 1970's and 80's in China just after *wushu* burst on the scene and then exploded in popularity with little to rival it. This book contains my memories and my personal life experiences of that special time.

In writing this book, there was no intention of hurting anyone or seeking revenge. Although in the past I had feelings of being treated unfairly that led to resistance and anger on my part, I now want to thank everyone in my life, both the people who supported me and those who gave me a hard time. I am the person I am today and have gained maturity because of everything that happened in my life. I thank everyone for my life's lessons.

Although I may not have completely forgiven everything, I have let go of all anger. If what I have written makes anyone feel uncomfortable or hurt, please know that this is not a personal attack. It is my truth, as seen through my eyes only, and I hope people will not attempt to discover the identities of characters in this book. They have their own truths.

My heartfelt appreciation goes to Dawn Cerf. With remarkable patience, she pulled little by little until all the memories hiding in my brain like a black cloud trapped in a box were revealed. This book could not have been written without you.

I, Dawn Cerf, began taking taiji classes from Liu Yu in 1994. While touring China with Liu Yu and friends in 1996, I heard many wonderful stories from her. I then proposed to Liu Yu that we work together putting her experiences in writing. At first, it was difficult for her to talk about her team years, so deeply buried were the memories. As she opened up, she suffered from the same recurring nightmares that tormented her as a girl. She persevered, however, and feels the process had therapeutic value. She sees more of the good things that resulted from those difficult years.

I want to express my deep gratitude to Liu Yu for sharing her story with me. It has been an adventure, with a book and a friendship as a result.

We both are sincerely thankful to our families. To Norm Petredean, who believed this accomplishment should be Liu Yu's without interference from him, thank you for being supportive. He only asks that Johnny Depp play his part in any movie rendition. To Han Ling Petredean, you were the inspiration behind this project so your mother's story could be shared with you. To Doug, Cody, and Ryan Cerf, thanks for your sacrifices and enormous support. We deeply appreciate the contributions of Liu Yu's parents, siblings, coaches, teammates, and college classmates.

Carol L. Craig's insightful questions and editing helped tremendously to make this a better book. Thanks to all our friends and Liu Yu's talented students who read chapters and offered artistic suggestions, especially Karen Rogers, Jennifer des Plantes, and Carolee Jenkins. Other support was received from Dawn's memoir sisters (Patti Kohlen and Anne Quinn), Regina Martinez Jackson, Donna Aiken, Paul Ogren, Susan Edwards McKee, Mal Towery, and many others. Thank you all.

"Flying Tiger" Calligraphy
by Grandmaster Chen Xiaowang